The .NET Developer's Guide to Directory Services Programming

Microsoft .NET Development Series

John Montgomery, *Series Advisor*
Don Box, *Series Advisor*
Martin Heller, *Series Editor*

The **Microsoft .NET Development Series** is supported and developed by the leaders and experts of Microsoft development technologies including Microsoft architects and DevelopMentor instructors. The books in this series provide a core resource of information and understanding every developer needs in order to write effective applications and managed code. Learn from the leaders how to maximize your use of the .NET Framework and its programming languages.

Titles in the Series

Brad Abrams, *.NET Framework Standard Library Annotated Reference Volume 1: Base Class Library and Extended Numerics Library*, 0-321-15489-4

Brad Abrams and Tamara Abrams, *.NET Framework Standard Library Annotated Reference, Volume 2: Networking Library, Reflection Library, and XML Library*, 0-321-19445-4

Keith Ballinger, *.NET Web Services: Architecture and Implementation*, 0-321-11359-4

Bob Beauchemin, Niels Berglund, Dan Sullivan, *A First Look at SQL Server 2005 for Developers*, 0-321-18059-3

Don Box with Chris Sells, *Essential .NET, Volume 1: The Common Language Runtime*, 0-201-73411-7

Keith Brown, *The .NET Developer's Guide to Windows Security*, 0-321-22835-9

Eric Carter and Eric Lippert, *Visual Studio Tools for Office: Using C# with Excel, Word, Outlook, and InfoPath*, 0-321-33488-4

Eric Carter and Eric Lippert, *Visual Studio Tools for Office: Using Visual Basic 2005 with Excel, Word, Outlook, and InfoPath*, 0-321-41175-7

Mahesh Chand, *Graphics Programming with GDI+*, 0-321-16077-0

Krzysztof Cwalina and Brad Abrams, *Framework Design Guidelines: Conventions, Idioms, and Patterns for Reusable .NET Libraries*, 0-321-24675-6

Anders Hejlsberg, Scott Wiltamuth, Peter Golde, *The C# Programming Language*, 0-321-15491-6

Alex Homer, Dave Sussman, Mark Fussell, *ADO.NET and System.Xml v. 2.0—The Beta Version*, 0-321-24712-4

Alex Homer, Dave Sussman, Rob Howard, *ASP.NET v. 2.0—The Beta Version*, 0-321-25727-8

James S. Miller and Susann Ragsdale, *The Common Language Infrastructure Annotated Standard*, 0-321-15493-2

Christian Nagel, *Enterprise Services with the .NET Framework: Developing Distributed Business Solutions with .NET Enterprise Services*, 0-321-24673-X

Brian Noyes, *Data Binding with Windows Forms 2.0: Programming Smart Client Data Applications with .NET*, 0-321-26892-X

Fritz Onion, *Essential ASP.NET with Examples in C#*, 0-201-76040-1

Fritz Onion, *Essential ASP.NET with Examples in Visual Basic .NET*, 0-201-76039-8

Ted Pattison and Dr. Joe Hummel, *Building Applications and Components with Visual Basic .NET*, 0-201-73495-8

Dr. Neil Roodyn, *eXtreme .NET: Introducing eXtreme Programming Techniques to .NET Developers*, 0-321-30363-6

Chris Sells, *Windows Forms Programming in C#*, 0-321-11620-8

Chris Sells and Justin Gehtland, *Windows Forms Programming in Visual Basic .NET*, 0-321-12519-3

Paul Vick, *The Visual Basic .NET Programming Language*, 0-321-16951-4

Damien Watkins, Mark Hammond, Brad Abrams, *Programming in the .NET Environment*, 0-201-77018-0

Shawn Wildermuth, *Pragmatic ADO.NET: Data Access for the Internet World*, 0-201-74568-2

Paul Yao and David Durant, *.NET Compact Framework Programming with C#*, 0-321-17403-8

Paul Yao and David Durant, *.NET Compact Framework Programming with Visual Basic .NET*, 0-321-17404-6

For more information go to www.awprofessional.com/msdotnetseries/

The .NET Developer's Guide to Directory Services Programming

- Joe Kaplan
- Ryan Dunn

✦ Addison-Wesley

Upper Saddle River, NJ • Boston • Indianapolis • San Francisco

New York • Toronto • Montreal • London • Munich • Paris • Madrid

Capetown • Sydney • Tokyo • Singapore • Mexico City

Many of the designations used by manufacturers and sellers to distinguish their products are claimed as trademarks. Where those designations appear in this book, and the publisher was aware of a trademark claim, the designations have been printed with initial capital letters or in all capitals.

The .NET logo is either a registered trademark or trademark of Microsoft Corporation in the United States and/or other countries and is used under license from Microsoft.

The authors and publisher have taken care in the preparation of this book, but make no expressed or implied warranty of any kind and assume no responsibility for errors or omissions. No liability is assumed for incidental or consequential damages in connection with or arising out of the use of the information or programs contained herein.

The publisher offers excellent discounts on this book when ordered in quantity for bulk purchases or special sales, which may include electronic versions and/or custom covers and content particular to your business, training goals, marketing focus, and branding interests. For more information, please contact:

U.S. Corporate and Government Sales
(800) 382-3419
corpsales@pearsontechgroup.com

For sales outside the United States please contact:

International Sales
international@pearsoned.com

 This Book Is Safari Enabled

The Safari® Enabled icon on the cover of your favorite technology book means the book is available through Safari Bookshelf. When you buy this book, you get free access to the online edition for 45 days.

Safari Bookshelf is an electronic reference library that lets you easily search thousands of technical books, find code samples, download chapters, and access technical information whenever and wherever you need it.

To gain 45-day Safari Enabled access to this book:

- Go to http://www.awprofessional.com/safarienabled
- Complete the brief registration form
- Enter the coupon code 1JJZ-5DXK-TIT6-PKKN-ERA9

If you have difficulty registering on Safari Bookshelf or accessing the online edition, please e-mail customer-service@safaribooksonline.com.

Visit us on the Web: www.awprofessional.com

Library of Congress Cataloging-in-Publication Data:

Kaplan, Joe.
  The .NET developer's guide to Directory Services programming / Joe Kaplan, Ryan Dunn.
     p. cm.
  Includes bibliographical references and index.
  ISBN 0-321-35017-0 (pbk. : alk. paper)
  1. Computer software—Development. 2. Directory services (Computer network technology)
  3. Microsoft .NET Framework. I. Dunn, Ryan 1976- II. Title.

  QA76.76.D47K363 2006
  005.2'768—dc22
                                                                    2006004150

ISBN 0-321-35017-0
Text printed in the United States on recycled paper at Courier in Stoughton, Massachusetts.
First printing, April 2006

To my wife, Karen, and son, Evan.
—J.K.

To the developers that struggle so hard each day with integrating Active Directory and ADAM meaningfully into their applications. Remember: "This is not 'Nam, this is software development; there are rules."
—R.D.

Contents

Listings

Tables

Foreword

A COUPLE OF YEARS AGO, I began work on an identity-aware application that would involve programming against Active Directory. At that time, the .NET Framework was at version 1.1, and `System.Directory-Services` clearly was where I wanted to invest my energy. I was shocked that a book search revealed virtually no hits on this topic. There were a few older books on ADSI programming, many of which were targeted at system administrators who use ADSI scripts to automate much of their day-to-day chores. But there was nothing for me, a .NET developer who simply wanted to write an identity-aware application.

Knowing the tremendous value of having a great technical book by my side, I tried something crazy. I posted an entry on my blog[1] suggesting that if any subject matter experts were interested in putting such a book together, I'd be happy to help by reviewing their work and introducing them to the editors at Addison-Wesley. Apparently, that post rekindled a latent interest in the minds of a bunch of Microsoft MVPs, who just needed a little push to get going. Joe Kaplan and Ryan Dunn threw themselves on the grenade and now here I sit, writing this foreword!

In the meantime, I have been fortunate to be able to review much of this book, and I've learned a great deal about programming `System.Directory-Services` by reading the draft chapters. Chapter 3 was invaluable when I was building the identity-aware application I mentioned earlier, and overall the book provided a number of insights that I share with students when

---

1. http://pluralsight.com/blogs/keith/archive/2004/10/15/2831.aspx

I teach my security course at Pluralsight. If you are currently doing (or even considering) any work with `System.DirectoryServices`, simply take this book to the checkout counter now, and continue reading this foreword at home. You'll be glad you did.

Directories surround us, but many enterprise programmers aren't aware of the wealth of information on their own domain controllers. For example, it would be wise to avoid building your own "Users" table in SQL Server if you can simply leverage user data in Active Directory. It would be utter folly to create a password database and roll your own authentication protocol on an intranet where you could simply leverage Kerberos. One neat technique I learned from this book was how to use "SID binding" to look up a user's record in Active Directory once you've authenticated that user. These are the sorts of practical techniques used every day by directory programming experts, but you'd be hard-pressed to find them by simply reading the documentation.

I've seen a lot of books written by professional technical writers. For some of them, you can tell that the only leg up the author has over your own experience is that he read the documentation a few weeks before you did. This is not one of those books. Joe and Ryan together have answered literally thousands of questions in public forums such as the ADSI USENET newsgroup at microsoft.public.adsi.general. They know the pain points that you'll encounter when you program against Active Directory, and this book overflows with practical wisdom as a result.

Thanks for the great work, guys!

—*Keith Brown*
Pluralsight
February 2006

Preface

WE WROTE THIS BOOK with the vision that it would be the definitive guide for helping developers leverage directory services from Active Directory and Active Directory/Application Mode (ADAM) in their .NET applications. Even though version 1.0 of the .NET Framework shipped in 2001 with a namespace called System.DirectoryServices (SDS) for doing this kind of work, the resources available to developers using these technologies have lagged behind. This is the book that we fervently wished we had back when we were first developing software for Active Directory. It was an idea that took a little while to come to fruition: Perhaps a bit of our back story will help to frame our perspective.

Ryan was working at a very large professional services firm that was selling off its consulting services capabilities. As part of the separation, a new IT infrastructure needed to be created. It fell to Ryan to figure out how to automate HR data feeds to provision Active Directory accounts and how to manage all of it with only a skeleton crew and a few custom apps. This was in the .NET version 1.0 beta 2 timeframe and .NET seemed promising.

Separately, but in an eerily similar vein, Joe was working in the IT organization of a large professional services firm that was contemplating a massive email system migration from a popular groupware platform to Microsoft's Exchange 2000 Server. Exchange works on top of Active Directory, and Joe was asked to help out on the integration project between Active Directory and the groupware system's directory.

Both projects required a heavy dose of directory services magic to tie the systems together and migrate from the competing platforms. The applications were not simple scripts, but complex systems and web applications requiring a more in-depth approach. But as we began to wade into the code, we noticed there were quite a few rough edges to be sorted out. Exactly how do we make the Lightweight Directory Access Protocol (LDAP) code work correctly in ASP.NET? What were all of those flags used for? How do we make these objects behave the way we expect? How do we extend the schema to accommodate our own custom business logic?

Naturally, we went to the web-based message boards and newsgroups seeking advice, but found very little. Some people had some of the answers if we translated their logic from scripts or C++ programs, but more people were asking than answering. With hard work and sometimes-fortuitous chance, we eventually pieced it together, but it was far more difficult than it needed to be.

Flash forward to 2006: The .NET Framework has matured significantly, with a milestone 2.0 release, and so has the .NET development community. Books and resources abound for just about every topic you could imagine. However, directory services programming still remains obscure and confusing.

This lack of guidance is somewhat ironic given that the enterprise directory continues to gain prominence in the organization. It is no longer just the province of a team of administrators writing scripts. It has become a key source of data for many full-scale applications, with some even building complex identity life cycle management processes on top of it.

We stuck around the message boards, and over the last several years, we worked actively in the online development community to help developers of all stripes solve their directory services development problems. We know from our work in the community that there tends to be a lot of confusion on how best to leverage what became of Active Directory Service Interfaces (ADSI) in the new managed model of `System.DirectoryServices`.

We took the most common problems that developers wrestle with in this space and tried to address them in turn. By the time you finish reading this book, we hope that your directory services programming will be much more effective than before.

Our approach for this book tends to be very pragmatic. We focus heavily on code samples showing how to do things the right way, sometimes at the expense of brevity. However, we do not hesitate to dig under the covers and provide answers for how things really work. We start with the basic skills that every directory services developer should understand and build a solid foundation. We then layer on more advanced topics and scenarios that we have run into firsthand and that we know from our work in the community that developers still struggle with. When we are done, you should have all the tools needed to tackle the advanced scenarios and build the types of applications you need.

Outside of this book, we endeavor to support our readers by making examples, errata, additional topics, and tools available on our companion web site, www.directoryprogramming.net.

What Is Covered?

The book primarily focuses on programming LDAP with the `System.DirectoryServices` namespace. At times, we address the new additions to .NET, `System.DirectoryServices.ActiveDirectory` (SDS.AD) and `System.DirectoryServices.Protocols` (SDS.P), when there is functionality or a scenario that is not addressed with `System.DirectoryServices`, although complete coverage of all of the new bits will require another book.

We take the approach of covering both the 1.1 and 2.0 versions of the .NET Framework. We realize that many developers will be working in both environments for years to come. Even for developers who may never use older versions, it is useful to learn the newer features by understanding the previous shortcomings.

The book also focuses on Microsoft's primary LDAP directory service product, Active Directory, with a fair amount of coverage of ADAM as well. While we do not provide specific examples of targeting non-Microsoft directories, we do try to point out the issues that are most likely to affect you, and how to avoid them.

The book is divided into two parts. Part I (Chapters 1–9) is all about the fundamentals of LDAP programming. It introduces the key concepts and provides a solid foundation upon which to build any type of directory services application. Part II (Chapters 10–12) is about applying the fundamentals from Part I to real-world problems and provides more of a "cookbook" approach. The topics in these last chapters come from what we see developers wrestling with everyday and our own experiences as we struggled to learn this.

Chapter 1 introduces the basic concepts of LDAP and discusses the key directory services that the book focuses on, Active Directory and ADAM. In Chapter 2, we continue the introduction with a survey of the APIs available for programming LDAP using the .NET Framework and discuss how they relate to each other.

Starting with Chapters 3 and 4, we cover the basic mechanics of accessing Active Directory or ADAM. In Chapter 3, we focus in detail on connecting to the directory, as well as creating, moving, renaming, and deleting objects. Chapter 4 covers the basics of searching. Searching is the fundamental activity of LDAP programming, so a solid grounding is essential.

Chapter 5 continues with the searching theme, but goes into detail on the advanced topics. The 2.0 release of the .NET Framework has added a host of new searching features, so we cover all of these here and provide complete samples.

Chapter 6 focuses on the intricacies of reading and writing attributes in the directory. We discuss all of the different attribute syntaxes, including the ones that tend to give developers the most trouble.

Chapter 7 covers LDAP schema and extensions, explaining key points that the enterprise developer should know for designing new schema.

We delve into the Windows security model in Chapter 8, addressing not only LDAP security and how it integrates with Windows security, but also the challenges of the security context in the ASP.NET environment. We will show you how to use Kerberos delegation and teach you common issues to look for. We also cover access control lists (ACLs) in Active Directory and ADAM and discuss the code access security (CAS) model in the .NET Framework, as well as how it applies to directory services programming.

Chapter 9 explores `System.DirectoryServices.ActiveDirectory`. This new namespace was introduced with .NET 2.0 and included many new capabilities for managing Active Directory and ADAM. We focus on one of the most useful features, the Locator service built into Active Directory that finds domain controllers on the network.

In Chapters 10, 11, and 12, we shift our focus from fundamentals to practical solutions for common problems. Some of these scenarios are advanced, but by this point, we should have you prepared to tackle them. Chapter 10 discusses user management in detail and provides a wealth of useful samples, as well as real answers to common problems. Chapter 11 covers group management in detail. We conclude in Chapter 12 with a variety of different approaches for authentication with LDAP, including a discussion of the alternatives.

We also include three appendices. Appendix A shows some different approaches for doing COM interop in .NET. COM interop is often required when working with these technologies, so it is useful to know the options here. Appendix B provides our list of "must-have" tools for LDAP programmers working with Active Directory and ADAM. Finally, Appendix C attempts to provide a cross-reference of common errors to topics in the book that deal with those problems. If you are stuck and need an answer fast, Appendix C might help you to use the book more effectively. We also tell you how to get in touch with us if you can't find what you are looking for here.

Target Audience

This book was written with the .NET enterprise application developer in mind. While it is generally applicable to any .NET developer doing directory services programming, we have included many topics of specific interest to the enterprise audience, including performance, scalability, and security scenarios. If you are new to .NET or programming in general, this may not be the book for you. We assume an overall moderate level of comfort and do not explain basic programming techniques.

The samples in the book are primarily in C#, but we do not specifically target C# developers. The samples try to focus on the usage of the classes themselves and not on the specific programming language. In cases where there are substantial differences beyond curly braces and semicolons, we show Visual Basic .NET samples as well. Additionally, all of the book's samples are available in both C# and Visual Basic .NET on the book's web site.

Prerequisites

To run the samples in this book, you will need the following.

- The .NET Framework (either SDK or redistributable). Version 2.0 is preferred, but 1.1 will suffice to a lesser extent.
- Active Directory on Windows 2000 Server or Windows Server 2003, or ADAM on Windows XP or Windows Server 2003.
- For ASP.NET examples, Windows 2000 Server, Windows Server 2003, or Windows XP running IIS is required.

Visual Studio .NET (either the 2005 or the 2003 version) is helpful, but not required.

Acknowledgments

From Joe Kaplan

They always say that writing a book is a lot of work, but only those who have done so can truly understand what that means.

First of all, thanks to our technical reviewers: Carlos, Matt, Weiqing, Richa, Smitha, Joe R., Keith, Dominick, and Joe S. You improved the quality of this material immensely. If anything is still wrong, it is not your fault.

Thanks to Ryan, who initially jumped on Keith's request for someone to write this book and kindly asked me to help. We barely knew each other when this started, but I now consider you a friend.

Thanks to Keith Brown, not only for introducing us to his publisher, but for reviewing as well. After reading your articles and seeing you speak for years, it has been a privilege to work with you directly.

The Active Directory team at Microsoft not only creates these APIs and products, but also actually listens to suggestions about how to make them better. Thanks especially to Dmitri Gavrilov and Eric Fleischman for their limitless knowledge and willingness to share it.

Thanks to everyone at Addison-Wesley for making this happen. You put a lot of faith in two new authors and demonstrated incredible patience along the way as we struggled mightily with our deadlines. Joan Murray and Jessica D'Amico kept us on the path and actually managed to wring a book out of us after all. Julie Nahil got our raw material turned into a finished product and the intrepid Audrey Doyle painstakingly proofed every word, even correcting the grammar in our code comments. The clients of our production software should be so lucky! Curt Johnson figured out how to get this thing in front of you.

Thanks especially to my wife, Karen, and son, Evan, for their patience, love, and support. Evan, I'm not sure if you will remember this when you are older, but I'm sure Mommy will never be old enough to forget this.

Finally, thanks to the directory services community at large, MVPs and random strangers alike, for being on the front lines every day and bringing a never-ending stream of real-world problems to the table. This would not have been possible without you.

From Ryan Dunn

Writing this book has taken a lot of time and effort over the last year. It was not accomplished in a vacuum and both Joe and I have a lot of appreciation for the people who really made this happen. In no particular order, I would like to acknowledge and thank the following people.

- Keith Brown, for helping us get started and providing so much support. Born of a possibly frustrated request to have a book on `System.DirectoryServices`, this book probably would not have happened if he didn't ask.

- Joan Murray, Jessica D'Amico, Karen Gettman, Audrey Doyle, Julie Nahil, and everyone at Addison-Wesley for being so extraordinarily helpful and patient with two first-time authors. Joan and Jessica were marvelous to work with as they guided us through this process.

- Our reviewers (Carlos, Dominick, Joe R., Weiqinq, Keith, Matt, Smitha, Richa, and Joe S.) for checking our facts (in some cases, suffering our questions), and for their great suggestions. This book would not be the same without all of your efforts.

- Joe, for being a great coauthor, conference companion, and friend. We met for the first time in Chicago over lunch to discuss how we would write this beast. A little over a year later, it is finally done. Suffice it to say, it just would not be the same book without Joe's knowledge baked in here as well.

- My wife, Shailaja, who supported me constantly and never complained when book time cut into our time. I love you.

About the Authors

Joe Kaplan works in Accenture's internal IT organization, building enterprise applications using the .NET Framework. He specializes in directory services programming, for which he has been recognized as a Microsoft MVP. An industry veteran of more than thirteen years, he also thrives on working with the development community and solving real-world problems.

Ryan Dunn of Avanade is a .NET developer and architect with experience in a wide range of industries and technologies. He has consulted on a number of projects to integrate clients' applications with Active Directory and ADAM. Ryan is a Microsoft MVP for ASP.NET, though he currently focuses primarily on directory services. Ryan can be reached on the Web in the ASP.NET forums or through his blog at http://dunnry.com/blog.

PART I

Fundamentals

■ 1 ■

Introduction to LDAP and Active Directory

THIS CHAPTER DESCRIBES the fundamental underpinnings of the material in the rest of the book. Since this book is essentially about programming directory services using the Lightweight Directory Access Protocol (LDAP) with Microsoft's .NET platform, we introduce the basic concepts of LDAP directories and protocols here.

The first part of the chapter introduces directory services and some specific directory technologies. The second part is more technical and delves into some of the details concerning the LDAP specification itself.

A Brief History of Directory Services

Anyone who has ever used a phone book or library card catalog realizes that directories are very useful tools. For software developers, having a single place to store enterprise-wide user data such as email addresses and passwords is equally as useful. Essentially, a directory service is simply an electronic rolodex of sorts.

Our experience with the Internet shows us that having simple, standardized protocols is one of the keys to broad adoption of a technology. Try imagining the Internet today if there were no standard DNS system to resolve names into numeric IP addresses or an HTTP protocol to deliver web content! However, as is often the case in this industry, it took a while for a standard protocol (LDAP) to emerge and later become the underpinnings to one of the most successful data repositories today.

Directory services within organizations started out as point solutions to particular problems. As developers of these systems began to realize that many of the systems they worked on needed the same set of services, open products and tools began to emerge in the marketplace. However, these products tended to use proprietary network protocols, programmatic interfaces, and metaphors for organizing and naming the content they stored. At a certain point, people realized that a standard for directory services would allow huge interoperability within industry, government, and academia, saving everyone enormous amounts of time and money. Thus, the X.500 standard was born.

X.500 was adopted in 1988 under the ITU-T Recommendation X.500 (also known as ISO/IEC 9594: Information Technology-Open Systems Interconnection-The Directory). It formalized many important concepts that are essential to directory services today. These include a hierarchical metaphor for storing objects in the directory, a naming standard for referring to objects in the directory, and standard protocols for clients accessing the directory and other directories interacting with the directory.

One essential part of X.500 is the Directory Access Protocol, or DAP. DAP defines a client/server protocol for accessing an X.500 directory using the application layer of the Open System Interconnection (OSI) model. The OSI model was originally adopted because the implementers of the standard were interested in using X.500 to manage email addresses for the OSI message-handling application known as X.400.

Unfortunately, the OSI model is somewhat complex to implement and many thought an easier standard would be more useful for most clients. The University of Michigan had the idea of developing to the existing protocol and binding it directly to the TCP/IP network protocol for use over the Internet. They called their implementation Lightweight Directory Access Protocol, or LDAP.

Definition of LDAP

The Lightweight Directory Access Protocol (LDAP) specification was ratified in July 1993, in RFC 1487. Its inventors at the University of Michigan originally created it as a complement to the heavier-weight DAP X.500 protocol. At first, the LDAP designers just wanted a simple gateway interface to X.500 for the TCP/IP protocol that was easy to implement and program against. The idea was that the LDAP server component would translate LDAP calls into their corresponding DAP X.500 calls, and would translate the X.500 server responses back into LDAP for the client.

However, with the explosive growth of TCP/IP and Internet technologies in the 1990s, the new protocol took on a life of its own. The divergence from X.500 began when LDAP gained its own database and structuring conventions and became a directory specification on its own. Much as LDAP was created to simplify access to X.500, implementers began to realize that simplifying deployment of X.500 held a lot to be desired as well. Directories that supported an LDAP interface but did not support the entire X.500 specification began to appear. This is what we largely see today, with the majority of directory products in the marketplace supporting LDAP, but only small parts of the complete X.500 specification. Since this book is primarily about LDAP and .NET, this is the last you will hear of X.500 from us.

LDAP was revised several more times under RFC 1777–1779 in 1995 (LDAP version 2) and RFC 2251–2256 in 1997 (LDAP version 3). We are primarily concerned with LDAP version 3 today. It is interesting to note that LDAP version 3 was never formally approved, but exists today as a recommendation and de facto standard of sorts. As you can imagine, this has led to some bickering within the industry, with some of Microsoft's implementation decisions for Active Directory being the target of this criticism. However, this book is all about practicality and these distinctions rarely prevent us from getting real work done. We will leave most of that criticism for the academics to grapple with.

Much of the rest of this chapter explores the basic concepts of LDAP.

Definition of Active Directory

Active Directory is Microsoft's directory service and Enterprise Network Operating System (ENOS) for Windows 2000 Server and Windows Server 2003. Active Directory is an integral part of the Windows server product, in that you cannot purchase or install it separately. Any Windows 2000/2003 server (besides the Web Edition) can be "promoted" to be an Active Directory domain controller. Active Directory serves as the store for user and computer accounts within an organization, as well as many other types of objects.

It is not possible to explain something like Active Directory thoroughly in just a few paragraphs. Some fantastic books already cover the subject in detail, such as *Active Directory, Third Edition*.[1] However, a few key concepts are especially relevant to developers.

Domain

The **domain** is the fundamental organizing concept for objects in Active Directory. A domain defines a directory partition or naming context (discussed shortly) where objects such as users, groups, and computers are stored and organized in a hierarchy. The domain also forms a replication boundary, in that the objects in a domain replicate only with other domain controllers for that domain.

Domain Tree

A **domain tree** is a collection of domains organized in a hierarchy and sharing the same DNS namespace. A domain tree also shares a common security relationship through trust relationships.

Forest

A **forest** is essentially a collection of domain trees that share a common schema, global catalog, and security relationship via trust relationships. We like to say that a forest is an Active Directory. Note that a forest need not contain more than one domain, but may contain many domains that can have complex hierarchical relationships to each other. Forests also do not need to have a contiguous namespace. For example, a forest can include two domain trees, such as "bigcompany.biz" and "mydomain.com".

Domain Controller

A **domain controller** is a Windows server that is specifically designated to provide directory services to a particular domain. Some directory services provided by the domain controller include LDAP access to the directory

---

1. Allen, R., and J. Richards. 2006. *Active Directory, Third Edition*. Sebastopol, Calif: O'Reilly.

store, a Kerberos Key Distribution Center (KDC) for Kerberos authentication services, and replication services to synchronize information in the directory with other domain controllers in the domain. A domain controller provides other directory services, such as DNS, but we are primarily interested in LDAP from a programming perspective.

A domain controller has at least three directory partitions, or naming contexts, that can be searched via LDAP. In addition to the domain partition that contains familiar objects such as users, groups, and computers, a domain controller has a configuration partition and a schema partition. As their names imply, the **configuration partition** contains configuration information such as replication topology, and the **schema partition** contains a description of the schema. Note that the configuration and schema partitions are replicated throughout the whole forest, unlike the domain partition, which is replicated only to other domain controllers in its domain.

Global Catalog

The **global catalog** provides a mechanism that enables us to search the entire forest at once instead of searching in a specific domain. It exists to solve the problem of "I know the object is in the forest somewhere, but I have no idea which domain it is actually in." The global catalog contains a partial replica of every object in every domain in the forest that includes the data we are most likely to want to use in a search. Global catalog searches are essentially just LDAP searches on a different TCP/IP port. Note that not every domain controller is a global catalog server, although that is certainly possible. We definitely need to have at least one!

Definition of ADAM

ADAM stands for Active Directory/Application Mode. ADAM is the Microsoft product that provides a stand-alone directory service without any of the network operating system features of Active Directory. Microsoft created ADAM in response to demand from customers for a platform that applications could use to provide simple directory service features without all of the additional features, limitations, and deployment complexity that come with Active Directory. The analogy we like to use is that ADAM is like an empty SQL Server database with an LDAP interface. It doesn't really do anything until you add some schema elements and data to it and write some code to access it. Let's explain ADAM by way of comparison with Active Directory and then mention a few possible scenarios where one might use ADAM.

Comparing ADAM with Active Directory

Since ADAM is based on Active Directory technologies, ADAM and Active Directory share many similarities, but also some important differences.

- ADAM is based on the underlying Active Directory database and technologies, and it provides similar scalability and performance, as well as the same replication engine. ADAM instances can be replicated.

- ADAM does not function as a network operating system and has no integrated DNS services.

- ADAM does not use the organizational concept of forests and domains. Instead, ADAM instances that replicate specific directory partitions are said to be part of the same configuration set.

- ADAM is not a store for Windows user and computer accounts. We cannot log on to Windows with accounts stored in ADAM.

- ADAM does not provide Kerberos services (Ticket Granting Service, etc.), like Active Directory does. ADAM cannot be used as a Kerberos realm.

- ADAM installs with a very basic schema. We are supposed to extend the schema to contain the classes and attribute definitions that our application needs. It is possible to add most of the Active Directory schema to ADAM, but this is not done by default.

- ADAM runs as a standard Windows service, not as an integral part of the operating system (a system service), like Active Directory does. This means that we can run multiple ADAM instances on the same machine on different network ports and under different service accounts. ADAM is not integrated with the Local Security Authority system service, as Active Directory is. Unlike the current version of Active Directory, we can start and stop ADAM whenever we like.

- ADAM allows us to use other LDAP naming attributes, such as "O" and "C," that are used in other LDAP directories. Additionally, we can root the directory in any namespace we want, such as `O=foobar` or `CN=myadaminstance`. Active Directory restricts us to using DNS names such as `DC=foobar,DC=com` for the root of a naming context.

- We can create user account objects in ADAM that can be authenticated with a simple LDAP bind. This makes ADAM useful as a user store for applications.

- ADAM can also use an LDAP bind to authenticate Windows users. By Windows users, we mean users that are stored in a domain such as Active Directory, or users stored on the local server where ADAM is installed. This feature is called **pass-through authentication**. Here, no object representing the Windows user is actually stored in ADAM. ADAM simply forwards the authentication request on to the machine itself.

- ADAM does not require an additional license beyond the license you purchased for the host operating system. We also can redistribute ADAM with our own products, subject to the terms of the license agreement, of course (we are not lawyers; read the fine print).

Based on our experience so far, many people have had difficulty determining exactly what ADAM is, or more importantly, what they are supposed to do with it. So, what exactly did Microsoft have in mind when it released this thing? Here are some common scenarios that we hope will help to illustrate the concept.

- Let's say we are building a public-facing web site that can hold thousands (or hopefully millions) of accounts for our (hopefully paying) customers. We do not want to use Active Directory, as we do not need all of its features; we simply want a user store. ADAM gives us an alternative to using a traditional relational database such as SQL Server to store these accounts, authenticate our users, and manage the life cycle of their accounts. Because it already has first-class support for things like secure password storage, password policies, account life cycles, and groups, ADAM provides many benefits over SQL out of the box.

- Now, let's take the same example we just described, but instead of a public-facing web site, we have an extranet scenario with internal users who are stored in Active Directory but external users who are not. Again, we can use ADAM and its pass-through authentication feature to store the external users in ADAM and authenticate both types of users with an LDAP bind. This keeps the application design simple and prevents us from having to duplicate our internal user accounts in a separate directory, reducing the complexity of managing the identity life cycle on our internal accounts.

- ADAM is a great place to store company-wide directory information that we might not want to include inside Active Directory—for example, items such as pictures that can take up a lot of space and consume precious replication bandwidth. We also can use ADAM in this case as a central aggregation point for many disparate directories, including non-Microsoft directories and perhaps even directories that are not implemented with LDAP at all.

- Perhaps we are building a commercial product, such as a certificate authority that issues certificates for SSL, end-user encryption, or code signing, and we are targeting our product for the Windows platform. We would like to provide an LDAP interface into our certificate store. ADAM allows us to use Microsoft's LDAP database to provide these features, saving us the trouble of building such a store ourselves and giving us all of the enterprise-scale features that Active Directory is known for (a robust store for large numbers of objects, replication, deployment flexibility, etc.). We can then redistribute ADAM with our product, assuming it already targets Windows Server 2003.

This book deals primarily with Active Directory, but much of it applies directly to ADAM as well. When there are interesting differences, we point them out and try to provide relevant examples whenever possible.

LDAP Basics

Even though this book is primarily about programming directory services in .NET, we are generally using the LDAP protocol under the hood, so it behooves us to know a little bit about it. It is actually quite simple.

The key aspects of the LDAP protocol are as follows.

- LDAP is bound directly to the TCP/IP network protocol. This distinguishes it from DAP, which incurs more of the overhead of the full OSI network stack.
- Much of the data exchanged with LDAP is encoded as ordinary strings rather than as obscure binary representations.
- LDAP uses a set of request/response message pairs performed on a persistent connection to define the basic operations in the protocol.

Under the hood, LDAP uses something called Basic Encoding Rules, or BER, to encode all elements of the protocol. BER is part of the ASN.1 specification for data encoding. ASN.1 is used extensively for binary encoding of structured data, and it shows up all over the place. BER is unlike XML, in that humans cannot really read BER-encoded data directly, as it is in a binary format. Fortunately, it is like XML, in that many libraries out there can parse the data for us, so we rarely have to deal with it directly in practice. The APIs we'll be using in this book are no exception, so suffice it to say that BER is in there, under the hood, and we'll leave it at that. If you want to find out more, please refer to the references on the book's web site, or type "ASN.1" into your favorite search engine and party on.

LDAP Distinguished Names

LDAP distinguished names (DNs for short) are a fundamental part of all LDAP programming, so let's take some time to explain them in detail. At its heart, an LDAP directory is a hierarchical store of objects, much like a typical filesystem. Like any good filesystem, LDAP has a path syntax to uniquely identify objects in the store. Let's start with an example of a DN and break it down:

```
CN=Jane.Doe,OU=People,DC=domain,DC=local
```

This DN is composed of four relative distinguished name (RDN) parts.

1. `CN=Jane.Doe`
2. `OU=People`
3. `DC=domain`
4. `DC=local`

Like a DNS name (such as `www.mydomain.com`), the DN reads from the most specific node on the left to the least specific node on the right. In the LDAP style, the root of the tree (`DC=local`) is at the end. Each RDN is a child of the object whose RDN is to its right. The object deepest in the tree in this DN is the object pointed to by `CN=Jane.Doe`.

This is conceptually quite similar to a filesystem path, except that the order is reversed. In a typical Windows filesystem path, we might have the following:

```
c:\local\domain\people\jane.doe.txt
```

As we know, `c:` is the drive in this case, and it represents the root of the namespace. `local`, `domain`, and `people` represent directories, and `jane.doe.txt` represents a document object in the filesystem. Here, the most specific part (the file itself) is on the right, at the end of the path.

The filesystem analogy holds up remarkably well when approaching an LDAP directory, and it is probably our most common interaction with a hierarchical data store in day-to-day life. The key differences are that the naming concept is different, and we tend to think of filesystems as containing either containers (directories) or objects (files). In an LDAP directory, containers are also first-class objects that contain their own data (attributes) as well.

As we can see, each RDN is composed of two parts: the name of the attribute that provides the primary name of the object, and the value of that attribute. In our example, `CN`, which stands for common name, is the name of the attribute that provides the primary name for objects of its class. `Jane.Doe` is the value of this attribute. We also see RDN attributes for `OU` (organizational unit) and `DC` (domain component).

Like a filesystem, the name for an object in an LDAP container must be unique. Thus, CN=Jane.Doe uniquely identifies this object within its container (OU=People). As a result, the entire DN uniquely identifies this particular object in the entire directory tree.

Another important difference is that the root of the namespace in LDAP is not necessarily equivalent to the highest-level RDN. In fact, in the previous example, the naming root is likely to be DC=domain,DC=local, not DC=local. To push our analogy a little further, DC=domain,DC=local is roughly equivalent to the c: drive on the filesystem in that the path c:\ is the highest-level place to put files on the c: drive. In our LDAP directory, the name of highest-level container to store objects in the partition is DC=domain,DC=local. There isn't actually a container object called DC=local that holds a container called DC=domain. This aspect of LDAP naming is probably one of LDAP's less intuitive features, but it is easy to deal with once we accept it. More detail follows, when we discuss naming contexts.

Now, let's look at some of the picky details.

- The characters <, ;+\"> cannot appear within a DN unless they are escaped with a \ character. Additionally, # must be escaped if it is the first character in the DN. Because escape sequences are allowed, parsing DNs can be more complicated than one might have originally hoped. Forward slashes do not need to be escaped for LDAP, but since they are used as path separators for ADSI (see Chapter 2), they must be escaped when used in ADSI-based APIs.

- Name components may contain spaces, although they are ignored if they are at the beginning or end of the string (unless they are escaped; see the previous bullet).

- Provisions also exist for encoding special characters using a binary syntax of the two hex characters representing a byte of data, preceded by a backslash. For instance, to use every developer's favorite example of an unprintable character, we might encode a newline character with the sequence \0A. Thus, a DN with a newline character might look like CN=Jane\0ADoe,OU=People,O=myorg.

Let's look at a couple of examples.

- `CN=spaces in name,O=Test`. This DN has spaces in the name. They are perfectly legal and do not require escapes.
- `CN=embedded\,comma,O=Test`. This DN has an embedded comma in the common name that needs to be escaped. The CN for the object is `embedded,comma`. However, the DN will always be returned in the escaped form.

■ WARNING   Avoid DNs That Require Escapes!

It is not always your decision to make, but life is always easier when you can avoid DNs that require escape sequences. If you have any influence over the naming policy in the directories you will be programming, please use it to discourage names with escape characters. You will thank us later.

Especially annoying are names that include a /, as LDAP does not require this to be escaped, but ADSI does. As a result, when using ADSI-based APIs, we may read an attribute from the directory that contains a DN, but then may need to escape it ourselves in order to use it in an LDAP path. It's best to avoid this kind of complexity.

If you are interested in digging up all the details, including the wonderful BNF grammar that describes the full DN syntax, we invite you to read RFC 2253 in all its glory.[2]

Naming Contexts

A **naming context** is the name of the object that represents the root of a directory tree. Naming contexts are also called directory partitions. Objects in that part of the tree will have a DN based on the name of the naming context. For example, if we have an Active Directory–style naming context

---

2. Though the current DN specification, RFC 2253, is fairly strict, the previous version for LDAP version 2, RFC 1779, is much more flexible. It allows the use of ; as a separator, it uses alternate escape mechanisms, and it is very lenient with the use of whitespace. LDAP version 3 implementations must accept input in LDAP version 2 format, but must always return values in LDAP version 3 syntax. Luckily, we do not have to deal with LDAP version 2 very often, but we may need to be aware of it.

called `DC=yourdomain,DC=com`, then all objects in that part of the tree have a name such as `CN=users,DC=yourdomain,DC=com`.

A directory may define multiple naming contexts that represent different directory trees. Typically, a directory will define a default naming context where the main objects are stored. As previously stated, Active Directory also defines a configuration naming context where configuration about the domain is stored, as well as a schema naming context where the schema objects are stored.

Another interesting aspect of naming contexts is that they may seem to have overlapping namespaces, but they are not actually part of the same tree. For example, an Active Directory domain such as `DC=mydomain,DC=com` will also contain a configuration partition, `CN=configuration,DC=mydomain,DC=com`, and a schema partition, `CN=schema,CN=configuration,DC=mydomain,DC=com`. Even though the actual names appear to form a hierarchy, the configuration partition cannot be accessed when searching inside the main domain partition and the schema partition cannot be searched from within the configuration partition. They are separate partitions that form their own roots.

ADAM is especially interesting here. It places no restrictions on root naming contexts, allowing us to call them whatever we want and allowing us to have practically as many as we want. Because ADAM instances are not rooted to a specific DNS namespace, as Active Directory must be, the configuration and schema partitions for an ADAM instance will always be rooted to an arbitrary GUID generated when the instance is first set up. For example, an ADAM instance configuration and schema partition DN might look like this:[3]

```
CN=Configuration,CN={94E8B161-1EBC-45E5-9407-1961AD6A9EDC}
CN=Schema,CN=Configuration,
    CN={94E8B161-1EBC-45E5-9407-1961AD6A9EDC}
```

Schema Basics

LDAP schema is composed of object class definitions that describe the types of objects that the directory may hold, along with attribute definitions that

---

3. Do not worry about the nasty GUID names here. We generally do not need to remember these, as we can discover these names dynamically using the `RootDSE` object that we describe in Chapter 3.

items that class instances may contain. LDAP inherits most
antics from its X.500 roots.

writing a book for enterprise developers, it seems like a
lain LDAP schema in terms of other schemas that we
know. By way of analogy, LDAP schema probably most
resembles a single-inheritance, object-oriented-type system such as
that used in the .NET common language runtime (CLR) or Java runtime,
but with some very specific differences. The obvious difference is that
LDAP schema defines only data, not behavior. It is, after all, a database.
However, the other important distinction is that LDAP objects are composed of largely primitive types (the attributes) rather than other objects.
There is also no notion of visibility scoping, such as public and private.

If you are familiar with XML schema, you may be thinking that LDAP
seems similar. On the surface, this may seem true, as LDAP also provides a
way to define hierarchical data. However, LDAP is quite a bit more
straightforward, and the analogy begins to fall apart as soon as we start to
consider XML complex types and such weird notions as "derive by restriction." We won't really use this analogy as we move forward, and we will
just be glad that LDAP schema is so much easier to comprehend.

Additionally, LDAP holds little resemblance to the table and column
schemas familiar to most relational database developers. Programmers
that are used to thinking about data sources only from the relational perspective will find LDAP to be remarkably different. However, there are a
few interesting similarities to SQL that we will refer to from time to time.

LDAP Classes

All LDAP class definitions share some basic characteristics.

Class Name. The class name indicates the type of an instance of a class
in the directory tree. Each object in the tree will have an `objectClass`
attribute with the name of the class of which it is an instance. Because
classes use inheritance, this attribute will also include the names of the parent classes.

Subclass. The subclass value indicates from which class the class inherits.
Only one subclass can be specified. All classes in the schema inherit from a
common root. The root of the class tree is the `Top` class (appropriately

named), which is defined to inherit from itself by convention, meaning that it has no parent. Note that the use of the word *subclass* here is exactly opposite from what objected-oriented programmers are used to saying, but try not to let that throw you.

Possible Superiors. A class includes a list of possible superiors. This list indicates which object classes may contain instances of this object in the directory tree. This is how the hierarchy of the tree is defined, similar to how directories work in a filesystem. However, unlike a filesystem, an LDAP directory allows many different types of objects to be containers. To push the analogy a little further, LDAP objects can be both files and folders.

Auxiliary Classes. A class may include multiple auxiliary classes. Auxiliary classes define additional attributes and characteristics that a class may contain and that can be shared among classes that have no direct inheritance relationship. For example, in Active Directory, both users and groups are mail recipients and security principals, but both have different inheritance hierarchies. As such, auxiliary classes are similar to interfaces in .NET, Java, and C++. In Windows Server 2003 Active Directory and ADAM, the directory also allows auxiliary classes to be added to specific objects dynamically at runtime.

RDN Attribute ID. The RDN attribute ID specifies the name of the attribute that is used to create the RDN for the object. For example, if the RDN is CN=Joe, then the RDN attribute ID is CN, which refers to the common name attribute. Note that at present, Active Directory uses only three different RDN attribute IDs: CN, OU, and DC. CN is the most common. Most other LDAP directories, including ADAM, can use a variety of other RDN attribute IDs.

Must Contain Attributes. Must contain attributes is a list of attributes that instances of the class must contain to be valid. These attributes are supplied by the caller during an LDAP Add operation or are generated by the system automatically. This is exactly like a column in SQL that does not allow nulls.

May Contain Attributes. May contain attributes is a list of attributes that class instances may optionally contain, but are not required by the schema. The vast majority of attributes fall under this category. It is very common for a large percentage of the available attributes for a class not to be populated. Technically, this is semantically different from having a null column value in a row in an SQL database, as an attribute that has no data is said not to exist on the object at all, whereas in SQL, the column for the row still exists but has a null value. However, from a programming perspective, the result is fairly similar. SQL developers who go to great lengths to exclude nulls from table schemas are in for a rude awakening with LDAP.

As usual, we've omitted a fair amount of detail at this point. We'll talk a bit more about some of the other interesting points about object classes when we discuss schema extensions in Chapter 7.

LDAP Attributes

Attributes define the data stored in objects in the directory tree. Fundamentally, attribute definitions consist of a name, a syntax, and a flag indicating whether the attribute can contain only one value or multiple values. The syntaxes describe the primitive data-type definitions for the directory, and generally, they are based on externally defined types, many originating from the initial X.500 specifications.

Names. Although we said that attribute definitions consist of a *name*, there are actually four important names for attributes, all of which are unique (for the same name type), and important in different circumstances.

The *LDAP display name* is probably the most important, as it generally is used in most directory operations, including searching, reading values, and performing modifications.

The *common name* represents the object defining the attribute in the schema, but it is used most often in schema definition. It is often (but definitely not always) the same as the LDAP display name.

The *attribute ID* is the Object Identifier (OID) for the object. LDAP requires that all attributes have an OID to define it uniquely to the public. OIDs are hierarchical naming devices that typically are represented in "decimal dot" notation—for example, 2.5.5.1. OIDs typically are registered with a centralized authority. A registered owner of an OID prefix may issue additional nodes underneath that prefix. In this way, OIDs are similar to the DNS system used on the Internet.

An interesting point about OIDs is that they are required in several places by the LDAP specifications, but Microsoft rarely uses them in practice, favoring GUIDs instead for internal processing because GUIDs are easier to generate and store, are fixed in size, and are easy to index. In fact, the fourth unique name for an attribute is the **schema ID GUID**, which is generally a well-known, published GUID value. It is used primarily for integrating with the Windows security system, used throughout Active Directory and ADAM. The Windows access control entry (ACE) structure allows GUIDs to be used to specify additional properties, and these are used to provide features such as attribute-level access control by specifying the schema ID GUID in its place.

Syntaxes. Attributes are defined to have a specific syntax. Syntaxes make up the primitive data types of LDAP, and generally, they are defined in some external source. They are roughly analogous to types in the .NET Framework, such as `System.Byte`, `System.Int32`, `System.DateTime`, and `System.String`. Many LDAP syntaxes come directly from X.500. There are syntaxes for representing different types of strings, numbers, dates, and arbitrary binary data, to name a few. Thus, even though we said that LDAP uses strings and BER encoding to transmit and store data, the attribute syntax specifies the exact nature of the data the attribute may contain.

DN Syntax and Linked Attributes. One of the most interesting syntax types that LDAP defines is the DN syntax. A DN attribute is essentially a pointer to another object in the directory. You can think of DN attributes as being similar to foreign keys in a SQL database. For example, a `manager` attribute defined as having DN syntax could contain the DN of the object in the directory containing that object's manager.

DNs are very useful because the directory maintains the correct value for the DN, even when the target is moved or renamed. DNs can also be set up to use forward and backward links, where a backward link is maintained automatically by the directory service. Using our original example, the `manager` attribute may have a back-linked attribute called `managerOf` that contains a list of the objects the current object manages. Because the directory maintains the back link, we need only specify the object's manager to be able to tell which objects another object manages. This concept is very powerful and is used throughout LDAP to create relationships between objects across the directory hierarchy.

Single and Multivalued Attributes. Attributes can be defined to hold single or multiple values. For those used to thinking about data from the perspective of traditional relational databases, this is an important distinction. SQL databases support a single value per column. In SQL, we typically need to normalize our data into separate tables to support similar semantics. Multivalued attributes simply contain a list of values that all share the same syntax.

There is more to attributes than what we have described here, but this gives you a basis for understanding how they work. Chapter 6 explores attribute values from the .NET perspective in great detail. Chapter 7 also digs into more specifics of the schema itself, from the programmer's perspective.

LDAP Protocol and API Basics

Before jumping into the .NET programming model for LDAP, it helps to look at the LDAP Protocol and API as it is defined by the standards and implemented in Microsoft's unmanaged LDAP library, wldap32.dll.

The LDAP Protocol uses a connection-based metaphor at the heart of its model. We begin our LDAP conversation by creating a persistent connection to the LDAP server. Then, we perform operations on top of this connection until we are done, when we close it. The operations are defined in a short set of request/response message pairs. For developers familiar with .NET's SQL programming model, this connection-based model should feel right at home. Instead of issuing SQL queries to the database, though, we send out request messages and wait to receive a corresponding response.

The following subsections provide a high-level introduction of the basic operations we perform on the LDAP server. The gory details are available in the LDAP RFCs and in Microsoft's LDAP API documentation, which you can browse at your leisure. As we explore the .NET APIs in depth in the rest of the book, we will pick the pieces that are important in the context of .NET development.

Init

Also known as "connect," this is where we establish the connection with our LDAP server based on its DNS name or numeric IP address and the TCP/IP port we wish to use for our requests. TCP port 389 is the standard registered port for normal LDAP and 636 is the standard port for SSL/ LDAP. Active Directory uses these ports exclusively, but an LDAP server such as ADAM may respond on any port. This operation returns the connection handle that we will use in all of our remaining operations.[4]

Bind

This is where we supply some credentials and authenticate with the server. The base LDAP API supports supplying a username and password and passing that over the network. However, LDAP also supports an extensibility mechanism where other types of authentication can be used. We will discuss many of these options in much more detail in Chapter 8.

We should make a few interesting points here, however, before we move on. First, the actual bind occurs on the connection handle that we established through our `Init` function (explained earlier). In Chapter 2 when we talk about ADSI, we'll talk about binding to an object, but under the hood, the bind is performed on the connection.

Another important point is that once we bind, the state of our connection changes to the authenticated state, and it stays that way until we "unbind" or disconnect. If we bind again as a different user, the connection is authenticated as the new user, not as the old user.[5]

Finally, we should point out that although most LDAP API calls are thread-safe, the bind operation changes the state of the connection as a whole, and so we must be careful to consider that issue when sharing a connection among multiple threads.

Binding is so important to understand that we cover it in detail in not just one chapter, but two! Chapter 3 explores binding in general, and Chapter 8 focuses on binding from the perspective of security.

Search

Search is arguably the most important operation in LDAP. This is how we find objects in the directory tree and read their attribute values. Given that

---

4. Init is not actually an LDAP operation as defined in the LDAP specification. However, from the perspective of Microsoft's LDAP API, it is how we establish the initial connection to the directory in order to perform subsequent operations, so we list it here.
5. This is not true in the case of "concurrent binds," which are a feature of Active Directory on Windows Server 2003 and ADAM.

LDAP directories are hierarchical, the semantics are somewhat different from more familiar query syntaxes such as SQL. However, LDAP is also much simpler than SQL with SQL's joins, subqueries, ordering, and grouping.

An LDAP query is composed of four basic parts: a search root, a search scope, a filter, and a list of attributes to return. There are actually more parameters and options, but these are our primary concern. We will delve more deeply into LDAP searching as it relates to .NET in Chapter 4.

Search Root. The search root determines the place in the tree from which the search will start. This value is passed in as a DN in string format. To search the entire directory, we pass in the DN of the object that is the root of the tree. To search lower in the hierarchy, we specify a lower-level DN. The search root can also be null. In this case, the search root is used to return a special object called RootDSE, or to search across multiple namespaces in the Active Directory forest with the global catalog.

Search Scope. This parameter allows us to specify three different scopes: subtree, one-level, and base. A subtree search says to search the entire tree below the level of the search root, including the search root itself. Subtree searches generally are used for directory-wide searches or deep searches within a branch of the tree. A one-level search will search only within the immediate children of the search root object, excluding the search root object itself.

The base-level search is probably the least obvious. It searches only within the search root object itself. It generally is used for retrieving attribute values from the search root object. Additionally, some attributes can be retrieved only via a base-level search.

Search Filter. The filter determines which objects will be returned in the query. It is analogous to the WHERE clause in an SQL statement. Each object in the scope of the query will be evaluated against the filter to determine whether it matches. LDAP filters are specified using a special syntax based on attribute matching and simple grouping. Fans of the LISP programming language or Excel formula language will feel very comfortable with the use of parentheses. We'll be discussing LDAP filters in Chapter 4. RFC 2254 describes the formal specification for the filter syntax.

Attribute List. Finally, a list of attributes to return for each object can be specified. If the returned object has a value populated for that attribute (and we have permission to see it), the value will be returned in the result. Note that it is possible to specify a null attribute list, in which case all normal attributes that have a value for the object are returned.

In some directories, such as Active Directory, certain types of attributes can be returned only if they are specifically requested because they are constructed programmatically by the server or are otherwise restricted from being returned by default. As such, they are much like a calculated column in a relational database.

We have skipped such details as timeout values, client and server controls, and such, but the point here is to get a feel for how search works and not to dwell exhaustively on the finer points. We cover all of that when we discuss searching with .NET in Chapters 4 and 5.

Add

As you might have guessed, the purpose of the add operation is to add an object to the directory tree. This operation is quite straightforward and requires only the DN of the entry to add and a set of additional attributes to set on the object during creation. As we discussed in the section Must Contain Attributes, earlier in this chapter, many classes in the schema require that certain values be populated at all times. Some of these attributes are intended to be supplied by the creator of the object, not by the system, so they must be specified during the add operation to satisfy the requirements of the schema. Other nonmandatory attributes can also be specified in the add operation.

Another important thing to point out is that we add objects to the tree one at a time. There is no notion of a bulk insert, as we see in some SQL implementations.

Delete

The delete operation removes an object from the directory tree. The operation is also quite simple to call, as it requires only the DN of the object to be removed.

Observant readers may wonder what happens when we delete an object that has children, or how deletion actually works in a replicated, multimaster directory such as Active Directory. Using a filesystem analogy, we might expect that deleting a container will delete all of its descendents as well.

However, that is not the default behavior in LDAP. We actually have to do some extra work to get that behavior. Additionally, most objects really are not permanently deleted from Active Directory right away, as we still need to be able to replicate out that change. Instead, the object is turned into a special "tombstone" object that is moved into a special "Deleted Objects" container. Tombstones retain only a fraction of their original attribute data, such as their GUID and a few other key identifying attributes. This is enough data to allow the deletion to replicate successfully to other replication partners. It is rarely enough to restore them back to their exact original state, however.

Modify

The `modify` operation is used to change the attribute values of an object in the directory. We specify the DN of the object to modify and a list of "modify operations" that specify the value(s) to change and the type of modification to make to each attribute. LDAP supports `add`, `delete`, and `replace` semantics.

- `Add` appends an additional value or values to an existing attribute, or creates an initial value for the attribute if it was not defined previously.
- `Delete` removes a specific value or values from an existing attribute, possibly removing the attribute from the object completely.
- `Replace` erases the existing value or values and places the specified value(s) in the attribute, or removes the attribute entirely from the object, depending on whether a new value or a null value is supplied.

One interesting thing about the values specified for a modification is that they are specified as either strings or binary encoded data. Even though LDAP supports the notion of specific syntaxes for attributes, the actual input and output are performed using only strings and binary data. Additionally, any attribute value can be interpreted in either way, so it is up to the caller to choose what is most appropriate to use!

The .NET interfaces we typically use return data as strongly typed .NET or COM data types such as integers, Booleans, and dates, as well as strings and raw binary data. Obviously, something magical is going on under the hood to make this happen. Chapter 6 covers this topic in detail.

Rename

This operation allows us to change the DN of an object in the tree. Changing the DN can have the effect of just renaming it within its current container, or it can also move the object and its children to a different location in the tree.

The `rename` operation has an interesting history, because the original versions of this API only allowed for changing the RDN of the object, meaning that we could not use it to move an object to a new parent in the tree. This turned out to be too limiting, so the API was expanded in later versions and the previous operations were largely deprecated.

Compare

The `compare` operation allows us to determine whether an attribute value in an object in the directory contains a certain value. The operation has no direct ADSI equivalent, so it is less familiar to many developers who do not use the LDAP API directly.

LDAP Controls

LDAP controls provide a standard extensibility mechanism in the LDAP version 3 protocol that allows LDAP directories to implement directory-specific functionality. Active Directory uses controls extensively to implement functions such as paged searches and virtual list views, which we discuss in Chapter 5. We generally do not interact with controls directly, as the underlying programming model usually takes care of this for us. However, it is helpful to know that they exist. Many of the standard operations allow an optional list of controls to be specified that will modify the behavior of the operation in an implementation-specific way.

SUMMARY

This chapter provided a high-level look at directory services in general, as well as a brief discussion of some of the directories we are primarily interested in, such as Active Directory and ADAM.

We concluded with a survey of the LDAP basics, including a discussion of schemas and the basic operations in the LDAP Protocol.

We skipped a lot of details and purposely avoided showing any C-style function signatures. The various RFCs, as well as Microsoft's own documentation of its LDAP API implementation, cover all of this in gory detail. While we only dipped our toes into a lot of this information, we did so that when we get into some of the sticky topics later on and we talk about what is going on under the hood, we will have a little background.

■ 2 ■
Introduction to .NET Directory Services Programming

T HIS CHAPTER INTRODUCES .NET developers to the world of Lightweight Directory Access Protocol (LDAP) directory services programming. We will discuss the overall landscape of .NET directory services
programming as well as how .NET relates to the underlying native
Windows APIs. We will touch upon the three relevant namespaces for
.NET developers—System.DirectoryServices, System.Directory-
Services.ActiveDirectory, and System.DirectoryServices.Proto-
cols—and discuss how to choose among the various options available to us.

.NET Directory Services Programming Landscape

Now that we know a little bit about directory services and LDAP, it is time
to discuss how we access these services from the .NET Framework. The
inaugural release of .NET version 1.0 included a namespace called (appropriately enough) System.DirectoryServices. This namespace was
packaged in its own assembly, System.DirectoryServices.dll. Throughout
this book, we'll refer to System.DirectoryServices as SDS.

The next major .NET release (version 1.1) saw no major changes to
SDS, with only a few bug fixes and no major new features. However,
.NET 2.0 introduces two important new capabilities for directory services

programming. `System.DirectoryServices.ActiveDirectory` (SDS.AD) is a brand-new namespace included in the existing System.DirectoryServices.dll assembly that adds significant new capabilities specifically for accessing Active Directory and Active Directory/Application Mode (ADAM). It builds on top of the general API provided by SDS and integrates tightly with it. Additionally, it wraps a few of the native Windows Ds* API calls for Active Directory- and ADAM-specific operations.

`System.DirectoryServices.Protocols` (SDS.P) is also new in .NET 2.0 and is a complete departure from SDS. It provides a lower-level API for LDAP-only programming. It can speak LDAP via the native LDAP TCP/IP protocol or via the Directory Services Markup Language (DSML) protocol, which uses XML, SOAP, and HTTP to encapsulate LDAP messages. SDS.P is packaged in its own assembly, System.DirectoryServices.Protocols.dll, and it does not rely on any SDS or ADSI features. SDS.P provides the highest level of control and performance for managed LDAP programming at the expense of being more complex than SDS.

Since SDS.P provides a completely different API for .NET directory services programming, .NET developers now have a choice of which API to use. We'll discuss when to use which interface later in this chapter, and we'll even use SDS.P in a few examples in later chapters. Unfortunately, complete coverage of SDS.P is beyond the scope of this book. You smart SDS.P developers will have to translate most of the examples yourselves!

For those of us still using .NET 1.1 or (gasp!) 1.0, the decision about which API to use is much easier to make given we do not really have an option (we can only use SDS). We understand that many of us will need to go back and forth between all versions of the platform for at least a few more years. This book attempts to bridge the gap between .NET 1.x and 2.0. We will try to show how to do things both ways when version 2.0 provides something significantly new and different.

A variety of other dark horse contestants are in the .NET directory services landscape as well. Windows Management Instrumentation (WMI), the ubiquitous API that is very popular in the systems scripting world and seems to provide wrappers for just about everything in Windows, provides some directory service features. A few third-party providers also have some interesting .NET APIs that we can use. Finally, Microsoft is building a brand-new scriptable command shell code-named "Monad" that is based on .NET-managed code and provides some directory service features. Sadly, we are going to ignore all of these for the rest of the book, as we don't think that they are as interesting to our primary audience, the .NET enterprise developer, and we already have plenty to cover without them.

Native Directory Services Programming Landscape

Windows includes a variety of APIs for working with directory services in native or "unmanaged" code. Since all of the .NET APIs we'll be discussing in this book build on these native APIs, it is helpful to know a little bit about them as well.

Native LDAP

wldap32.dll is a DLL included with Windows that contains Microsoft's implementation of the standard LDAP API defined in the RFCs we mentioned in Chapter 1. It works directly on the TCP/IP protocol and is designed to be used from C and C++. This native LDAP implementation is the lowest-level API included with Windows for working with LDAP directories. It is not designed to be accessed via COM automation clients such as VBScript, JScript, and Visual Basic. The new SDS.P namespace is actually using this library for a lot of its functionality via P/Invoke.

The Net* APIs

Microsoft has a set of APIs in the Windows Platform SDK that are designed to provide access to the Windows Security Account Manager (SAM) infrastructure. All of these APIs are prefixed with the word "Net," so we refer to them as the Net* APIs. These APIs were originally designed to work with the Windows NT4 domain controller model and local machine accounts, but they also have limited support in Active Directory for backward compatibility. They communicate with remote machines via the Windows remote procedure call (RPC) infrastructure.

The Ds* Active Directory APIs

When Microsoft introduced Active Directory with Windows 2000, it included with the Windows Platform SDK a set of APIs for performing tasks specific to Active Directory. All of these APIs are prefixed with the letters "Ds" (e.g., DsGetDCName), so we refer to them collectively as the Ds* APIs. Even though the primary interface for managing Active Directory is LDAP, a variety of functions, such as locating an appropriate domain controller and managing replication, cannot be accomplished via LDAP alone. These APIs fill that gap. As with all APIs in the standard platform SDK, these are designed to be accessed via C and C++. They also communicate with Active Directory through the Windows RPC infrastructure.

Active Directory Service Interfaces (ADSI)

Active Directory Service Interfaces (ADSI) is a COM-based native API included with all versions of Windows for accessing a variety of different directory services using a provider model. Different ADSI providers implement the ADSI COM interfaces and provide access to specific directory service protocols via these standard interfaces. For example, the LDAP ADSI provider allows access to LDAP services and the WinNT provider allows access to the SAM system. Windows ships with a variety of different ADSI providers, including the two we already mentioned. The ADSI provider model is open, so third parties may also implement their own providers for their directories.

Unlike the other APIs we have been discussing, ADSI is higher level and designed primarily for use from automation clients such as VBScript and JScript, as well as from (non-.NET) Visual Basic and C++. As a result, ADSI is significantly easier to use than the other APIs and opens up the world of directory services programming to the scripting community. The ease with which developers and administrators can use and create scripts to maintain all of Microsoft's directory services has been crucial to its successful adoption.

As with any higher-level abstraction, ADSI generally performs more slowly than the APIs it encapsulates as we get further from the metal, so to speak. This is the price we pay for abstraction. However, because all of these APIs tend to access network resources, the network itself is often the limiting factor in performance. When used thoughtfully, ADSI can

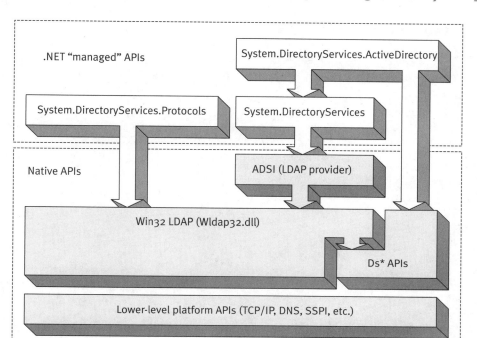

FIGURE 2.1: Directory Services Programming Landscape

offer extremely good performance that would be more than acceptable in most situations.

It is probably fair to say that the LDAP provider for ADSI is the most full featured of the ADSI providers and fits in with the ADSI interface model the best. For example, the ADSI search interface, IDirectorySearch, is fully exploited only by the LDAP provider.[1] As with any API that tries to provide a "one size fits all" interface to a variety of different systems, there are definitely some rough edges and missing features with all of the ADSI providers. For our purposes, ADSI (and its managed counterpart, System.DirectoryServices) represents the sweet spot for most of the work we want to do. The remaining rough spots and subtleties are what a lot of the rest of this book is about.

Figure 2.1 shows the familiar architectural "layer" model for the entire API stack.

---

1. IDirectorySearch also works with the NDS provider, but it is rarely used and we do not cover it in this book.

System.DirectoryServices Overview

The `System.DirectoryServices` namespace contains the core classes a developer will need to find, access, create, and update information in Active Directory or ADAM. In this section, we will cover the main classes and key aspects that every developer should know.

SDS uses .NET's ability to interoperate with COM to provide a managed code wrapper around some (but not all) of the ADSI interfaces, while still providing a set of classes that are consistent with the overall design of the .NET Framework.

A Word about ADSI Providers

Because SDS is based on ADSI, it can use all of ADSI's various providers to access different directory services. As we already stated, we are primarily interested in LDAP in this book, but SDS is designed to support the other providers as well (at least to some extent). However, most of these other providers don't fit in as well with the design as LDAP does, and they will eventually move into other manifestations in the .NET Framework.

SDS has been part of the .NET Framework since version 1.0 and is the only directory service API available on all versions of the framework. In .NET 2.0, the SDS namespace was overhauled to include a variety of new classes and features, and even more bug fixes. However, the API changes in 2.0 have been designed to maintain backward compatibility. Code compiled in versions 1.0 and 1.1 should also continue to run on the version 2.0 runtime.

We mentioned earlier that SDS is packaged in the System.Directory-Services.dll assembly. While this may seem obvious to many, it bears mentioning that we have to add an assembly reference to it in order to use the types in the namespace. Since no project types in Visual Studio include this assembly reference by default, we must remember to add it before proceeding.

Class Overview

We can divide the functionality in the `System.DirectoryServices` namespace into four subcategories:

- Directory object access
- Directory searching
- Directory object security
- Code access security

In Chapter 1, we discussed the LDAP API and mentioned that the primary metaphor for LDAP is based on sending and receiving messages on a persistent connection. However, in SDS (and ADSI), the primary metaphor is based on finding and manipulating objects in the directory. When we compare a directory service to a filesystem, the metaphor seems more natural. We are mainly interested in the files in the filesystem and are not so worried about how we were connected to it. As such, it makes sense that we would be interested primarily in the objects in the directory as well. However, in order to make this metaphor work, ADSI has to jump through some interesting hoops behind the scenes. Usually we can ignore this and just go about our work. Sometimes, however, there is enough friction between the two models that we must pay more attention to what's going on under the hood.

Directory Object Access

The `DirectoryEntry` class is the primary class used in SDS to represent objects in the directory. It provides the ability to read all of the properties (or attributes, in LDAP terms) of a directory object, as well as to modify objects. The `DirectoryEntry` class is based largely on top of the `IADs` interface in ADSI, which is the primary interface in ADSI. This primary class uses the `PropertyCollection` and `PropertyValueCollection` classes to read and modify attribute data, as well as a few additional enumerations to control things like authentication behavior. Closely related to the `Directory-Entry` class is the `DirectoryEntries` class, which allows for enumeration over a collection of `DirectoryEntry` objects and provides the means for adding and removing objects from the directory hierarchy. Most importantly, DirectoryEntry also controls the security context used to access the directory. It is essentially the core of the entire system.

Finally, a new DirectoryServicesCOMException has been added in the version 2.0 release to help developers more easily trap SDS exceptions and relay meaningful information that was previously somewhat obscured with the standard COMException. Although this new exception class alleviates some of the pains associated with exception handling in version 2.0, developers are still hamstrung to some extent because the underlying ADSI components tend to throw very generic and uninformative errors.

Directory Searching

The DirectorySearcher class provides the mechanism for searching LDAP directories in .NET. While DirectoryEntry is the core of the SDS system, DirectorySearcher is what sets SDS apart from other APIs. The DirectorySearcher class wraps the IDirectorySearch ADSI interface and provides a straightforward class for performing both simple and complex search functions that support nearly all of the features supported by LDAP and Active Directory. The DirectorySearcher class uses a DirectoryEntry object to define the location from which to start the search in the directory tree, and to define the security context used to perform the search.

DirectorySearcher uses a variety of other classes for support, such as the SearchResult, SearchResultCollection, ResultPropertyCollection, and ResultPropertyValueCollection classes. These allow enumeration of search results and read-only access to the attribute data from each result. Additionally, some other types and enumerations are used to support things such as search scope and sorting.

The biggest changes to SDS in .NET 2.0 surround the DirectorySearcher class. We can now perform virtual list view searches, attribute-scoped queries, and searches for deleted items, and we can get extended distinguished name (DN) information, among other things. All of these are welcome new additions, and we will discuss them in more detail in Chapters 4 and 5.

IDirectorySearch

Technically, we can use `DirectorySearcher` with any ADSI provider that supports the `IDirectorySearch` interface. However, in practice, this is limited to a single provider—the `LDAP` provider. In previous ADSI-based APIs, directory searching was a mixed bag. Automation clients such as VBScript had to use a fairly clunky ADO-based interface and only C++ clients could use `IDirectorySearch`. .NET brings the power and speed of `IDirectorySearch` to all .NET languages in an easy-to-use design.

Directory Object Security

The .NET Framework 2.0 introduces first-class support for Windows security descriptors and access controls lists (ACLs). Referred to affectionately as MACL, the Managed ACLs are now integrated into nearly every .NET object that supports a Windows ACL, such as files and synchronization objects like mutexes. Active Directory and ADAM objects are no exception to this. SDS includes a variety of new classes to support the special ACL settings that Active Directory uses to provide its granular security model.

This substantially improves the developer's ability to read and write security descriptors on Active Directory resources. Previously, this was possible only by dropping down into the ADSI using COM interop, and the experience was often slow and unpleasant. Used in conjunction with the new `IdentityReference` class in the `System.Security.Access-Control` namespace, it is now simple to modify and maintain enterprise security in .NET. We will cover managing security and permissions in more detail in Chapter 8.

Code Access Security

The .NET Framework includes a system called code access security (CAS), which provides a mechanism to limit the actions that code can perform based on the identity of the code and independent from the identity of the user running the code. SDS integrates with the CAS system by providing a `DirectoryServicesPermission` class and an accompanying attribute

(`DirectoryServicesPermissionAttribute`) for declarative security. A few additional supporting classes also are included to round out CAS support. We discuss CAS in detail in Chapter 8.

ADSI Providers

ADSI was designed to be extensible. Different vendors can create providers to allow developers access to any data store using ADSI. Shipping with ADSI today are providers for the following data stores:

- `LDAP`. Used to communicate with LDAP servers
- `WinNT`. Used to communicate with Windows NT 4.0 domain controllers and the local SAM database
- `NDS`. Used to communicate with Novell Directory Servers
- `NWCOMPAT`. Used to communicate with older Novell implementations
- `IIS`. Used to read and manipulate the IIS metabase
- `Ads`. Used to enumerate providers on the system

Since this book deals only with LDAP directories and primarily with Active Directory and ADAM, we are mainly concerned with the `LDAP` provider. The `LDAP` provider actually comes in two flavors: `LDAP` and `GC`. GC stands for global catalog, which is the component of Active Directory that contains a partial read-only replica of all of the data in the entire forest. However, the `GC` provider still speaks LDAP, just on different TCP/IP ports. Aside from the fact that the global catalog is read-only, it can really be considered just a special case of LDAP in Active Directory. When using a lower-level LDAP API to talk to the global catalog, we just change our TCP/IP port and keep doing whatever we were doing before.

The `WinNT` provider still has its place for use with older NT4 domains (although we don't cover those in this book, as we already mentioned) and local machine accounts. Because Active Directory is backward compatible with the SAM interfaces, `WinNT` can be used to access Active Directory in a pinch. However, it is unable to access all of Active Directory's capabilities. For this reason, we recommend avoiding the `WinNT` provider when working with Active Directory and sticking with `LDAP`. In distributed environments such as web applications, we have seen flaky behavior with this provider, though SDS does actually work fairly well with the `WinNT` provider in a local desktop context.

We mentioned `NDS` and `NWCOMPAT` for completeness only. In practice, these providers for Novell are not used widely and have been deprecated. Most Novell shops have converted to eDirectory by now and can speak LDAP natively anyway.

The `IIS` provider is interesting in that it requires many additional provider-specific ADSI interfaces to do the advanced work. This results in the need for a lot of reflection code or COM interop in .NET to access these features. Just using SDS may not be enough. These issues make using the `IIS` provider with SDS harder than it probably should be. While we can still use it to do what we need to do, this is a case of where we should be looking for other APIs. As such, `IIS` is probably the worst fit to the ADSI model of all of the providers, because it requires the use of so many of these additional interfaces. We have heard rumors that Microsoft will eventually release a domain-specific .NET API for IIS (once rumored to be called `Microsoft.Iis.Metabase`) that will address many of these issues and will provide a good managed-code experience for .NET developers. Until then, it is probably best to look to WMI for IIS support. We have heard that it is pretty good and that WMI has a nice .NET story with the `System.Management` namespace.

Other Useful ADSI Interfaces

As we already discussed, SDS provides a .NET wrapper around some but not all of the ADSI interfaces. Typically, we can do the vast majority of our work using just the few interfaces that it does wrap. However, it is occasionally useful or necessary to use some of the interfaces defined in ADSI, as there is no .NET equivalent.

When We Need to Use ADSI

The following primary categories of use cases represent instances when we will need to drop a little lower than SDS to get to ADSI and use its interfaces instead:

- Handling some specific data types
- Performing some specific operations on users or groups

- Managing security on directory objects (.NET 1.x only)
- Performing specific utility functions

Handling Some Specific Data Types. Some attribute values from Active Directory and ADAM are returned from the `DirectoryEntry` object as type `System.__ComObject` rather than as something more intuitive or useful, such as `String`, `Int32`, or `DateTime`. Actually, these types are pointers to ADSI COM interfaces. Specifically, three Active Directory data types are marshaled back to .NET in this way: `LargeInteger` (syntax 2.5.5.16), `DN-With-String` (syntax 2.5.5.14), and `DN-With-Binary` (syntax 2.5.5.7). `LargeInteger` is by far the most common. We discuss LDAP data types in detail in Chapter 6, including a discussion of the history behind this apparently strange behavior.

Performing Specific Operations on Users or Groups. ADSI includes an `IADsUser` and `IADsGroup` interface to help make some operations on user and group objects in Active Directory easier to perform. SDS does not include a wrapper around these interfaces, so we sometimes need direct access to these interfaces to get work done. The most notable of these functions are the `IADsUser SetPassword` and `ChangePassword` methods. We cover the specific details of these two interfaces in our sections on user and group management in Chapters 10 and 11.

Managing Security on Directory Objects. We already discussed how SDS includes a set of classes for managing the security of objects in the directory with the Managed ACL or MACL classes. However, all of these classes are brand new for .NET 2.0. In .NET 1.x, the story is not as good. To accomplish the same goals, we need to use the ADSI `IADsSecurityDescriptor`, `IADsAccessControlList`, and `IADsAccessControlEntry` interfaces or resort to other, more complex means. As usual, we will dig into the details on this in Chapter 8 and demonstrate how to get by in both worlds.

Performing Specific Utility Functions. ADSI also includes a variety of other utility interfaces that have no .NET equivalent. They tend to vary in usefulness from "sometimes necessary" to "would never miss it." `IADsNameTranslate` probably ranks highest among the nice-to-have features in ADSI. `IADsObjectOptions` and `IADsObjectOptions2` have a managed wrapper in .NET 2.0, `DirectoryEntryConfiguration`, but not in 1.x. These interfaces are often required for some ADAM tasks and contain a few nice-to-have features that are useful in some scenarios. We will ignore the rest for now, and will mention them later in the context in which they are useful.

How to Use ADSI When Necessary

There are two approaches to using ADSI features within .NET:

- Reflection-based approach
- Direct COM interop approach

Reflection is essentially just the ability to discover information about a type at runtime and to call members on that type. There are three ways to do reflection to access ADSI features in SDS.

- Use the `Invoke/InvokeGet/InvokeSet` methods from `Directory-Entry`.
- Write our own reflection code using `System.Reflection`.
- Use late binding (not for C#; this requires a language that supports late binding such as Visual Basic .NET or JScript .NET).

The most practical approach is to use the Invoke* methods on `DirectoryEntry`. They allow us to call any property or method defined on any COM interface that is valid for the current directory object. Note that in .NET 1.x, this is limited to method calls only, as there is only one `Invoke` method and it only supports methods. Property invocation requires using the second approach.

The other general approach is to use COM interop directly. Normally, we do this by creating an interop assembly using the tlbimp.exe command-line tool or by simply setting a reference to activeds.tlb in Visual Studio. It is actually possible to roll our own interop assembly by declaring the interop types manually. We cover various interop approaches in more detail in Appendix A.

System.DirectoryServices.ActiveDirectory Overview

New with .NET 2.0 comes the `System.DirectoryServices.ActiveDirectory` (SDS.AD) namespace. While this namespace is primarily targeted at administrators, it does contain a few nuggets of functionality that might appeal to the .NET developer.

Class Overview

One of the challenges in working with Active Directory programmatically is that we cannot perform all of the operations we need to perform using standard LDAP calls. As we mentioned before, Active Directory ships with a variety of API functions that provide access to many of these additional functions. We collectively refer to these as the Ds* APIs. The challenge was that these APIs were designed to be called only from C/C++ and did not have an equivalent COM interface that allowed them to be called via scripting clients. Because of this, the primary audience for these APIs—namely, the administrators—did not have an easy means to use them.

Microsoft addressed this problem by creating the SDS.AD namespace. SDS.AD is new functionality built on top of SDS that expands the tools a developer might use to manage or control Active Directory and ADAM. Many of the concrete concepts of Active Directory find themselves represented as classes in SDS.AD. Some of these include:

```
Forest
ActiveDirectoryPartition (instantiable as Domain)
DirectoryServer (instantiable as DomainController,
   GlobalCatalogServer, and ADAMInstance)
ActiveDirectorySchemaClass
ActiveDirectorySite
ActiveDirectorySubnet
ReplicationConnection
TrustRelationshipInformation
```

SDS.AD does a nice job of marrying together the SDS ADSI model with the Ds* APIs, which actually don't use ADSI at all. A lot of work goes on under the hood to make all of this work together. The result is really the best of both worlds for the .NET developer.

Using these classes or derived subclasses, we can exercise very granular control over Active Directory and ADAM operations such as replication, schema updates, and trust management between domains. For the rest of this section, we will cover some of the more important classes or groups of classes, and we will discuss what they contain.

ActiveDirectoryPartitions

Introduced with this namespace is the concept of the `ActiveDirectoryPartition` class. This abstract class manifests itself in concrete implementations of things like `Domain`, `ApplicationPartition`, and `ActiveDirectorySchema`. These classes have drastically simplified what was once difficult and obscure functionality.

Domain. We assume that you are familiar with domains and the purposes they serve, so we won't spend a lot of time talking about the specifics of setting up domains. Oftentimes, decisions to set up domains are not based on technical criteria as much as they are based on political decisions that take into account differing security needs or segregation of the objects they contain. Briefly, **domains** are logical units of security and replication. Only domains within the same forest share the same schema, but they do not share objects or security policies. In order for one domain to communicate with another domain, some sort of communication channel must exist. A **trust** is used to secure this communication channel, and trusts are the mechanism by which security contexts and objects can be resolved from one domain into another. In practical terms, a trust allows users or objects in one domain to be authenticated in another domain. There are different types of trusts (transitive and nontransitive), as well as directions (one-way and two-way). With the `Domain` class, it is now possible to do things such as enumerate, create, and verify trusts, enumerate domain controllers, and enumerate child domains. Previously, many of these capabilities were available only using C/C++, or they required nontrivial searches to extract this information.

ApplicationPartition. Application partitions are a new type of directory partition available in Windows 2003 that typically are specific to a particular domain controller. The data that resides in these types of partitions is usually useful only locally and is relevant to a particular application that uses this domain controller. By default, the data that resides in the partition will not replicate outside of the local domain controller where it resides. This has the benefit of reducing replication traffic on the network when that data is not relevant for the entire domain. It is now possible to manage and create these application partitions with the aptly named `Application-Partition` class. Furthermore, it is possible to selectively set up replicas, or replication partners, for these partitions in Windows 2003 for backup or redundancy purposes.

ActiveDirectorySchema. **Schema** defines the shape of a directory object. That is, it defines its properties (what it contains) and its relationships to other objects (what it is). Out of the box, Active Directory and ADAM ship with hundreds of classes and attributes which serve the interests of developers and users in the vast majority of situations. For reasons of specificity or clarity, it is often useful to define our own schema instead of bludgeoning data into an unused (and unrelated) attribute on an object. When this is done, it is called **extending the schema** (for more on schema and extensions, see Chapter 7). The `ActiveDirectorySchema` class is responsible for all things related to Active Directory and ADAM schema. It is now possible to easily retrieve, inspect, and if necessary, modify schema classes and attributes. Additionally, we can now easily locate the schema master to perform operations such as reloading the schema.

DirectoryServer

The abstract `DirectoryServer` class exists in concrete implementations to operate directly on domain controllers, ADAM instances, and global catalog servers. It encapsulates much of the functionality needed to maintain, promote, or modify the server and its roles.

DomainController. The `DomainController` class encapsulates many of the operations an Active Directory admin would like to perform on her domain controllers. For instance, with this class, it is possible to find other domain controllers, enable global catalog operations, determine OS version and IP address, check replication consistency, find replication partners, and even determine FSMO roles. We can also determine the site, forest, and current time on any domain controller. Whew! If you don't know what all of those things are, or why they are useful, don't sweat it. Administrators are going to be the likely consumers of these classes, and we will cover the parts that the average enterprise developer should know.

The `DomainController` class allows us to use the domain controller Locator service (packaged in the `DsGetDCName` API) directly from within our code. This is our favorite feature in the namespace for enterprise developers, as it allows us to use the full power of the locator service to do things like dynamically find domain controllers in any site and force rediscovery of a domain controller in a failure situation. We'll come back to this class in Chapter 9.

GlobalCatalog. The global catalog server is a special type of domain controller that holds a subset of all of the data in the forest. This powerful functionality exists to make searching across domains efficient. It means that in multidomain forests, it is possible to connect to a global catalog in one domain and search it for objects that reside in another domain. There is an associated cost with creating a global catalog in terms of replication traffic, as all global catalog replicated objects and their subset of attributes are replicated across domains. The `GlobalCatalog` class wraps all the functionality of the `DomainController` class, but adds the ability to find, create, demote, and enumerate other global catalogs.

AdamInstance. The `AdamInstance` class operates for ADAM in much the same way as the `DomainController` class operates for Active Directory. ADAM instances don't participate in trusts, so we won't find any support here for that. However, we can find ADAM instances and set up replication using this class model.

System.DirectoryServices.Protocols Overview

Unlike SDS and SDS.AD, SDS.P has no dependencies upon the ADSI COM-based system for directory access. Instead, it supports LDAP by calling directly into the Windows LDAP library (wldap32.dll) or by using SOAP/HTTP to talk to a DSML server (see the sidebar What Is DSML? for more about DSML).

What Is DSML?

DSML stands for Directory Services Markup Language. It is essentially an XML specification for describing directory information, querying directories, and performing modification operations. DSML is actually described in two different standards. Version 1 defines the XML structure of the directory as a set of XML schemas. Version 2 defines how directories are queried and modified using the SOAP specification to define message patterns for the various directory operations. The net result is that DSML provides a web services–based protocol for accessing directory information.

Microsoft actually provides a DSML server for Active Directory and ADAM that is freely downloadable (http://msdn.microsoft.com/library/en-us/dsml/dsml/portal.asp). So far, the reception for DSML has been fairly muted, with very few customers using DSML for much more than experimentation. However, this may be due in part to the difficulty of creating a SOAP client for the server. Previously, the SOAP messages had to be crafted and processed by hand, which made DSML at least as difficult to use as the LDAP API it tries to wrap. However, now that SDS.P provides a very simple API for using DSML, we may see an increase in usage.

Overall Design

SDS.P is factored into a separate assembly and has no inherent dependency on `System.DirectoryServices` (with one minor exception that we'll discuss later). Like the LDAP API itself, SDS.P uses a persistent connection to the server as the primary metaphor for working with the directory, instead of the object metaphor favored by SDS and ADSI. A `DirectoryConnection` connection is established (either as `LdapConnection` or `DsmlSoapHttpConnection`), and then operations such as search, add, modify, and delete are performed on the connection using a request/response message-passing pattern. As you may recall from our brief introduction to the LDAP API in Chapter 1, this is how LDAP works.

One of the triumphs of SDS.P is its use of a provider model to abstract the underlying transport mechanism from the operations being performed. Once we have selected a transport (either direct LDAP over TCP/IP or the

DSML protocol using SOAP/HTTP), the operations performed are largely identical. We could presumably write an application that allows the user to select her transport at runtime with little difficulty! Of course, we must observe some subtle differences to make this work in practice, but it is certainly possible.

Because SDS.P is essentially a complete wrapper around LDAP, it provides a number of features to developers that are missing in SDS. One of the things we will notice immediately is that SDS.P provides complete support for asynchronous invocation using the standard .NET asynchronous design pattern (`Begin/End` semantics, delegates, `IAsyncResult`, etc.). This makes it much easier to use the LDAP API's native support for asynchronous messaging, which might be very important in high-performance, multithreaded server applications.

Another important distinction between SDS.P and the ADSI model is that just like the LDAP API, SDS.P does not attempt to convert the raw data in the store to a "stronger" type. Programmers used to ADSI may be shocked to discover that LDAP actually stores integers, Booleans, and dates as strings! In the LDAP world, everything is interpreted as either a string or binary data. If we want to reinterpret the data as a type that is more convenient for processing in a strongly typed language such as .NET, then we have to perform a lot of extra work. The upside of this is that we eliminate the overhead that ADSI imposes with its mapping, along with any possible errors related to ADSI not being able to do the mapping in the first place. Data-mapping errors often surface with non-Microsoft directories, especially those that don't support LDAP version 3.

Finally, several other LDAP features are available in SDS.P that simply are not available in SDS. Some of these include access to the full set of secure binding mechanisms supported by LDAP, fast concurrent binding in Windows 2003 Active Directory and ADAM, and full client and server certificate processing for SSL/LDAP connections.

How Is it Organized?

One of the first things we will notice when looking at the SDS.P namespace is that nearly 100 types are defined there. It seems like a lot compared to

SDS, but once you get the hang of it, it is straightforward. The namespace can be loosely grouped into the following categories:

- Connection types
- Operation types
- Data (attribute) types
- Control types

Connection Types

As we just mentioned, the primary metaphor for SDS.P is the connection to the server, so this is where we start.

DirectoryConnection. `DirectoryConnection` defines the abstract base class for the other connection classes.

LdapConnection and DsmlSoapHttpConnection. These are the actual classes we instantiate to establish a connection to the directory using our protocol of choice. Note that `DsmlSoapHttpConnection` derives from another abstract base class, `DsmlSoapConnection`, in order to provide session state support. Presumably, this class could also be used as a base for adding DSML support on other transports, such as what is promised by technologies like Windows Communication Framework (WCF, previously called Indigo).

DirectoryIdentifier, LdapDirectoryIdentifier, and DsmlDirectory-Identifier. These classes are used to provide different mechanisms for identifying a directory server. LDAP typically uses DNS names and DSML typically uses URIs, but Microsoft's LDAP API also supports serverless binding to Active Directory using the locator service. We'll discuss serverless binding in more detail in Chapter 3, in the context of SDS.

A variety of other classes and enumerations also are used to support various authentication mechanisms and server options used by LDAP, including `LdapSessionOptions` and its various options, as well as `Auth-Types`, which defines which type of secure authentication to use. Detailed control over session options is one of the most distinguishing features that sets SDS.P apart from SDS. For example, SDS.P offers very fine-grained control over the behavior of referrals, the version of LDAP to use, and SSL options, to name just a few.

LDAP Operation Types

These classes define how various operations are performed on the directory, such as searches, additions, deletions, and modifications. All of these come in matching request/response pairs to be used on the `Directory-Connection.SendRequest` method and its peers. These classes form the key abstraction over the connection classes, as they are used interchangeably over LDAP and DSML.

The `DirectoryRequest` and `DirectoryResponse` classes are the abstract base classes for all of the other message pairs. The actual concrete classes for the directory operations are implemented in the following classes:

- `AddRequest/AddResponse`
- `CompareRequest/CompareResponse`
- `DeleteRequest/DeleteResponse`
- `ExtendedRequest/ExtendedResponse`
- `ModifyDNRequest/ModifyDNResponse`
- `ModifyRequest/ModifyResponse`
- `SearchRequest/SearchResponse`

The `SearchRequest` and `SearchResponse` pair comprises the most commonly used operation. Searching has a variety of options and other classes associated with it for accessing the results of searches, including partial result sets. These classes include `SearchResultEntry`, `SearchResultEntryCollection`, `SearchResultAttributeCollection`, `SearchResultReference`, and `SearchResultReferenceCollection`. A number of LDAP controls also are used to modify the behavior of searches.

LDAP Data Types

Data in LDAP revolves around attributes and their values. The `DirectoryAttribute` class is the core class for representing this in SDS.P. As we discussed earlier, LDAP essentially stores all data as strings. Data can be interpreted as either a string or binary data (a byte array).

Even though LDAP attributes support specific syntaxes such as strings, Booleans, numeric data, and dates, the actual storage is a string representation of the data. Thus, a Boolean is actually stored as the string TRUE or FALSE and an integer value of 1234 is stored as the string `"1234"`. The directory service enforces the syntax rules for the attribute when it is saved, but does not convert to any kind of platform-native binary data type.

This is probably the aspect of SDS.P that is the most different from the ADSI-based providers. ADSI goes through great effort to read a directory's schema and devise helpful mapping of LDAP data to standard COM variant data types such as `VTI4` (variant holding a 4-byte integer) and `VTBool` (variant holding a Boolean). SDS.P gives us the raw data and leaves any sort of syntactic mapping to the devices of the developer.

As a result, the primary methods on `DirectoryAttribute` for getting the data will return either a string or a byte array. Under the hood, `DirectoryAttribute` attempts to convert the binary data into a UTF8 string. If that succeeds, it will return a string by default. If it fails, it will return a byte array. We can also request the data as either strings or byte arrays by calling the `GetValues` method.

A few other classes support `DirectoryAttribute`, such as `DirectoryAttributeCollection`, `DirectoryAttributeModification`, and `SearchResultAttributeCollection`. We may use them in some examples later on, but we won't cover them in more detail.

LDAP Control Types

LDAP controls are used to modify the behavior of an LDAP operation on the server. They provide an extensibility mechanism for the server to support operations that are more advanced. LDAP controls may be generally supported by the LDAP specification or may be proprietary to the specific directory implementation. SDS.P ships with many of the supported controls for Active Directory and ADAM.

Finally, SDS.P has a base class for all of these controls, called `DirectoryControl`. Unlike many of the base classes used in SDS.P, this one is not abstract, which means we can instantiate it directly. This gives developers the ability to use controls that may be supported on their directory server, of which SDS.P has no strongly typed representation. The developer simply needs to know the control's Object Identifier (OID), whether it is server-side or client-side, and what the binary input data for the control must look like. Developers may also use this base class to create their own strongly typed controls.

Selecting the Right Technology

.NET provides us with a few different approaches for programming directory services, so how do we know which one to choose? If we are still using .NET 1.x, the answer is simple, as SDS is really our only choice. However, in version 2.0, the landscape is a little broader. We can now choose between using SDS and SDS.P.

As you can probably tell by looking through this book, we think that SDS is the sweet spot for most of what a serious enterprise developer is going to want to do. The programming model is a bit more straightforward, the performance is quite good (especially if we are careful), and we can get a lot of work done with it. However, sometimes using the more powerful model provided by SDS.P is a good idea, or perhaps even necessary. Here are some examples.

- If performance is of the utmost importance, SDS.P is going to be faster for equivalent operations, as it is "closer to the metal" than ADSI.
- Certain LDAP features are available only via SDS.P. We'll be covering a lot of these points in more detail throughout the book, but some examples we can mention here include using the stats control for query statistics and using certain specific binding features.
- If we want to use LDAP in a firewall-friendly manner over SOAP and XML via a DSML server, SDS.P is the only way to go.
- When we need an asynchronous programming model for multi-threaded server scenarios, SDS.P has this built in.
- If we are programming against a non-Microsoft LDAP server, SDS.P may be our only hope, as many of the things that help make SDS so productive are also designed with Microsoft servers in mind.

Another thing to consider is that developers coming to .NET from an LDAP C API or Java Native Directory Interface (JNDI) background might feel more at home with SDS.P. In that case, go with what makes you productive.

Finally, do not underestimate the usefulness of ADSI's mapping of LDAP schema to COM data types. This is a hard problem to solve in the general sense, and we will inevitably end up reinventing this wheel many times when dealing with LDAP data directly. ADSI and SDS save us valuable time here.

The Argument against Using activeds.dll Directly via COM Interop

It is possible today to create a runtime-callable wrapper (RCW) in .NET and use ADSI from managed code directly, since ADSI is in fact just a set of COM interfaces. In Visual Studio .NET, this is as simple as adding an assembly reference to activeds.tlb from the COM tab in Visual Studio. For longtime ADSI developers, this can feel more comfortable than getting used to the new object model introduced with SDS. However, for a large percentage of today's enterprise developers, the newer SDS model is better suited to .NET development than the RCW interop model.

The benefits of using SDS over importing an RCW of ADSI lie in its object model. There is a simplicity and an "object-orientedness" to SDS that is not present using the native ADSI functionality. SDS relies on relatively few objects to provide the bulk of functionality that was previously exposed by a larger number of separate ADSI interfaces. These objects encapsulate a good deal of the functionality and the nuances with which ADSI developers previously had to struggle. Most tasks today can be directly accomplished using SDS without relying on an ADSI RCW. Here are some examples of such tasks.

- `DirectorySearcher` is infinitely better to use for searching LDAP than ADO or the OleDb .NET classes. It is designed specifically for this purpose and will always be faster for equivalent search filters.

- The `DirectoryEntry` class is easier to use from a programming model perspective and gives us strong typing at runtime. This is critical for C# developers and Visual Basic .NET developers who run with `Option Strict`.

- SDS is designed to work well with the .NET CAS system, which is important when our code is running in a partially trusted environment. The story here is different between .NET 1.x and 2.0 (see Chapter 8), but it is always the case that using `ActiveDs` directly will require Unmanaged Code permissions, which precludes us from running in a partially trusted environment.

- In 2.0, SDS has even better integration with .NET, and SDS.AD provides a host of useful features for working directly with Active Directory.

If these arguments are not strong enough to dissuade you from using the RCW-interop approach, here is another one: We aren't covering the ADSI interop approach in this book, so you might as well get with the program!

SUMMARY

In this chapter, we introduced the LDAP programming technologies in the .NET Framework. We started with a high-level overview of the landscape and delved into some of the details about how the .NET-managed code interfaces interact with the various Windows-native platform interfaces such as ADSI and the LDAP API (wldap32.dll). We spent some additional time focusing on ADSI, since it is the underpinnings of the primary .NET directory services programming interface, SDS.

We then provided a high-level overview of the facilities available in the .NET Framework, including `System.DirectoryServices`, as well as `System.DirectoryServices.ActiveDirectory` and `System.DirectoryServices.Protocols`, which are new additions in .NET version 2.0.

With SDS, we get the basic functionality necessary to do most types of LDAP programming in .NET, and it is included in all of the released versions of the .NET Framework. Most of the rest of the book focuses here.

With SDS.AD, we have full control over how Active Directory and ADAM operate directly using .NET. The somewhat arcane API calls previously used to manage Active Directory are now gone: trusts, replication, domain controllers, schema, sites, and subnets are all directly modifiable using the new SDS.AD namespace.

SDS.P provides a completely different approach for working with LDAP that conforms directly to the LDAP API. It also uses a provider model to allow seamless interoperability with the DSML protocol.

We concluded with some guidance on when to use the various options available.

3

Binding and CRUD Operations with DirectoryEntry

D irectoryEntry is the primary class in `System.DirectoryServices` (SDS). It represents an object in the underlying connected directory. This object can be any type of object in the directory. Typically, it represents things like users, computers, groups, and containers. The majority of what we can accomplish with SDS relies on the use of `DirectoryEntry` in some manner or another.

In addition to what `DirectoryEntry` represents, it is solely responsible for all binding to connected directories and provides the security context with which to operate. Any changes or updates to the connected directories occur through use of `DirectoryEntry`, including the addition of new objects or the deletion of existing ones. SDS relies on `DirectoryEntry` for the vast majority of its heavy lifting.

This chapter is divided into roughly three parts. In the first part, we take a lap around the `DirectoryEntry` class and examine its properties, methods, and supporting classes. The second part of the chapter dives deep into the details of connecting to the directory and explains how the various available options work and affect the way the connection will behave. In the last part, we discuss how the standard create, read, update, and delete (CRUD) operations familiar to database developers are performed.

Property and Method Overview

Before we start diving into details on `DirectoryEntry`, let's introduce all of the class members.

Constructors

`DirectoryEntry` contains five public constructors that allow us to initialize the class state with varying default values. The constructors allow us to initialize the `Path`, `Username`, `Password`, and `AuthenticationTypes` properties directly. We can also change these values after constructing the object by setting the corresponding properties.

In general, we recommend using the full constructor that takes all four of these parameters:

```
DirectoryEntry entry = new DirectoryEntry(
    "LDAP://rootDSE",
    null,
    null,
    AuthenticationTypes.Secure);
```

The advantage is that we are more explicit in our intentions and it takes less code to set all of the values than it would to set the properties individually. There are also some subtle differences between how .NET 1.x and 2.0 set default values that could lead to potential migration surprises (see Chapter 8), so being explicit can help mitigate those risks.

The fifth constructor allows us to pass in an existing object derived from `IADs` to initialize a new `DirectoryEntry`. While we rarely use this constructor in practice, it is nice to have it there if we need it.

Properties

`DirectoryEntry` contains 16 properties that are used for a variety of purposes. We'll be using these properties extensively throughout the book, so it is important to explain them now.

AuthenticationTypes

This is a read-write property that allows us to change the way the object behaves when it connects to the directory. It can also be initialized via one of the constructors. Understanding what all of the `AuthenticationTypes` values do is critical to our success with SDS. We cover them in detail later in this chapter, in the section AuthenticationTypes Explained.

Children

This is a read-only property that provides a way to enumerate the children of `DirectoryEntry` using a `DirectoryEntries` object. This property is used for adding and removing objects from the directory tree as well as for enumerating children.

Guid

This is a read-only property that provides direct access to the `objectGUID` attribute from Active Directory or ADAM as a `System.Guid` struct.

Name

This is a read-only property that provides the relative distinguished name (RDN) attribute value for this entry in the LDAP directory as a string. This value is supplied by the underlying `IADs` ADSI object.

NativeGuid

This is a read-only property that provides direct access to the `objectGUID` attribute from Active Directory or ADAM as a string using the octet string format actually returned by the LDAP API. The `Guid` property is actually based on this value, which is derived directly from the underlying `IADs` ADSI object. We discuss `Guid` and `NativeGuid` in more detail in the upcoming section on GUID binding.

NativeObject

This is a read-only property that provides direct access to the underlying `IADs` ADSI object that `DirectoryEntry` wraps. It is primarily used in COM interop scenarios.

ObjectSecurity (New in 2.0)

This new read-write property in .NET 2.0 allows access to the Active Directory and ADAM security descriptor using the new .NET 2.0 managed access control list (MACL) classes. These new classes provide a unified

> **▪ WARNING**   Keep DirectoryEntry Alive When Using NativeObject!
>
> When using `NativeObject`, we need to be sure to keep the `Directory-Entry` object alive. Otherwise, the .NET garbage collector may collect the `DirectoryEntry` object and close the underlying COM object that `NativeObject` represents. This can lead to some very subtle bugs at runtime! An explicit call to `Dispose` on `DirectoryEntry` after we are done using `NativeObject` should suffice. We cover the proper use of `Dispose` later in this chapter.

system for modifying Windows security descriptors across the entire framework. We discuss Active Directory and ADAM security in Chapter 8.

Users of .NET 1.x may still read and modify the security descriptor, but they must use a less desirable COM interop scenario to achieve the same goal. We also discuss this in detail in Chapter 8.

Options (New in 2.0)

Also new in .NET 2.0, this read-only property returns an `ActiveDirectoryConfiguration` object that we can use to read and write specific configuration options. In .NET 1.x, COM interop is once again required to achieve the same results. Chapters 8 and 10 provide some examples of using this class.

Parent

This is a read-only property that returns a new `DirectoryEntry` object representing the parent of the current `DirectoryEntry` object in the directory tree if it is not a root node. The parent object inherits its security context and settings from the child that created it.

> **▪ NOTE**   Properties Return New DirectoryEntry Instances
>
> A new object is returned each time the property is accessed. The `DirectoryEntry` object does not maintain a copy internally. If we want to access the same object represented by the `Parent` property multiple times, we should create a local variable to reference it and use that. Since a new object is allocated each time, we are responsible for cleaning it up as well, through proper use of the `Dispose` method.

Password

This property allows us to set the password that will be used when binding to the directory, if supplied. In .NET 1.x, this property is read-write, but it has been changed to write-only in .NET 2.0 for security purposes. It can also be initialized via two of the constructors.

■ **NOTE** Password Property Cannot Change a User's Password

This property is not related to the password value of a user object in the directory and we cannot use it to change that. See Chapter 10 for more details on managing user passwords.

Path

This is a read-write property specifying the path to the object as a string. Most of the constructors allow us to initialize this property directly. Paths are the fundamental way we locate servers and objects in the directory, and we devote an entire section to them in this chapter.

Properties

This is a read-only property that provides access to the attributes on the underlying object in the directory as a `PropertyCollection` object.

SchemaClassName

This is a read-only property that provides a string containing the name of the schema class for the directory object. This value is provided by the underlying `IADs` ADSI object.

SchemaEntry

This is a read-only property that provides a `DirectoryEntry` object representing the schema object upon which the `DirectoryEntry` object is based. This property is much like the `Parent` property in that it uses the same security context and settings as the current object and generates a new instance on each access.

UsePropertyCache

This read-write Boolean property allows us to enable and disable the ADSI property cache. The property cache helps with performance by batching together LDAP search and modify operations and generating less network traffic and overhead. We recommend always leaving this in the default state of "true". There is no good reason to turn this off.

Username

This is a read-write property showing the username used to authenticate with the directory. It can also be initialized via two of the constructors. As with the `Password` property, it is not used to read or change the username on a user object in the directory. The section Username Syntaxes in Active Directory and ADAM, later in this chapter, focuses on the available options.

Methods

In addition to its properties, the `DirectoryEntry` object implements 11 methods that we will also use throughout the rest of the book.

Close

`Close` is used to clean up underlying resources used by ADSI. We generally recommend using the `Dispose` method rather than the `Close` method. For more information, please refer to the sidebar titled Close or Dispose?

CommitChanges

If we have made modifications to the attribute values in the object and are using the property cache (which is on by default and should always be left on!), then we must call this method to have our changes flushed back to the directory. See Chapter 6 for details.

CopyTo (Overloaded)

LDAP does not support these methods, and since LDAP is all we are talking about here, we will ignore them from now on.

DeleteTree

This method deletes this entry from the directory, as well as every entry under it in the tree. It uses the `IADsDeleteOps` ADSI interface under the hood to do this.

Dispose

This method is similar to `Close`, but it supports the `IDisposable` interface. In general, we recommend using `Dispose` rather than `Close` and we explain why in the upcoming sidebar, Close or Dispose?

Exists

This static method attempts to tell us whether an object exists in the directory.

■ NOTE   Limitations of the Exists Method

This method works well only when we are not supplying credentials to the `DirectoryEntry` object. Since it does not allow us to specify the security context used to make this determination, it may not work as desired and may even throw an exception instead of returning false. It is useful in some situations, but it is important to know its limitations. We recommend implementing a custom existence checking method when supplying credentials.

Invoke

This method is a handy wrapper that allows us to invoke methods exposed by the various IADs* interfaces via late binding using the .NET reflection system under the hood. It is most commonly used for Active Directory and ADAM password management, but it useful whenever we need to access an ADSI method that has no direct .NET counterpart.

InvokeGet (New in .NET 2.0)

This method is nearly identical to the `Invoke` method, except that it allows us to get the value of an ADSI property. The original .NET 1.x implementation only allowed calling ADSI methods via `Invoke`, so reading properties required more verbose reflection code. This was likely a simple oversight, and it has been corrected with the addition of this method.

InvokeSet (New in .NET 2.0)

This method is just like `InvokeGet`, except that it sets ADSI property values.

MoveTo

This method allows us to change the location of an object in the directory tree. The overload also allows us to rename an object in the directory. It uses the `IADsContainer.MoveHere` method under the hood to perform the operation.

RefreshCache

`RefreshCache` is used to load the ADSI property cache from the LDAP directory. Loading the property cache reads the attribute values for the corresponding directory object and allows us to read and modify them with `PropertyCollection` and `PropertyValueCollection`.

The overloaded version is useful for loading specific attribute values into the cache. This is required for attributes such as constructed attributes in Active Directory and ADAM that are not returned by default. It can also be used to limit the list of attributes we wish to read in order to increase performance.

Note that calling this method will erase any changes we have made in the local property cache unless we have already saved them with `Commit-Changes`, so we must be careful with it.

Rename

This method is similar to the `MoveTo` method that allows us to rename the object in the directory, except that the object is not also moved. Like `MoveTo`, it also uses the `IADsContainer.MoveHere` method under the hood to perform the operation.

Close or Dispose?

The `DirectoryEntry` class offers both a `Close` method and a `Dispose` method (inherited from the `System.ComponentModel.Component` base class). What do these methods do, and when should we use them?

Both `Close` and `Dispose` are intended to be used to clean up the underlying COM object. The primary difference between the two is that `Dispose` also suppresses .NET finalization, and `Close` does not. Suppressing finalization means that the garbage collector will not bother to run the `Finalize` method on the object because we have signaled that we have already cleaned up the underlying resource that the finalizer needed to take care of. Objects that need to be finalized are automatically promoted one garbage collection generation, so they tend to hang around in memory longer, which is something we probably want to avoid if possible.

The other difference is that `Close` allows the `DirectoryEntry` instance to be bound to a different object and reused. We do not recommend doing this, however, as it might throw exceptions or not work as expected. If we instead tried rebinding with a `DirectoryEntry` that had been `Disposed`, it would throw an `ObjectDisposedException`.

In summary, use `Dispose`. It does everything that `Close` does, and it takes care of the finalization.

Better yet, use the built-in language features to ensure that objects are `Disposed` properly. In C#, always use the `using` construct:

```
using (DirectoryEntry entry = new DirectoryEntry())
{
    //do some work here
}
```

To reinforce this point, we try to use this syntax consistently throughout the book, even though it is slightly more verbose.

In .NET 2.0, Visual Basic also offers a similar construct:

```
Dim entry As DirectoryEntry
Using (entry = New DirectoryEntry())
    'Do some work here
End Using
```

In .NET 1.x Visual Basic, we should always use a construct like this:

```
Dim entry As DirectoryEntry
Try
    entry = New DirectoryEntry()
    'Do some work here
Finally
    If Not entry Is Nothing Then entry.Dispose()
End Try
```

> ■■ **WARNING**   Dispose Is Not Optional in .NET 1.x
>
> It is especially important to ensure that `Dispose` is being called consistently if we are using older versions of the .NET Framework. As of this writing, .NET 1.x contains a number of bugs related to how the finalization was implemented in SDS that caused the underlying COM object never to be released if we failed to call `Dispose` explicitly! Essentially, the `Finalize` method called by the finalizer thread does not release the underlying COM object. This caused significant memory leaks in long-running applications with substantial SDS use. These bugs are fixed as of .NET 2.0, but we really do not want to be relying on the garbage collector to clean up our objects anyway, so we should do it ourselves.
>
> Remember also that all of the properties and methods in SDS that return a `DirectoryEntry`, such as `Parent` and `SchemaEntry`, actually return a new instance of a `DirectoryEntry` object, not a value held in the class' internal state. Therefore, not only is it OK to call `Dispose` on these objects without fear of corrupting the containing object's internal state, but it is actually our responsibility! Make sure to wrap all of those objects in a `using` block as well.

Binding to the Directory

In this section, we start diving into detail on the mechanics of binding to the directory using the `DirectoryEntry` object.

Binding Syntax

In ADSI and SDS, we use the term "binding" to describe the process of connecting to an object in an LDAP directory to read or modify its data. Use of the term "bind" is slightly different from the technical definition in LDAP, but we use this convention here. Please see the sidebar in Chapter 8, titled LDAP Bind vs. ADSI Bind, for more details.

To bind successfully to either Active Directory or ADAM, we need some key information:

- The ADSI provider to use
- The server and port to connect to
- Where in the directory hierarchy to bind
- The credentials with which to bind
- Any provider-specific options

Using the pseudocode representation in Listing 3.1 to demonstrate, this information corresponds exactly to one of the constructors available on DirectoryEntry.

LISTING 3.1: Pseudocode Representation of Binding Syntax

```
DirectoryEntry entry = new DirectoryEntry(
    "{Provider}://{server:port}/{Hierarchy Path}",
    "{username}",
    "{password}",
    {Provider Options}
    );
```

Listing 3.2 shows a concrete example of what a typical Active Directory binding looks like.

LISTING 3.2: Typical Active Directory Binding Demonstrating the Four Parameters

```
using System.DirectoryServices;
//note the LDAP: is case-sensitive
DirectoryEntry entry = new DirectoryEntry(
    "LDAP://DC=domain,DC=com",
    null,
    null,
    AuthenticationTypes.Secure
    );
```

In Listing 3.2, we are using the LDAP provider and no server name at all (called a **serverless bind**) to bind to the directory and access the domain root object. Since we did not supply a username or password (collectively referred to as **credentials**) and we specified `AuthenticationTypes.Secure`, the current Windows security context is used to access the directory automatically.

At this point, we have not actually bound to the directory. Because `DirectoryEntry` allows us to change the properties represented by the parameters on the constructor (such as `Path` and `Username`) after the object is constructed, it does not connect to the directory until it is forced. The first action, such as reading, or an action such as modifying the underlying directory object's properties, initiates the bind. This design gives us flexibility, but it can be confusing to people coming from an ADSI background, as it does not work this way in ADSI.

Any property or method that forces the connection will do. Typically, we use the `RefreshCache` method or the `NativeObject` property if we want to quickly force a bind:

```
//bind occurs at access here
object nativeObj = entry.NativeObject;

//or we could do this
entry.RefreshCache();
```

ADSI Path Anatomy

Let's start drilling down on the various pieces that determine how `DirectoryEntry` binds to the directory, starting with `Path`. SDS uses the ADSI `ADsPath` syntax for specifying how objects in the directory are identified.

`ADsPath` is composed of these component parts:

```
<provider>://<server>/<object name>
```

Table 3.1 shows a few concrete examples.

TABLE 3.1: Example LDAP ADsPaths

Example	ADsPath
1	`LDAP://mydc.mydomain.com/DC=mydc,DC=mydomain,DC=com`
2	`GC://mydc/<GUID=02d18309-b56a-4d86-b454-f5b907f07f8c>`
3	`LDAP://RootDSE`
4	`LDAP://10.10.11.100:50000` `/OU=somecontainer,O=mydirectory`

As we can see, `ADsPaths` look a lot like URLs, and this is no coincidence. This string syntax is instantly familiar to most developers today, given the ubiquity of URLs.

Provider Syntax

In ADSI and SDS, the `<provider>` portion (which might be called the **scheme** if we were describing it in terms of URLs) determines the ADSI provider used to service the request. Because this book is about LDAP, we'll be using the `LDAP` provider in most cases. As we discussed in Chapter 1, Active Directory has the notion of a global catalog that contains a forest-wide, read-only copy of all of the objects in the forest (minus some of the attributes), so Active Directory supports a `GC` provider as well. The `GC` provider essentially just instructs ADSI to use the LDAP protocol, but to connect on port 3268 rather than port 389 (or on port 3269 rather than port 636, in the case of SSL/LDAP).

⬛ WARNING   ADSI Providers Are Case Sensitive!

When specifying the provider in an `ADsPath`, do not use the spelling "ldap" or "Ldap," and so on, or it will not work and will result in the cryptic COM error message "0x80005000 Unknown error" when binding. The `LDAP` and `GC` providers must be specified in all capital letters.

Server

As we might imagine, the `<server>` portion of `ADsPath` determines what server we wish to use. The server is extremely flexible in ADSI, especially when used with Active Directory. Active Directory supports

- DNS-style names (see example 1 from Table 3.1)
- NetBIOS names (see example 2)
- IP addresses (see example 4)
- No server at all (also called serverless binding; see example 3)

Example 3 (no server at all) bears special mention, and we actually cover that in the upcoming section called Serverless Binding to Active Directory.

With DNS-style names, Active Directory supports

- The fully qualified DNS name of the domain controller or global catalog server
- The fully qualified DNS name of the domain or forest
- The unqualified name of the domain or forest (which is often but not always the same as the NetBIOS)

If we do not specify a specific server name, either with serverless binding or by using the name of the domain, the Windows runtime will try to find an appropriate Active Directory server for us. Note that ADAM does not support this option, as ADAM is not a domain.

Serverless Binding to Active Directory. Serverless binding is available in Active Directory as a means to select any available domain controller in the local site to serve as the binding domain controller. By avoiding the specification of a particular server, we reduce the chances of overloading that server with requests, or of complete failure if that particular domain controller is down for maintenance or otherwise unavailable. A serverless bind will simply select the next available domain controller to bind with, first by site and then outside the site, thereby avoiding having to rely on a particular server to always be up and available. This leads to more scalable and robust applications.

In its simplest form, a serverless bind looks like this:

```
DirectoryEntry de
    = new DirectoryEntry("LDAP://DC=domain,DC=com");
```

Notice that we have an ADsPath that specifies an object name by its distinguished name (DN), but we have omitted the server.

So, how does it magically know what domain to use? It infers a domain to use based on the security context of the current thread. This will be either the account that the process was created with or an impersonated account. If the account is an Active Directory domain account (and not a local machine account), then the domain of that account is used to find a domain controller. The technology that enables serverless binding is called the Locator service and is covered in detail in Chapter 9.

Serverless binding works remarkably well in many scenarios when the current user's security context is a domain account. We use serverless binding liberally throughout the examples in this book, as the syntax is more compact and most of our samples are simple console applications, where it is probably reasonable to assume a domain account.

The main problem here is that serverless binding does not work at all under a local machine account. If used with a local machine account, a `DirectoryEntry` bind will generally yield a `COMException` of "0x8007203A The server is not operational". In this case, we must use one of the other valid server name syntaxes instead.

However, since so many examples (including most of ours) use serverless binding, it is often unclear that they are making this fundamental assumption about how the code will be executed.

Serverless binding tends to cause the most trouble in ASP.NET applications, where the security context can have so many variables and many of those involve the use of local machine accounts. See Chapter 8 for more details.

We also mentioned that Active Directory supports using the DNS name of the domain as valid server name syntax. An `ADsPath` with this syntax might look like this:

```
LDAP://domain.com/DC=domain,DC=com
```

This option is interesting, as it combines built-in failover capabilities offered by serverless binding without relying on the current security context to determine a domain to use in the first place. It is often a great choice to use in ASP.NET applications for the same reasons they are often problematic with serverless binding.

Recommendations for Server Name Syntax for Active Directory. Obviously, a lot of choices are available. However, we will attempt to simplify this with a single mandate:

Always use serverless binding or fully qualified DNS names!

SSL generally requires the use of the DNS name and Kerberos does not work well with IP addresses, often resulting in an NTLM authentication instead (which we would like to avoid if possible). We should not use NetBIOS and IP addresses, with the possible exception of test setups.

Never use them in production deployments. Avoid unqualified DNS names as well.

We want to avoid using specific server names in Active Directory unless we are performing operations that require a specific server, such as synchronization.

Recommendations for Server Name Syntax for ADAM. For ADAM, we recommend using the fully qualified DNS domain name of the ADAM instance, if possible. The same reasons for using DNS names that apply to Active Directory apply to ADAM as well.

Recommendations for Specifying the Port. As with the server component in a web URL, the port part is optional unless we are using a nonstandard port. When using Active Directory, we never need to supply the port. Active Directory works only on the standard LDAP ports 389 and 636 for SSL. The global catalog is accessible only on ports 3268 and 3269 (again, for SSL). All we need to do is supply the correct provider (LDAP or GC) and set the appropriate binding flag to add SSL support, and ADSI will do the rest.

When using ADAM, it is more likely that it will be configured to listen for LDAP requests on different ports. The main reason is that multiple ADAM instances often coexist on the same machine. As such, it may become a requirement when using ADAM to supply the port information as well in the ADsPath.

Object Name Syntax in ADsPaths

The <object name> component specifies which object in the directory we wish to reference. In general, we will use the LDAP DN of the object for this. We discussed LDAP DNs in some detail in Chapter 1. Referring back to Table 3.1, examples 1 and 4 demonstrate using the DN. Example 1 shows a typical DN for a domain root-naming context in Active Directory, and example 4 shows a non-Active Directory DN, perhaps from ADAM. We can tell this is not an Active Directory DN because Active Directory does not use the o attribute (which stands for "organization") for object naming.

Example 2 shows an alternate object name syntax supported by both Active Directory and ADAM, which uses the object's GUID directly to specify the name. Active Directory and ADAM support a variety of special binding syntaxes that we explore in the upcoming sections on GUID, SID, and WKGUID binding.

The LDAP specification allows a directory to define provider-specific object naming syntaxes and to signify them by enclosing the name in <> characters. Active Directory and ADAM have done just that. Other directory platforms may define their own using this extension mechanism.

Finally, the third example shows the use of the RootDSE object. The object name RootDSE is a special "ADSI syntax" for referring to something called the LDAP V3 base DSA query. RootDSE is also covered in the section Binding to RootDSE, later in this chapter.

Special Character Considerations in Object Names. Largely, we do not have to worry about special characters in ADsPaths with LDAP. Most of the important rules apply to the DN in the <object name> part and the normal rules for DNs apply. However, there is one important exception to this rule. In a DN, the / character is legal, but in an ADsPath, this is a part separator, so it must be escaped with a \ character. Please refer back to the section LDAP Distinguished Names, in Chapter 1, for more details.

GUID Object Name Syntax. One of the special object name syntaxes supported by Active Directory and ADAM is the GUID style:

```
<GUID=guidvalue>
```

The angle brackets and the GUID keyword are required to inform the directory that an object should be referenced by its objectGUID attribute, rather than by its normal DN. The binding syntax itself is not that complicated; the treatment of guidvalue is what confounds most first-time ADSI and SDS users. Where does that value come from?

In ADSI, we could retrieve the GUID for any object by first searching for it, or binding to it, and then retrieving the objectGuid attribute, using the various GUID properties on DirectoryEntry or perhaps an extended DN search. It should be a simple matter of taking the returned GUID and binding to it. In .NET, there is even a managed Guid class to make string representations easier. However, there are some subtle issues to doing this correctly.

The first thing to understand is that Active Directory and ADAM support two syntaxes for guidvalue.

- The first is the standard COM GUID format, without the {} (e.g., `db78ba89-b85f-447f-bd06-e3a40996a9a8`). We get this value by calling `Guid.ToString("D")` in .NET on a normal `System.Guid` structure, such as that returned by the `Guid` property on `Directory-Entry`.

- The second is the "octet string" format used by the directory natively, which is a sequence of ASCII character pairs representing the hexadecimal value of each byte in the binary format of the GUID (e.g., `89BA78DB5FB87F44BD06E3A40996A9A8`, using the same GUID as in the first syntax). This is the format returned by the `NativeGuid` property on `DirectoryEntry`.

Thus, using this same GUID value, our GUID binding syntax could be either of these (neither is case sensitive for the value):

```
<GUID=db78ba89-b85f-447f-bd06-e3a40996a9a8>
<GUID=89BA78DB5FB87F44BD06E3A40996A9A8>
```

We can use whichever syntax we like, but we need to be careful not to get them mixed up or to build them incorrectly.

So, what exactly is the difference between these two formats? If we look closely, we can see that they contain the same data, but in a slightly different order. For the 16 bytes in the GUID (represented by the 32 hex characters), the COM GUID follows this pattern:

```
4 3 2 1 - 6 5 - 8 7 - 9 10 - 11 12 13 14 15 16
```

The first four bytes are in reverse order, then the second two, and then the third two. Bytes 9–16 are in the same order. Why is this?

The answer lies in the fact that the first eight bytes in a GUID structure are considered a 4-byte integer followed by two 2-byte integers. As you may know, integers in the Intel x86 world (which is historically almost synonymous with Windows) are stored in "little endian" order, which means that the least significant bytes come first. However, the COM GUID representation shows the values as hex-format integers in "reading" format, with the most significant bytes first, as we are used to seeing numbers printed and written.

Thus, the binary representation of the GUID is always different from the standard COM string syntax that we are used to seeing when we see GUIDs in print. Active Directory and ADAM store the GUID in the binary syntax, thus the `NativeGuid` property is shown in byte-order. The bottom line is that the `Guid` property, the `NativeGuid` property, and the `object-GUID` attribute in the directory all represent the exact same data.

Listing 3.3 demonstrates all of this.

LISTING 3.3: Demonstration of Different GUID Binding Approaches

```
using System;
using System.DirectoryServices;

public static void GuidBindingTest()
{
    DirectoryEntry rootDSE;
    DirectoryEntry domainRoot;
    DirectoryEntry entry1;
    DirectoryEntry entry2;
    DirectoryEntry entry3;
    string dnc;
    Guid objectGuid;
    Guid guidProperty;
    Guid convertedGuid;
    string nativeGuidString;
    string octetGuidProperty;


    using (rootDSE = GetEntry("rootDSE"))
    {
        dnc = (string)
            rootDSE.Properties["defaultNamingContext"].Value;
    }


    using (domainRoot = GetEntry(dnc))
    {
        guidProperty = domainRoot.Guid;
        nativeGuidString = domainRoot.NativeGuid;
        objectGuid = new Guid((byte[])
            domainRoot.Properties["objectGuid"].Value);

    }

    octetGuidProperty =
        BitConverter.ToString(guidProperty.ToByteArray());
    octetGuidProperty =
        octetGuidProperty.Replace("-", "").ToLower();
```

```
byte[] nativeGuidBytes = new byte[16];
for (int i = 0; i<16; i++)
{
    nativeGuidBytes[i] = Byte.Parse(
        nativeGuidString.Substring(i*2, 2),
        NumberStyles.HexNumber
        );
}
convertedGuid = new Guid(nativeGuidBytes);

Console.WriteLine("Guid property (COM syntax):      {0}",
    guidProperty.ToString("D"));
Console.WriteLine("NativeGuid (octet style):        {0}",
    nativeGuidString);
Console.WriteLine("Guid property (dashes removed): {0}",
    guidProperty.ToString("N"));
Console.WriteLine("objectGuid (COM syntax):         {0}",
    objectGuid.ToString("D"));
Console.WriteLine("Guid Property as octet string:  {0}",
    octetGuidProperty);
Console.WriteLine("NativeGuid converted to Guid:   {0}",
    convertedGuid.ToString("D"));

string comBindingSyntax =
    String.Format("<GUID={0}>", guidProperty.ToString("D"));
string nativeBindingSyntax =
    String.Format("<GUID={0}>", nativeGuidString);
string invalidBindingSyntax =
    String.Format("<GUID={0}>", guidProperty.ToString("N"));

using (entry1 = GetEntry(comBindingSyntax))
{
    entry1.RefreshCache(); //force bind
    Console.WriteLine(
        "{0} worked as expected.", comBindingSyntax);
}
using (entry2 = GetEntry(nativeBindingSyntax))
{
    entry2.RefreshCache(); //force bind
    Console.WriteLine(
        "{0} worked as expected.", nativeBindingSyntax);
}
using (entry3 = GetEntry(invalidBindingSyntax))
{
    try
    {
        entry3.RefreshCache(); //force bind
    }
    //this should fail unless there just happens
    //to be another object with the other GUID.
    //This is extremely unlikely!
```

```
            catch (COMException ex)
            {
                Console.WriteLine(
                    "{0} failed as expected.",
                    invalidBindingSyntax);
            }
        }
        //OUT:
        //
        //Guid property (COM syntax):
        //    f5433a51-e10a-419e-8472-b368cc2abf2c
        //NativeGuid (octet style):
        //    513a43f50ae19e418472b368cc2abf2c
        //Guid property (dashes removed):
        //    f5433a51e10a419e8472b368cc2abf2c
        //objectGuid (COM syntax):
        //    f5433a51-e10a-419e-8472-b368cc2abf2c
        //Guid Property as octet string:
        //    513a43f50ae19e418472b368cc2abf2c
        //NativeGuid converted to Guid:
        //    f5433a51-e10a-419e-8472-b368cc2abf2c
        //<GUID=f5433a51-e10a-419e-8472-b368cc2abf2c>
        //    worked as expected.
        //<GUID=513a43f50ae19e418472b368cc2abf2c>
        //    worked as expected.
        //<GUID=f5433a51e10a419e8472b368cc2abf2c>
        //    failed as expected.


    }
    private static DirectoryEntry GetEntry(string dn)
    {
        return new DirectoryEntry(
            "LDAP://" + dn,
            null,
            null,
            AuthenticationTypes.Secure
            );
    }
```

From this, we can see that the `Guid` and `NativeGuid` properties and the `objectGUID` attribute represent the same data in different formats, and that we can transform between all three easily.

We also see that using the `Guid.ToString("N")` method does not do what we want. It looks like it produces a GUID in octet string syntax (no dashes), but really it just uses the standard COM GUID string format with dashes removed. This is not what we want!

When creating GUID binding strings, just remember that if the string contains dashes, the GUID must be in COM string format, and if it does not contain dashes, it must be in binary octet string format.

■ NOTE   GUID DN Syntax Is an LDAP Feature

The GUID DN syntax is not a feature of ADSI, but it is supported by LDAP and the directory itself. This means that any API talking to Active Directory or ADAM can use this syntax in place of a DN, not just ADSI or SDS. It works perfectly fine in the Win32 LDAP or `System.DirectoryServices.Protocols`. However, it is an Active Directory and ADAM feature. Other directories may not support this syntax. This rule applies to all of the special binding syntaxes we are describing here.

Internally, `objectGUID` is essentially the primary key for objects in Active Directory and ADAM. Unlike the DN, it is rename-safe, even in cross-domain moves. All objects in the directory have an `objectGUID` attribute and it is impossible to change it without doing some dangerous hacking. As such, it makes an ideal primary key for storage in other systems. In SQL Server, for example, a column of type "unique identifier" is perfect for storing the `objectGUID` attribute. This creates a durable, immutable foreign key pointing to Active Directory or ADAM data for application scenarios that may require it, such as custom synchronization tasks. Since we are storing the directory object's GUID in the database, it makes perfect sense to use the GUID binding syntax to find the object in the directory.

Well-Known GUID Object Name Syntax. One of the problems that applications must contend with is that we often need to access certain "well-known" objects in Active Directory, such as the Domain Controllers container, but we may not always know their names from one install to the next. The names may vary with different internationalized installations of Windows.

Microsoft solves this particular naming issue the same way it solves many other similar problems in Windows. It specifies a well-known GUID that can be used to alias a particular object, regardless of its "normal" name. This well-known GUID will be the same in all deployments of

Active Directory. In order to use the well-known GUID in a bind, there is another, special DN syntax:

```
<WKGUID=XXXXXXXXXXXXXXXXXXXXXXXXXXXXXXXX,DC=domain,DC=com>
```

This DN syntax is similar to the `<GUID=xxxx>` syntax, except there are two parts to it:

```
<WKGUID=(GUID part),(DN of the domain partition)>
```

`(GUID part)` is the well-known GUID of the object and it *must* be specified in octet string syntax. This is unlike normal GUID binding syntax, where both octet string and COM GUID formats are allowed. `(DN of the domain partition)` is the actual DN of the domain partition, assuming we are looking for well-known objects in the domain partition. We need this, of course, because a well-known GUID is not unique (hence, it is well known!) and we still need to know which Active Directory domain we are referring to. There are also three well-known objects in the Configuration container that would use its DN here instead. These DNs will vary from directory to directory but can be determined dynamically from `RootDSE`.

Listing 3.4 demonstrates how to bind to the `'CN=Users'` container in a domain.

LISTING 3.4: Well-Known GUID Binding

```
string adsPath = "LDAP://<WKGUID=a9d1ca15768811d1aded00c04fd8d5cd," +
    "DC=domain,DC=com>";

using (DirectoryEntry de = new DirectoryEntry(
    adsPath,
    null,
    null,
    AuthenticationTypes.Secure
    ))
{
    Console.WriteLine("Successfully Bound To: {0}",
        de.Properties["distinguishedName"].Value);
}

//OUT: Successfully Bound To: CN=Users,DC=domain,DC=com
```

Table 3.2 shows the well-known GUIDs that are defined.

> **■ NOTE   The Well-Known GUID and objectGUID Are Not the Same**
>
> The well-known GUID is not the same as the target object's `object-GUID` attribute. The well-known GUID will be the same in all implementations, whereas the actual `objectGUID` will vary with each installation. They are used for two different purposes.

TABLE 3.2: Well-Known Defined GUIDs

Container	GUID Identifier
Users	GUID_USERS_CONTAINER_W
Computers	GUID_COMPUTERS_CONTAINER_W
Systems	GUID_SYSTEMS_CONTAINER_W
Domain Controllers	GUID_DOMAIN_CONTROLLERS_CONTAINER_W
Infrastructure	GUID_INFRASTRUCTURE_CONTAINER_W
Deleted Objects	GUID_DELETED_OBJECTS_CONTAINER_W
Lost and Found	GUID_LOSTANDFOUND_CONTAINER_W

The value for these GUID Identifier constants is defined in the ntdsapi.h header file in the Windows Platform SDK.

The well-known object mechanism is extensible via the `other-WellKnownObjects` attribute, so it is possible to add our own well-known objects to the directory if we wish.

SID Object Name Syntax. Similar to GUID binding, SID binding is an alternate way to locate an object in Active Directory or ADAM using its security identifier (SID). SIDs are the unique identifiers used by Windows for security principals. The SID used for binding in Active Directory and ADAM is stored in the `objectSid` attribute. However, unlike the `object-GUID` attribute, not every object in the directory has a SID. Only objects that have the `securityPrincipal` auxiliary class will have an `objectSid` attribute. Luckily, this includes many of the objects we are interested in, such as users, groups, and computers.

Similar to `objectGUID`, the `objectSid` value remains the same even if that object has been renamed or moved. A major difference between `objectSid` and `objectGuid` is that since a SID is tied to a domain, it cannot be moved across domains. Instead, if an object moves across domains, it will be assigned a new SID for the domain (the `objectGUID` will remain the same), and the previous SID will be added to the object's `sidHistory` attribute.

The SID DN style uses the following syntax:

```
<SID=sidvalue>
```

Like the GUID syntax, `sidvalue` can be one of two different syntaxes:

- The hexadecimal octet string
- The Security Descriptor Description Language (SDDL) format, which looks like `S-1-5-xxxx`

▪▪ NOTE **SDDL Format Works Only with Windows Server 2003 Active Directory and ADAM**

We have to be careful which environment we are targeting when using a SID bind. Only the Windows Server 2003 version of Active Directory and ADAM supports the SDDL syntax, so we must use the octet string syntax with Windows 2000. If we have a mixed environment or are uncertain which platform will be used, it is better to err on the side of caution and use the octet string format. It is possible to determine the directory version at runtime by examining several different attributes on `RootDSE`, such as `supportedCapabilities`.

.NET 2.0 has a convenient new `SecurityIdentifier` class with a `ToString` method that will produce SDDL output given the binary form. However, for .NET 1.x, the SDDL format of the SID is not available without P/Invoking a Win32 API (`ConvertSidToStringSid`), or using the ADsSecurity.dll library. As such, it is often easier to bind with the SID using the octet string syntax if we are given the binary version to start with. When retrieving the SID from Active Directory with the `objectSid` attribute, the binary format is returned.

Listing 3.5 shows a handy function for generating octet strings from binary data such as GUIDs and SIDs. It is so handy, in fact, that we reference it several more times throughout the book!

LISTING 3.5: BuildOctetString Function

```
using System.Text;

private string BuildOctetString(byte[] bytes)
{
    StringBuilder sb = new StringBuilder();
    for(int i=0; i < bytes.Length; i++)
    {
            sb.Append(bytes[i].ToString("X2"));
    }
    return sb.ToString();
}
```

Listing 3.6 demonstrates how we might use this function.

LISTING 3.6: Demonstrating SID Binding

```
DirectoryEntry user = new DirectoryEntry(
    "LDAP://CN=User1,CN=Users,DC=domain,DC=com",
    null,
    null,
    AuthenticationTypes.Secure
    );

//retrieve the SID
byte[] sidBytes =
    user.Properties["objectSid"].Value as byte[];

//format the bytes using the BuildOctetString function
string adPath =
    String.Format(
        "LDAP://<SID={0}>",
        BuildOctetString(sidBytes)
        );

DirectoryEntry sidBind = new DirectoryEntry(
    adPath,
    null,
    null,
    AuthenticationTypes.Secure
    );

//force the bind
object native =  sidBind.NativeObject;
```

As with the earlier GUID binding sample, this example is somewhat contrived because we would not first bind to an object and then retrieve its SID, only to rebind again. A more realistic use for this is to examine the user object's `tokenGroups` attribute, which is a multivalued attribute that contains the SIDs of all of the security groups of which the user is a member. We could create a bindable SID string, use it to bind to any of the security groups, and then examine the group object. A sample in Chapter 10 demonstrates this.

Like GUIDs, SIDs can also be stored in external databases and used as keys into Active Directory data. They are not as convenient to use as GUIDs, as the binary data is of a variable length and not all objects have a SID to begin with. However, there are certain applications where this might be appropriate.

> **■ WARNING** SID Binding Does Not Work with the Global Catalog
>
> Unlike the other special binding syntaxes, SID binding is available only over the LDAP port on Active Directory. Attempting to do a SID bind against the global catalog will result in an error.

Providing Credentials

Throughout most of this book, we use samples like Listing 3.7 for binding to the directory.

LISTING 3.7: Binding with Default Credentials

```
DirectoryEntry entry = new DirectoryEntry(
    "LDAP://DC=domain,DC=com",
    null,
    null,
    AuthenticationTypes.Secure
    );
```

Here, we are specifying `null` for the `username` and `password` parameters. This is also called **supplying default credentials** and it instructs Windows to use the current security context to access the directory.

However, we do not always wish to access Active Directory or ADAM with our currently logged-on credentials. We may need to bind using an ADAM account (which requires explicit credentials) or we may be running

> **■ NOTE**　Using the AuthenticationTypes.Secure Flag
>
> We are using the `Secure` option with the provider in order to protect the credentials we have specified and to keep them from being transmitted in plain text over the wire. Note also that the username and password we have specified are used to create the security context that will be used to bind to the directory. You can find more detail on secure binding later in this chapter and in Chapter 8. We generally use secure binding throughout the samples in this book, where appropriate, because secure binding is generally a good thing to do.

under a local machine account that cannot access the domain. To accommodate this, the `DirectoryEntry` supports accepting alternate credentials in plaintext, as shown in Listing 3.8.

LISTING 3.8:　**Binding with Explicit Credentials**

```
DirectoryEntry entry = new DirectoryEntry(
    "LDAP://DC=domain,DC=com",
    @"domain\adminuser",
    "password",
    AuthenticationTypes.Secure
    );

//equivalent syntax
DirectoryEntry entry = new DirectoryEntry(
    "LDAP://DC=domain,DC=com"
    );
entry.Username = @"domain\adminuser";
entry.Password = "password";
entry.AuthenticationType = AuthenticationTypes.Secure;
```

Suppose we wanted to bind directly to a user object rather than to the root domain, as we did in Listing 3.8. Listing 3.9 demonstrates what this might look like.

LISTING 3.9:　**Binding to a Specific User with Default Credentials**

```
DirectoryEntry entry = new DirectoryEntry(
    "LDAP://CN=Joe Somebody,CN=Users,DC=domain,DC=com"
    );
entry.Username = @"domain\adminuser";
entry.Password = "password";
entry.AuthenticationType = AuthenticationTypes.Secure;
```

It can be confusing to first-time SDS users what is happening here, because the credentials we have specified are not those of `Joe Somebody`, the user to which we are binding! Don't we need to supply Joe's username (`domain\jsomebody`) and know his password in order to bind correctly?

The answer is, of course, no. Remember, we said earlier that the credentials supplied were used to create the security context with which to bind to the directory. Those credentials do not represent the object to which we are binding. Instead, they are the credentials of whatever user we wish to use to perform the task we need to perform. This could be a very low-privileged account that can just read a few attributes on a few objects, an administrator with power over every object in the domain, or something in between.

Chapter 8 thoroughly explores the security aspects of binding and the implications of supplying and omitting credentials.

Username Syntaxes in Active Directory and ADAM

One of the most confusing aspects about supplying credentials is to know the right format with which to specify the username parameter. The LDAP specification states that the user's full DN must be accepted as a username when doing simple binds. However, it allows directories to accept additional username syntaxes as well. Active Directory supports four different username syntaxes that we can use:

- Full DN (e.g., `CN=user,DC=domain,DC=com`), contained in the `distinguishedName` attribute (as per the LDAP spec)
- NT Account Name (e.g., `domain\user`)
- User Principal Name (UPN) (e.g., `user@domain.com`), contained in the `userPrincipalName` attribute
- Plain username (e.g., `user`), contained in the `sAMAccountName` attribute

However, we cannot use all of them interchangeably. Different flags, set via the `AuthenticationTypes` enumeration, control which username format we can use. Here are the rules governing use for each of them.

- We can always use the NT Account Name, regardless of the `AuthenticationTypes` flags.
- We can always use the UPN.
- We can use the plain username only if `AuthenticationTypes.Secure` is set.
- We can use the DN only if `AuthenticationTypes.Secure` is *not* set.[1]

Table 3.3 summarizes the allowed combinations.

TABLE 3.3: AuthenticationTypes Requirements for Username Syntaxes

Username Syntax	AuthenticationTypes Requirement
NT Account Name	Any
User Principal Name	Any
Plain Account Name	`AuthenticationTypes.Secure`
Distinguished Name	Not `AuthenticationTypes.Secure`

Recommendation: Use the NT Account Name or UPN

Given that the NT Account Name and the UPN may always be used, it seems to make the most sense to use those consistently in our code.

The UPN is the new recommended username syntax in Windows 2000 and higher, and it should generally be favored over the NT Account Name. However, there is one potential gotcha with the UPN in that Active Directory does not enforce uniqueness on the `userPrincipalName` attribute, even though it is required for every UPN to be unique in the entire Active Directory forest. If two or more users share the same UPN, none of them will be able to authenticate using their UPN. These issues do not

---

1. DN syntax actually can be used with `AuthenticationTypes.Secure`, but only if the user's common name (CN) is the same as the `sAMAccountName`. ADSI will take the user's CN from the DN and use this as the username in a secure bind. Given that the CN does not necessarily equal the `sAMAccountName`, this technique is inherently unreliable and we recommend against using it. It is also not documented by Microsoft, so the behavior may change at any time.

occur with the NT Account Name, as every account has a user name (sAMAccountName) that is guaranteed to be unique by the directory and every domain has a unique domain name.

There may be occasions where using the plain username is important. For example, we may not know the domain name or have the UPN. In that case, make sure to use AuthenticationTypes.Secure.

There may also be occasions where we want to bind with the DN. For example, the DN is the username binding syntax that is actually defined by the LDAP simple bind specification, so many applications that try to work across different LDAP servers may choose to use this as a lowest common denominator format. In this case, make sure you do *not* use AuthenticationTypes.Secure so that a simple bind will be used instead. Please see the section AuthenticationTypes Explained for precautions regarding using a simple bind.

Username Syntaxes in ADAM

ADAM is a little less complicated than Active Directory when authenticating ADAM users. By ADAM users, we mean user objects stored in ADAM, not in Active Directory (see Chapters 8 and 10 for more details). Two username formats may be used in ADAM:

- Full DN (e.g., CN=user,DC=domain,DC=com), contained in the distinguishedName attribute
- UPN (e.g., user@domain.com), contained in the userPrincipalName attribute

The DN is required by the LDAP specification, as we previously explained. The UPN in ADAM is a little bit different from the UPN in Active Directory, though. ADAM has no concept of a forest and does not integrate with Kerberos, so the syntax requirements for UPN in ADAM are more relaxed in that it does not even need to contain an "@" sign. Essentially, we can put whatever value we wish in the ADAM UPN attribute, as long as it is unique. Note that the UPN is not a mandatory attribute in the ADAM user object schema, so it may not be set. If we wish to use it for binding, we must populate the value first.

In the case of ADAM users, we use an LDAP simple bind to authenticate them with SDS, so we must use `AuthenticationTypes.None` to accomplish this.

AuthenticationTypes Explained

The last component that determines the behavior of the `DirectoryEntry` bind was called "provider-specific options." In SDS terminology, we mean authentication types, which are represented by the `Authentication-Types` enumeration.

`AuthenticationTypes` specify options that change the mechanisms used by SDS to connect and communicate with the directory. It is vitally important to understand what each one does and how they work together, so we will now examine each member of the enumeration in detail.

Enumeration Members

Listing 3.10 shows the members of the `AuthenticationTypes` enumeration.

LISTING 3.10: AuthenticationTypes Enumeration Members

```
[Flags]
public enum AuthenticationTypes
{
    Anonymous = 0x10,
    Delegation = 0x100,
    Encryption = 2,
    FastBind = 0x20,
    None = 0,
    ReadonlyServer = 4,
    Sealing = 0x80,
    Secure = 1,
    SecureSocketsLayer = 2,
    ServerBind = 0x200,
    Signing = 0x40
}
```

We will explore each member in detail. Instead of proceeding in alphabetical order, we will group the values together in terms of their importance to each other.

None. This is the default value for the enumeration. `None` is most often used when an LDAP simple bind is desired (see Chapter 8 for more details on what simple bind really means). An LDAP simple bind is the only binding mechanism defined in the actual LDAP version 3 specification, so it has excellent compatibility across LDAP server vendors. Unfortunately, it relies on a plaintext exchange of credentials, so it is completely insecure by itself.

> **▪ WARNING   This Option Is Not Secure!**
>
> We repeat again, this option is not secure by itself. Please do not use None unless it is combined with SecureSocketsLayer or some other external means of transport security such as IPSEC. Do not pass plaintext credentials on an unencrypted network channel!

Note that this is not the default value for any of the DirectoryEntry constructors that do not specify AuthenticationTypes in .NET 2.0. .NET 2.0 uses Secure by default. Unfortunately, in .NET 1.x, the behavior varies depending on the constructor used. Chapter 8 contains an important caveat about the behavior differences this change can cause.

Secure. This option indicates to use the Windows Security Support Provider Interface (SSPI) authentication system when binding to the directory. In terms of SDS use, this is roughly synonymous with using the Windows Negotiate protocol.[2] Negotiate authentication selects between Kerberos and NTLM authentication through a negotiation process (hence the name). Negotiate is the native authentication protocol of Windows in Windows 2000 and later. Secure binding supports both explicit credentials and using the current Windows security context for authentication, which is incredibly useful in many situations. Chapter 8 discusses these options in detail.

Sealing. This flag says to use the encryption capabilities of SSPI to encrypt traffic after the security context is established. Because it relies on SSPI, it must be combined with the Secure flag in order to work.

---

2. Windows Server 2003 can use Digest authentication when Secure authentication is selected, and it detects that the server supports Digest authentication but does not support Negotiate, as might be more likely on a non-Windows directory. This behavior may also make its way into other operating systems. However, Secure authentication almost always means Negotiate authentication for typical scenarios.

Not all SSPI authentication protocols support encryption, and they behave differently on different operating system versions. Kerberos authentication always supports encryption (although different operating systems support different encryption strengths). However, NTLM support for encryption was not originally available in Windows 2000 and instead made its appearance originally with Windows XP. To discover which operating systems support SSPI encryption on which protocol, it is best to check the most recent documentation, as this even tends to vary from one service pack to another and not just with full operating system releases.

Signing. Signing uses the signing capabilities of SSPI to sign network traffic and verify whether someone has tampered with it. As with `Sealing`, it must be combined with the `Secure` flag in order to work.

`Signing` and `Sealing` are very often used together. `Signing` also has the same caveats as `Sealing` in terms of support with various protocols on different operating system revisions.

Delegation. `Delegation` refers to the ability of a service to use an authenticated user's security context to access another service on the network. `Delegation` is a feature offered by the Kerberos authentication protocol. Like `Sealing` and `Signing`, it must again be combined with the `Secure` flag, or it has no effect.

A lot of confusion surrounds this particular value because it seems to indicate that somehow delegation will occur if it is used, or that it must be specified when using delegation. In fact, neither of these is true. It is entirely possible for delegation to be available if we do not explicitly request it, and it is possible to request it and not get it. However, if we want delegation, it is always best to use this flag to signal our intent. We discuss delegation scenarios in detail in Chapter 8, including how to detect whether delegation is available.

Anonymous. This option tells ADSI not to perform a `Bind` operation before attempting other operations, such as searches. As such, the state of the LDAP connection will not be authenticated.

In order to use `Anonymous` successfully, we must also supply username and password credentials with an empty string (`" "` or `String.Empty`). We cannot use `null`/`Nothing`. If we try to use a null reference for our credentials, we will receive a somewhat cryptic "invalid parameter" exception.

This flag is not typically used with Active Directory, as unauthenticated users can do very little in the directory. In fact, Windows Server 2003 Active Directory and ADAM do not allow anonymous operations by default. This flag is generally used with non-Microsoft directories that allow completely anonymous access.

SecureSocketsLayer. `SecureSocketsLayer` specifies that the SSL/TLS protocol will be used to encrypt the network traffic with the directory server, including the `Bind` request. When specifying this option, an SSL certificate must be installed and available in Active Directory and ADAM.

Under the covers, ADSI will change the TCP port (if it is not already specified) from the default port 389 to port 636, and SSL will be used to secure the communication.

SSL is often supported by third-party LDAP directories and should be the preferred method of protecting credentials when communicating with directories other than Active Directory and ADAM. `SecureSocketsLayer` is also helpful in some situations when using the ADSI `SetPassword` and `ChangePassword` methods (see Chapter 10).

Note that we can combine `Secure` authentication with `SecureSocketsLayer`, but we cannot combine `SecureSocketsLayer` with `Sealing` or `Signing`.

Troubleshooting Binds with SecureSocketsLayer

Because `SecureSocketsLayer` binds rely on the SSL protocol, they have some additional ways of failing that can be frustrating to diagnose if we do not understand the requirements. SSL uses certificates on the server (and possibly the client as well) to determine the identity of the server and negotiate an encrypted channel between the client and server. Because certificates are used, SSL binds are subject to all of the various failure modes for certificates as well. In order for a client to accept a server's certificate, the following must be true.

- The server must have an SSL certificate installed.
- The DNS name used to contact the server must be the same name stored in the server's certificate.
- The client must trust the issuer of the server's certificate.
- The certificate must not have been revoked by the issuer.
- The current date must be within the certificate's valid issue dates.

Obviously, a number of things can go wrong here. For one, the server must have an SSL certificate. This may seem obvious, but remember that Active Directory and ADAM servers do not have SSL certificates by default. These must be provisioned and installed before SSL is even an option.

The second problem occurs frequently when using an IP address for the server name. Generally, certificates are issued to servers with the DNS name of the server in the certificate, and this name must match the name the client used to access the server in order for the client to trust the identity of the server. If we follow the recommendation of always using DNS names, this is rarely a problem.

The third problem involves certificate trust. Certificate trust is determined by hierarchies of certificate authorities that issue certificates. These authority hierarchies "chain up" to a root certificate authority. Root authorities are the top of the food chain, and in Windows, they are installed in the Trusted Roots certificate container. If the server's certificate does not chain up to a trusted root certificate on the client's system, the client will not trust the server.

Certificate authorities can also revoke certificates, at which point the certificate is no longer valid. Certificate revocation is determined by a list that the issuer publishes at a well-known HTTP address. Not all clients actually check the revocation list, but a certificate may still be rejected for this reason.

Finally, a certificate is valid for a specific period. If the server's certificate has expired or is not yet valid, the client will not accept it either.

If all of these failure modes remind us of the certificate warning dialog displayed by Internet Explorer when it has a problem with a server's certificate, this is because LDAP and IE use the same SSPI provider, Schannel, for SSL services. The glaring difference between the two is that in IE, we are presented with a warning dialog that we may dismiss, and in LDAP, the connection simply fails for the same conditions. All of the requirements must be met in order for LDAP to negotiate an SSL connection.

Windows provides a variety of different tools and techniques for debugging Schannel problems, including Schannel debugging to the Event Log and the SSL Diagnostics Tool.

Encryption. This enumeration value is actually the same as the `SecureSocketsLayer` value and they do exactly the same thing. However, `Encryption` is the deprecated name and should not be used.

ServerBind. Unlike many of the other flags described so far, this flag affects the DNS lookup behavior of `Bind`. `ServerBind` essentially says "I am supplying an exact server name in my `ADsPath`, so do not bother using DNS to try to dynamically discover a domain controller using the Locator service." It is a performance optimization only, as it eliminates the extra DNS traffic involved in the dynamic discovery process. It is never required.

Given this, we should never combine `ServerBind` with serverless binding or binding with the domain name.

`ServerBind` is most often used with ADAM and non-Microsoft directories. It can be used with Active Directory, but it eliminates Active Directory's automatic failover capabilities and can cause brittleness as a result. It is useful with scenarios when a specific domain controller is required, such as for synchronization or for specific FSMO operations.

We can combine `ServerBind` with any other flags.

FastBind. In order to provide some of the special ADSI interfaces for an object, such as `IADsUser`, that correspond to specific types of objects in the directory, ADSI attempts to determine the object's schema type when the object is first accessed. It does this by retrieving the object's `objectClass` attribute. Once the `objectClass` attribute is known, ADSI can map all of the extra ADSI interfaces to the object. This initial search is done *in addition to* the search operation used to fill the property cache.

In effect, ADSI does two searches every time it accesses an object and reads its properties. When accessing a large number of objects in batch operations (for instance, to update a particular attribute), all of these little search operations can add up to a huge performance hit.

`FastBind` disables this initial search to determine the `objectClass` attribute. This can cause remarkable performance increases. Unfortunately, it comes with a drawback. Only the following high-level ADSI interfaces will be available to the object:

- `IADs`
- `IADsContainer`
- `IDirectoryObject`
- `IDirectorySearch`
- `IADsPropertyList`
- `IADsObjectOptions`
- `ISupportErrorInfo`
- `IADsDeleteOps`

One thing that is interesting about this list is that all of the operations performed by the `DirectoryEntry` class in normal usage use only these ADSI interfaces under the hood. We need the other interfaces that `Fast-Bind` prevents only when using the various `Invoke` methods to access members of other interfaces, such as `IADsUser` and `IADsGroup`. As such, this flag can probably be used for an effective performance boost much more often than it is.

Additionally, this option does not verify that the object exists during binding, which can complicate error handling should this situation not be expected. For example, with `FastBind`, we cannot use the `NativeObject` property to verify an object's existence. We must perform an operation that loads the property cache, such as `RefreshCache`, as only then is an actual search performed.

We can combine `FastBind` with all other `AuthenticationTypes`.

ReadonlyServer. In Active Directory and ADAM as of Windows Server 2003, all servers are writable, so this flag has no effect. It is generally there for use with Windows NT4 and the `WinNT` provider where backup domain controllers exist.

However, the next version of Windows Server (currently code-named "Longhorn Server") will introduce something called the "read-only DC," so perhaps this flag will take on new meaning then.

Recommendations for AuthenticationTypes

So, which values should we use? Because `AuthenticationTypes` is a bitwise type of enumeration, we can combine the values, so there are many options. We cannot provide guidance on every single combination, but we can make some recommendations.

- The `Secure` flag should almost always be used with Active Directory.
- Any time explicit credentials are used, they should be secured on the wire. The `Secure` flag should be used with Active Directory and with ADAM if pass-through authentication of a Windows user is being used. Otherwise, the `SecureSocketsLayer` value should be specified.
- For complete over-the-wire security, we recommend using the `Secure`, `Signing`, and `Sealing` flags together. This will ensure that the network traffic is encrypted and tamper resistant.
- The `FastBind` flag can be used to increase performance with any other combination of values as long as its drawback is not an issue.
- If a particular server is specified, the addition of the `ServerBind` flag is recommended in conjunction with any other flags.
- If delegation is required, we recommend using the `Delegation` flag in addition to the `Secure` flag to indicate clearly that we want delegation.

So, in a scenario where we are talking to Active Directory using a specific server and we need delegation, secure communications, and maximum performance, we would use this:

```
AuthenticationTypes.Secure | AuthenticationTypes.Sealing |
AuthenticationTypes.Signing | AuthenticationTypes.Delegation |
AuthenticationTypes.FastBind | AuthenticationTypes.ServerBind
```

Table 3.4 summarizes the rules for use of `AuthenticationTypes`.

TABLE 3.4: Valid AuthenticationTypes Combinations and Restrictions

Value	Requires	Often Combined With	Do Not Combine With
Secure			Anonymous
Sealing	Secure	Signing, Delegation	SecureSocketsLayer
Signing	Secure	Sealing, Delegation	SecureSocketsLayer
Delegation	Secure	Signing, Sealing	
Anonymous			Secure
SecureSocketsLayer			Signing, Sealing
ServerBind		Any	
FastBind		Any	
ReadonlyServer		Any	

Binding to RootDSE

One of the shortcomings of the original LDAP specification was that there wasn't an easy way to know information about a given directory at runtime. For example, it is nice to know the DNs of the naming contexts exposed by the directory, the schema it exposes, and the various capabilities it supports.

The primary LDAP version 3 specification, RFC 2251, addresses this by defining a well-known root DSE object (a DSA-specific entry, where DSA is a standard X.500 term for the directory server itself) available on all servers that provides specific information about the directory. The root DSE object is accessible by performing a base-level search against a null DN as the search root with a filter of `(objectClass=*)`.

ADSI provides a shortcut for accessing the root DSE object by providing a special DN for it, called (predictably) `RootDSE`. Thus, an `ADsPath` for the root DSE object would look like this:

```
LDAP://RootDSE
LDAP://mydc.mydomain.com/RootDSE
```

As with all DNs, `RootDSE` is not case sensitive. We can capitalize it any way we want. Because there is no actual object named "RootDSE" in the directory, we cannot perform a search looking for it. The `RootDSE` DN is just syntactic sugar understood by ADSI to give us a shortcut to find it. Thus, in a lower-level API such as `System.DirectoryServices.Protocols` (SDS.P), we would actually have to perform the base-level search on the null search root DN, as the term "RootDSE" is valid only in ADSI.

RootDSE Attribute Data

RFCs 2251 and 2252 define the following attributes that all LDAP version 3 servers must support.

- **namingContexts.** The DNs of the naming contexts held in the server. In Active Directory, this will always contain the Configuration container and the schema container, as well as the default context for the server.

- **subschemaSubentry.** The DN of the subschema entries (or subentries) known by this server. The subschema entries describe the schema supported by the server in a standard format that any client can parse and use to understand the schema at runtime. For example, ADSI uses this to map LDAP data types to ADSI and COM data types.

- **altServer.** Alternative servers in case this one is unavailable later. Note that Active Directory and ADAM do not publish this attribute.

- **supportedExtension.** List of supported extended LDAP operations specified by their Object Identifiers (OIDs).

- **supportedControl.** List of supported LDAP controls specified by their OIDs.

- **supportedSASLMechanisms.** List of supported Simple Authentication and Security Layer (SASL) security features by their names, such as GSS-SPNEGO and DIGEST-MD5.

- **supportedLDAPVersion.** LDAP versions implemented by the server.

Furthermore, Active Directory and ADAM support the following additional properties.

- **currentTime.** The current time based on the server.
- **dsServiceName.** The DN of the NTDS Settings object.
- **defaultNamingContext.** In Active Directory, this is the DN of the domain partition object. ADAM does not advertise a defaultNamingContext by default, but it can be set to any partition defined by the server.
- **schemaNamingContext.** The DN of the schema partition. In Active Directory, this is the forest schema container. In ADAM, this is the schema container for the configuration set.
- **configurationNamingContext.** The DN for the configuration partition. In Active Directory, this is the configuration context for the forest. In ADAM, it is the configuration context for the server.
- **rootDomainNamingContext.** In Active Directory, this is the DN for the naming context of the forest root domain. This attribute is not published in ADAM, as it does not have forests.
- **supportedLDAPPolicies.** A list of the LDAP management policies supported by the server. In Active Directory and ADAM, this will include things such as MaxValRange and MaxPageSize.
- **highestCommittedUSN.** Active Directory and ADAM use update sequence numbers (USNs) for tracking changes, for replication purposes. This shows the highest USN committed on the server.
- **dnsHostName.** The DNS name of this particular server.
- **ldapServiceName.** In Active Directory, this is the service principal name (SPN) of the server that the Kerberos system uses for mutual authentication.
- **serverName.** The DN for the server object for the server, as defined in the Configuration container.
- **supportedCapabilities.** Values identifying the supported capabilities of the server as OIDs.

Uses for RootDSE

RootDSE is extremely useful for determining information about the server dynamically at runtime. One of the most common things we will do in LDAP programming is perform subtree searches on the default naming context of the server. Instead of having to know the DN of this object to use as a search base, we can use RootDSE to tell us this information. Listing 3.11 demonstrates this.

LISTING 3.11: Retrieving the Default Naming Context with RootDSE

```
DirectoryEntry rootDSE = new DirectoryEntry("LDAP://RootDSE");
String dnc = (string)
    rootDSE.Properties["defaultNamingContext"].Value;
DirectoryEntry searchRoot = new DirectoryEntry("LDAP://" + dnc);
```

If you are at all like us, you will likely use code such as this in nearly every project. We use the default naming context for building the DN of not only the domain root, but also the known children in the domain. Given that these values rarely change, it is probably a good idea from a performance perspective to cache these values if they are being used in a larger application framework.

Another very helpful attribute is the dnsHostName attribute. If we did not specify a specific server name in our binding string, we may wish to know to which server we actually connected. This is one easy way to find out. All of the other attributes have varying degrees of usefulness depending on the application.

RootDSE is also useful if we need to authenticate a user's credentials via ADSI. Chapter 12 discusses LDAP authentication in detail.

Here are a few other useful things to keep in mind about RootDSE.

- The LDAP version 3 specification dictates that all clients can access it anonymously. No authentication or authorization is required.
- Since only the seven core attributes are dictated by the specification, keep this in mind with code that seeks to be directory-server neutral.

ADSI Connection Caching Explained

As we explained in Chapter 1, the LDAP API is based on the concept of operations performed on a persistent connection to the server. However,

ADSI and SDS are based on a metaphor of reading and modifying objects in the directory. Since we know ADSI is using LDAP under the hood, we know that there must be an LDAP connection being used somewhere. So, how exactly does that work? Does ADSI create and destroy a new connection with each object access? Does it somehow reuse an existing connection that it maintains?

As you may have guessed by the title of this section, ADSI does in fact cache and reuse LDAP connection handles under the hood when it can. This is important because there is significant overhead in establishing a connection and binding to authenticate it. We would not want to do this repeatedly if we could avoid it. Furthermore, in high-volume server scenarios where many different connections are being opened and closed quickly, we run the risk of running out of TCP "wildcard ports," which could cause the underlying network layer to fail. We will not explain wildcard ports in detail here, but suffice it to say that if we are building a server application with high scalability requirements, we don't want to run out of them. This section is important!

Here is how it works. If a client in a particular process makes a connection to a server by creating and binding a `DirectoryEntry` object, the connection will be reused if all three of the following are true.

- The same server, port, and credentials are used.
- The same authentication flags (`AuthenticationTypes` enumeration) are used, with the exception of the `ServerBind` and `FastBind` flags.
- The original `DirectoryEntry` object, or at least one object that has been opened, subsequently stays open.

Listing 3.12 shows an example.

LISTING 3.12: Demonstrating Proper Connection Caching

```
DirectoryEntry rootDSE = new DirectoryEntry(
    "LDAP://myserver.mydomain.com/RootDSE"
    );
//this will force the connection to be established
Object bindTest = rootDSE.NativeObject;

//server, port and credentials are the same.
//connection will be reused, even though the object
```

```
//"user" will be released when the using block exits
DirectoryEntry user;
string cn;
using (user)
{
 user = new DirectoryEntry(
     "LDAP://myserver.mydomain.com/" +
     "CN=myuser,CN=Users,DC=myserver,DC=mydomain,DC=com"
     );
 cn = (string) user.Properties["cn"].Value;
}

DirectoryEntry newUser;
string cn2;
using (newUser)
{
 //This will start a new connection because the
 //AuthenticationTypes are different
 newUser = new DirectoryEntry(
     "LDAP://myserver.mydomain.com/" +
     "CN=myuser2,CN=Users,DC=myserver,DC=mydomain,DC=com",
     null,
     null,
     AuthenticationTypes.SecureSocketsLayer
     );
 string cn2 = (string) newUser.Properties["cn"].Value;
}
//The second connection is closed as we leave the using block
//and the newUser DirectoryEntry is disposed

//We are now cleaning up the original object.
//The connection will be closed
rootDSE.Dispose();
```

Let's review some of the finer points here. The first thing to remember is that the connection stays open as long as at least one object that uses the connection stays open. This means that at least one object must not be Disposed or finalized by the garbage collector. In order to prevent finalization, we have to keep a live root to the object in memory. That generally means maintaining the object in a long-lived object member, such as in a static variable in a class.

Another thing to remember is that connections are cached per process. This is especially important to remember in the context of ASP.NET, where a single process may host multiple AppDomains containing different web applications that are not related. If we reuse servers, ports, credentials, and

`AuthenticationTypes` between different web applications in the same server process, the various web applications will reuse each other's cached connections.

Connection Caching with Serverless Binds

When we use serverless binding, the LDAP API will determine an Active Directory server for us automatically, using the Locator service. So then, if we repeatedly create `DirectoryEntry` objects in this way and we don't explicitly control the server being used, will connection caching still work?

The short answer is maybe. The Locator service will generally continue to return the same server, which will allow connection caching to work. It does this by caching the Locator call. However, after some time, the Locator service is contacted again to avoid stale data. It is also possible for other processes on the machine to force a cache refresh. The point here is that it is entirely possible for a serverless bind to return a different domain controller. We should keep in mind the fact that we do not have a guarantee that we will always get the same domain controller and avoid writing code that expects this behavior. If a new domain controller is returned because of a cache refresh, we will get a new connection.

The story with binding with default credentials is pretty much the same. As long as the security context stays the same, connection caching will continue to work. However, if the security context changes (due to a change in thread impersonation, for example), then a new connection will be created. This last point is important to remember, because if we are impersonating many different users in a high-volume application, a new connection will be opened for each one and we may have scalability issues as a result.

Directory CRUD Operations

The ability of the SDS developer to create, read, update, and delete (CRUD) directory objects is obviously core to all operations using Active Directory. Unlike with SQL databases, which are optimized to balance read and write operations, LDAP databases are optimized for reads and the vast majority of operations we perform are geared toward this. In fact, we dedicate the next three chapters to a discussion of searching for objects in the directory and reading and writing their attribute values. In this section, we will focus on the ability to create and delete them, with a few highlights on reading and updating. We also discuss moving and renaming objects, which is a special case of an update that is different from other types of update operations.

Reading Attributes of Directory Objects

Reading and writing data with `DirectoryEntry` is a sufficiently complicated subject to warrant an entire chapter, so Chapter 6 is dedicated to just that. For now, we will just touch on a few highlights.

The `Properties` property on `DirectoryEntry` provides access to the list of attributes for a directory object and the values of each attribute. `Properties` returns a `PropertyCollection` that represents the list of attributes. Each element in the `PropertyCollection` in turn contains a `PropertyValueCollection` that represents the attribute values. Even though LDAP attributes may allow single or multiple values, we always use a `PropertyValueCollection` to represent the data so that we can cover both cases. A single-valued attribute will simply be represented by a `PropertyValueCollection` with a `Count` property of 1.

Accessing attribute values is fairly simple:

```
object val = entry.Properties["attributeToRead"].Value;
```

Here, the `Value` property on the `PropertyValueCollection` is used to access all of the attribute values as an object. The object can be an array of a more specific type, a scalar value of a more specific type, or `null`, depending on what data is actually stored in the directory. We can also use the various standard collection methods on the collection classes to perform typical collection operations:

```
if (entry.Properties.Contains("attributeToRead"))
{
    //safe to access now
    object val = entry.Properties["attributeToRead"][0];
}
```

Modifying Attributes of Directory Objects

The `DirectoryEntry` class provides read-write access to attribute data in an LDAP directory. As with reading directory attributes, we use `PropertyCollection` and `PropertyValueCollection` to modify the data within the directory.

Once again, reading and writing data to the directory is complex enough that we have an entire upcoming chapter dedicated to the subject. However, here is a brief sample that demonstrates the basics:

```
entry.Properties["attributeName"].Value = value;
entry.CommitChanges();
```

Here we see the `PropertyValueCollection` being used to overwrite all of the values in the attribute with a new value (defined by the variable `value`, which we left vague on purpose). Then, we call the `CommitChanges` method to flush our locally cached changes back to the directory.

That is just the tip of the iceberg, but we'll leave it at that for now and move on to the other CRUD methods. Once again, Chapter 6 covers the rest of the details.

Creating Directory Objects

Creating objects in Active Directory requires a small understanding of the underlying schema. We are not actually creating a new `DirectoryEntry` as much as we are creating an Active Directory object that is defined by the underlying schema. Given that the nature of LDAP directories is hierarchical, objects must be created in context with their parent.

Binding to the Parent Container

The first step to creating an object is determining where the object will reside. We need to choose a valid container object that will house the new object once it is created. We initiate a bind to the container, and use the `Add` method on its `Children` property. Listing 3.13 demonstrates this.

LISTING 3.13: Creating an Object in the Directory

```
string parentOU = "LDAP://OU=Domain Users,DC=domain,DC=com";
using (DirectoryEntry entry = new DirectoryEntry(
    parentOU,
    null,
```

```
        null,
        AuthenticationTypes.Secure
        ))
{
        using (DirectoryEntry newUser =
            entry.Children.Add("CN=John Doe", "user"))
        {
            //add mandatory attribs
            newUser.Properties["sAMAccountName"].Add("jdoe1");

            //add optional ones
            //Last Name
            newUser.Properties["sn"].Add("Doe");
            //First Name
            newUser.Properties["givenName"].Add("John");
            //description
            newUser.Properties["description"].Add("Average Guy");
            //phone number
            newUser.Properties["telephoneNumber"].Add("555-1212");
            //this is how it will be presented to users
            newUser.Properties["displayName"].Add("Doe, John");

            //update the directory
            newUser.CommitChanges();
        }
}
```

In this example, we chose to create a user named John Doe. The first thing to notice is that the Add method takes two parameters, the first being the RDN of the object and the second being the name of the schema class for the new object. For most users and objects, the RDN will start with CN=; however, when creating objects like Organizational Units (OUs), we need to use the OU= prefix. That may seem obvious, but it is important to note that not every object has an RDN starting with CN= in Active Directory.

Specifying Mandatory Attributes

In our example, let's assume that we were using the Windows 2000 version of Active Directory. Windows 2000 Active Directory requires that we set the sAMAccountName attribute (a.k.a. the pre-Windows 2000 login name) before trying to commit the object to the directory.

How did we know that it was mandatory? Unfortunately, this can be a little bit of black magic. The LDAP schema gives us some clues, but sometimes we need to use some trial and error to know for sure.

To start, each object class defines a list of mandatory and optional attributes in the schema (more on schema in Chapter 7). We can look this up with an LDAP browser tool or by using the MSDN documentation. In our example, we will find that the schema for the `user` class defines the following attributes as mandatory:

- `Common-Name`
- `Instance-Type`
- `NT-Security-Descriptor`
- `Object-Sid`
- `SAM-Account-Name`

Unfortunately, this list does not tell the whole story. All of these attributes are definitely mandatory, but two of them—`Instance-Type` and `Object-Sid`—are also marked with the `systemOnly` attribute in the schema, which means that only the directory itself updates these attributes. This means that we cannot change them, even if we want to.

This is where the trial and error begins. The other attributes are not marked `systemOnly`, so we might want to conclude that we are responsible for providing the rest of them, but in fact, we are not. The directory supplies default values for some of them.

In fact, in Windows Server 2003, the directory now supplies a default value for `sAMAccountName` as well, so there are no mandatory attributes for creating a user on Windows Server 2003. However, we do not have a way to determine this by examining the schema, so this is where the trial and error comes in. Note that we still recommend setting `sAMAccount-Name` explicitly when creating users, since we may not like the default name that Active Directory gives us.

Deleting Directory Objects

In classic ADSI, we had two methods for removing objects from the directory. We could bind to the container and call the `IADsContainer.Delete` method, or we could use the utility interface, `IADsDeleteOps`, and remove the object and any children. The main difference between the two methods is that the first targeted one object and the second targeted the object and

> **■ NOTE**   **Do Not Try to Use GUID or SID Binding for Add and Delete Operations**
>
> We introduced GUID and SID binding earlier in the chapter, as an alternate way of binding to objects with `DirectoryEntry`. It is important to note that this binding syntax is not supported when adding or deleting objects from the directory, or with any other method or property that uses the `IADsContainer` ADSI interface under the hood.

any children. We have the same functionality today in SDS, but it exists with different names.

Removing a Single Object

The SDS equivalent of `IADsContainer.Delete` is the `DirectoryEntries.Remove` method. The first thing to notice is that this method exists on a collection of `DirectoryEntry` objects. To use this, we must bind to the parent container, access the `Children` property, and call the `Remove` method, passing the child `DirectoryEntry` to be removed. We are subject to the restrictions of the ADSI method that `Remove` wraps—namely, the object to be deleted must itself be childless (either a leaf node or an empty container). If we have the proper permissions and meet these restrictions, the object will be deleted from the directory immediately, without any need to call `CommitChanges` on the containing object. Listing 3.14 demonstrates this.

LISTING 3.14: Removing a Single Object from the Directory

```
string parentPath =
    "LDAP://OU=ParentContainer,DC=domain,DC=com";

DirectoryEntry parent = new DirectoryEntry(
    parentPath,
    null,
    null,
    AuthenticationTypes.Secure
    );

using (parent)
{
    //find the child to remove
    DirectoryEntry child = parent.Children.Find("CN=John Doe");
```

```
    using (child)
    {
        //immediately delete
        parent.Children.Remove(child);
    }

}
```

If instead we already have a `DirectoryEntry` for the object that we want to delete, we can also use the `Parent` property shortcut, as shown in Listing 3.15.

LISTING 3.15: Deleting an Object via an Existing Reference

```
string adsPath =
    "LDAP://CN=ObjectToBeDeleted," +
    "OU=ParentContainer,DC=domain,DC=com";

DirectoryEntry entry = new DirectoryEntry(
    adsPath,
    null,
    null,
    AuthenticationTypes.Secure
    );

using (entry)
using (DirectoryEntry parent = entry.Parent)
{
    parent.Children.Remove(entry);
}
```

Deleting Multiple Objects with DeleteTree. When we wish to remove an entire container or OU, we can use the aptly named `DirectoryEntry.DeleteTree` method. Care must be taken when using this method, as all child objects, including any nested containers and their children, will also be removed. Listing 3.16 demonstrates this.

LISTING 3.16: Deleting Many Objects with DeleteTree

```
string objectPath =
    "LDAP://CN=ObjectToBeDeleted," +
    "OU=ParentContainer,DC=domain,DC=com";
using (DirectoryEntry entry = new DirectoryEntry(objectPath))
{
    entry.AuthenticationType = AuthenticationTypes.Secure;
    entry.DeleteTree(); //remove object and all children
}
```

Moving and Renaming Directory Objects

It might seem strange that when we speak of moving an object in ADSI, we are speaking of renaming it as well. A quick peek at the following `IADs-Container.MoveHere` ADSI method signature shows us why this is. We can see that the signature accepts the `ADsPath` of the object to be moved, and optionally, the new RDN name that the object will assume. If we do not supply the new name parameter, the object will simply be moved. If we supply the object's current location and a new name, the object will only be renamed.

```
HRESULT MoveHere(
  BSTR bstrSourceObject,
  BSTR bstrNewName,
  IDispatch** ppbstrNewObject
);
```

Since SDS uses `MoveHere` under the hood, this behavior is still relevant. However, to make it a little easier to use, the SDS designers wrapped this ADSI method with the `DirectoryEntry.MoveTo` method. We must slightly adjust our thinking from the ADSI method to use this SDS functionality correctly. The ADSI `MoveHere` method exists on the container. To use this method, we would first bind to the container, call `MoveHere`, and then pass the name of the object to be moved. However, the SDS method is from the point of view of the object to be moved. That is, we bind to the object to be moved, and then we pass a `DirectoryEntry` representing the new parent container. We can optionally provide an RDN and the object will be renamed as well. Thankfully, for us, the SDS designers realized that it was not intuitive only to rename an object, so they provided us with a separate method, `DirectoryEntry.Rename`, for this.

Moving a Directory Object

Two overloads on the `DirectoryEntry.MoveTo` method are available to us. One will move the object, and the other will both rename and move the object. Listing 3.17 demonstrates the latter.

LISTING 3.17: Moving an Object and Simultaneously Renaming It

```
string objectPath =
    "LDAP://CN=ObjectToBeMoved," +
    "OU=ParentContainer,DC=domain,DC=com";
```

```
using (DirectoryEntry entry = new DirectoryEntry(
    objectPath,
    null,
    null,
    AuthenticationTypes.Secure
    ))
{
    string parentPath =
        "LDAP://OU=NewParentContainer,DC=domain,DC=com";
    using (DirectoryEntry newParent =
        new DirectoryEntry(parentPath))
    {
        //choose one or the other
        //entry.MoveTo(newParent); //move
        entry.MoveTo(newParent, "CN=NewObjectName");
        //move and rename
    }
}
```

Renaming a Directory Object

Renaming an object is more straightforward. We simply bind to the object to be renamed, and call the `Rename` method, supplying the new RDN. Listing 3.18 demonstrates this.

LISTING 3.18: Renaming an Object

```
string adsPath =
    "LDAP://CN=ObjectToBeRenamed," +
    "OU=ParentContainer,DC=domain,DC=com";

DirectoryEntry entry = new DirectoryEntry(
    adsPath,
    null,
    null,
    AuthenticationTypes.Secure
    );

using (entry)
{
    entry.Rename("CN=NewObjectName"); //rename only
}
```

This is equivalent to the `MoveTo` operation shown in Listing 3.19.

LISTING 3.19: An Alternate Approach to Renaming an Object

```
string adsPath =
    "LDAP://CN=ObjectToBeRenamed," +
```

```
            "OU=ParentContainer,DC=domain,DC=com";

DirectoryEntry entry = new DirectoryEntry(
    adsPath,
    null,
    null,
    AuthenticationTypes.Secure
    );

using (entry)
using (DirectoryEntry parent = entry.Parent)
{
    entry.MoveTo(parent, "CN=NewObjectName");
    //rename only
}
```

As demonstrated, the first example seems more intuitive for a developer, and the second (equivalent) method would make a developer pause and think, "Wait! I don't want to move this object!" For this reason, we recommend using the `Rename` method for purposes of clarity.

SUMMARY

In this chapter, we dove into detail on the `DirectoryEntry` class. `DirectoryEntry` is the core object in SDS and it controls how most of our interaction with the directory works. Even `DirectorySearcher`, the other core object in SDS, relies on `DirectoryEntry` to establish a connection to the directory and a security context to use for searching.

We focused heavily on the parameters used for constructing `DirectoryEntry` objects because the syntax for each is important. We also discussed how the various settings affect each and what some of the behaviors of specific directories require to achieve specific results.

We also took a tour through some of the more exotic binding methods, such as GUID, SID, and the well-known GUID binding.

Finally, we demonstrated how `DirectoryEntry` is used to perform the key CRUD operations on an LDAP directory, and how objects in the directory are moved and renamed.

■ 4 ■

Searching with the DirectorySearcher

IN THIS CHAPTER, we introduce LDAP searches with the `Directory-Searcher` class. We start with an overview of searching in general and provide a tour through the properties and methods of `Directory-Searcher` and its supporting classes. After that, we start to dig into the mechanics of searching with an explanation of the search base, scope, and security contexts.

Next, we take a deep look at building LDAP query filters, as they are the mechanism by which we can restrict the results of our searches and find specific objects. They are essential to effective searching.

After that, we look at how to control the results returned from a search. We demonstrate the methods available for executing a search, and we show how to enumerate the results we receive.

We wrap up with a discussion on performing large searches using a technique called paging, and we talk about how to have the server sort our results.

LDAP Searching Overview

In Chapter 3, we covered how we can connect to Active Directory or ADAM, bind to an object, and perform create, read, update, and delete (CRUD) operations. In each of the scenarios, we knew exactly where our object was located in the directory in order to construct our binding string (ADsPath). What happens when we do not know where the object is located, or we want to return a number of related objects? The facilities and methods for searching the directory are distinctly different from what we have used thus far.

LDAP Searches in ADSI

In ADSI, we had two sets of technologies that allowed us to search Active Directory. First, for automation languages like Visual Basic 6 and VBScript, we had ADO and its OleDb LDAP provider. This provider allowed us to use either a SQL-like syntax to specify our search, or a more typical LDAP style, and behind the scenes, ADO would connect to the OleDb provider, which in turn would connect to ADSI and the IDirectorySearch interface, which would ultimately connect to the native Win32 LDAP library that would perform the search. A number of layers were involved there, as well as some clunkiness in terms of trying to use an ADO Recordset to represent a hierarchical tree of data or to specify advanced search options, but it was easy to use and it performed relatively well.

On the other side, C/C++ developers could bypass all of the ADO and OleDb layers and directly tap into the ADSI IDirectorySearch interface, a low-level, nonautomation interface that is not available to scripting languages. This was a powerful alternative, but its downside was in the details. IDirectorySearch forces the developer to deal with many structures and pointers that need to be freed properly, and it requires significant chunks of code to properly initialize a search and interpret the results. The C++ requirement scares away most developers right off the bat, and the complexity of using the interface deters many more that try.

LDAP Searches in System.DirectoryServices

In System.DirectoryServices (SDS), we use the DirectorySearcher class to query the directory and read the attributes of the objects found. DirectorySearcher is the class that makes SDS so much more powerful than traditional ADSI scripting. It combines the ease of use of typical .NET Framework classes, while providing the full compliment of search features. Like ADO, it wraps the ADSI IDirectorySearch interface and all of its messy details. However, since the object model is specifically tailored to support LDAP searches, we are not compelled to accept any of the compromises forced on us by the ADO `Recordset` model. We get the power and performance previously available only to C++ developers, with the simplicity of ADO and a better programming model than that available with either of them!

DirectoryEntries.Find versus DirectorySearcher

First-time SDS users tend to stumble upon a method called `Find` on the `DirectoryEntries` collection class. One might wonder what the difference is between this method and the `FindAll` and `FindOne` methods on `DirectorySearcher`. The main difference is that the `DirectoryEntries.Find` method actually wraps the `IADsContainer.GetObject` method. It takes only the relative distinguished name (RDN), and optionally, the class of the object to find, as arguments. It will also search only the immediate container (no children containers) and will throw an exception that must be handled if the object is not found. As such, its use is fairly limited.

`DirectorySearcher` supports the full gamut of search features and does not suffer from these limitations. It is especially nice that it will not throw an error if no results are found! We tend to stick to `DirectorySearcher` for finding objects and use `DirectoryEntries` for the operations that actually require it, such as creating and deleting objects.

DirectorySearcher Overview

Let's drill down on the members of the `DirectorySearcher` class so that we can begin to get a feel for how it works.

DirectorySearcher Properties

We have grouped the various properties of the `DirectorySearcher` class together by their intended use to help demonstrate how they work together.

Scope Limiting

The following properties help us limit how much of the directory we search and which objects we want to find in the parts we are searching. For performance and efficiency reasons, we should always try to keep our search as narrow as possible.

- `Filter`
- `ReferralChasing`
- `SearchRoot`
- `SearchScope`

Client Search Performance/Efficiency Options

These settings affect how the search will perform from the client's perspective. These options can increase the efficiency of the client, or in the case of timeout settings, make it appear so.

- `Asynchronous`**[1]
- `CacheResults`
- `ClientTimeout`

Searching Features

These features change how the search will perform or what it will return—sometimes dramatically. These properties expose the different behaviors of the underlying directory. When we use any of these, we are no longer asking for a simple search, we are fundamentally changing the search behavior at some level.

- `AttributeScopeQuery`**
- `DerefAlias`**[2]
- `DirectorySynchronization`**
- `ExtendedDN`**

---

1. Asynchronous support is not available using .NET 2.0. While this setting will toggle the underlying `IDirectorySearch` option, all that will happen is that SDS will consume it synchronously, so the net effect is that everything is synchronous in SDS. If asynchronous support is desired, `System.DirectoryServices.Protocols` (SDS.P) must be used.

2. Aliases are not used in Active Directory or ADAM, so this feature is not discussed. In other LDAP directories, it is possible to have aliases on objects, and this feature controls how they are decoded.

**Available in .NET 2.0 only.

- SecurityMasks**
- Sort
- Tombstone**
- VirtualListView**

Many of these features are advanced and are the topic of Chapter 5.

Server Performance/Efficiency Options

We can maximize performance or minimize strain on our servers with careful application of the following properties. Some of these are covered later in this chapter, and others are more advanced topics and are covered in Chapter 5 in the sections on timeouts and performance optimization.

- PageSize
- PropertiesToLoad
- PropertyNamesOnly
- ServerPageTimeLimit
- ServerTimeLimit
- SizeLimit

Methods

Two key methods actually execute the search.

FindAll()

The FindAll method returns a SearchResultCollection containing all the search results for a given search configuration. Internally, this method will initiate a bind to the SearchRoot DirectoryEntry (if it was not previously bound), and will use the IDirectorySearch interface to execute the search.

FindOne()

The FindOne method returns a single SearchResult, representing the first result in the underlying result set. Internally, this method is calling the Find-All method and returning the first SearchResult from the SearchResult-Collection. Developers are sometimes under the mistaken impression that this method is somehow faster or more efficient than the `FindAll` method. Since `FindAll` is always called, this of course is not the case.

Related Classes

While the vast majority of the functionality in SDS is contained in the `Directory-Entry` and `DirectorySearcher` classes, they use a few ancillary classes for support. For searching purposes, we typically use two related classes.

SearchResult

A `SearchResult` represents a single item from a result set. This class contains the `ResultPropertyCollection` class that holds the attributes and values specified by the `PropertiesToLoad` collection. If no additional attributes are specified in `PropertiesToLoad`, all nonconstructed attributes are returned by default. `SearchResult` also contains a handy method called `GetDirectoryEntry` that returns a `DirectoryEntry` object representing the result.

■ NOTE   **Use GetDirectoryEntry Only When a Modify Operation Is Required**

Beginners with SDS often get used to using the `DirectoryEntry` object to read the properties of objects and are tempted to use `GetDirectoryEntry` to convert a `SearchResult` into a `DirectoryEntry` so that they can read its attribute values. Do not do this! Creating a new `DirectoryEntry` object will trigger at least one and maybe two or more additional searches to the directory in order to read an object's attributes. This is very expensive from a performance perspective, especially when performed in a loop over many results.

By comparison, `SearchResult` already has all of the attributes we need. They were returned as part of the search operation, so there is no additional network overhead to read them. If we are careful with our use of the `PropertiesToLoad` property, we can also just get the attributes we need and reduce the size of the data moved over the network, increasing our performance some more.

The primary reason to call `GetDirectoryEntry` from `SearchResult` is if we need to modify something. We already discussed CRUD methods in Chapter 3, and we go into detail on modify attribute values in Chapter 6.

SearchResultCollection

This collection of `SearchResult` instances represents the result set as accumulated by the server for a specific query. This class internally holds references to unmanaged resources, and as such should always explicitly be disposed using the `Dispose` method, just like `DirectoryEntry` and `DirectorySearcher`.

The Basics of Searching

While LDAP allows us to do many things, searching is really the primary activity of LDAP programming. As such, it makes sense that we spend two whole chapters talking about it. Before we can execute a search, we need to answer some important questions.

- Where should the search start?
- How deep in the directory tree should the search go?
- Which objects should be found?
- What attribute data from each object found should be returned?
- How many objects should be found?
- How will security affect my search?

If we take each of these questions in turn, we can start to formulate a simple plan for how to design and perform a search in the most efficient manner. If all of this is starting to look too complicated, don't worry, it will become second nature as your experience using SDS grows.

Deciding Where to Search

Our search starts at the location in the directory defined by the `SearchRoot` property. `SearchRoot` contains a `DirectoryEntry` that represents both the binding context that will be used for connecting to the directory as well as the starting location for the search.

For example, let's say we want to do a search starting at the normal `Users` container of our Active Directory domain, and the distinguished name (DN) of the domain naming context is as follows:

```
DC=domain,DC=com
```

We would first create a DirectoryEntry object pointing to the Users container and pass that to the SearchRoot of the DirectorySearcher, as Listing 4.1 demonstrates.

LISTING 4.1: Initializing the SearchRoot of the DirectorySearcher

```
DirectoryEntry users = new DirectoryEntry(
    "LDAP://CN=Users,DC=domain,DC=com",
    null,
    null,
    AuthenticationTypes.Secure
    );

DirectorySearcher ds1 = new DirectorySearcher(users);

//this is equivalent

DirectorySearcher ds2 = new DirectorySearcher();
ds2.SearchRoot = users;
```

The DirectorySearcher will search in some part of the directory tree, starting at the CN=Users container.

> **▪ NOTE**   **Use the Default SearchRoot with Caution**
>
> The default value for SearchRoot is null. This has several implications of which we should be aware. First, the LDAP provider will be assumed. Next, the RootDSE of the current domain will be contacted and the default naming context will be queried to determine the starting search location (which means we are searching the entire domain). Finally, the security credentials of the current thread will be used to determine our permissions. Needless to say, these are a lot of assumptions to make, and the result might not be exactly what we wanted. For the sake of clarity, we recommend specifying a SearchRoot using either this property or one of the DirectorySearcher constructors. This makes it much easier to decipher our intent.

How Security Affects Searching

The binding context of the DirectoryEntry object set as our SearchRoot determines the security context for all of the related searching operations. This means that whatever credentials our SearchRoot uses will determine what our `DirectorySearcher` can and cannot return. Since not all accounts in the directory may have rights to see every object and attribute value, choosing different `DirectoryEntry` credentials for our `SearchRoot` may result in completely different search results.

This really comes into play when using nonprivileged accounts and searching for attributes that only more privileged accounts can normally view. In these scenarios, it will appear as though the attribute does not exist on the object. In some cases, we may not have permission to see the whole object or even list the contents of a specific container.

It is important to note that no error will occur when searching for an attribute or location for which the user does not have the proper read privileges. Instead, the returned result set will simply be empty of the prohibited objects or attributes and no indication will be given as to the reason.

One thing a developer can do to troubleshoot these types of issues is to use one of the many freely available LDAP browsers (see Appendix B for our LDAP tools list). By binding as a standard user in such a tool and browsing to an object, we will immediately see what is and is not available in our targeted context.

Controlling Depth of Search with SearchScope

The `SearchScope` property controls the depth of our search below the `SearchRoot` object in the directory hierarchy. `SearchScope` uses an enumeration (also called `SearchScope`) to define the three possible depths: `Subtree`, `OneLevel`, and `Base`. The default value is `SearchScope.Subtree`.

Subtree

The `Subtree` option is typically the one that most developers will use, as it will search the current `SearchRoot` and all children below it, including any child containers. This is the largest of the scope settings and we typically use it when we do not know where objects are located, or when we want to search for similar objects across disparate containers.

OneLevel

The `OneLevel` option searches all immediate children of the current `SearchRoot`, excluding the `SearchRoot` itself. Unlike the `Subtree` scope, descendants below the immediate children will not be included. This option is best used when we know which container holds our target objects and we want to tighten our scope.

Base

A Base-scoped search looks within the SearchRoot object itself. This scope is generally used for retrieving constructed attributes of a particular object from the directory. The search does not select any objects below the SearchRoot in the directory hierarchy. As such, we typically set the Filter property to (objectClass=*), which will match any object, as all objects by definition must have an objectClass.

We rarely use this option in SDS to retrieve constructed attributes, because the DirectoryEntry object mirrors this functionality with the RefreshCache method. Given that we need to create the DirectoryEntry anyway to populate the SearchRoot property, using RefreshCache often requires less code and is cleaner (see Chapter 6).

The question becomes, when should we use this scope? It turns out that one of our advanced searches, called an attribute scope query (see Chapter 5), requires this option. We might also use this scope to take advantage of the different data marshaling behaviors of Directory-Searcher compared to DirectoryEntry (see Chapter 6).

Figure 4.1 illustrates the three scope options. In the diagram, we see a root object with three immediate children. Two of the child objects have children as well.

Building LDAP Filters

The filter in an LDAP query restricts the objects that the search will return. It is the equivalent of the WHERE clause in the ubiquitous SQL SELECT statement in the RDBMS world. For example, we could use a filter to limit a search of an entire Active Directory domain naming context to find a specific user's object by their login name.

We rarely want to search for every object in the directory or within a certain scope, so it is critical to learn to use LDAP filters effectively.

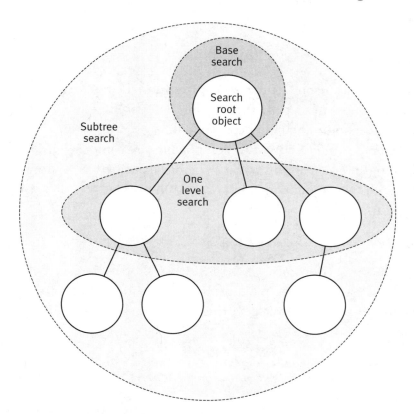

Figure 4.1: Search Scope Options Illustrated

The grammar and rules for LDAP filters are part of the LDAP version 3 specification and they are defined in RFC 2254. The syntax is actually quite simple compared to that of many other query languages. We can be productive creating LDAP filters in just a few minutes.

We specify the `DirectorySearcher`'s filter using its `Filter` property. If no value is specified, the default `(objectClass=*)` filter is used. This filter matches any object and is similar to using `SELECT *` in the SQL world.

Basic Syntax

At their most basic level, filters are composed of what are called **filter comparisons** or **components**. Here is the basic format for any individual comparison:

```
(<attribute name><filter type><attribute value>)
```

For example:

```
(displayName=John Doe)
```

In this example, the attribute name is `displayName`, the filter type is `=`, and the attribute value is `John Doe`. The surrounding parentheses, `()`, are required to delimit an individual filter component.

To create a complex filter, individual components are composed into a **filter list** using logical AND, OR, and NOT operations (specified as `&`, `|`, and `!`). For a filter with two components that must both be true, the filter list might look like this:

```
(&(displayName=John Doe)(telephoneNumber=5551212))
```

Here the two comparisons are nested inside an `&` operation, so both must be true to satisfy the filter. This nesting can be done to arbitrary depths to create some very complex expressions. Here is a more complicated example.

```
(|(&(displayName=John Doe)(telephoneNumber=5551212))
(&(displayName=Mike Smith)(telephoneNumber=5551000)))
```

This filter requires that the object have either a `displayName` of `John Doe` and a phone number of `5551212`, or a `displayName` of `Mike Smith` and a phone number of `5551000`.

Filter Types

The comparison itself is often called the **filter type**, and there are seven valid filter types, as listed in Table 4.1.

TABLE 4.1: Filter Types

Filter Type Symbol	Filter Type Description
=	Equal
~=	Approximately equal
>=	Greater than or equal
<=	Less than or equal

TABLE 4.1: Filter Types *(Continued)*

Filter Type Symbol	Filter Type Description
`attrib:matchingrule`	Extensible
`=*`	Presence
`= [initial] any [final]`	Substring

Equal

This filter type is the most straightforward. It simply checks for equality and can be used with all attribute types if the value part can be interpreted correctly. Here are some examples:

```
(sn=dunn) - Last Name equals "dunn"
(isDeleted=TRUE) - Boolean equality
```

Approximately Equal

This filter type is intended to indicate that a value is approximately equal to the actual value. In practice, this filter type does not seem to produce predictable results and it is not used frequently.

Greater Than or Equal

This filter type compares the value to see if it is greater than or equal to the attribute value. For instance:

```
(lockoutTime>=1)
```

Note that not all attribute syntaxes may use this filter type, although it is generally available to strings, dates, and numbers.

Less Than or Equal

This filter type is similar to >= and has the same restrictions on usage. Note that LDAP filters do not support the simple > and < semantics. The = logic is always included. As such, we must sometimes remember to add or subtract one from our comparisons.

Extensible

Extensible filters also allow provider-specific matching rules to be used. The rule is defined by an Object Identifier (OID) and it uses syntax like this:

```
(userAccountControl:1.2.840.113556.1.4.803:=2)
```

Active Directory and ADAM define two extensible filter types for doing bitwise AND and OR comparisons on numeric attributes. In this example, we are searching for objects that have bit 2 set, indicating in this case that the account is disabled.

Presence

This filter type allows us simply to check whether an object has a specific attribute. *The presence filter type does not specify a value in the comparison.* The value is not *. Instead, the whole filter type is =*. This may seem like a minor point, but a presence filter type is different from a substring filter type, even though they both use *. Please do not confuse them.

As an example, the following filter will find objects with a displayName attribute:

```
(displayName=*)
```

All attribute syntaxes may use presence filter types.

Substring

The substring filter type allows us to match part of a string using the familiar * character as a wildcard placeholder. For example, the following filter would find anyone named Frank or Frances:

```
(givenName=fran*)
```

The wildcard character may be placed anywhere in the string, including at the beginning or end, and multiple wildcard characters may be used. As such, all of these are valid as well:

```
(givenName=*rank)
(givenName=Fr*nk)
(givenName=F*an*)
```

The value must have at least one character other than the wildcard placeholder in order to differentiate a substring filter type from a presence filter type.

Not all attribute syntaxes support substring searches, but all of the standard string syntaxes do.

Substring Performance Tips

Substring searches are best used when at the end of the filter and not at the beginning or in the middle. The server is unable to use the standard indices unless the wildcard is placed at the end of the value.

A new option introduced to Active Directory in Windows 2003 and included in ADAM allows a special "tuple" index to be built. This greatly improves the performance of substring searches where the wildcard comes at the beginning of the value. Note that these types of indices consume significantly more resources than a typical index and most attributes do not use this feature. Chapter 7 discusses how these types of indices are specified.

Reserved Characters in Values

Much as we would in any other language, we need to escape reserved characters if we wish to search for the intrinsic value itself. To escape reserved characters, we need to replace the character with its ASCII hex value equivalent. Table 4.2 lists the reserved characters and their escape sequences. Notice that the escape sequence comprises just the \ character (indicating binary data) and the hex of the ASCII character equivalent.

TABLE 4.2:   Reserved Characters

Character	Escape Sequence
*	\2A
(	\28
)	\29

TABLE 4.2: Reserved Characters *(Continued)*

Character	Escape Sequence
\	\5C
NUL	\00
/	\2F

For example, we can use the following to search for an object that has the * character in its description attribute:

```
(description=A description with \2A)
```

Specifying Comparison Values in Search Filters

In Chapter 1, we discussed how LDAP attributes have a defined syntax that represents the primitive data type of the attribute. The LDAP filter syntax defines the query filter syntax for each of these attribute syntaxes. We drill down on the various syntaxes in Chapter 6 extensively, but let's take a quick look at them now in terms of query filters.

Table 4.3 summarizes the valid Active Directory and ADAM attribute syntaxes and the rules governing them.

As we can see, different attribute syntaxes require different formatting rules for specifying the value in the LDAP filter. Additionally, not all syntaxes support every operator.

We will now dig into the details of these rules and show examples of how to format all of these different strings.

Searching for Strings

Searching for attributes with one of the standard string syntaxes is pretty straightforward. By standard strings, we mean Teletex, Printable, IA5, Numeric, and Unicode. The comparison value is just the string itself and this hardly warrants a full-blown code sample, so we just show a filter showing a search for a string value:

```
(displayName=John Doe)
```

All of these string syntaxes allow the >= and <= operators and well as substring matches.

TABLE 4.3: Summary of Attribute Filter Syntaxes and Allowed Operators

Syntax Name	Syntax OID	Filter Description	Allows >= and <=	Allows Substring
Object(DS-DN)	2.5.5.1	The string version of the DN	No	No
String(Object-Identifier)	2.5.5.2	The string version of the OID	No	No
String(Teletex)	2.5.5.4	The string itself	Yes	Yes
String(Printable)	2.5.5.5	The string itself	Yes	Yes
String(IA5)	2.5.5.5	The string itself	Yes	Yes
String(Numeric)	2.5.5.6	The string version of the number	Yes	Yes
Object(DN-Binary)	2.5.5.7	The binary filter string encoding of the standard string representation of the attribute	No	No
Boolean	2.5.5.8	TRUE or FALSE	No	No
Integer	2.5.5.9	The number as a string	Yes	No
String(Octet)	2.5.5.10	The binary filter string encoding of the binary data	Yes	Yes

Continues

TABLE 4.3: Summary of Attribute Filter Syntaxes and Allowed Operators (*Continued*)

Syntax Name	Syntax OID	Filter Description	Allows >= and <=	Allows Substring
String (UTC-Time)	2.5.5.11	The string in the format YYYYMMDDHHMMSS.oZ	Yes	No
String (Generalized-Time)	2.5.5.11	The string in the format YYYYMMDDHHMMSS.oZ	Yes	No
String (Unicode)	2.5.5.12	The string itself	Yes	Yes
Object (DN-String)	2.5.5.14	The binary encoded version of the standard string representation of the attribute	No	No
String (NT-Sec-Desc)	2.5.5.15	nTSecurityDescriptor is an operational attribute and we cannot use it in a filter	NA	NA
Interval/LargeInteger	2.5.5.16	The number as a string	Yes	No
String (Sid)	2.5.5.17	The binary filter string encoding of the binary data	Yes	No

There are a few additional details to remember.

- `Teletex`, `IA5`, and `Printable` strings are case sensitive for searching. This means that the value in the query filter must match the attribute value case exactly.
- `Unicode` strings are not case sensitive for searching. The case in the query filter does not matter.
- `Teletex`, `Printable`, `IA5`, and `Numeric` strings have limited character sets.
- `Unicode` strings may contain any Unicode character. UTF8 encoding should be used for non-ASCII values and some values may require escape sequences as a result.

Searching for Numbers

Creating filters for numeric attributes is trivial, as the value is just the decimal version of the number. For example:

```
(badPwdCount=5)
```

The same rules apply for normal and `LargeInteger` syntaxes. Note that when `LargeInteger` values actually represent time values, we may need to do a little bit more work to format them correctly. We cover how to do this in the upcoming section, Searching for Time Values.

Numeric values support the >= and <= operators, but do not support substring searches.

Searching for Boolean Data

Searching for Boolean data is actually very simple, yet it seems to be a constant source of confusion. The only thing to remember is that a Boolean value is case sensitive. We must use either `TRUE` or `FALSE` to represent the value for a Boolean search filter. Notice that the values are all uppercased. Thus, we can have this:

```
(isDeleted=TRUE)
```

...or this:

```
(isDeleted=FALSE)
```

Searching for Distinguished Names and Object Identifiers

Distinguished names (syntax 2.5.5.1 in Table 4.3) and object identifiers are similar to strings. To match a DN, our filter might look like this:

```
(distinguishedName=CN=Users,DC=domain,DC=com)
```

To match an OID, we might do this:

```
(attributeSyntax=2.5.5.1)
```

This looks very similar to the standard string syntaxes, but there are two key differences. These attributes do not allow substring matches or the >= and <= filter types. The value must be supplied exactly.

These limitations are not obvious at first and they can cause confusion. For example, we might want to find all of the members of a group who are in a certain Organizational Unit (OU). We would like to do this:

```
(member=*,OU=MyOU,DC=domain,DC=com)
```

Unfortunately, that does not work.

Searching for Binary Data

A number of attributes in Active Directory and ADAM contain binary data. These attributes use the basic 2.5.5.10 Octet String syntax for arbitrary binary data, or the 2.5.5.17 SID syntax that is used specifically for security identifiers (SIDs), as shown in Table 4.3. It might seem quite difficult to search for binary data, given its nature. However, it is possible, and in the case of GUIDs and SIDs, it is used quite often.

Listing 3.5 from Chapter 3 demonstrates a utility function called Build-OctetString that converts binary data into the native LDAP Octet String format. Search filters also use octet strings to specify binary data, but they must escape each byte with an additional \ character in order to work. Listing 4.2 demonstrates another version of this function especially designed for search filters.

LISTING 4.2: Converting Binary to String for Search Filters

```
using System.Text;

private string BuildFilterOctetString(byte[] bytes)
```

```
    {
        StringBuilder sb = new StringBuilder();

        for(int i=0; i < bytes.Length; i++)
        {
            sb.AppendFormat(
            "\\{0}",
            bytes[i].ToString("X2")
            );
        }
        return sb.ToString();
    }
```

Once we have the binary data in string format, it is a simple matter to use it to search. Let's suppose we know that this is a particular object's GUID:

```
{4a5a0fa7-1200-4198-a3a7-31ee9ba10fc9}
```

Listing 4.3 shows how we can use the `BuildFilterOctetString` function to generate the appropriate filter value.

LISTING 4.3: Converting a GUID to a Filter String

```
Guid objectGuid = new
    Guid("4a5a0fa7-1200-4198-a3a7-31ee9ba10fc9");
string filter = string.Format(
    "(objectGUID={0})",
    BuildFilterOctetString(objectGuid.ToByteArray())
    );
Console.WriteLine(filter);
//OUT: (objectGUID=
// \A7\0F\5A\4A\00\12\98\41\A3\A7\31\EE\9B\A1\0F\C9)
```

We can easily apply this to any other type of binary data stored in the directory, including SIDs or even more esoteric data like JPEGs and X509 certificates, if we wish.

One other interesting point to mention about these attribute syntaxes is that they allow the >= and <= operators. Note, though, that standard octet strings also support substring searches, but SIDs do not. We rarely need to use these special filter types with binary data; it is useful occasionally. We are uncertain as to why SIDs do not support substring searches and normal octet strings do, but we cannot think of a good reason to search for SIDs this way either, so perhaps that explains it.

Searching for Time Values

Searching by date/time is a fairly common task in Active Directory and ADAM. However, the syntax representations for dates/times in a search filter are not immediately obvious.

The main issue here is that Active Directory actually uses several different syntaxes to represent a date value. These break down into two categories:

- Dates stored as `Generalized` or `UTC` time values
- Dates encapsulated in the Windows `FILETIME` format that are stored as `LargeInteger` values (equivalent to a .NET `Int64`)

The reason for this is largely historic. The LDAP specification defines the `Generalized` and `UTC` time syntaxes and specifies many standard attributes that use them, so Active Directory uses the LDAP specification to represent those values. However, Windows also uses the `FILETIME` structure extensively for storing and processing values. For many of the features in Active Directory that integrate directly with Windows, such as account expiration dates, it makes sense to store those values in the native format to avoid any possible loss during translation.

Once we know what syntax the attribute in question actually uses, we know how to proceed.

Searching for Generalized and UTC Time Values. `Generalized` and `UTC` time syntaxes use a human-readable string in the following format:

```
YYYYMMDDHHMMSS.0[+/-]HHMM
```

In case you were wondering what the `+/-` relates to, Active Directory and ADAM date/time values are always stored in the Greenwich Mean Time (GMT) standard time zone. By adding or subtracting our time zone offset relative to GMT, we can specify the correct time for our location.

For example, the Eastern Standard Time (EST) offset is `-0500`, so August 1, 2005, at 6:00 AM would be represented as follows:

```
20050801060000.0-0500
```

If we want to use the GMT time zone itself, the offset is specified as `.0Z`. The same time in GMT would be:

```
20050801060000.0Z
```

With some languages and platforms, we might need to perform tedious string concatenation operations to build this format. However, the .NET Framework makes this easy. Listing 4.4 demonstrates how to use `DateTime.ToString` to accomplish this.

LISTING 4.4: Generating UTC and Generalized Time Filters

```
public static string GetUtcFilter(DateTime date)
{
    return date.ToString("yyyyMMddhhmmss.0Z");
}

public static string GetGeneralizedFilter(
    DateTime date,
    TimeSpan offset
    )
{
    string sign =
        TimeSpan.Compare(offset, TimeSpan.Zero) == -1? "" : "+";
    return string.Format(
        "{0}.0{1}{2}{3}",
        date.ToString("yyyyMMddhhmmss"),
        sign,
        offset.Hours.ToString("00"),
        offset.Minutes.ToString("00")
        );
}
```

The UTC version is a bit more straightforward, so it makes sense to use it and to convert the date parameter to UTC in advance.

Creating Filters for Dates in FILETIME Format. The 2.5.5.16 `LargeInteger` syntax can be used to represent any standard 8-byte integer value, just like the .NET `Int64` (`long`) type. Because the number syntaxes in filters are just specified as the standard decimal string representation of the number, there is not much to the filter itself:

```
(accountExpires<=127787436516581785)
```

However, when the `LargeInteger` syntax value actually represents a `FILETIME` and we wish to create the filter given a date value, we must convert the date into a number representing the `FILETIME` first. Since most `LargeInteger` syntax attributes in Active Directory and ADAM represent `FILETIME` values or time spans, this is what we usually need to do.

Luckily, .NET makes this easy too. The `ToFileTime` method on the `DateTime` struct returns an `Int64`. This is exactly what we need. Listing 4.5 shows a complete sample of applying this to find passwords that are more than 30 days old.

LISTING 4.5: Creating a LargeInteger Date Filter to Find Old Passwords

```
string adsPath = "LDAP://dc=domain,dc=com";

//Explicitly create our SearchRoot
DirectoryEntry searchRoot = new DirectoryEntry(
    adsPath,
    null,
    null,
    AuthenticationTypes.Secure
    );

using (searchRoot) //we are responsible for Disposing
{
    //find anything with a password older than 30 days
    string qry = String.Format(
        "(pwdLastSet<={0})",
        DateTime.Now.AddDays(-30).ToFileTime() //30 days ago
        )

    DirectorySearcher ds = new DirectorySearcher(
        searchRoot,
        qry
        );

    using (SearchResultCollection src = ds.FindAll())
    {
        Console.WriteLine("Returning {0}", src.Count);

        foreach (SearchResult sr in src)
        {
            Console.WriteLine(sr.Path);
        }
    }
}
```

Bitwise Operations

Some attributes in Active Directory and ADAM are numbers that represent a collection of bitwise flags. Most developers will deal with the most common of these attributes, `userAccountControl`, at some point in time. In fact, we deal with it extensively in Chapter 10. This particular attribute defines many aspects of a user account's security settings.

Bitwise searches are enabled by the extensible filter type in Active Directory and ADAM. The format for these filters looks something like `(attribute:extension:=value)`. Extensions match a rule OID, so we can express our previous format as `(attribute:ruleOID:=value)`. For bitwise filters, there are two relevant extensions and matching rule OIDs:

- **Bitwise OR (called LDAP_MATCHING_RULE_BIT_OR).** 1.2.840.113556.1.4.804
- **Bitwise AND (called LDAP_MATCHING_RULE_BIT_AND).** 1.2.840.113556.1.4.803

Note that there is no bitwise NOT equivalent.

Using a bitwise filter is fairly straightforward; the developer only really needs to worry about the value portion of the filter. The bitwise filter format dictates that the value portion of our filter is in decimal format. This simply means that we must convert the hexadecimal or binary flag value to decimal and use it instead. As shown in Listing 4.6, if we want to find all disabled accounts, we should determine the relevant flag (in this case, `UF_ACCOUNTDISABLE`) and attach the bitwise AND rule OID to our filter, converting the flag value to decimal first.

LISTING 4.6: Finding Disabled Accounts with a Bitwise Filter

```
string adsPath = "LDAP://dc=domain,dc=com";

//Explicitly create our SearchRoot
DirectoryEntry searchRoot = new DirectoryEntry(
    adsPath,
    null,
    null,
    AuthenticationTypes.Secure
    );

using (searchRoot)
```

```
{
    //UF_ACCOUNTDISABLE = 0x2, which is 2 decimal
    //find all disabled accounts
    string filter =
        "(userAccountControl:1.2.840.113556.1.4.803:=2)";

    DirectorySearcher ds = new DirectorySearcher(
        searchRoot,
        filter
        );

    using (SearchResultCollection src = ds.FindAll())
    {
        Console.WriteLine("Returning {0}", src.Count);

        foreach (SearchResult sr in src)
        {
            Console.WriteLine(sr.Path);
        }
    }
}
```

The performance on bitwise filters is not spectacular, since any indices on the attribute cannot be used. As such, it is best to use this type of filter comparison in conjunction with other indexed attributes in the filter criteria to minimize the impact.

Restrictions on Attributes That May Be Used in a Filter

Most attributes in Active Directory and ADAM can be used in a query filter, but a few cannot. Specifically, constructed and operational attributes are not available for use in search filters. Attributes such as `canonicalName` and `tokenGroups` are actually constructed on the fly by the directory, so they are restricted from usage in query filters.

Note that we can still return these attributes as part of a search result (with restrictions, in some cases). We just cannot use them to find the actual object in the first place.

Ambiguous Name Resolution

Ambiguous name resolution (ANR) is an Active Directory feature that makes it easier to find objects in the directory when we have only a fragment of a name and we do not know exactly to what attribute the name corresponds.

ANR is essentially a shortcut that creates a more complex filter for us under the hood, using indexed attributes to help improve performance.

For example, this simple filter expands to the much larger filter shown in Listing 4.7:

```
(anr=dunn)
```

LISTING 4.7: ANR Filter Expansion

```
(|
    (displayName=dunn*)
    (givenName=dunn*)
    (legacyExchangeDN=dunn)
    (msDS-AdditionalSamAccountName=dunn*)
    (physicalDeliveryOfficeName=dunn*)
    (proxyAddresses=dunn*)
    (name=dunn*)
    (sAMAccountName=dunn*)
    (sn=dunn*)
)
```

As Listing 4.7 demonstrates, ANR is doing a lot of work for us behind the scenes. ANR is searching nine attributes for us instead of one and has changed the filter type to substring. Luckily, the wildcard is at the end of the string and all of these attributes are generally indexed in Active Directory by default, but ANR can still have an adverse effect on performance if abused. A filter containing a single ANR criterion is not much to worry about, however multiple ANR expressions in the filter can quickly grow out of hand. Consider Listing 4.8.

LISTING 4.8: Beware ANR Filter Expansion

```
Searching for the authors or their hometowns gets messy quickly.

(|(anr=dunn)(anr=kaplan)(anr=chicago)(anr=seattle))

expands to:
```

```
( |
    (displayName=dunn*)
    (givenName=dunn*)
    (legacyExchangeDN=dunn)
    (msDS-AdditionalSamAccountName=dunn*)
    (physicalDeliveryOfficeName=dunn*)
    (proxyAddresses=dunn*)
    (name=dunn*)
    (sAMAccountName=dunn*)
    (sn=dunn*)
    (displayName=kaplan*)
    (givenName=kaplan*)
    (legacyExchangeDN=kaplan)
    (msDS-AdditionalSamAccountName=kaplan*)
    (physicalDeliveryOfficeName=kaplan*)
    (proxyAddresses=kaplan*)
    (name=kaplan*)
    (sAMAccountName=kaplan*)
    (sn=kaplan*)
    (displayName=chicago*)
    (givenName=chicago*)
    (legacyExchangeDN=chicago)
    (msDS-AdditionalSamAccountName=chicago*)
    (physicalDeliveryOfficeName=chicago*)
    (proxyAddresses=chicago*)
    (name=chicago*)
    (sAMAccountName=chicago*)
    (sn=chicago*)
    (displayName=seattle*)
    (givenName=seattle*)
    (legacyExchangeDN=seattle)
    (msDS-AdditionalSamAccountName=seattle*)
    (physicalDeliveryOfficeName=seattle*)
    (proxyAddresses=seattle*)
    (name=seattle*)
    (sAMAccountName=seattle*)
    (sn=seattle*)
)
```

Chapter 7 briefly describes the schema value that determines if an attribute is included in ANR.

Controlling the Content of Search Results

So far, we have discussed some of the basics of searching, including the search root and scope. We also took a deep dive into LDAP filters. At this time, we have a few points left to cover from our original list, before we actually execute the search and examine the results.

- What attribute data from each object found should be returned?
- How many objects should be found?

Specifying Attribute Data to Be Returned

The DirectorySearcher class allows us to limit the attributes returned for an object found in a search. This allows us to ship significantly less data across the network than we might otherwise, and it can dramatically improve the performance of our queries.

This is done using the PropertiesToLoad property, which is a simple collection class. We use its Add and AddRange methods, as shown in Listing 4.9.

LISTING 4.9: Specifying Attributes to Return

```
DirectorySearcher ds = new DirectorySearcher();
ds.PropertiesToLoad.Add("distinguishedName");
ds.PropertiesToLoad.Add("displayName");

//or alternately

ds.PropertiesToLoad.AddRange(
    new string[] {"distinguishedName", "displayName"});
```

If we specify attributes that the target objects do not contain, they are simply ignored. Additionally, if we specify attributes we do not have permission to read, they are also not returned.

DirectorySearcher always loads one additional mystical property, called ADsPath, to the list, even if we do not specify anything. ADsPath is not actually an LDAP attribute, but ADSI builds this using the DN of the object returned.

Returning No Attribute Data

The DirectorySearcher also allows us to disable the retrieval of actual attribute data and instead just get the attribute names in the ResultPropertyCollection of the SearchResult object. We do this by setting the PropertyNamesOnly property to true. The default is false,

> **▪ NOTE   Not All Attributes May Be Returned from All Search Scopes**
>
> For the most part, we can return any attribute we want from a query, including the constructed variety. However, a few of the constructed attributes, such as `tokenGroups`, are available only from a base search. Attempting to return them from any other scope will result in the dreaded 0x80072020 `COMException`, which indicates an operations error.

meaning that the `DirectorySearcher` will retrieve the attribute names and their values.

In practice, we use this option infrequently, as we are typically interested in the attribute data. However, some scenarios may require knowing only which attributes are populated on a given object, or perhaps we know we will be modifying the underlying object and only want to use the `Get-DirectoryEntry` method to get a `DirectoryEntry`. This option makes that easy and the search is more efficient when used.

Limiting the Number of Results to Return with the SizeLimit Property

Sometimes we want to return a single object and other times we may need to find every object in the naming context. There are valid reasons to do both, but if we want to return a limited number of objects, it is a good idea to specify how many we want to return. We do this with the `SizeLimit` property, as shown in Listing 4.10.

LISTING 4.10: Setting the Size Limit

```
DirectorySearcher ds = new DirectorySearcher();
ds.SizeLimit = 2;
```

A `SizeLimit` of zero (`0`, the default) indicates that we want to return the maximum number of objects allowed. If `SizeLimit` is greater than zero, it instructs the server to return the specified number of results instead.

Note that the server may not always honor this request. Active Directory and ADAM define a certain maximum number of objects that can be returned in a single search page, and this number cannot be exceeded, no matter how many we ask for. These limits are put in place to help protect the directory from resource exhaustion that could compromise its stability.

The other important thing to remember with the `SizeLimit` property is that it is honored only if we are not performing a paged search. Paged searches are discussed in detail in this chapter, in the section titled Returning Many Results with Paged Searches. Once paging is enabled, ADSI will attempt to return every object that matches the query, no matter what `SizeLimit` is specified.

Executing the Query and Enumerating Results

Once we have chosen the search root, scope, filter, attribute list, and number of results to return, we are actually ready to execute the query and examine the results. The `FindOne` and `FindAll` methods do this.

Finding a Single Object with FindOne

`FindOne` is a convenient shortcut when we want only one result back and do not want to write the extra code to enumerate the `SearchResultCollection`. If no object matches the query, `FindOne` simply returns `null`.

`FindOne` internally calls `FindAll` under the hood to perform the actual query and returns the first result found. As such, it is never faster than `FindAll` and we can never guarantee that only one object matched the query. `FindOne` is best used in conjunction with a filter designed to match only a single object in the query scope. Listing 4.11 demonstrates a typical use of `FindOne`.

LISTING 4.11: A Typical Invocation of FindOne

```
DirectoryEntry root = null;
DirectorySearcher ds = null;
SearchResult result = null;

using (root = new DirectoryEntry(
    "LDAP://CN=Users,DC=domain,DC=com",
    null,
    null,
    AuthenticationTypes.Secure
    ))
{
    using (ds = new DirectorySearcher(root))
```

```
        {
            ds.Filter = "(sAMAccountName=jkaplan)";
            ds.SizeLimit = 1;
            result = ds.FindOne();
        }
    }
    if (result != null)
        Console.WriteLine(result.Path);
```

Listing 4.11 demonstrates how we might use `FindOne` to locate a user whose log-on name is `jkaplan` by doing a subtree search starting in our domain's `Users` container using the current thread's Windows credentials to access the directory. Here, the filter uses the Active Directory `sAMAccountName` attribute, which happens to be unique within a given domain, so we have some certainty that using the = filter type will match at most only one object in the scope of a single domain. We have taken the defaults for most of the properties, such as `SearchScope` and `PropertiesToLoad`, but we can obviously change those as needed.

We have also applied the C# `using` statement to wrap both of the objects that implement the `IDisposable` interface. We discussed this in Chapter 3 several times, including in the Close or Dispose? sidebar. It is important to apply this technique to all `IDisposable` objects to ensure timely resource cleanup, especially in long-running server processes like web applications, even if the code is slightly more verbose.

Beware the FindOne Memory Leak Bug

Users are discouraged from using the `FindOne` method in versions of .NET prior to 2.0 because of a bug culminating in a memory leak. Essentially, the bug will manifest itself whenever `FindOne` is called and no result is returned. The underlying `SearchResultCollection` that was obtained was not properly disposed in this situation, leading to a leak. This code demonstrates what we mean:

```
//given a DirectorySearcher ds
SearchResult result = ds.FindOne();
if (result==null)
{
    //WARNING: memory leak here under the hood!
}
else
{
    //No memory leak here; we found an object
}
```

This bug is obviously quite easy to run across, as we often wish to search for objects that may not exist. In a long-running server process such as a web application, these leaks can build up over time and cause instability.

Luckily, we can create a simple function to work around this problem:

```
SearchResult FindOne(DirectorySearcher ds)
{
    SearchResult result = null;
    ds.SizeLimit = 1;
    using (SearchResultCollection results =
        ds.FindAll())
    {
        foreach (SearchResult res in results)
        {
            result = res;
            break;
        }
        return result;
    }
}
```

This bug is fixed as of .NET 2.0.

Getting Multiple Results with FindAll

FindAll allows us to return multiple results that match our query. Its usage is similar to FindOne, except that FindAll returns a SearchResultCollection that we must enumerate to retrieve the individual results. Let's modify Listing 4.11 to find the first 100 objects in the same container that have an email address, and then dump the addresses to the console (see Listing 4.12).

LISTING 4.12: Finding Objects with Email Addresses Using FindAll

```
DirectoryEntry root = null;
DirectorySearcher ds = null;
SearchResultCollection results = null;

using (root = new DirectoryEntry(
    "LDAP://CN=Users,DC=domain,DC=com",
    null,
    null,
    AuthenticationTypes.Secure
    ))
{
    using (ds = new DirectorySearcher(root))
    {
        ds.Filter = "(mail=*)";
        ds.SizeLimit = 100;
        ds.PropertiesToLoad.Add("mail");
        using (results = ds.FindAll())
        {
            foreach(SearchResult result in results)
            {
                Console.WriteLine(result.Properties["mail"][0]);
            }
        }
    }
}
```

In Listing 4.12, we have added the `mail` attribute to the list of attributes to return. This causes the search to return this single attribute instead of returning all of the object's nonconstructed attribute values. A tiny change like this can have enormous performance impacts on a search, especially if the objects matched by the query contain large amounts of data.

We have once again wrapped the use of the `SearchResultCollection` in a `using` statement, as it too implements the `IDisposable` interface. Have we harped on this enough?

Enumerating the Results

We tend to use the `foreach` statement to enumerate the results. Unlike some other collection classes in the .NET Framework, `SearchResultCollection` internally implements its own private `IEnumerator` object that pulls the results from the directory. Any access to the `SearchResultCollection` properties, such as inspecting the `Count` property, will cause the entire result set to be retrieved from the directory and then enumerated. This can have a large impact, especially when returning many results, for a couple of reasons. First, using a `foreach` loop would allow us to break off the search if necessary, without enumerating all the results completely. This is more efficient, as we break off the search early and do not force the server to return all of the results first. Second, we can process each result as it comes from the server using a `foreach` loop without waiting for the entire search to complete. Using a `for` loop in conjunction with the `Count` property prevents both of these scenarios. As such, we generally recommend using the `foreach` loop when enumerating our results.

Since we knew that each result returned in Listing 4.12 would have a `mail` attribute (our filter dictated that), we can safely dig into the collection results without fear of getting a `NullReferenceException` or `Index-OutOfRangeException`. If we were not sure whether the `SearchResult` actually contained a particular attribute value, we would want to check first, using the `Contains` method.

Returning Many Results with Paged Searches

In large directories, it is easy to specify a search that might match many items. However, Active Directory and ADAM impose a policy on LDAP queries that limits the maximum number of results that may be returned in a single search page. This allows the directory to conserve machine resources and helps prevent LDAP queries from launching (accidentally or otherwise) denial of service attacks against the server!

This query policy is defined by the `MaxPageSize` setting. By default, it is set to 1,000 objects for both Active Directory and ADAM.

Active Directory and ADAM directories frequently contain thousands if not millions of objects, though. Given that many important scenarios would not be possible if we could not retrieve more than 1,000 objects, we need a way to get around this limitation.

Active Directory and ADAM solve this dilemma by offering a search technique called **paging**. Paging splits the entire result set of a query into smaller subsets called, appropriately enough, pages. The client continues requesting search pages from the server until all results within the query scope have been found.

Paging using the LDAP API actually requires specific code to retrieve individual pages and is much more complex to implement than a non-paged search. However, the ADSI `IDirectorySearch` interface abstracts away all of this complexity and makes paging seamless to the client. `DirectorySearcher` piggybacks on top of this, making paged searches seamless to .NET clients as well.

■ WARNING   Do Not Change the MaxPageSize Policy

Active Directory and ADAM offer the ability to change the `MaxPage-Size` policy and they will even accept enormous values. Do not do this! `MaxPageSize` is there to help protect our servers. Paging is so easy in .NET and all other ADSI clients that there is no compelling reason to change this anyway.

Also, what would we change the policy to? Our goal is probably to return all matches to a query, but we must choose an actual number. What if we choose a number based on the maximum number of objects in the directory and the directory adds more objects later? We end up in an escalating cycle that never ends.

Enabling Paging

Paging is controlled by the `PageSize` property on the `Directory-Searcher`. Setting `PageSize` to a value greater than zero will change the behavior of the search by enabling paging.

The rest of our code changes very little. We enumerate the `SearchResultCollection` as before, but this time many results are returned. Listing 4.13 shows an example of how to use paging in SDS.

LISTING 4.13: Enabling Paging Support

```
string adsPath = "LDAP://dc=domain,dc=com";

//Explicitly create our SearchRoot
DirectoryEntry searchRoot = new DirectoryEntry(
    adsPath,
    null,
    null,
```

```
    AuthenticationTypes.Secure
    );

using (searchRoot) //we are responsible for Disposing
{
    DirectorySearcher ds = new DirectorySearcher(
        searchRoot,
        "(&(objectCategory=person)(objectClass=user)" //any user
        );

    //enable paging support
    ds.PageSize = 1000;

    //wait a maximum of 2 seconds per page
    ds.ServerPageTimelimit = TimeSpan.FromSeconds(2);

    using (SearchResultCollection src = ds.FindAll())
    {
        Console.WriteLine("Returning {0}", src.Count);

        foreach (SearchResult sr in src)
        {
            Console.WriteLine(sr.Path);
        }
    }
}
```

Choosing an Appropriate Page Size

Listing 4.13 shows the page size set to 1,000. In general, it is a good idea to set this value to the maximum page size for simple searches. By setting it to the maximum value, we are minimizing the network roundtrips necessary to retrieve each page, which tends to be the more expensive operation for simple searches.

While it is possible to specify a PageSize greater than the system's MaxPageSize, the server will ignore it and use the MaxPageSize instead. No exception will be generated in this case.

In some cases, we may need to specify a smaller page size to avoid time-outs or overtaxing the server. Some queries are especially expensive, so limiting the number of results in a single page can help avoid this.

Using the ServerPageTimeLimit

We can also control paging, not only by setting a specific number of results, but also by limiting the time that the server should spend retrieving any one page. As Listing 4.13 also demonstrates, when used in conjunction with the `PageSize` property, the `ServerPageTimeLimit` specifies a `TimeSpan` that represents the maximum time that a server will spend retrieving a page of results before returning what it has. We can use this with more complex and expensive queries to allow the server to process other requests more efficiently.

As an example, suppose a search returned 20,000 objects. We could set our `PageSize` to be the `MaxPageSize` value of 1,000, and set our `ServerPageTimeLimit` to 10 seconds. This would mean that our page would contain either 1,000 results, or as many as the server could retrieve in 10 seconds. Each subsequent page will follow the same logic until the entire result set is returned. All of this happens seamlessly to the client, so it may not be noticeable.

Finally, using the `ServerPageTimeLimit` without also setting the `PageSize` has no effect, as paging support must be enabled by setting a nonzero `PageSize` before this setting takes effect.

Caching Result Sets

We find, on the `DirectorySearcher` class, an interesting property called `CacheResults`. If we read relevant ADSI documentation, we gather that manipulating this property will set an underlying ADSI feature that determines whether the search results are cached locally at the client. It turns out that in .NET, this property does very little for us. Internally, since the `SearchResultCollection` holds every `SearchResult` in an `ArrayList`, we never hit this unmanaged ADSI client cache when enumerating our collection repeatedly. As such, it is safe to turn this off and reduce client-side memory usage. We will not notice the reduced memory usage by viewing our .NET program's memory profile. Instead, turning off the ADSI caching feature will reduce our unmanaged memory requirements, so keep this in mind.

Sorting Search Results

With ADSI and SDS, we have the ability to perform a limited type of sorting to the results before sending them to the client. The important distinction here is that the sorting is performed server side, before the client is involved. This means that the server must collect all the search results (with some exceptions) first, perform the sorting operation, and then return. This will always incur a performance penalty over sending an unsorted result set and allowing the client to sort the results. The size of the penalty depends on a number of factors, but it will always exist.

Sorting in Active Directory and ADAM is fairly limited. We are able to sort on only one attribute at a time, in ascending or descending order. Additionally, not all types of attributes can be sorted on. More sophisticated sorting must be done client side. When possible, we recommend implementing our own custom sorting on the client to relieve the server of this burden. Listing 4.14 shows an example of how to apply sorting to an attribute.

LISTING 4.14: Server-Side Sorting

```
string adsPath = "LDAP://dc=domain,dc=com";

//Explicitly create our SearchRoot
DirectoryEntry searchRoot = new DirectoryEntry(
    adsPath,
    null,
    null,
    AuthenticationTypes.Secure
    );

using (searchRoot)
{
    DirectorySearcher ds = new DirectorySearcher(
        searchRoot,
        "(&(objectCategory=person)(objectClass=user))"
        );

    //sort by last name starting with 'Z'
    ds.Sort = new SortOption(
        "sn",
        SortDirection.Descending
        );

    using (SearchResultCollection src = ds.FindAll())
    {
        Console.WriteLine("Returning {0}", src.Count);

        foreach (SearchResult sr in src)
        {
```

```
        Console.WriteLine(sr.Path);
    }
  }
}
```

> ■■ **TIP**   **Improving Performance with Sorted Searches**
>
> Whenever possible, sorting should be done on an indexed attribute. Otherwise, Active Directory will have to retrieve all the results first before sorting them and sending them to the client. This can have a very adverse performance impact. In the best scenario, if the sorting option is indexed and included as part of the filter, Active Directory can further optimize the search and performance will be enhanced. For example, if `attribute1` is an indexed attribute, the most efficient sort would be to specify `attribute1` in the `SortOption`, and use a filter containing the attribute (perhaps `(attribute1=s*)`).

SUMMARY

In this chapter, we introduced the basic concepts of searching the directory. We discussed how to specify the location in the directory to start the query, and the depth in the tree that the search may traverse.

We then dug deeply into LDAP query filters, showing the query syntax as well as the rules governing how comparison values are specified for the various attribute syntaxes supported by Active Directory and ADAM. We also showed a few tricks for doing bitwise comparisons and using ANR.

We discussed how to execute a query and how to enumerate the results, limiting the number returned as needed. We also discussed how paging enables Active Directory and ADAM to support returning large numbers of search results without compromising the directory.

We concluded with a discussion of sorting results on the server.

5

Advanced LDAP Searches

B EYOND THE BASICS OF SEARCHING, System.DirectoryServices (SDS) exposes some powerful options to the developer. This chapter takes a look at the advanced options and demonstrates how and when to use them.

We start with some of the advanced behaviors that apply to many different kinds of searches, such as:

- Administrative limits
- Timeouts
- Performance optimization
- Global catalog searches in Active Directory
- Referral chasing

The second part of the chapter switches to the advanced searching features supported by Active Directory and ADAM that were introduced to SDS in version 2.0 of the .NET Framework. These include:

- Virtual List Views (VLVs)
- Deleted object searches
- Directory synchronization
- Attribute scope queries

- Extended distinguished name (DN) queries
- Security descriptor searches

We finish up with a discussion of asynchronous searches using the `System.DirectoryServices.Protocols` (SDS.P) namespace.

Administrative Limits Governing Active Directory and ADAM

In Chapter 4, in the section titled Returning Many Results with Paged Searches, we briefly mentioned an LDAP query policy called `MaxPage-Size`. As it turns out, `MaxPageSize` is just one of many policies enforced by Active Directory and ADAM that can affect the behavior of our searches. Since the server enforces these policies, they always override any settings requested by the client when sending a search request.

As such, it is important for developers to know which settings will have an impact on their code. Table 5.1 summarizes the limits.

TABLE 5.1: Administrative Limits for LDAP Searches with Active Directory

Value	Description	Default
InitRecvTimeout	Initial Receive Timeout. This is the amount of time a server will wait for the client to send the initial request after receiving a new connection.	120 seconds
MaxConnections	Maximum open connections allowed. Any connections after this limit mean that another connection will be dropped.	5,000 connections
MaxConnIdleTime	Maximum amount of time an open connection can be idle before disconnection.	900 seconds
MaxActiveQueries	Maximum number of queries that will execute at one time. If this limit is reached, subsequent queries will receive a "busy" notification error.	20 queries

TABLE 5.1: Administrative Limits for LDAP Searches with Active Directory *(Continued)*

Value	Description	Default
MaxNotification-PerConnection	Maximum number of notifications a client can request per connection. Client will receive a "busy" error when this limit is exceeded.	5 notifications
MaxPageSize	Maximum number of results returned per page. If the number of selected results exceeds this value, only this limit is returned, unless paging is performed. If paging is used, this limit is enforced per page.	1,000 results
MaxQueryDuration	Maximum length of time a query can execute. If this limit is exceeded, a timeLimitExceeded error will be raised. To exceed this limit, paging must be used, but then this limit is enforced per page as well.	120 seconds
MaxTempTableSize	Maximum size of temporary storage allocated for queries. This storage is used to sort and select intermediate results. A size smaller than the expected result set will result in decreased performance.	10,000 results
MaxResultSetSize	Maximum size of the intermediate data stored in a paged search. The server might store this intermediate data between pages in a paged search to speed subsequent pages. When this value is exceeded, the server will discard older data.	262,144 bytes
MaxPoolThreads	Maximum number of threads created for query execution and listening for network input/output. This is a per-processor value.	4 per CPU
MaxDatagramRecv	Maximum size of a datagram that can be processed. Datagram requests larger than this limit will be discarded.	1,024 bytes

Understanding Searching Timeouts

Timeouts affect whether our searches will finish completely or return partial results. In addition to the limits imposed by the server, the client has the ability to request specific timeout behaviors as well.

Precedence of Timeouts

Within the `DirectorySearcher` class are a number of members that represent a timeout value of some type or another. It can often be confusing to determine exactly when each timeout value is used and what precedence each has. In this section, we will hopefully dispel some of that confusion. Let's start by examining the available timeout settings:

- `ClientTimeout`
- `ServerPageTimeLimit`
- `ServerTimeLimit`

ClientTimeout

This `TimeSpan` represents the maximum amount of time that the client will wait for the server to return results before abandoning the search and returning no results. By default in SDS, this is set to wait indefinitely. If a `TimeSpan` greater than zero is provided, the client will wait the minimum of this value, or until an administrative server timeout is generated. Clients should set this to a reasonable value when expecting particularly long searches.

ServerPageTimeLimit

When used in conjunction with a paged search (see the section Returning Many Results with Paged Searches, in Chapter 4), this `TimeSpan` represents the maximum amount of time that the server should spend generating search results for a particular search page, before returning it to the client. As such, it is used only when searching for large result sets greater than the `MaxPageSize` that use paging (usually 1,000 results). Values greater than the `MaxQueryDuration` will essentially be ignored, as that will become the limiting factor per page. By default, this is set to wait indefinitely, so this means that in practice, the `MaxQueryDuration` will be used.

ServerTimeLimit

This `TimeSpan` specifies the maximum amount of time that the server will wait for a search to complete. If this value is exceeded, only the results accumulated to that point will be returned. By default, SDS is set to wait indefinitely. In practice, the limiting factor is the server's administrative LDAP search time limit of 120 seconds (`MaxQueryDuration`). All non-paged searches must complete before the minimum of the `ServerTime-Limit` or `MaxQueryDuration` (the default is 120 seconds), or only the results accumulated to that point will be returned. Paged searches are not affected by this value.

Nonpaged Searches

When using a nonpaged search (i.e., `PageSize` equals zero), there are only three arbitrators of when a search will end. Table 5.2 summarizes these settings in a concise format.

TABLE 5.2: Nonpaged Timeout Precedence

Timeout Operator	Default Value	Precedence	Notes
`MaxQuery-Duration`	120 seconds	First	This is an administrative limit found on the `LDAPAdminLimit` attribute. It is the maximum time any nonpaged search will be executed before the server generates a timeout. While it can be changed, it is not advisable to change this value from the default.
`Server-TimeLimit`	Indefinite	Second	Values larger than `MaxQuery-Duration` will essentially be ignored, since the `MaxQuery-Duration` will be the limiting factor.
`Client-Timeout`	Indefinite	Third	The `ServerTimeLimit` takes precedence over this setting, so any value specified larger than the `Server-TimeLimit` will essentially be ignored.

Paged Searches

For a paged search (i.e., `PageSize` is greater than zero), there are again three arbitrators of when a search will end. Table 5.3 summarizes these settings.

TABLE 5.3: Paged Search Timeout Precedence

Timeout Operator	Default Value	Precedence	Notes
`ServerPage-TimeLimit`	Indefinite	First	The `ServerPageTime-Limit` controls how much time the server will spend collecting an individual page. It does not control how long the entire search will last. A paged search will continue for as long as there are result pages, until it is finished.
`Client-Timeout`	Indefinite	Second	During a particularly long paged search, the client has the option of abandoning it using this timeout.
`MaxQuery-Duration`	120 seconds	Third	This limit does not come into effect in practice very often, because this limit is applied per page and not per search.

Optimizing Search Performance

As with any query language, many factors affect the overall performance of an LDAP query. As developers, we typically want our queries to be fast. We also know that it usually takes a while to learn all the tips and tricks, but it is this knowledge that separates the novices from the pros.

This section focuses on making the right choices to get the fastest queries possible.

Choosing the Right Search Root

One of the most important performance improvement tips is to use a `SearchRoot` that is the closest parent to the objects we wish to find. We then must scope the search correctly. Here are the binding locations and scopes, presented in order from best to worst.

1. If we know where our objects are located, we bind directly to the objects' parent container using the container's DN and scope the search using `SearchScope.OneLevel`.

2. If our objects are in separate containers, we set the `SearchScope` to the closest common parent container and specify the `SearchScope.Subtree` option. If the objects are widely distributed across many containers and levels in the directory hierarchy, we may need to use the root of the partition. As we described in Chapter 3, we generally use the `RootDSE` object to find the DN of the naming context for the directory partition. Typically, the partition's DN that we will use is specified by the `defaultNamingContext` attribute of the `RootDSE` object.

3. Finally, if we are not sure which domain our objects are in (or if local replicas are not available), we set the `SearchRoot` to the global catalog server and perform a subtree search. Keep in mind that the global catalog contains only a subset of the full object attributes, so it may become necessary to rebind to the object using its DN to return all of its attributes.

Choosing the Right Scope

Looking at our available search scopes (`Base`, `OneLevel`, and `Subtree`), it would seem intuitively obvious to choose the narrowest scope available that will return what we want. Indeed, this is exactly the case, but the importance of this cannot be overstated. The difference between using a `OneLevel` search versus a `Subtree` search can mean an order of magnitude difference in speed and efficiency. Putting aside base-level searches (`Base`) for now, the biggest performance differentiator is going to be between using `OneLevel` and `Subtree`. This especially holds true when searching with nonindexed attributes. If we are vigilant in using an indexed attribute in our filter at all times, we can usually extract pretty good performance as well.

Now, if we happen to know the exact DN of the object we wish to search for, we can use a `Base` search to return its attributes. While there are definitely some uses for `Base` searches (attribute scope queries, for example), keep in mind that it might actually be easier simply to create a `Directory-Entry` for the object instead. This is actually how the `DirectoryEntry` retrieves an object's attributes under the hood in the first place!

Creating Efficient Queries

Once the search scope and starting location are as efficient as possible, we can focus on other areas to help us improve the performance and efficiency of our queries. Table 5.4 lists some common areas that a developer can focus on to bring performance gains.

TABLE 5.4: Performance Tips

Tip	Effect
Use indexed attributes in filters when possible.	Try whenever possible to have at least one indexed attribute listed in the query filter. As an example, in Windows 2000, using `objectCategory` in lieu of or in conjunction with the `objectClass` attribute is more efficient, as the former is indexed. It turns out that `objectClass` is indexed by default in Windows 2003, but the premise is the same for other attributes.
Return only the data required.	By default, a search will return all of the normal attribute values for an object. If we need only a few of these, we can improve performance tremendously, simply by specifying the values we need.
Request only the number of results needed.	We should always try to specify the number of results we wish to receive with the `SizeLimit` property, unless we are executing a paged search.
Avoid ANR searches.	Ambiguous name resolution (ANR) is a terrific feature, but it can quickly get out of control in queries that are more complicated. It is important to remember that the actual ANR filter internally expands into a much larger filter that might drag down performance.
Avoid careless substring searches.	Use substring search filters with care. Whenever possible, place the wildcard at the end of the value (`"sn=d*"`) in order to preserve index usage. Avoid other wildcard positions when possible (`"sn=*unn"` or `"sn=*un*"`). If this is not possible, then create a medial or "tuple" index on this attribute. Avoid unnecessary substring searches in general.

TABLE 5.4: Performance Tips *(Continued)*

Tip	Effect
Avoid sorting.	Sorting can be a big performance killer. Even when performing it in the most efficient manner (see Sorting Search Results, in Chapter 4), it still can suck performance from our applications. We should always consider whether we can push the sorting to the client. If we can, this will always be more efficient than performing the sort server side.

Properly place AND and OR operators.	This is a tricky one to understand sometimes. Suppose we had the following type of filter (in English): "Select all users that have a last name of either kaplan or dunn." We could express that filter using something like this:
	
	`(&`
	`(objectCategory=person)`
	`(objectClass=user)`
	`(|`
	`(sn=dunn)`
	`(sn=kaplan)`
	`)`
	`)`
	
	It turns out this is not the most efficient way to do this. We really want to do something like this:
	
	`(|`
	`(&`
	`(objectClass=user)`
	`(objectCategory=person)`
	`(sn=dunn)`
	`)`
	`(&`
	`(objectClass=user)`
	`(objectCategory=person)`
	`(sn=kaplan)`
	`)`
	`)`
	
	The query processor has been improved in Windows 2003, making this not as big an issue, but it should be kept in mind.

Avoid bitwise comparisons.	We demonstrated how to use bitwise comparisons in Chapter 4 and also suggested using them sparingly. The reason is that a bitwise comparison prevents the use of an index for that attribute. Therefore, when using these types of comparisons, it is important to keep in mind the first tip in this table and to use other indexed attributes when possible to limit the impact.

TABLE 5.4: Performance Tips *(Continued)*

Tip	Effect
Avoid using the NOT (!) operator.	This is a subtle point, but the query processor processes objects that we might not have permission to view, and attributes that do not have a value as meeting the filter criteria, resulting in unnecessary matches. Additionally, this operator prevents the use of indices on affected attributes.
Use connection caching.	Opening and closing connections is inefficient. In the section ADSI Connection Caching Explained, in Chapter 3, we describe how to do this properly.
Query an object only once.	Instead of constantly requerying an object and generating network traffic and overhead, we should query the object only once and cache the data locally.
Avoid referral chasing if possible.	Referral chasing can send us bouncing from server to server looking for objects. This can be very time consuming to perform. When querying for objects that might exist in another domain in the same forest, consider using the global catalog rather than referrals. This is generally more efficient.

Turn Caching Off When Possible

The `CacheResults` property of `DirectorySearcher` manipulates an underlying ADSI feature that enables client-side caching. By default, this property is set to `true` and caching is enabled in SDS. As we mentioned previously in Chapter 4, this property has little bearing for us in .NET. Internally, the entire result set is held in an `ArrayList` object in our `SearchResultCollection` object, so we will not actually contact the ADSI local cache when enumerating a result set more than once. It is safe to set this to `false` and lower the unmanaged memory requirements for our application.

Searching the Global Catalog

The **global catalog** is a special data store that contains a partial replica of every object in the entire forest. That is, a global catalog spans every domain in the entire forest. This special repository allows us to easily search in multiple domains in an efficient manner. Without using the global catalog, we

> ### ▪ TIP   Profile Your LDAP Queries
>
> Active Directory and ADAM both support a special control that supports returning query statistics about how a query performed. The information contains details on the number of objects visited and indices used, among other things. This kind of information can be extremely helpful in understanding why different queries perform differently.
>
> We do not have an easy way to use these statistics from within our own code, but several of the tools we discuss in Appendix B, such as ldp.exe and ADFind, support query statistics. We generally recommend using one of these types of tools for modeling queries before committing to code anyway. Remember, though, that using the statistics control requires administrative privileges on the server, as the user must have the ability to debug the server in order to invoke this feature. Hopefully we have a highly privileged account that we can bind with for these special occasions.

would need to use referral chasing (see Chasing Referrals, later in this chapter) to find objects in other domains, which takes considerably longer.

A global catalog server is simply a domain controller that has been dual-purposed not only to serve its joined domain, but also to hold a partial replica of the entire forest and to service global catalog search requests.

Important Considerations for Using the Global Catalog

The global catalog contains only a partial replica of each object in the directory. This means that we are limited to searching using only filter criteria from the available attributes. The attributes included for replication to the global catalog are actually defined in the schema and can be set by an administrator (see Table 7.4 in Chapter 7 for details). It also means that in order to read any additional attributes, we must perform another bind to the object directly in the domain to retrieve that information. One last point is that the global catalog is a read-only data repository. We cannot bind to it directly and add, modify, or delete information contained within it.

Binding Syntax for the Global Catalog

While normal LDAP operations are serviced off of port 389 (port 636 using SSL), the global catalog is serviced off of port 3268 (port 3269 using SSL).

Listing 5.1 shows a sample of how to use the global catalog to find objects across the forest.

LISTING 5.1: **Searching the Global Catalog**

```
class Invoker
{
    static void Main(string[] args)
    {
        Console.WriteLine(
            GetUserInfo("dunn")
            );

        Console.ReadLine();
    }

    public static string GetUserInfo(string lastName)
    {
        DirectoryEntry gc = new
            DirectoryEntry("GC:");

        DirectoryEntry _root = null;

        using (gc)
        {
            //there is only 1 child under "GC:"
            foreach (DirectoryEntry root in gc.Children)
            {
                _root = root;
                break;
            }
        }

        StringBuilder sb = new StringBuilder();

        //note the filter must be searching
        //  for a GC replicated attribute!
        string filter = String.Format(
            "(sn={0}*)",
            lastName
            );

        DirectorySearcher ds = new DirectorySearcher(
            _root,
            filter,
            null,
            SearchScope.Subtree
            );
```

```
    using (SearchResultCollection src = ds.FindAll())
    {
        foreach (SearchResult sr in src)
        {
            sb.AppendFormat("{0}\n", sr.Path);
        }
    }

    return sb.ToString();
}
```

Note that the GC: moniker has been substituted for the standard LDAP: provider. Beneath the covers, it will automatically be converted to LDAP:/ /<server>:3268/, as the only difference is the port that the global catalog listens on.

Chasing Referrals

A single naming context on a server may not contain all of the data we might wish to find. Instead, the data may be distributed over different partitions and servers on the network. When a server does not have information requested by the client in a query, it can issue what is called a **referral** to direct the client to another location where that information might be found. As such, the client does not have to know where particular data can be found and can instead choose to continue the search on additional servers in the domain. We can specify four different referral behaviors.

- **None.** The client will ignore all referrals.
- **Subordinate.** The client will chase continuation references. Continuation references occur when the server hosts the naming context, but a subordinate context is requested. For instance, the server might return a subordinate referral to the configuration context when the default naming context is searched.
- **External.** The client will chase referrals in external domains. This occurs when the server does not host the naming context, but refers to another server that might host it. This is the default behavior.
- **All.** This is simply the bitwise-OR of .Subordinate and .External, indicating that both behaviors should be followed.

> **▪▪ NOTE   Do Not Combine Subordinate Referrals with Paged Searches**
>
> If paged searching is used, the Subordinate option cannot be used. No error or other indication will occur; it will simply be ignored if specified.

Chasing referrals can be an expensive operation, so it is best to avoid it or to use the global catalog when possible. They can also have complex security implications when the same credentials are used to attempt to access disparate directories.

Virtual List View Searches

Virtual List View (VLV) searches were introduced with Windows 2003 as an efficient way to return subsets of otherwise very large result sets. The secret to the speed and efficiency of a VLV search is that unlike traditional searches, VLVs do not need to retrieve all entries before returning a portion of the result set.

A common task for many enterprise application developers is to create a form (web or desktop) to allow users to search Active Directory. This application might have a few text boxes into which the user can enter search terms—perhaps a last name by which to search (a custom phonebook of sorts). The results will then be displayed in a paged DataGrid or ListBox.

Inevitably, the first thing a user will do is type S* and search for every single user in the directory that has a last name starting with the letter S. For a small domain with only a few thousand users, this probably won't make much of a difference. For a very large Active Directory installation, however, we might time out before this thing returns (especially if this is a web request).

From a performance perspective, this was always a critical test: If we waited to load all the results before displaying the ListBox, there would be a noticeable lag that the user would dislike (likely causing her to pound on the Search button again). We could try to solve these problems either by loading asynchronously, or by smart paging (i.e., loading only what the user might see in her current `ListBox` view). Built-in asynchronous support for LDAP searching was available only for C/C++ developers prior to .NET 2.0, and properly working asynchronously can be challenging, especially when we are working with a web page and not a local desktop application. While asynchronous searching with partial results might solve the sluggishness the user perceives, it does nothing to alleviate the horror the directory administrator feels as she watches helplessly while her domain controller CPU is pegged at 100% for 5 minutes as someone tries to return 30,000 results (nonindexed, of course).

A better solution that both conserves resources and behaves responsively is to return only the portion of the larger result set that the user is presently looking at. With databases, we would offload the paging to the database server and have it selectively return a portion of the results using standard SQL statements. Until Windows Server 2003 and ADAM, this was not possible with LDAP searches—it was an all-or-nothing proposition. Using VLV searches, however, we can easily mimic the smart-paging behavior that was previously possible only with database servers. In this section, we will outline where a VLV search is most appropriate and the different methods by which to use this powerful feature.

> ### ▪▫ WARNING   VLV Might Not Behave Well in Active Directory
>
> As of this writing, there are some known issues in the VLV implementation in Active Directory that cause it not to work as expected. The implementation in ADAM seems to work fine, however. We believe Microsoft is working to address these issues, but a fix may not be available as you are reading this. Use caution if you are targeting VLV for Active Directory.

Offset versus Target Searches

There are two different mechanisms for performing a VLV search. The first uses the `Offset` property, and the second uses the `Target` property. It might be confusing, but we only ever use one or the other of these properties at a time. The basic difference between the two methods is that the `Offset` type of search is specified by a numeric location within our result set, and the `Target` search is specified by some value within the result set. From a conceptual level, let's assume that our data can be represented by an array of letters sorted alphabetically, like this:

```
{"A", "A", "A", "F", "G", "L", "N," "O", "O", "S", "T", "W", "Z"}
```

As an example of an `Offset` search, we could specify that we wished to retrieve one result from either side, centered on the middle of the result set. We would do this by specifying an `Offset` of 7 and a `BeforeCount` and `AfterCount` of 1 each. The seventh result in this case is `N`, and we would choose the `L` and `O` surrounding it. In reality, this is an approximation, so the result might differ slightly, but this is a conceptual exercise at this point.

For this type of search, we can also use a handy shortcut in the `Target-Percentage` property that represents `Offset/ApproximateTotal`. This use of the VLV search is appropriate when we want information by position in the result set and not necessarily by value.

Separately, we could also define our VLV search to use the `Target` property. The way this works with respect to the previous example is that we specify a value representing the attribute that was used for sorting. In our case, we might not know or care what values are near the center of our result set. Instead, perhaps we want to return results that surround results starting with `S` (this might actually lie anywhere in the sorted results). We can do this by specifying the `Target` as `S`, and a `BeforeCount` and `After-Count` of 1 each. This type of search is appropriate when we don't know where in our approximate total our values might be positioned, but we do know what the data might look like.

Using the DirectoryVirtualListView Class

Before we dig too deep into examples, we should cover what properties are available on the requisite helper class, `DirectoryVirtualListView`, and what they are used for.

AfterCount

This represents the number of results to select after the target offset. Adding the `AfterCount` and `BeforeCount` together should yield the approximate total number of results to select.

ApproximateTotal

Much as it sounds, this represents the approximate total number of results that will be retrieved. When set by the client, this helps the server quickly determine where in the offset to search. By default, this value is 0, which indicates that the server should determine and use its own estimate. This value will be updated with the server's estimate after the first search is performed. It can then be used to calculate things like pagination.

BeforeCount

This represents the number of results to select before the target offset. We would use this only when we're not selecting the first subset of results (i.e., the target indices that are greater than zero). Added to the `AfterCount`, this should equal the approximate number of results in the returned VLV subset.

DirectoryVirtualListViewContext

This utility class represents the underlying context that is created when performing a VLV search. For efficiency, subsequent VLV searches should use the same context when performing subsequent searches. This is taken care of automatically using the `DirectoryVirtualListView` class, so developers need not concern themselves too much with this utility class.

Offset

When set by the client, this represents the index in the underlying result to approximate the search. After the server performs the search, this value is updated to represent the server's best estimate of where the target result set truly resides. As an example, if we had approximately 1,000 results and wished to retrieve the last one-third of the result set, we could specify an `Offset` of 667 and an `AfterCount` of 333.

Target

We don't always have to use the `Offset` when searching using a VLV. Instead, we can have a sorted result set and use a string as the index. For example, if we had 1,000 results sorted by last name (the `sn` attribute), we could search for all the entries starting with the word "Dunn" by specifying this string as the `Target` value. The number of entries determined by the `AfterCount` and `BeforeCount` would be returned surrounding the `Dunn` index. The `Target` value should always represent the attribute that was used to sort the result set.

TargetPercentage

The `TargetPercentage` is nothing more than a convenience to represent the `Offset`/`ApproximateTotal`. We could use this to specify things like returning the surrounding 50 entries at the 60% mark of the result set (`TargetPercentage=60`, `AfterCount=25`, `BeforeCount=25`). As such, this is used with `Offset` searches and not `Target` searches (though the name might be confusing).

Searching by Offset

Using code similar to that shown in Listing 5.2, we can search using the `Offset` through a portion of the result set.

LISTING 5.2: Searching by Offset

```
string adsPath = "LDAP://DC=domain,DC=com";

//Explicitly create our SearchRoot
DirectoryEntry searchRoot = new DirectoryEntry(
    adsPath,
    null,
    null,
    AuthenticationTypes.Secure
    );

using (searchRoot)
{
    DirectorySearcher ds = new DirectorySearcher(
        searchRoot,
        "(objectCategory=person)"
        );

    //sorting must be turned on
    ds.Sort = new SortOption(
        "cn",
        SortDirection.Descending
        );

    //grab first 50 users starting at 1st index
    ds.VirtualListView =
        new DirectoryVirtualListView(0, 50, 1);
```

```
using (SearchResultCollection src = ds.FindAll())
{
    Console.WriteLine("Found {0}", src.Count);

    foreach (SearchResult sr in src)
    {
        Console.WriteLine(sr.Path);
    }
}

Console.WriteLine(
    "Approx: {0} Found",
    ds.VirtualListView.ApproximateTotal
);

int offset = 50;

//this is how we would search again using the same VLV
while (offset < ds.VirtualListView.ApproximateTotal)
{
    //update our offset and continue to search
    ds.VirtualListView.Offset = offset;


    using (SearchResultCollection src = ds.FindAll())
    {
        Console.WriteLine("Found {0}", src.Count);

        foreach (SearchResult sr in src)
        {
            Console.WriteLine(sr.Path);
        }
    }

    //increment our offset
    offset += 50;
}
}
```

Listing 5.2 also demonstrates how we reuse the same `DirectoryVirtualListView` to perform additional searches while changing the `Offset`.

Searching by String

Another powerful option for VLV searches comes in the form of the `Target` property. Since we must use a server-side sort for a VLV search to work, we can specify by string value where in the sort index we would like to retrieve.

For instance, if we created an application that searched for all users in the directory by last name, this would provide an ideal use of the VLV and the `Target` example. Listing 5.3 shows such an example.

LISTING 5.3: Searching by String

```
string adsPath = "LDAP://DC=domain,DC=com";

//Explicitly create our SearchRoot
DirectoryEntry searchRoot = new DirectoryEntry(
    adsPath,
    null,
    null,
    AuthenticationTypes.Secure
    );

using (searchRoot)
{
    DirectorySearcher ds = new DirectorySearcher(
        searchRoot,
        "(objectCategory=person)"
        );

    //sorting must be turned on,
    //sort by last name
    ds.Sort = new SortOption(
        "sn",
        SortDirection.Descending
        );

    //grab 50 users starting with sn="D*"
    ds.VirtualListView =
        new DirectoryVirtualListView(0, 50, "D");

    using (SearchResultCollection src = ds.FindAll())
    {
        Console.WriteLine(
            "Returning {0}",
            src.Count
            );

        foreach (SearchResult sr in src)
        {
            Console.WriteLine(sr.Path);
        }
    }
    Console.WriteLine(
        "Approx: {0} Found",
```

```
            ds.VirtualListView.ApproximateTotal
        );
}
```

As Listing 5.3 demonstrates, this powerful solution allows us to return a subset of a much larger result set quickly, without needing to retrieve all of the entries first. In the case of a user trying to search for other users by last name, this provides an easy mechanism to pull only enough results surrounding the `Target`, and it is much more efficient.

It is important to note that in both listings, we applied server-side sorting to the result set. This is a necessary step when using VLV searches, and an error will occur when sorting is not applied. Both the `Target` and the `Offset` refer to a location within a sorted result set, but with different purposes. We can use only one or the other as a basis for a starting location in our search. Finally, we should also be cognizant that the VLV is returning an estimate and not an exact match around the `Offset` or `Target`. There might be an overlap or gaps in those results if we were to try to iterate sequentially through the result set, as shown in Listing 5.2.

VLV searches provide a powerful option for SDS developers when dealing with otherwise large result sets and ad hoc queries. Thoughtful implementation of a VLV search can provide huge performance wins for both the end user and the directory servers themselves.

> **■ NOTE   VLV Requires Windows XP or Higher**
>
> Even though the target server may support it, as of this writing the ADSI client itself added support for VLV only as of the Windows XP version. Developing a solution on Windows XP and attempting to deploy it to a Windows 2000 application server will result in a disappointing surprise. Note that Microsoft may choose to add this feature to Windows 2000 at some point, so check the documentation for the latest information.

Searching for Deleted Objects

For most types of objects in Active Directory and ADAM, once an instance has been deleted, it is moved to the Deleted Objects container and it becomes a **tombstone**. This container is not normally visible to users and by default can be searched only by administrators.

> ■ **NOTE** Tombstones Are Limited with DirectoryEntry
>
> When working with tombstones, it is important to note that we cannot use `DirectoryEntry` to modify them. Operations on tombstones require that a special control be added to the LDAP operation and `DirectoryEntry` does not do this.

The process to search for deleted objects is as follows.

1. Using the WKGUID syntax, bind to the Deleted Objects container with the `AuthenticationTypes.FastBind` option.
2. Specify the `SearchScope.OneLevel` option (`Subtree` will also work, but it returns the container as well).
3. Use a filter with `(isDeleted=TRUE)`, plus any other filtering criteria.
4. Set the `Tombstone` property on `DirectorySearcher` to `true`.

Listing 5.4 shows how this might be accomplished. Note that we are binding using the WKGUID format from Chapter 3.

LISTING 5.4: Searching for Deleted Items

```
string adsPath =
    "LDAP://<WKGUID=18e2ea80684f11d2b9aa00c04f79f805," +
    "dc=domain,dc=com>";

//Explicitly create our SearchRoot
DirectoryEntry searchRoot = new DirectoryEntry(
    adsPath,
    null,
    null,
    AuthenticationTypes.Secure
    | AuthenticationTypes.FastBind //use fastbind
    );

using (searchRoot)
{
    DirectorySearcher ds = new DirectorySearcher(
        searchRoot,
```

```
        "(isDeleted=TRUE)" //all deleted objects
        );

    ds.SearchScope = SearchScope.OneLevel;
    ds.Tombstone = true;

    using (SearchResultCollection src = ds.FindAll())
    {
        Console.WriteLine("Returning {0}", src.Count);

        foreach (SearchResult sr in src)
        {
            Console.WriteLine(sr.Path);
        }
    }
}
```

While it is not strictly necessary to bind to the Deleted Objects container, it is recommended. A search similar to Listing 5.4 would work fine if binding directly to the root application or domain partition. However, it would not be as efficient, given that we know that our deleted objects will be found in the Deleted Objects container.

Reasons to Search for Deleted Objects

Most of the time, we actually do not care about deleted objects at all and are happier to ignore them. However, if we are building a custom synchronization application using a technique called change polling, we actually do need to track object deletions. The target data source generally needs to know when to delete an object from its store as well, or it is not really staying in sync!

We may also occasionally just need to find a deleted object for various administrative reasons, but the change polling application is by far the most common.

Directory Synchronization Queries

It is a fact of life that there is no one source of truth for all data in most enterprises of any size. As such, we often need to build applications that integrate various sources of data through synchronization processes.

In both Active Directory and ADAM, we can track changes to the directory using an LDAP extension called the `DirSync` control. This extension allows a user to return the difference between the initial state of the directory and some later state. To do this, an initial search is performed that records the current state into a cookie. On a subsequent search, this cookie is handed back and is used to determine which objects have changed, and an updated cookie is returned. Since an object change could include the actual deletion of an object, this type of search automatically includes tombstones.

■■ **WARNING   Some DirSync Options Require Windows 2003 Clients!**

As of this writing, some parts of the ADSI support for `DirSync` require a Windows Server 2003 client. Please refer to the sidebar DirectorySynchronizationOptions, later in this chapter, for additional details.

Limitations on Search Root and Scope

We must use the root of one of our directory or application partitions as the `SearchRoot` (application, domain, configuration, or schema). The only scope allowed for this type of search is `Subtree`. Typically, we would use paging for a large `Subtree`-scoped search. However, in this type of search, paging is not allowed.

Permissions

To use this type of search, the caller must have the "directory get changes" privilege (`SE_SYNC_AGENT_NAME`) for the current root directory partition being searched. By default, this means only an administrator or `SYSTEM` will be able to perform this search. Finally, the caller must have the `DS-Replication-Get-Changes` **control access right** (which is a special type of entry applied to the security descriptor on the partition root object). As we can see, this prevents all but the most privileged users from using this functionality. These privileges are needed specifically because in essence, we are allowing the running account to view any changed attribute on every object, regardless of the underlying access control list (ACL) permission.

For Windows 2003, we have the option of using `DirectorySynchro-nizationOption.ObjectSecurity`, which allows the current user to see the changes on objects that she would already have permission to see based on her current security context. Objects that the current security credentials would not normally be allowed to see will not be returned. This is a good way to give this ability to less-privileged accounts and still allow this type of search.

By default, we should be aware that no ADAM security principal will have the `DS-Replication-Get-Changes` control access right by default. This will have to be added to a group or user using a tool such as ADAM's version of dsacls.exe.

Filter

Any valid filter is usable; however, we have to keep in mind that only the objects that match that filter will be tracked on the initial search and on subsequent searches. For instance, if we specified `(sn=Dunn)` for the initial search, only objects with a last name equal to "Dunn" would be tracked for subsequent searches. Instead, if we initially specified `(object-Class=user)`, all users would be tracked (as well as computers). A subsequent search to find changes could specify `(sn=Dunn)`, which would filter the results equivalently to using `(&(objectClass=user)(sn=Dunn))`.

Attributes

We can specify specific attributes we are interested in tracking by adding them to the `PropertiesToLoad` collection. If we pass `null` (`Nothing` in Visual Basic .NET), this is an indication that we wish to track all attributes. Any specified attributes in the `PropertiesToLoad` collection will also act as an additional filter, as only those objects on the initial search that have at least one of these attributes populated will be tracked. Subsequent searches will include only those objects where at least one of the tracked attributes has been updated. When inspecting the returned `SearchResult`, only the attributes that have changed will be included, regardless of whether the attribute is populated. In addition to any changed attributes, `ADsPath`, `objectGuid`, and `instanceType` will always be included in a `SearchResult`.

DirSync Samples

Listing 5.5 demonstrates a complete `DirSync` implementation.

LISTING 5.5: **Sample DirSync Class**

```
public class DirSync
{
    //snip... just the juicy parts left for brevity

    public void InitializeCookie(string qry)
    {
        //this is our searchroot
        DirectoryEntry entry = new DirectoryEntry(
            this.adsPath,
            this.username,
            this.password,
            AuthenticationTypes.Secure
            );

        using (entry)
        {
            //we want to track all attributes (use null)
            string[] attribs = null;

            DirectorySearcher ds = new DirectorySearcher(
                entry,
                qry,
                attribs
                );

            //we must use Subtree scope
            ds.SearchScope = SearchScope.Subtree;

            //pass in the flags we wish here
            DirectorySynchronization dSynch = new
                DirectorySynchronization(
                    DirectorySynchronizationOptions.None
                    );

            ds.DirectorySynchronization = dSynch;

            using (SearchResultCollection src = ds.FindAll())
            {
                Console.WriteLine(
                    "Initially Found {0} objects",
                    src.Count
                    );

                //get and store the cookie
```

```
                StoreCookie(
                    dSynch.GetDirectorySynchronizationCookie()
                    );
            }
        }
    }

    public void GetSynchedChanges(string qry, bool saveState)
    {
        //this is our searchroot
        DirectoryEntry entry = new DirectoryEntry(
            this.adsPath,
            this.username,
            this.password,
            AuthenticationTypes.Secure
            );

        using (entry)
        {
            string[] attribs = null;

            DirectorySearcher ds = new DirectorySearcher(
                entry,
                qry,
                attribs
                );

            //we must use Subtree scope
            ds.SearchScope = SearchScope.Subtree;

            //pass back in our saved cookie
            DirectorySynchronization dSynch = new
                DirectorySynchronization(
                    DirectorySynchronizationOptions.None,
                    RestoreCookie()
                    );

            ds.DirectorySynchronization = dSynch;

            using (SearchResultCollection src = ds.FindAll())
            {
                Console.WriteLine(
                    "Subsequently Changed: {0} objects",
                    src.Count
                    );

                //return each object that has changed
                //and what attributes have changed,
                //keeping in mind that the attributes:
                //'objectGuid', 'instanceType', and
```

```
                    //'ADsPath' will always be returned as well
                    foreach (SearchResult sr in src)
                    {
                        Console.WriteLine(
                            "Detected Change in {0}",
                            sr.Properties["AdsPath"][0]
                            );

                        Console.WriteLine("Changed Values:");
                        Console.WriteLine("==============:");

                        foreach (string prop in
                            sr.Properties.PropertyNames)
                        {
                            Console.WriteLine(
                                "\t {0} : {1}",
                                prop,
                                sr.Properties[prop][0]
                                );
                        }
                    }

                    if (saveState)
                    {
                        //get and store the cookie again
                        StoreCookie(
                          dSynch.GetDirectorySynchronizationCookie()
                            );
                    }
                }
            }
        }

        //quick method to save the byte[] array to disk
        private void StoreCookie(byte[] cookieBytes)
        {
            //snipped for brevity!
        }

        //quick method to restore the byte[] array from disk
        private byte[] RestoreCookie()
        {
            //snipped for brevity!
        }
    }
```

The class shown in Listing 5.5 has been abbreviated to cut down on the size of this book, but we provide a complete listing on the book's web site.

Our sample class can be consumed using a technique similar to that shown in Listing 5.6.

LISTING 5.6: Demonstrating DirSync Class Use

```
//optionally add credentials if not running
//with privileges
DirSync ds = new DirSync();

//initialize our search and look for all users
ds.InitializeCookie(
    "(objectClass=user)"
    );

//..update the directory somehow

//now retrieve what has changed
//this can be called much later
//or in another program as state
//is stored to the local drive
ds.GetSynchedChanges(
    "(objectClass=user)",
    true
    );
```

It is important to note that we are essentially comparing two snapshots in time. Actually, that is not entirely true—it is more as though we are viewing a partial snapshot full of changes since a given point in time. We actually do not know the initial values of any object directly. We know only when something has changed, and we know its final value. We should also note that object state can differ between domain controllers, even at the same moment in time. As such, it is advisable to bind to the exact same domain controller each time when comparing snapshots. This eliminates the natural discrepancy that can occur between object states based on localized but nonreplicated changes.

One last point that bears mentioning is that we really have no way of tracking any of the intermediate changes that might have occurred between an object's initial state and its final state right before the search. An object's state can vary drastically between its initial and final states, but these intermediate values will not be captured by this type of search. Only the final state of the object will be directly viewable in these cases.

As we can see, the `DirectorySynchronization` class is extremely powerful if we can live with some of the limitations imposed on us.

DirectorySynchronizationOptions

The `DirectorySynchronizationOptions` enumeration represents additional settings we can specify for a search. The possible values are as follows.

- **`IncrementalValues`.** Supported only on Windows 2003 server. If this flag is specified, only the changed values from a multivalued attribute (up to the limit) will be returned.
- **`None`.** This is the default flag setting.
- **`ObjectSecurity`.** Supported only on Windows Server 2003. If not specified, the user must have the replicate changes privilege (SE_SYNC _AGENT_NAME). When present, the user can view objects and attributes accessible to the caller.
- **`ParentsFirst`.** Return the parent object before the children if both have changed.
- **`PublicDataOnly`.** Private, nonreplicated data is omitted from the results.

Using Attribute Scope Query

Windows 2003 Server and ADAM include an exciting new feature called attribute scope query (ASQ).

As the term implies, an ASQ changes the scope of a query to search the list of objects specified by an attribute value in a specific object, instead of performing a traditional search scope. The attribute to be used must use DN syntax (Object-DN, 2.5.5.1), as those are the types of attributes that specify lists of objects in the directory.

For example, what if we want to find all of the email addresses of the members of a specific distribution list? Since the member list of a group is essentially arbitrary and may contain objects from all over the directory, we do not traditionally have an efficient way to target them specifically. The common approach is to enumerate the group's `member` attribute and query each object in the list for their email address. This is both tedious and inefficient.

ASQ changes this. We can now directly search the objects referenced in the `member` attribute of a group and retrieve their email addresses.

An ASQ can only be performed against a single DN-syntax attribute in one object at a time. Because of this, our `DirectorySearcher` must be configured with the scope set to `Base` and the `SearchRoot` pointing to the object whose attribute is the target of the query.

With ASQ, the `PropertiesToLoad` property now instructs `DirectorySearcher` to retrieve those attributes from the target of the search, not from the `SearchRoot` object itself. It is also worth noting that we cannot retrieve attribute values from the `SearchRoot` object at the same time we are performing an ASQ. We need two separate searches for that.

Listing 5.7 demonstrates this example.

LISTING 5.7: Using an Attribute Scope Query to Retrieve Data from the Members of a Group

```
string adsPath =
    "LDAP://CN=Group1,OU=Groups,dc=domain,dc=com";

//Explicitly create our SearchRoot
DirectoryEntry searchRoot = new DirectoryEntry(
    adsPath,
    null,
    null,
    AuthenticationTypes.Secure
    );

using (searchRoot) //we are responsible for Disposing
{
    string[] attribs = new string[]{
        "distinguishedName",
        "sAMAccountName",
        "name",
        "mail"
         };

    DirectorySearcher ds = new DirectorySearcher(
        searchRoot,
        "(&(objectClass=user)(objectCategory=person))",
        attribs
        );
```

```
//must be SearchScope.Base
ds.SearchScope = SearchScope.Base;

//we choose any DN-type attribute
ds.AttributeScopeQuery = "member";

using (SearchResultCollection src = ds.FindAll())
{
    Console.WriteLine("Returning {0}", src.Count);

    foreach (SearchResult sr in src)
    {
        foreach (string s in attribs)
        {
            if (sr.Properties.Contains(s))
            {
                Console.WriteLine(
                    "{0}: {1}",
                    s,
                    sr.Properties[s][0]
                    );
            }
        }
    }
}

//OUTPUT:
//distinguishedName: CN=User4925,OU=Users,DC=domain,DC=com
//sAMAccountName: User4925
//name: User4925
//mail: user4925@domain.com
//distinguishedName: CN=User4935,OU=Users,DC=domain,DC=com
//sAMAccountName: User4935
//name: User4935
//mail: user4935@domain.com
//...
```

Wow! That is an extremely useful feature that was not only easier to program, but also faster and more efficient than binding to each member to get our information. Once again, it is important to note that the value specified in the AttributeScopeQuery property must be a string that represents a DN syntax attribute (either single- or multivalued).

Clever developers will realize that this is probably the easiest way to enumerate a large group's membership. Instead of using attribute range retrieval (Chapter 6), we can simply specify a base-level search on the group of interest and perform an ASQ on the `member` attribute.

> **■ NOTE** ASQ Requires Windows XP or Higher
>
> Like VLV searches, as of this writing the ADSI client supports only ASQ as of the Windows XP version. Developing a solution on Windows XP and attempting to deploy it to a Windows 2000 application server will not work.

Extended DN Queries

An Extended DN query allows us to retrieve the formatted GUID and security identifier (SID) of an object as well as the normal DN when retrieving objects in the domain. Typically, the DN is returned in the traditional format:

```
CN=Someone,CN=Users,DC=domain,DC=com
```

However, when we set the `DirectorySearcher`'s `ExtendedDN` property to either the `Standard` or the `HexString` value, the extended DN search feature is enabled and our DNs will look like this:

```
<GUID=01a3e601-7b3a-42f1-8b25-f5cc2dc41565>;
<SID=S-1-5-21-329068152-1454471165-1417001333-227109>;
CN=Someone,CN=Users,DC=domain,DC=com
```

…or this:

```
<GUID=01e6a3013a7bf1428b25f5cc2dc41565>;
<SID=0105000000000005150000000782e9d13fd77b15675b9755425770300>;
CN=Someone,CN=Users,DC=domain,DC=com
```

The DN now includes a semicolon-delimited list of the GUID and SID DN syntaxes that we described in Chapter 3, in addition to the traditional DN. Note that only objects that are security principals—for example, users and groups—have a SID, so the SID is included only with these types of objects. The GUID is always returned, as every object has an `objectGUID` attribute.

Listing 5.8 shows a simple example.

LISTING 5.8: Using the ExtendedDN Query

```
string adsPath = "LDAP://DC=domain,DC=net";

//Create our SearchRoot
DirectoryEntry entry = new DirectoryEntry(
    adsPath,
    null,
    null,
    AuthenticationTypes.Secure
    );


using (entry)
{
    //Create our searcher
    DirectorySearcher ds = new DirectorySearcher(
        entry,
        "(sAMAccountName=User1)", //find 'User1'
        new string[] { "distinguishedName" }
        );

    //Specify the Standard Syntax
    ds.ExtendedDN = ExtendedDN.Standard;

    SearchResult sr = ds.FindOne();

    string dn =
        sr.Properties["distinguishedName"][0].ToString();

    //ExtendedDN is in
    //"<GUID=XXX>;<SID=XXX>;distinguishedName" format
    string[] parts = dn.Split(new char[]{';'});

    //Output each piece of the extended DN
    foreach (string part in parts)
    {
        Console.WriteLine(part);
    }
}

//OUT: <GUID=4fe5eed1-e8a5-4831-af3f-0be590f879ca>;
//       <SID=S-1-5-21-4089392435-310822506-2481186512-1115>;
//       CN=User1,OU=Domain Users,DC=domain,DC=net
```

Given that we must manually parse the returned values for each DN to find the GUID or SID, why is this even useful? Well, sometimes we might want to return the GUID and SID for each object returned in the search, and this method is definitely more efficient than binding to each object and retrieving the GUID or SID from the `DirectoryEntry`.

Had this functionality been exposed in .NET 1.x, it would have given us a nice way to get the string format of a SID without using P/Invoke. However, in .NET 2.0, this is an easy task now with the `SecurityIdentifier` class. We expect to need the `ExtendedDN` feature much less often than most of the other advanced features available to us.

> ■ **WARNING**   ExtendedDN Requires Windows 2003 Clients!
>
> As of this writing, the ADSI code that supports `ExtendedDN` is implemented only in the Windows Server 2003 version of the ADSI library. This means that we cannot use Windows XP workstations or lower for issuing `ExtendedDN` queries with `DirectorySearcher`. Attempting to use `ExtendedDN` on an unsupported platform will result in an `InvalidOperationException` from `DirectorySearcher`.

Reading Security Descriptors with Security Masks

Every object in Active Directory and ADAM contains an attribute called `ntSecurityDescriptor`. This attribute contains a Windows security descriptor object that contains the discretionary access control list (DACL), the system access control list (SACL), group, and owner information that controls the object's access control behavior.

In .NET 2.0, a new property called `SecurityMasks` has been added to `DirectorySearcher` that allows us to control which components of the security descriptor are returned in the data when we request the `ntSecurityDescriptor` attribute in a search operation.

We cover security descriptors in great detail in Chapters 6 and 8. Chapter 6 contains a complete discussion of reading and writing security descriptors as a whole, and Chapter 8 actually focuses on the internal structure of security descriptors. Please refer to both of those chapters for an explanation of why this property is important and what we can do with the data once we have it.

In this chapter, we will simply demonstrate how to use the new property of the `DirectorySearcher` effectively. Listing 5.9 contains a sample.

LISTING 5.9: Retrieving a Security Descriptor

```
string adsPath = "LDAP://dc=domain,dc=com";

//explicitly create our searchroot
DirectoryEntry searchRoot = new DirectoryEntry(
    adsPath,
    null,
    null,
    AuthenticationTypes.Secure
    );

using (searchRoot) //we are responsible for disposing
{
    DirectorySearcher ds = new DirectorySearcher(
        searchRoot,
        "(cn=User1)",
        new string[]{"ntSecurityDescriptor"}
        );

    //Get the Security for this object
    ds.SecurityMasks = SecurityMasks.Dacl
        | SecurityMasks.Group
        | SecurityMasks.Owner;

    SearchResult sr = ds.FindOne();

    if (sr == null)
        throw new Exception("No user found");

    byte[] descriptorBytes =
        (byte[])sr.Properties["ntSecurityDescriptor"][0];


    ActiveDirectorySecurity ads = new ActiveDirectorySecurity();

    ads.SetSecurityDescriptorBinaryForm(
        descriptorBytes,
        AccessControlSections.All
        );

    //helper function
    PrintSD(ads);

    AuthorizationRuleCollection rules = ads.GetAccessRules(
        true,
        true,
        typeof(NTAccount)
        );
```

```
        foreach (ActiveDirectoryAccessRule rule in rules)
        {
            //helper function
            PrintAce(rule);
        }
    }

Sample output:

=====Security Descriptor=====
    Owner: S-1-450115865-2557621802-512
    Group: S-1-450115865-2557621802-512
=====ACE=====
    Identity: NT AUTHORITY\SELF
    AccessControlType: Allow
    ActiveDirectoryRights: ExtendedRight
    InheritanceType: None
    ObjectType: ab721a53-1e2f-11d0-9819-00aa0040529b
    InheritedObjectType: <null>
    ObjectFlags: ObjectAceTypePresent
```

We show the code for the two helper functions mentioned in Listing 5.3, called `PrintSD` and `PrintAce`, in Chapter 8, Listing 8.2. We omitted them here for brevity.

Asynchronous Searches

We have finally come to the point in the book where we have hit the wall with SDS and can go no further. While there is a property on `Directory-Searcher` called `Asynchronous`, it has no effect because it is used in a synchronous manner. We have always been able to use SDS in an asynchronous pattern using delegates and events, or directly creating new background threads, but none of this was built into SDS per se; it was a result of a general .NET asynchronous pattern. To get direct support for asynchronous searches, we need to dip into a lower-level API and use `System.DirectoryServices.Protocols` (SDS.P).

Asynchronous searches provide a couple of benefits to developers. For long-running or complex searches, we often do not want to block the main thread and make our user interface unresponsive. Using an asynchronous pattern allows us to have our main thread continue operations while the search performs on another thread. A callback mechanism will inform us when the search has completed.

We can also use asynchronous searches to increase stability in high-volume server applications, for similar reasons.

It is important to note here that while the client application might appear to be more responsive, the directory server still has to do the same amount of work as it would if it were called synchronously. We are not making our search any easier for our directory servers!

The benefit of offloading the work to another thread is available whether we use the built-in support of SDS.P, or we simply put SDS into a general .NET asynchronous pattern. However, the second benefit for these types of searches is that we can get partial results during long-running searches. This benefit is available only when using SDS.P. That is, we don't have to wait for the entire search to complete before we can get some results, which we would have to do using SDS regardless of whether we invoked it asynchronously.

■ WARNING   SDS.P Sample Ahead!

We have spent most of the book so far discussing SDS in detail, but we provided only a brief introduction to SDS.P in Chapter 2. So far, we have not even shown a sample using it.

Unfortunately, we would need another book to cover SDS.P in similar detail, so we must take a different approach. Whenever we have a compelling sample that demands it, we are simply going to dive into the SDS.P code headfirst, even if the first sample involves multiple threads and callbacks. We believe this is more useful than not providing the sample at all. However, if this leaves you feeling lost, it is probably best just to skip ahead.

Creating an Asynchronous Search

Developers familiar with using delegates in the more general .NET asynchronous pattern will be familiar with how this is done using SDS.P. We typically have a `BeginInvoke/EndInvoke` and a callback mechanism. The same is true using SDS.P, but we have a few more options. At the most basic level, we have, as Listing 5.10 shows, a simple search with a callback function.

LISTING 5.10: Using Asynchronous Searching

```
class Program
{
    static Mutex mutex = new Mutex();
    static LdapConnection connect;

    static void Main(string[] args)
    {
        this.connect = new LdapConnection(
            new LdapDirectoryIdentifier("SERVER:389"),
            new System.Net.NetworkCredential(
                "CN=Admin,OU=Users,O=Dunnry,C=US",
                "secret"
            ),
            AuthType.SecureSocketsLayer
            );

        this.connect.Bind();

        this.connect.SessionOptions.ProtocolVersion = 3;
        this.connect.SessionOptions.ReferralChasing =
            ReferralChasingOptions.None;

        SearchRequest request = new SearchRequest(
            "O=Dunnry,C=US",
            "(cn=user9*)",
            SearchScope.Subtree,
            null
            );

        request.SizeLimit = 500;

        Console.WriteLine(
            "Main Execution on thread #{0}",
            Thread.CurrentThread.ManagedThreadId);

        IAsyncResult result = this.connect.BeginSendRequest(
            request,
            PartialResultProcessing.NoPartialResultSupport,
            new AsyncCallback(InternalCallback),
            null
            );

        //let the async thread signal
        result.AsyncWaitHandle.WaitOne();

        //wait until the other thread finishes output
        this.mutex.WaitOne();

        Console.WriteLine(
            "Finished...Press Enter to Continue"
```

```
                );

        this.mutex.ReleaseMutex();

        Console.ReadLine();
    }

    static void InternalCallback(IAsyncResult result)
    {
        this.mutex.WaitOne();

        Console.WriteLine(
            "Callback on thread #{0}",
            Thread.CurrentThread.ManagedThreadId);

        SearchResponse response =
            this.connect.EndSendRequest(result)
                as SearchResponse;

        foreach (SearchResultEntry entry in response.Entries)
        {
            Console.WriteLine(entry.DistinguishedName);
        }

        this.mutex.ReleaseMutex();
    }
}
```

Developers familiar with using callback functions know that the threads are often different from the main application. This means that we have to deal with thread concurrency issues, especially when using shared resources. Listing 5.10 sidesteps this issue somewhat by writing to the `Console`, but developers should be aware that accessing a shared resource requires the use of a synchronization object such as a `Mutex`.

For long-running processes where results might trickle in, we can optionally use the `PartialResultProcessing.ReturnPartialResultsAndNotifyCallback` enumeration. This will allow us to catch results as they come in. Listing 5.11 shows an example of how this could be formulated.

LISTING 5.11: Retrieving Partial Results

```
class PartialResults
{
    static Mutex mutex = new Mutex();
    static LdapConnection connect;
```

```
static void Main(string[] args)
{
    this.connect = new LdapConnection(
        new LdapDirectoryIdentifier("Server:389"),
        new System.Net.NetworkCredential(
        "CN=Admin,OU=Users,O=Dunnry,C=US",
        "secret"
        ),
        AuthType.Basic
        );

    this.connect.Bind();

    this.connect.SessionOptions.ProtocolVersion = 3;
    this.connect.SessionOptions.ReferralChasing =
        ReferralChasingOptions.None;

    SearchRequest request = new SearchRequest(
        "O=Dunnry,C=US",
        "(objectClass=user)",
        SearchScope.Subtree,
        null
        );

    request.SizeLimit = 200;

    Console.WriteLine(
        "Main Execution on thread #{0}",
        Thread.CurrentThread.ManagedThreadId
        );

    IAsyncResult result = this.connect.BeginSendRequest(
        request,
    PartialResultProcessing.ReturnPartialResultsAndNotifyCallback,
        new AsyncCallback(InternalCallback),
        null
        );

    //let the async thread signal
    result.AsyncWaitHandle.WaitOne();

    //wait until the other thread finishes output
    this.mutex.WaitOne();

    Console.WriteLine(
        "Finished...Press Enter to Continue"
        );

    this.mutex.ReleaseMutex();
```

```
            Console.ReadLine();
    }

    static void InternalCallback(IAsyncResult result)
    {
        this.mutex.WaitOne();

        Console.WriteLine(
            "Callback on thread #{0}",
            Thread.CurrentThread.ManagedThreadId
            );

        if (!result.IsCompleted)
        {
            PartialResultsCollection prc =
                this.connect.GetPartialResults(result);

            for (int i = 0; i < prc.Count; i++)
            {
                SearchResultEntry entry = prc[i]
                    as SearchResultEntry;

                if (entry != null)
                {
                    Console.WriteLine(
                        "Partial Result: {0}",
                        entry.DistinguishedName
                        );
                }
            }
        }
        else
        {
            SearchResponse response =
                this.connect.EndSendRequest(result)
                    as SearchResponse;

            foreach (SearchResultEntry entry
                in response.Entries)
            {
                Console.WriteLine(entry.DistinguishedName);
            }
        }
        this.mutex.ReleaseMutex();
    }
}
```

As Listing 5.11 demonstrates, the callback will be notified periodically when partial results are available, and we can pull the partial results using the `GetPartialResults` method. When the call is finally completed, we still need to call `EndSendRequest` and retrieve the remaining results. It is important to note that the `SearchResponse` returned from `EndSend-Request` when using partial results contains only the remaining results not already retrieved by using `GetPartialResults`.

SUMMARY

The first part of the chapter dug into the advanced searching topics that tend to affect all types of queries and operations, such as timeouts and performance optimization. We also demonstrated how we can search for objects in multiple domains in the same Active Directory forest using the global catalog, or find objects in other naming contexts via referrals.

In the second part of the chapter, we covered the advanced searching features supported by Active Directory and ADAM that were introduced to SDS in version 2.0 of the .NET Framework. We included detailed explanations and samples for the following new features:

- Virtual List Views
- Deleted object searches
- Directory synchronization
- Attribute scope query(ies)
- Extended DN queries
- Security descriptor searches

We concluded with a departure from our normal discussion by demonstrating how we can perform asynchronous searches using the `System.DirectoryServices.Protocols` namespace.

■ 6 ■
Reading and Writing LDAP Attributes

I N THIS CHAPTER, we explore how to read and write LDAP data using `System.DirectoryServices` (SDS). As we discussed in Chapter 1, LDAP data is represented by attributes defined in the LDAP schema. It's interesting how attribute syntaxes in an LDAP directory are converted by the ADSI layer into COM data types, and how those COM data types are again translated into .NET data types. In fact, this is one of the aspects of directory services programming that developers often struggle with. We'll spend a significant portion of the chapter explaining how all of the different syntaxes relate to .NET and we'll provide samples for reading and writing each type. Finally, we'll touch on some interesting problems with attributes that contain many values.

Basics of Reading Attribute Values

As we discussed in Chapters 3 and 4, SDS provides two mechanisms for reading attribute data. The `DirectoryEntry` class allows us to read data for a particular object in the directory via the `PropertyCollection` and `PropertyValueCollection` classes. The `DirectorySearcher` class allows similar functionality through the `ResultPropertyCollection` and `ResultPropertyValueCollection` classes on the `SearchResult` class.

Use of the Term "Property" versus "Attribute"

One thing worth mentioning is that in SDS, the class library uses the word "property" to refer to directory object data, where LDAP uses the word "attribute". This is largely because SDS is a general API that deals with multiple data sources and a more general term is appropriate. These terms are basically interchangeable. However, since this book deals specifically with LDAP, we will largely ignore the SDS naming convention and refer to LDAP data as attributes.

The design of these two sets of classes is remarkably similar, so knowledge about one pair generally applies to the second. There are some subtle but important differences, however.

The Basic Design

Both `PropertyCollection` (from `DirectoryEntry`) and `ResultPropertyCollection` (from `SearchResult`) are typical .NET dictionary-type collection classes with a string key and the value as a `PropertyValueCollection` or `ResultPropertyValueCollection`, respectively. Each key corresponds to an attribute held by the parent object. There are no really important differences between these two property collection classes, so we can think of them the same way in practice.

The actual attribute values are stored in the `PropertyValueCollection` and `ResultPropertyValueCollection` classes. These classes are typical .NET array-style collections that use an integer value for indexing. The values are typed as `System.Object` because the directory may contain many different types of data (`byte[]`, `System.Int64`, `System.String`, etc.) and `System.Object` is the only common base class. Like all array-style collections in .NET, we may enumerate the value collections using either a `foreach` construct or a `for` loop that indexes values numerically.

Because the directory may contain multivalued attributes, the class library designers opted always to represent attribute values with a collection class. Attributes with a single value are simply represented by a collection class with one value and null values use an empty collection. This provides a consistent programming model.

While this leads to a common model, it also tends to be a source of confusion for first-time SDS developers, who expect to be able to differentiate easily between a single-valued attribute and a multivalued attribute. We will mention some tips in this chapter and point out that it becomes easier to identify these kinds of things with experience.

Key Differences between the Value Collections

There are a number of important differences between the two types of value collections.

- `ResultPropertyValueCollection` is read-only, and `PropertyValueCollection` allows editing.
- `PropertyValueCollection` has a helper property called `Value`, and `ResultPropertyValueCollection` does not.
- They use two different mechanisms for converting ADSI data types to .NET data types.

The last point is subtle, but it is the most important one to understand in order to avoid confusion later on. We will be covering this point in detail later in this chapter.

Collection Class Usage

We need to know just a few basic things about using the value collection classes in order to be productive. Let's examine this from a task-centric perspective. In each of these examples, assume we have a `DirectoryEntry` called `entry` and a `SearchResult` called `result` pointing to the same object in the directory.

Getting Single Values

This is probably the thing we will do most often. Typically, we will either use the `Value` property or access the first element in the collection:

```
object name = entry.Properties["name"].Value;
name = entry.Properties["name"][0];
name = result.Properties["name"][0];
```

Note that the first approach is slightly safer if we have not already checked for a null value, as the Value property will return null/Nothing. The other approaches will throw an exception if the attribute is null, as the array will not have a value at index 0.

Checking for Null Values

If we try to imagine an object in an LDAP directory as a row in a SQL database, the schema for the table would typically allow many null column values. The vast majority of attributes in most LDAP classes are optional and it is very common for objects to contain only a small fraction of the attributes allowed by the schema. This analogy is a little flimsy, and we explain why in the sidebar LDAP and Null Values, later in this chapter. However, it is useful for our purposes here.

As a result, we will be checking for null values frequently. This is just good defensive programming and will contribute greatly to the stability of our applications in production.

With PropertyValueCollection, we can do this by using the Value property:

```
if (entry.Properties["description"].Value != null)
{
    //do something interesting
}
```

An alternate approach is to check the Count property:

```
if (entry.Properties["description"].Count > 0)
{
    //do something interesting
}
```

Things change a bit with ResultPropertyValueCollection. Since it does not have a Value property, we cannot check it for a null value. This is also a situation where there are differences between versions 1.x and 2.0 of the framework. Namely, in version 1.x, a ResultPropertyValueCollection instance was not created if the attribute was not returned in the search, so checking a property like Count would generate a NullReferenceException. This behavior has changed in version 2.0, and a ResultPropertyValueCollection instance will be returned, making it safe to check the Count property without fear of an exception.

LDAP and Null Values

We are purposely being a little bit loose with the term "null" in our discussion. Unlike in the RDBMS world, where we have neat rows and columns that structure our data, the LDAP world does not correspond to this model exactly. If we consider an object to be a row, then the attributes are the columns in a table. If we check the intersection of any row and column, we expect either a value or null. However, this analogy breaks down a bit when we consider that null values do not really exist in LDAP. Either the object contains the attribute or it does not. If we compare it to the RDBMS world again, it would be as if each object was a row, and each row had different columns defined. It is not as if the object contained an attribute that we could find, and it contained a "null" value! The attribute simply does not exist, and from a developer's perspective, we infer this to mean it is null.

As such, when we say an attribute is null, we really mean that the attribute does not exist on the object. That our SDS objects return `null` for nonexistent attributes is only a result of our programming model.

Of course, it is less than ideal to have to remember how value collections will behave based on the version of the framework we are using, and it leads to fragile code. Instead, we should always check the `ResultPropertyCollection` or `PropertyValueCollection` first:

```
if (result.Properties.Contains("description"))
{
    //do something interesting
}

if (entry.Properties.Contains("description"))
{
    //do something interesting
}
```

It turns out that since the `Contains` method works for both `ResultPropertyCollection` and `PropertyCollection` classes, it tends to be easier to use this method consistently without needing to remember the details of either class or the differences due to versions of the framework.

For this reason, we generally recommend using the `Contains` method, as it will work well in all circumstances and scenarios.

Checking for Multiple Values

Many attributes in LDAP allow multiple values and the basic design of the value collections assumes that any attribute may contain multiple values. In order to find out if an attribute actually contains multiple values, we can use the `Count` property:

```
if (entry.Properties["memberOf"].Count > 1)
{
    //do something interesting
}

if (result.Properties.Contains("memberOf"))
{
    if (result.Properties["memberOf"].Count > 1)
    {
        //do something interesting
    }
}
```

We would do something similar with a `SearchResult/ResultProp-ertyValueCollection`.

Another option is simply to enumerate the collection with `foreach`:

```
foreach (string groupDN in entry.Properties["memberOf"])
{
    //do something interesting
}

if (result.Properties.Contains("memberOf"))
{
    foreach (string groupDN in result.Properties["memberOf"])
    {
        //do something interesting
    }
}
```

Using the Value Property

One of the primary differences between `PropertyValueCollection` and `ResultPropertyValueCollection` is that the former contains a `Value` property. The `Value` property does one of three different things when reading an attribute value.

- If the attribute does not exist on the object, it returns `null/Nothing`.
- If the attribute contains a single value, it returns an `Object` that represents a scalar value of the type as marshaled by the .NET Framework (see Table 6.1).
- If the attribute contains multiple values, it returns an `Object` that contains a single-dimensional array of similarly typed objects.

For example, let's take the `member` attribute on the `group` class. It is defined as syntax 2.5.5.1, which is represented in .NET as `System.String` (see Table 6.1). It is defined in the schema as multivalued and optional. As such, the `Value` property might return `null`, a `System.String`, or an array of `System.String` objects, depending on whether the group has zero, one, or multiple members.

This makes the `Value` property especially useful for getting attribute values directly, as we have seen in the earlier examples and throughout the book. It can also be used for writing attribute values, where it is even more useful.

Understanding the ADSI Property Cache

In normal use, ADSI maintains a property cache of values for an object from the directory. The property cache contains an in-memory representation of the data on the server. All reads and writes are performed on the local cache and updates do not take effect until the cache is flushed.

The property cache is a great performance booster, as it reduces the number of remote LDAP messages that must be sent and received in order to work with an object's attribute data. Experienced architects know that any type of remote call over the network tends to be expensive, so making the calls "chunkier" rather than "chattier" is a great way to boost performance. With SDS and ADSI, much of this work is taken care of for us.

The property cache can be filled using the `RefreshCache` method. Additionally, some types of operations will force the property cache to be filled if it is not already. For example, accessing the attributes of a `DirectoryEntry` via the `Properties` property will force the cache to be loaded (if it was not previously loaded by another operation), as will accessing the `Guid`, `Name`, `NativeGuid`, `SchemaClassName`, or `SchemaEntry` property.

Calling `RefreshCache` with no arguments will cause all of the nonconstructed attributes for the object to be loaded. Calling `RefreshCache` with arguments allows us to load specific attributes we want into the cache. It also allows us to load a special type of Active Directory and ADAM attribute called a **constructed attribute**. Constructed attributes are not actually stored in the directory but are calculated on the fly by the directory. Constructed attributes are different from back-link attributes (see Chapter 7) in that they cannot be used in LDAP query filters. Some examples of useful constructed attributes are `tokenGroups`, `allowedAttributesEffective`, and `canonicalName`.

■ TIP   **RefreshCache Can Increase Performance**

Careful use of `RefreshCache` with arguments can also improve our performance, as only the data we need is read. However, we must make sure to get every attribute we are using, or we will end up accidentally doing a full cache load anyway.

Flushing Changes Back to the Directory

In order to flush changes back to the directory, we must commit the changes using the `CommitChanges` method. Note that if `RefreshCache` is called explicitly, or because another operation triggers the cache to be refreshed, any uncommitted changes will be lost. We have seen developers spin their wheels for hours on this problem because they accessed the `Guid` property before flushing changes in order to do some simple logging and kept magically erasing all of their changes. It looked like `CommitChanges` was doing nothing. Do not let this happen to you!

LDAP Data Types in .NET

The data types in LDAP are defined by what are known as LDAP **syntaxes**. According to the LDAP specifications (see RFC 2252), the syntax describes

The Property Cache under the Hood

Those familiar with ADSI will recognize the `RefreshCache` methods being equivalent to the `GetInfo` and `GetInfoEx` methods on the `IADs` interface. Under the hood, `RefreshCache` pretty much invokes those methods directly. `CommitChanges` is also paired exactly with the `SetInfo IADs` method.

But how does the property cache actually work at the LDAP level? In order to fill the cache, the ADSI `LDAP` provider performs a base-level search on the object in question, with no attributes specified in the attribute list. When no attributes are specified, the default LDAP API behavior is to return all nonconstructed attributes. Constructed attributes must always be requested specifically. This is why we must use the version of `RefreshCache` that takes an array of strings as an argument.

■ WARNING   Do Not Disable the Cache

SDS provides a mechanism for disabling the property cache by setting the `UsePropertyCache` property on the `DirectoryEntry` object to `false`. In this mode, each attribute is read as needed and changes are flushed to the directory immediately.

Do not use this feature. The property cache makes things significantly faster and generally makes our programming lives easier. Neither of us can remember a time when disabling the cache was even useful.

the type of data that can be stored in the attribute and the format used to read and write to it via the LDAP API.

The syntax is defined by a combination of the LDAP syntax, which is defined as an Object Identifier (OID), and the OM syntax, which is an integer value.

Table 6.1 defines the syntaxes supported by Active Directory and ADAM.

TABLE 6.1: LDAP Attribute Syntaxes with Their Matching Programmatic Data Types

Syntax Name	Object(DS-DN)
LDAP Syntax	2.5.5.1
OM Syntax	127
ADSI Type	ADSTYPE_DN_STRING
COM Type	VT_BSTR
DirectoryEntry	System.String
DirectorySearcher	System.String
Notes	Standard distinguished name (DN) syntax

Syntax Name	String(Object-Identifier)
LDAP Syntax	2.5.5.2
OM Syntax	6
ADSI Type	ADSTYPE_CASE_IGNORE_STRING
COM Type	VT_BSTR
DirectoryEntry	System.String
DirectorySearcher	System.String
Notes	Contains only digits and "."

Syntax Name	String(Teletex)
LDAP Syntax	2.5.5.4
OM Syntax	20
ADSI Type	ADSTYPE_CASE_IGNORE_STRING
COM Type	VT_BSTR
DirectoryEntry	System.String
DirectorySearcher	System.String
Notes	Case insensitive for searching; Teletex characters only

Syntax Name	String(Printable)
LDAP Syntax	2.5.5.5
OM Syntax	19
ADSI Type	ADSTYPE_PRINTABLE_STRING
COM Type	VT_BSTR
DirectoryEntry	System.String
DirectorySearcher	System.String
Notes	Case sensitive for searching; printable characters only

Syntax Name	String(IA5)
LDAP Syntax	2.5.5.5
OM Syntax	22
ADSI Type	ADSTYPE_PRINTABLE_STRING
COM Type	VT_BSTR
DirectoryEntry	System.String
DirectorySearcher	System.String
Notes	Case sensitive for searching; IA5 string

TABLE 6.1:   LDAP Attribute Syntaxes with Their Matching Programmatic Data Types *(Continued)*

Syntax Name	`String(Numeric)`
LDAP Syntax	2.5.5.6
OM Syntax	18
ADSI Type	`ADSTYPE_NUMERIC_STRING`
COM Type	`VT_BSTR`
DirectoryEntry	`System.String`
DirectorySearcher	`System.String`
Notes	Contains only digits; rarely used in Active Directory

Syntax Name	`Object(DN-Binary)`
LDAP Syntax	2.5.5.7
OM Syntax	127
ADSI Type	`ADSTYPE_DN_WITH_BINARY`
COM Type	`VT_DISPATCH (IADsDNWithBinary)`
DirectoryEntry	`System.__ComObject`
DirectorySearcher	`System.String`
Notes	Also Object(OR-Name); used for associating a GUID with DN

Syntax Name	`Boolean`
LDAP Syntax	2.5.5.8
OM Syntax	1
ADSI Type	`ADSTYPE_BOOLEAN`
COM Type	`VT_BOOL`
DirectoryEntry	`System.Boolean`
DirectorySearcher	`System.Boolean`
Notes	Used for standard Boolean values

Syntax Name	`Integer`
LDAP Syntax	2.5.5.9
OM Syntax	2
ADSI Type	`ADSTYPE_INTEGER`
COM Type	`VT_I4`
DirectoryEntry	`System.Int32`
DirectorySearcher	`System.Int32`
Notes	Used for standard signed integers

Syntax Name	`Enumeration`
LDAP Syntax	2.5.5.9
OM Syntax	10
ADSI Type	`ADSTYPE_INTEGER`
COM Type	`VT_I4`
DirectoryEntry	`System.Int32`
DirectorySearcher	`System.Int32`
Notes	Used for enumerated values

TABLE 6.1: LDAP Attribute Syntaxes with Their Matching Programmatic Data Types *(Continued)*

Syntax Name	`String(Octet)`
LDAP Syntax	2.5.5.10
OM Syntax	4
ADSI Type	`ADSTYPE_OCTET_STRING`
COM Type	`VT_UI1│VT_ARRAY`
DirectoryEntry	`System.Byte[]`
DirectorySearcher	`System.Byte[]`
Notes	Used for arbitrary binary data
Syntax Name	`Object(Replica-Link)`
LDAP Syntax	2.5.5.10
OM Syntax	127
ADSI Type	`ADSTYPE_OCTET_STRING`
COM Type	`VT_VARIANT`
DirectoryEntry	`System.Byte[]`
DirectorySearcher	`System.Byte[]`
Notes	Used by the system only for replication
Syntax Name	`String(UTC-Time)`
LDAP Syntax	2.5.5.11
OM Syntax	23
ADSI Type	`ADSTYPE_UTC_TIME`
COM Type	`VT_DATE`
DirectoryEntry	`System.DateTime`
DirectorySearcher	`System.DateTime`
Notes	Used for date values; stored relative to UTC
Syntax Name	`String(Generalized-Time)`
LDAP Syntax	2.5.5.11
OM Syntax	24
ADSI Type	`ADSTYPE_UTC_TIME`
COM Type	`VT_DATE`
DirectoryEntry	`System.DateTime`
DirectorySearcher	`System.DateTime`
Notes	Used for date values; time zone information is included
Syntax Name	`String(Unicode)`
LDAP Syntax	2.5.5.12
OM Syntax	64
ADSI Type	`ADSTYPE_CASE_IGNORE_STRING`
COM Type	`VT_BSTR`
DirectoryEntry	`System.String`
DirectorySearcher	`System.String`
Notes	Case insensitive for searching; contains any Unicode character

TABLE 6.1:   LDAP Attribute Syntaxes with Their Matching Programmatic Data Types *(Continued)*

Syntax Name	Object(Presentation-Address)
LDAP Syntax	2.5.5.13
OM Syntax	127
ADSI Type	ADSTYPE_CASE_IGNORE_STRING
COM Type	VT_BSTR
DirectoryEntry	System.String
DirectorySearcher	System.String
Notes	Not really used in Active Directory either
Syntax Name	Object(DN-String)
LDAP Syntax	2.5.5.14
OM Syntax	127
ADSI Type	ADSTYPE_DN_WITH_STRING
COM Type	VT_DISPATCH (IADsDNWithString)
DirectoryEntry	System.__ComObject
DirectorySearcher	System.String
Notes	Not used in Active Directory schema; also defined as Object (Access-Point) which is not used and has no marshaling defined
Syntax Name	String(NT-Sec-Desc)
LDAP Syntax	2.5.5.15
OM Syntax	66
ADSI Type	ADSTYPE_NT_SECURITY_DESCRIPTOR
COM Type	VT_DISPATCH (IADsSecurityDescriptor)
DirectoryEntry	System.__ComObject
DirectorySearcher	System.Byte[]
Notes	Contains Windows security descriptors
Syntax Name	Interval/LargeInteger
LDAP Syntax	2.5.5.16
OM Syntax	65
ADSI Type	ADSTYPE_LARGE_INTEGER
COM Type	VT_DISPATCH (IADsLargeInteger)
DirectoryEntry	System.__ComObject
DirectorySearcher	System.Int64
Notes	Both types have same syntaxes, but Interval is treated as unsigned
Syntax Name	String(Sid)
LDAP Syntax	2.5.5.17
OM Syntax	4
ADSI Type	ADSTYPE_OCTET_STRING
COM Type	VT_UI1|VT_ARRAY
DirectoryEntry	System.Byte[]
DirectorySearcher	System.Byte[]
Notes	Contains Windows security identifiers

Note that most of the LDAP types have their own OID, but a few share the same OID and differ only by OM syntax. Additionally, a few types share the same OM syntax, but differ by OID. It does not help our cause to try to explain this right now, so we will let that go for now.

We have to get through a few conversions to use these types in .NET. First, each LDAP data type has a corresponding ADSI data type used to represent it within the ADSI world. Next, each ADSI data type has a default COM data type that it will be converted to by clients using the automation-compliant APIs. Finally, each COM data type has a default marshaling behavior in .NET determined by the .NET COM interop layer.

Looking at Table 6.1, we see that most LDAP data types have friendly .NET data type equivalents, with the vast majority being represented as normal .NET System.String and many of the others as things like DateTime, Int32, and Boolean. However, the table does contain a few strange things, most notably the System.__ComObject, which the experienced .NET programmer may recognize as not even being a public type! We also see that DirectoryEntry and DirectorySearcher marshal some of the types differently.

Figure 6.1 shows a typical layer diagram that illustrates the different places in the native code stack where the various .NET classes get their data.

Understanding the unusual cases is essential to being fully effective in working with Active Directory and ADAM in .NET. We will delve into the finer points in the next few sections. We will also talk more about the LDAP schema in Chapter 7.

ADSI Schema Mapping Mechanism

In the previous section, we discussed the various LDAP syntaxes and showed how they map into the various data types. We also know that ADSI will map each LDAP attribute to an appropriate ADSI data type and COM data type. So, how does ADSI know the syntaxes of all of the LDAP attributes so that it knows the proper data type mappings? Given that LDAP schemas are extensible and can thus be completely unique, this obviously must be done dynamically.

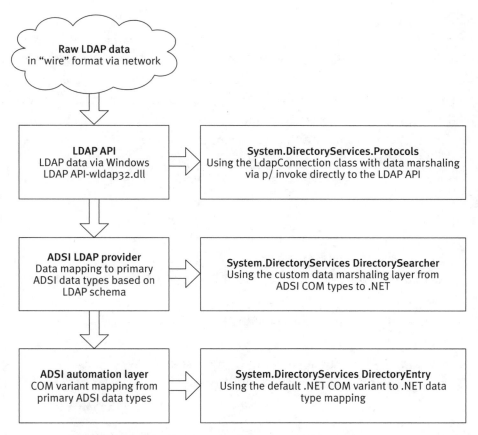

FIGURE 6.1: Directory Services API Layers and Data Type Marshaling

To make this work, ADSI takes advantage of the fact that LDAP version 3 requires that each directory expose its schema in a special abstract form via a specific object in the directory. The abstract schema, an object of type subSchema, describes each attribute in the directory and its syntax (among many other things). The object's location is published in a DN-syntax attribute called subschemaSubentry, on the RootDSE object.

To create a schema mapping for a given directory, ADSI first reads RootDSE to find the abstract schema, and then reads the abstract schema to create a mapping in memory for that directory. From there, ADSI can create an appropriate ADSI or COM mapping for any attribute it reads or writes. The schema for each directory is read only once for a given process the first time that directory is accessed.

Schema Caching

If you've ever looked at the aggregate schema object for an LDAP directory with a large schema, like Active Directory, you may have noticed that it is pretty large. There is a definite performance penalty for reading all of this data over the network each time a directory is accessed, especially in short-lived processes like scripts. To make things faster, ADSI will attempt to cache the schema locally on the filesystem so that the abstract schema can be read from disk.

Here is how it works. The first time ADSI encounters an LDAP version 3 directory, it will

1. Find the abstract schema for a directory by reading the subschema-Subentry in RootDSE.

2. Read the abstract schema data from the subSchema object, including the modifyTimeStamp attribute.

3. Create an in-memory model of the LDAP to ADSI and COM schema map.

4. Try to write the schema data to the filesystem in the <System-Root>\SchCache directory.

5. Try to create a registry key with the name matching the DN of the subschemaSubentry object in HKLM/Software/Microsoft/ADs/Providers/LDAP, which contains values pointing to the schema file and holding the modifyTimeStamp of the object.

On a subsequent visit to the same directory, ADSI will once again access the RootDSE object and find the subschemaSubentry object.

1. It then checks the registry in HKLM/Software/Microsoft/ADs/Providers/LDAP to see if a key exists that matches the DN value of the subschemaSubentry for the RootDSE object.

2. If the key exists, it checks to see if the value for the file exists and if the file is on disk.

3. If the file exists, it then reads the modifyTimeStamp attribute from the subSchema object.

4. If the `modifyTimeStamp` is the same as or older than the value stored in the registry, the schema is read from the filesystem rather than the network. This is where the major performance improvement comes from, as the abstract schema can easily be 1.5MB of data on a 2003 Active Directory with the Exchange Server 2003 schema loaded.

5. If the `modifyTimeStamp` on the `subSchema` object is newer than the one recorded in the registry, then the newer schema is downloaded and used, with the new data being recorded to disk and the new timestamp recorded to the registry, as explained earlier.

Troubleshooting ADSI Schema Cache

Normally, the ADSI schema cache just works behind the scenes and does what it is supposed to. However, there are several cases where it does not, and suddenly we lose the ability to read most attributes without weird exceptions. Some of the most frustrating problems we've seen developers suffer through are caused by schema caching. This is a topic that developers should understand well, since it tends to crop up with some regularity.

What Can Go Wrong?

Schema caching in ADSI imposes a number of preconditions that must be perfectly aligned for it to work correctly. The most obvious aspect is that we typically need an administrative-level account to write to HKLM in the registry or the Windows directory, yet this is something we obviously cannot be guaranteed of when our application runs. In fact, we can argue that in nearly all instances, we would *not* want this to be the case, especially in the context of an application servicing web browsers. In ASP.NET, the default settings for both IIS 5 and IIS 6 run the worker process as a low-privileged account, not an administrator.

The net result of reduced permissions is that the schema will simply not be cached and will be read directly from the directory for each process that loads ADSI against that LDAP directory. Luckily, this just makes things slower. It does not actually break anything.

However, what happens if we cannot read or interpret the schema at all? In this case, bad things are probably about to happen. If ADSI fails to get the schema for the current directory, it falls back to a built-in LDAP version 2 schema. If an attribute we happen to read or write is in this schema, then ADSI can map the LDAP data type to an ADSI and COM (and eventually .NET) data type and everything will work as we expect. However, if the attribute is not in the built-in schema, an exception will be thrown when trying to read or write it with the `DirectoryEntry`.

In .NET 1.x, the `DirectorySearcher` has the same problem, although the exception is different.

`DirectorySearcher` exception:

```
System.NotImplementedException - "Handling of this
ADSVALUE type is not yet implemented (type = 0xb)"
```

`DirectoryEntry` exception:

```
System.Runtime.InteropServices.COMException (error
code 8000500c) "The Active Directory datatype cannot
be converted to/from a native DS Datatype"
```

Things improve slightly in version 2.0 with `DirectorySearcher`, as any unknown data types will automatically be marshaled as a byte array (`byte[]`), so we should not see `System.NotImplementedException` anymore. We still have to contend with converting all the returned data from byte arrays back into strings and such, but at least we can read the data.

Addressing Schema Mapping Problems

ADSI can have schema-mapping problems for three primary reasons.

- The `subSchema` object cannot be read due to a security problem.
- The target directory is not LDAP version 3 compliant and does not support a `subSchema` object via the `subschemaSubentry` attribute on RootDSE.
- ADSI has an internal error parsing the schema.

Security-Related Schema Problems

Of the three errors, the first one is the only one that occurs with Active Directory and ADAM, so we will focus on that. Essentially, this problem tends to occur when the security context used to bind to the directory is not accepted by the server and the remote user ends up being authenticated as an anonymous user instead. Anonymous users do not have permission to read the `subSchema` object in either Active Directory or ADAM by default, so the LDAP version 2 schema is used.

This problem is especially significant in ASP.NET applications, as we should remember that the schema is cached only once per process.[a] In ASP.NET applications, multiple `AppDomains` are often loaded in the same process. When we find a situation where ASP.NET applications seem to have problems that are inconsistent, we need to make sure to check *all* of the applications in that process for any SDS or ADSI usage to make sure that none of them is binding anonymously. Otherwise, the first application to start up in that worker process will define the schema mapping for that particular directory for the life of the process. If that application happens to authenticate as an anonymous user, the schema will revert to LDAP version 2 and will cause problems for all applications running in the process.

The good news is that we can generally always find a way to correct this problem by fixing the security context. We discuss binding and security contexts in much greater detail in Chapters 3 and 8.

LDAP Compliance Problems

We probably can't do much to address LDAP compliance problems. For example, the directory may be an LDAP version 2 directory that does not support a `RootDSE` mechanism. It may also have a customized schema. In this case, no mechanism is available for ADSI to learn the schema, so it cannot map any data types for the custom attributes. The other version of this problem is that the directory has an incomplete LDAP version 3 implementation where there is no `subschemaSubentry` attribute on `RootDSE`.

---

a. In more-recent versions of ADSI, if a connection using different credentials accesses a directory and sees that the schema cache for that directory is in the default mode, it will attempt to download the schema again using the new credentials.

In this case, our best bet is to use `System.DirectoryServices.Protocols` (SDS.P) in .NET 2.0. As we discussed in Chapter 2, this API is lower level and does not attempt to do any data-type conversion. As long as the directory is otherwise LDAP compliant, we should be able to get on with our work (at the expense of having to write more code to do the same things). If we do not have the option of going with .NET 2.0, then things get a little ugly.

Using the `DirectoryEntry` object, we can cast the `NativeObject` property to an `IADsPropertyList` object and use its `GetProperty-Item` method to get an `IADsPropertyValue` object. From there, we can attempt to convert the attribute value to whatever data type we choose. It is unpleasant and potentially slow, but it should work. In this situation, if we avoid using `DirectorySearcher` except to access very basic attributes like `distinguishedName`, then we might be able to cobble together a solution.

Schema Parsing Problems

These are rare, but they are also the most insidious to diagnose. Although we do not have any specific examples, it has been known to happen with some non-Microsoft directories that the abstract schema presented cannot be parsed by ADSI successfully, due to a bug in the ADSI implementation or in the format of the directory's `subSchema` data. In this case, ADSI will silently fail, leaving us with the default backup LDAP version 2 schema.

So, how can we tell if this is the problem? If the `subSchema` appears to be where it should and we can rule out security context issues blocking us from reading it, then this is a possibility.

The workarounds are similar to those suggested earlier. However, if we are interested in getting this fixed, this is the point where we should consider contacting Microsoft support. The Directory Services team is genuinely interested in correcting any flaws in ADSI and will want to hear about it. These bugs exist mainly because they are rarely communicated back to the product group. Don't be shy; they might even build you a hotfix.

.NET Attribute Value Conversion

We now know that ADSI converts LDAP data to ADSI data types via schema mapping. Developers who are familiar with programming ADSI in an unmanaged language (Visual Basic 6, VBScript, C++, etc.) have also observed that ADSI data types are converted to normal COM variant types such as `BSTR` and `VT_I4` when using the automation-compliant ADSI interfaces. The final piece in the puzzle is to understand how these data types are converted into the .NET data types we actually use.

Things are a little bit complicated here because SDS uses two different mechanisms to convert ADSI data types to .NET data types. The `Directo-ryEntry` classes (`DirectoryEntry`, `PropertyCollection`, `PropertyVal-ueCollection`) use one mechanism, and the `DirectorySearcher` classes (`DirectorySearcher`, `SearchResult`, `ResultPropertyCollection`, `ResultPropertyValueCollection`) use another. As Table 6.1 shows, the net result is the same in most cases, but there are differences as well. First, let's understand how things work and then we'll talk about the differences.

Data-Type Conversion with the DirectoryEntry Family

As we previously explained, `DirectoryEntry` is essentially a wrapper around the `IADs` ADSI interface. `IADs` is an automation-compliant COM interface, so it returns standard COM automation data types when properties are accessed. The normal .NET/COM interop system has built-in marshaling for the standard variant types. For example, `BSTR` converts back and forth to `System.String`, `VT_I4` converts to `System.Int32`, and `VT_BOOL` converts to `System.Boolean`.

With the `DirectoryEntry` family of classes, SDS takes advantage of the platform's built-in support for the standard COM variant types and essentially does nothing. We access values in `PropertyValueCollection` as .NET data types, and in most cases, we can ignore their COM origins.

Data-Type Conversion with the DirectorySearcher Family

As we also know, `DirectorySearcher` is essentially a wrapper around the ADSI `IDirectorySearch` interface. Unlike with `IADs`, however, `IDirec-torySearch` is not automation compliant. It is designed for use by lower-level languages like C++ and it requires programmers to access the ADSI data types directly. It does not return standard COM variant types. In order to provide .NET programmers with standard .NET data types, the SDS implementers had to write their own marshaling code to do the conversion.

Why the Big Deal?

This is important to understand because not all ADSI data types convert directly to COM automation types. Specifically, ADSTYPE_LARGE_INTEGER, ADSTYPE_NT_SECURITY_DESCRIPTOR, ADSTYPE_DN_WITH_BINARY, and ADSTYPE_DN_WITH_STRING do not convert to standard variant types, but instead convert to an IDispatch that can be cast to a special ADSI interface that is automation compliant.

However, these IDispatch types in .NET are converted to a special internal .NET data type called System.__ComObject, instead of to something we know what to do with, such as System.String or System.Int32. In order to convert these values to .NET data types, some additional COM interop is required.

With the DirectorySearcher family, the same problem does not exist, since SDS contains an explicit mapping system for IDirectorySearch as well as conversions for these types. For example, ADSTYPE_LARGE_INTEGER is converted to System.Int64.

The result is that for most LDAP data types, DirectoryEntry and DirectorySearcher will convert to the exact same data type, but not always. Specifically, for the four types we mentioned previously, the marshaling is different. This inconsistency is a constant source of confusion for developers who are not expecting it.

Let's look at some specific types.

Standard Data Types

The majority of Active Directory and ADAM attributes have simple conversions to .NET data types, with strings being the most popular. We can generally just cast any data type from the System.Object returned by the collection class back to its corresponding actual runtime type:

```
//given a DirectoryEntry entry and a SearchResult result
//we access the single-valued attribute cn which at runtime
```

```
//will be a simple string
string name = (string) entry.Properties["name"].Value;
//or
name = (string) result.Properties["name"][0];
```

In Visual Basic .NET, the preceding code would look something like this:

```
Dim cn As String
cn = DirectCast(entry.Properties("cn").Value, String)
cn = DirectCast(result.Properties("cn")(0), String)
```

Note that we can also use CType in Visual Basic .NET. The only problem is that CType will happily try a coercive conversion if the direct conversion does not work, so we need to be careful. Since DirectCast will not do this, we generally recommend using it when we just want to cast.

The other basic conversions are very similar:

```
DateTime createDate =
    (DateTime) entry.Properties["whenCreated"].Value;
int userAccountControl =
    (int) entry.Properties["userAccountControl"].Value;
bool isSystemOnly =
    (bool) entry.Properties["systemOnly"].Value;
```

As demonstrated, the actual type conversion is straightforward. We will most likely want to check if the value can be null or multivalued before blindly using the Value property or directly accessing the array by index. (We omitted this here.)

Binary Data Conversion

The process of converting attributes that contain binary data is very similar to that used for the other standard data types. In this case, both Directory-Entry and DirectorySearcher will convert the attribute data to a single-dimensional array of bytes:

```
//given our DirectoryEntry entry
//and SearchResult result from our previous examples
byte[] sid =
    (byte[]) entry.Properties["objectSid"].Value;
sid = (byte[]) result.Properties["objectSid"][0];
```

What about Boxing of Value Types?

It is true that `System.Boolean`, `System.Int32`, `System.Int64`, and `System.DateTime` are all .NET value types or structures, yet the SDS collection classes cast them as `System.Object`. As developers, we should be aware that when value types are cast to and from reference types like `System.Object`, the .NET Framework does something called boxing and unboxing. A performance penalty is associated with boxing and unboxing, and many developers have been taught to try to avoid it when possible.

Unfortunately, this is one of the situations where we cannot avoid it. Because the LDAP data types are returned as a mix of reference types and value types, there really is no other way for the collection classes to work. Does this make things slower? Probably, but if we consider it in the overall scheme of things, it is not so bad. Nearly all of this data is retrieved via network calls and it goes through many layers before it gets to our code. Try to relax and not worry about it. Try some of the other performance tips we suggest in the book, and if you get desperate, you are probably using the wrong API. Check out SDS.P or consider dropping .NET entirely and look at the Win32 LDAP API instead.

If the attribute contains multiple values, we simply do the same thing in a `foreach` loop:

```
foreach (byte[] cert in entry.Properties["userCertificate"])
{
    //do something useful...
}
```

We can also use the `Value` property again here with `PropertyValue-Collection`. In the case of multiple values, it will return a jagged array of byte arrays.

COM Interop Data Types

We have already established that certain types of attributes require some form of COM interop with ADSI in order to use these values from

`PropertyValueCollection`, and we know why this happens. Now we will focus on the specifics for dealing with these types of attributes.

It is very helpful (and assumed for this book) that you have at least a basic understanding of COM interop in .NET. Specifically, we are talking about using a runtime-callable wrapper (RCW), a mechanism by which the .NET Framework can call into COM code.

Approaches for COM Interop

Essentially three different mechanisms are available for dealing with COM interop with ADSI.

- Create an RCW interop assembly with tlbimp.exe, or by setting a COM reference to activeds.tlb in Visual Studio .NET.
- Create our own interop assembly by hand, adding the specific type declarations needed to use the types in which we are interested.
- Use .NET reflection to late-bind to the ADSI types we wish to use.

We expand on these in detail in Appendix A. The code in this chapter shows a mix of the interop assembly and reflection approaches.

> **NOTE   DirectorySearcher Marshals These Types Differently**
>
> As we cover the following COM interop data types, we should keep in mind that `DirectorySearcher` marshals these values differently than `DirectoryEntry`, as previously explained. Where appropriate, we will attempt to show the differences between these classes when reading the COM interop types.

LargeInteger Values

Of the syntaxes that require COM interop, the `LargeInteger` syntax, 2.5.5.16, is the most common. A `LargeInteger` value is just an 8-byte integer. Active Directory uses this attribute syntax frequently for storing date/time values as well as the large numbers used for replication sequencing. ADSI returns this syntax using the `IADsLargeInteger` interface.

This interface exists primarily because the automation-compatible languages such as Visual Basic and VBScript do not support 8-byte integers directly. The ADSI designers solved this problem by returning a special type, IADsLargeInteger, which contains the eight bytes of data split into two properties, the HighPart and the LowPart, each containing four bytes of data in a standard VT_I4 variant that represents a 4-byte signed integer.

As developers, we are a little bummed that this type is not automatically marshaled directly into a System.Int64 for us using DirectoryEntry, given that .NET can easily support 8-byte integers.

■ **WARNING** **LowPart Is Not Really a Signed Integer!**

It seems like a very natural thing to fit one 8-byte integer into two 4-byte integers. We just split up the binary data into a HighPart and a LowPart and we are all set.

The problem is that both HighPart and LowPart are treated as normal signed integers, since that is what the COM variant types support. However, in reality, LowPart is not really a signed integer at all, but simply four bytes of data, or an unsigned integer at best. The main difference between a signed integer and an unsigned integer is that in a signed integer, the high bit indicates positive or negative, whereas in an unsigned integer, it just increases the value.

Thus, we cannot treat the sign of the LowPart as meaningful. Do not try to use addition to combine the values, or you may get intermittent surprises. If you see another sample that uses addition, it probably has a bug.

So, how do we actually read the value? Listing 6.1 shows how to do this in C#, with the reflection-based approach thrown in for good measure.

LISTING 6.1: Converting IADsLargeInteger to System.Int64 in C#

```
using System.DirectoryServices;
using ActiveDs;

DirectoryEntry entry = new DirectoryEntry(
    "LDAP://DC=domain,DC=com",
    null,
    null,
    AuthenticationTypes.Secure
    );
```

```
using (entry)
{
    object val = entry.Properties["lockoutDuration"].Value;

    Console.WriteLine(
        "Using ActiveDs Interop: {0}",
        GetInt64(val)
        );

    Console.WriteLine(
        "Using Reflection: {0}",
        LongFromLargeInteger(val)
        );
}


//using the RCW interop
static Int64 GetInt64(object largeIntVal)
{
    if (largeIntVal == null)
        throw new ArgumentNullException("largeIntVal");

    IADsLargeInteger largeInt;
    largeInt = (IADsLargeInteger) largeIntVal;
    return (long)largeInt.HighPart << 32 |
        (uint)largeInt.LowPart;
}

//decodes IADsLargeInteger objects into Int64 format (long)
//using Reflection instead of Interop
static long LongFromLargeInteger(object largeInteger)
{
    System.Type type = largeInteger.GetType();

    int highPart = (int)type.InvokeMember(
        "HighPart",
        BindingFlags.GetProperty,
        null,
        largeInteger,
        null
        );

    int lowPart = (int)type.InvokeMember(
        "LowPart",
        BindingFlags.GetProperty,
        null,
        largeInteger,
        null
        );

    return (long)highPart << 32 | (uint)lowPart;
}
```

In Listing 6.1, we showed two equivalent methods for decoding `IADs-LargeInteger` into a `System.Int64` (`long`). One method uses the RCW for activeds.tlb to create a strongly typed `IADsLargeInteger`, and the other method uses reflection to invoke back into the type at runtime and get the same properties. Notice how both functions use bit shifting and a cast to `uint` to convert the value? This is the proper approach. However, there is a problem if we are using Visual Basic .NET, as we may not have support for unsigned integers, depending on our version of the .NET Framework. Support for unsigned integers was only added to Visual Basic .NET in version 2.0 of the .NET Framework. In order to be fair, we include Listing 6.2, which will work in any version.

LISTING 6.2: Converting IADsLargeInteger to System.Int64 in Visual Basic .NET

```
Imports ActiveDs

Function ConvertToInt64(ByVal largeInt As Object) as Int64
    Dim data(7) As Byte
    Dim adsLargeInt As IADsLargeInteger
    adsLargeInt = Ctype(largeInt, IADsLargeInteger)

    BitConverter.GetBytes(adsLargeInt.LowPart).CopyTo(data, 0)
    BitConverter.GetBytes(adsLargeInt.HighPart).CopyTo(data, 4)

    return BitConverter.ToInt64(data, 0)
End Function
```

This one is going to seem a little weird at first. In order to get around the issues with unsigned integers in Visual Basic .NET, we use the `BitConverter` class to treat the data as raw binary. We essentially copy the individual byte arrays representing the component pieces to a new byte array, and convert that back to an `Int64` in the same way. Note that we copy the low part into the beginning of the array, as integer values on Intel platforms are "little endian."

Converting Int64 to DateTime

Oftentimes, we can represent the `IADsLargeInteger` that we convert to `Int64` by either a `DateTime` or a `TimeSpan` in .NET. Depending on the attribute, we just need to use one of the static methods on the `System.DateTime` class (`FromFileTime`, `FromFileTimeUtc`) or `TimeSpan`

(FromTicks) to do the conversion easily. We will have to know at some level whether the attribute represents an actual date/time (e.g., lockout-Time), or a duration (e.g., lockoutDuration), to decide which class to use for the conversion. Regardless, we must make sure to test the value to ensure that it is greater than zero (> 0) before passing it to the DateTime methods; otherwise, an exception will be thrown. Some attributes, like pwdLastSet, use 0 to indicate states other than an actual time, so caution must be used.

Using DirectorySearcher

When dealing with LargeInteger syntax attributes, it is often easier to use the DirectorySearcher marshaling behavior as opposed to using the IADsLargeInteger interface with DirectoryEntry. It returns an Int64 object directly, which is typically all we want in the first place. If we do not currently have a SearchResult, we can just use a base-scoped search on our DirectoryEntry and avoid the whole interop mess, as shown in Listing 6.3.

LISTING 6.3: Reading LargeInteger Syntax with DirectorySearcher

```
//use a base-scoped search
DirectorySearcher ds = new DirectorySearcher(
    user,  //this is our targeted entry
    "(objectClass=*)", //base level filter
    null,
    SearchScope.Base
    );

//we essentially convert our DirectoryEntry
//to a SearchResult to get the desired behavior
SearchResult result = ds.FindOne();

//now we get the different marshaling
//behavior we want (no IADsLargeInteger)
 long usnChanged =
     (long) result.Properties["usnChanged"][0];
//or...
 Int64 usnChanged =
     (Int64) result.Properties["usnChanged"][0];
```

Whenever possible, we should choose to use DirectorySearcher and SearchResult to read these attribute types. Trust us; it will make your life easier.

DN-With-Binary

The DN-With-Binary syntax, 2.5.5.7, is fairly rare and is primarily used by the wellKnownObjects and otherWellKnownObjects attributes in Active Directory. As we discussed in Chapter 3, when we talked about binding using WKGUID, these types of attributes associate a GUID value (the binary part) with a DN to allow an object to be identified by a published GUID value and still have a localized name in the DN.

DN-With-Binary syntax attributes are marshaled by the Directory-Entry classes as System.__ComObjects that can be cast to an IADsDN-WithBinary ADSI object. The interface is very simple and has no significant gotchas, as IADsLargeInteger does.

- The BinaryValue property contains the binary part and is marshaled as a byte[].

- The DNString property contains the DN part and is marshaled as a simple string.

Listing 6.4 shows an example of how we can get these two properties.

LISTING 6.4: Converting DN-With-Binary for WellKnownObjects

```
string adsPath = "LDAP://dc=domain,dc=com";

DirectoryEntry root = new DirectoryEntry(
    adsPath,
    null,
    null,
    AuthenticationTypes.Secure
    );

using (root)
{
    if (root.Properties.Contains("wellKnownObjects"))
    {
        foreach(object o in root.Properties["wellKnownObjects"])
        {
            byte[] guidBytes;
            string dn;

            //use our helper function
            DecodeDnWithBinary(
                o,
                out guidBytes,
```

```
                            out dn
                            );

                Console.WriteLine(
                    "Guid: {0}",
                    new Guid(guidBytes).ToString("p")
                    );

                Console.WriteLine(
                    "DN: {0}",
                    dn
                    );
            }
        }
    }


    //This is our reflection-based helper for
    //decoding DN-With-Binary attributes
    private void DecodeDnWithBinary(
        object dnWithBinary,
        out byte[] binaryPart,
        out string dnString)
    {
        System.Type type = dnWithBinary.GetType();

        binaryPart = (byte[])type.InvokeMember(
            "BinaryValue",
            BindingFlags.GetProperty,
            null,
            dnWithBinary,
            null
            );

        dnString = (string)type.InvokeMember(
            "DNString",
            BindingFlags.GetProperty,
            null,
            dnWithBinary,
            null
            );
    }
```

Similar to what we can do with IADsLargeInteger, we can use the
ActiveDs RCW interop approach, or we can simply use reflection to pull
both the BinaryValue and DNString properties at runtime. We chose to
show the reflection-based approach because this reduces runtime dependencies when deploying our application, but either approach is totally valid.

> **■ NOTE** DN-With-String
>
> Active Directory and ADAM also support another syntax, called DN-With-String, which is essentially just like DN-With-Binary, except that an arbitrary string is associated with the DN value instead of some binary data. We decided not to bother to show this because there isn't a single attribute in the Active Directory 2003 schema (Exchange Server 2003 installed and all) that actually uses the syntax. You would have to create your own in order to need to know how to do this. If you do, the mechanics are the same as those used with DN-With-Binary.

Using DirectorySearcher

The marshaling behavior on this type is interesting, as it is actually marshaled as a delimited string. We can simply parse the value to retrieve the GUID and DN values. Listing 6.5 shows one such example.

LISTING 6.5: Reading DN-With-Binary with DirectorySearcher

```
DirectoryEntry root = new DirectoryEntry(
    "LDAP://dc=domain,dc=com",
    null,
    null,
    AuthenticationTypes.Secure
    );

using (root)
{
    DirectorySearcher ds = new DirectorySearcher(
        root,
        "(objectClass=*)",
        new string[]{"wellKnownObjects"},
        SearchScope.Base
        );

    SearchResult sr = ds.FindOne();

    if (sr != null)
    {
        foreach (string s in sr.Properties["wellKnownObjects"])
        {
            string[] parts = s.Split(new char[]{':'});

            Console.WriteLine(
                "Guid: {0}",
```

```
                new Guid(parts[2]).ToString("b")
                );

            Console.WriteLine(
                "DN: {0}",
                parts[3]
                );
        }
    }
}
```

It can be advantageous to use `DirectorySearcher`, simply because we will not have to worry about the whole COM interop mess again. We just need to worry about safely parsing the returned string values.

Reading Security Descriptors

Security descriptors are interesting objects in Active Directory and ADAM. A **security descriptor** is actually a complex structure that contains several pieces, including a discretionary access control list (DACL) used for determining permissions on the object and a system access control list (SACL) that determines auditing behavior. However, the security descriptor itself is stored and retrieved as a single attribute value.

The really interesting part in all of this is that different types of users have different levels of access to the various parts of the security descriptor. For example, only administrators can read the SACL. Normal users cannot even see it!

So, if the entire security descriptor is read as a single piece of data, but only certain users can see the SACL, how exactly does that work? No other attributes in the directory allow us to see only certain parts based on our permissions, so this is a behavior we have not experienced so far.

The secret to making this work involves a special LDAP control that indicates to the directory what parts of the security descriptor should be returned as the result of a search. We may specify any combination of the owner, group, DACL, or SACL.

Here is where it gets tricky: If we request to read the security descriptor but ask for a part that we do not have access to (e.g., the SACL), it will silently fail and nothing will be retrieved at all. Additionally, if the special LDAP control is not used on the search, then the default behavior is to try to return the entire security descriptor. This will fail if we are not an administrator, as we do not have rights to read the SACL!

■ NOTE   Special Issues with Reading Security Descriptors with ADAM Principals

The actual problem with reading the SACL portion of the security descriptor is that it requires the `ACCESS_SYSTEM_SECURITY` privilege in the user's security token. Since this is given only to administrators by default, this effectively limits reading SACLs to administrators. ADAM users do not even have traditional Windows security tokens with privileges, so this effectively prevents an ADAM security principal from ever being able to read a SACL (or gain all administrative rights to an ADAM instance). According to our sources, Microsoft is looking at ways to solve this problem in a future version of ADAM.

The `DirectoryEntry` object makes this easy for us. By default, the underlying ADSI layer will automatically add the special control to search requests for the security descriptor and specify that everything but the SACL is returned. This default behavior gives us what we want nearly all the time, as we would rather have most of the security descriptor (and arguably the most important part: the DACL) than nothing at all. The downside here is that if we are actually binding to the directory with an administrative account and we really did want to read the SACL as well, we have to do some extra work.

The extra work is performed using the `IADsObjectOptions` interface, or by using the `DirectoryEntryConfiguration` class in .NET 2.0 or the `Invoke` method in .NET 1.x. All of these types provide ways of specifying which parts of the security descriptor should be returned. Listing 6.6 shows an example.

LISTING 6.6: Setting Security Masks for DirectoryEntry

```
//given a DirectoryEntry entry that we will
//retrieve the security descriptor on and wish
//to get the SACL for as well

//this approach works with .NET 2.0
entry.Options.SecurityMasks =
```

```
    SecurityMasks.Owner |
    SecurityMasks.Group |
    SecurityMasks.Dacl |
    SecurityMasks.Sacl;

//this approach works with any version of the framework
//but must be used on .NET 1.x

const int ADS_OPTION_SECURITY_MASK = 3;
const int ADS_SECURITY_INFO_OWNER = 0x1;
const int ADS_SECURITY_INFO_GROUP = 0x2;
const int ADS_SECURITY_INFO_DACL = 0x4;
const int ADS_SECURITY_INFO_SACL = 0x8;

int flags = ADS_SECURITY_INFO_OWNER |
    ADS_SECURITY_INFO_GROUP |
    ADS_SECURITY_INFO_DACL |
    ADS_SECURITY_INFO_SACL;

entry.Invoke("SetOption", new object[]
    {ADS_OPTION_SECURITY_MASK, flags} );
```

The behavior of `DirectorySearcher` is slightly different here. By default, it does not load the special control to modify security descriptor read behavior. As a result, the entire security descriptor is requested and we will receive a security descriptor only if we are bound as an administrator. In .NET 1.x, there is no way to modify this behavior.

.NET 2.0 addresses this by adding the ability to supply the security descriptor flags to `DirectorySearcher`. Chapter 5 contains a sample of how this is done.

Table 6.2 summarizes the behavior.

TABLE 6.2:   Security Descriptor Read Behavior

Type	Version	Default Security Descriptor Flags	Modifiable Behavior?
DirectoryEntry	1.x	owner, group, and DACL	Yes (Invoke method)
DirectorySearcher	1.x	ALL (no control sent)	No

TABLE 6.2: Security Descriptor Read Behavior *(Continued)*

Type	Version	Default Security Descriptor Flags	Modifiable Behavior?
DirectoryEntry	2.0	owner, group, and DACL	Yes (DirectoryEntry-Configuration)
DirectorySearcher	2.0	ALL (no control sent)	Yes (SecurityMasks property)

Data Types for Security Descriptors

Once again, the DirectoryEntry and DirectorySearcher classes behave differently here. When we read the ntSecurityDescriptor attribute directly from PropertyValueCollection, DirectoryEntry marshals security descriptors as a System.__ComObject data type containing an IADsSecurityDescriptor ADSI interface. This interface uses some additional ADSI interfaces to allow us to manage access control lists (ACLs) on directory objects. Access control itself is a fairly big topic that we cover in more detail in Chapter 8. Here, we will just show how the value is obtained using COM interop.

DirectorySearcher marshals security descriptors in binary format as a byte array. Various options are available to convert the binary format into something we can work with. See Chapter 8 again for more details.

The downside of the DirectoryEntry class' behavior is that we must use COM interop to work with this data type. .NET 2.0 solves this problem with a new property on the DirectoryEntry class, called ObjectSecurity. It allows us to read and write security descriptors using the new .NET managed access control list (MACL) classes. We will definitely prefer to use these new classes when possible. One important thing to note, though, is that this new property supports only the actual security descriptor on the object. If another attribute contains a security descriptor, as might be the case with some Exchange Server attributes, we will need to go back to COM interop.

Listing 6.7 shows a basic example.

LISTING 6.7: Reading Security Descriptors

```
using System.DirectoryServices;
using ActiveDs;

DirectoryEntry entry;
entry = new DirectoryEntry(
    "LDAP://DC=domain,DC=com",
    null,
    null,
    AuthenticationTypes.Secure
    );
using (entry)
{
    IADsSecurityDescriptor sd;
    sd = (IADsSecurityDescriptor)
        entry.Properties["ntSecurityDescriptor"]).Value;
    Console.WriteLine("owner={0}", sd.Owner);
}
```

In some cases, we may need to do an explicit RefreshCache to load the ntSecurityDescriptor attribute into the property cache before accessing it.

Using DirectorySearcher

Once again, we refer to the sample in Chapter 5 for a demonstration of using DirectorySearcher for reading a security descriptor.

Syntactic versus Semantic Conversion

At first blush, it may seem very straightforward to convert attribute values into the types we want. We can either check the type information at run-time using the .NET Framework's language support, or look up schema information (either programmatically or by hand, referring to the reference material). Using this, we should be able to convert any data type into a meaningful representation.

Unfortunately, this is not always straightforward. While we can certainly determine syntax via type information, it is a much more difficult (and interesting) problem to determine semantics. For example, let's say we encounter an attribute that contains binary data. We can easily convert this into a byte array using the techniques we have presented here, but what does the binary data actually mean? It could represent a GUID (objectGUID), a security identifier or SID (objectSID), an X509 certificate (userCertificate), a JPEG file (jpegPhoto), or practically anything else. Another good example is a LargeInteger syntax value. Windows often uses these to represent dates in FILETIME format (pwdLastLet), but also uses them to represent time intervals (lockoutDuration) and sometimes just uses them to represent really big numbers (uSNChanged). So, how can we determine this information?

In the general case, we cannot. There is simply not enough information stored in the schema or available from the .NET type system at runtime to make these kinds of judgments. At some level, we have to "know" what the attribute data means so that we can interpret it in a more meaningful way.

At some point, we will find ourselves in a position where we must make semantic interpretations about LDAP data. Every interesting problem will involve this kind of work to some degree or another. The more general the problem we are trying to solve, the more difficult this exercise will become.

Dealing with Attributes with Many Values

LDAP schema allows attributes to be either single valued or multivalued. However, in Active Directory and ADAM, multivalued attributes are really divided into two different categories: standard attributes and link value paired attributes. Link value paired attributes have a DN syntax (DS-DN, DN-With-Binary, DN-With-String) and have what is known as a linkID defined (see Chapter 7 for more details on the schema and linkIDs). DN syntax attributes without linkIDs and all other syntaxes have the standard multivalue behavior. In practice, nearly all DN attributes in the default schema are link valued, but they do not have to be.

The key difference here is the maximum limit on the number of values that are allowed for a multivalued attribute. Standard attribute values have a maximum number of elements, which is around 800 in Windows 2000 Active Directory and 1,300 in Windows 2003 and ADAM. Note that the actual maximum size may vary, but these numbers are as high as we can ever expect. However, link value paired attributes do not have a defined maximum number of values. In Windows 2000 Active Directory,

Microsoft recommends against DN link value paired attributes with more than 5,000 values because a variety of interesting problems can result, but the directory did not enforce this limit and many people exceeded it with mixed success. These issues were resolved in Windows 2003 and ADAM, so link value paired attributes are effectively unlimited again.

The problem for LDAP programmers is that Active Directory and ADAM limit the maximum number of attribute values that can be returned from a single attribute in a single search. Like paged searches (discussed in Chapter 4), this is done to improve the performance of the directory and to protect it from potential denial of service attacks. The maximum number of values that can be returned is determined by the `MaxValRange` LDAP policy, which is set to 1,000 in Windows 2000 and 1,500 in Windows 2003 and ADAM. This essentially means that `PropertyValueCollection` or `ResultPropertyValueCollection` will never have more than the `MaxValRange` number of values, regardless of how many values the attribute actually contains.

Given that the maximum number of allowed attribute values for standard attribute types is lower than these two limits, we see that standard attributes are not subject to this limitation and that only link value paired attributes are affected.

We could probably ignore this little detail altogether in most cases, except for the fact that one very important link value paired attribute, the `member` attribute, which determines membership in groups, runs into the `MaxValRange` limit with some frequency. If we are reading a group's membership, we probably would like to know all of the members, not just the first 1,500, so we have to do some extra work.

How to Use Range Retrieval in SDS

To get all of the attribute values, they must be retrieved using a process called **range retrieval**, where subsets of the attribute values are retrieved in subsequent requests. Instead of referencing the attribute by its normal name, we use a special syntax to specify the range of values we want to retrieve:

```
mvaAttributeToRead;range={low index}-{high index}
```

Here, `low index` and `high index` are numbers representing the range of results to be returned. Note that if `high index - low index` exceeds the `MaxValRange` policy, only a maximum of `MaxValRange` values will be returned. It is also acceptable to specify `*` for `high index` to always get back the maximum allowed number of results.

A typical algorithm will repeat the query using `low index = high index + 1` from the previous query. We know that we have retrieved all of the attribute values when the `high index` returned is `*` rather than a numeric value.

For example, we might request this:

```
member;range=0-*
```

...and receive this:

```
member;range=0-1499
```

In this case, we know that the attribute has at least 1,500 members, and probably more. However, we might also receive this in reply to the same request:

```
member;range=0-*
```

In this case, we can assume that the attribute has fewer values than the maximum range value, so additional searches are not required. This search contains all of the values. The tricky part about using range retrieval is that the `high index` of the attribute that we must look for will change to `*` when we request a range that exceeds the remaining number of values. However, we can use this to our advantage to detect when we have arrived at the last search in the range retrieval. Listing 6.8 demonstrates this technique.

Range retrieval works on only a base-level search. It is possible to use either `DirectoryEntry` or `DirectorySearcher` to do range retrieval, but our tests have shown that `DirectorySearcher` seems to perform a little bit better and is more straightforward to use.

LISTING 6.8: Range Retrieval Using DirectorySearcher

```
public static ArrayList RangeExpansion(
    DirectoryEntry entry,
    string attribute)
```

```
{
    ArrayList al = new ArrayList(5000);
    int idx = 0;

    //zero based index, so less 1
    int step = entry.Properties[attribute].Count - 1;

    string range = String.Format(
        "{0};range={{0}}-{{1}}",
        attribute
        );

    string currentRange = String.Format(range, idx, step);

    DirectorySearcher ds = new DirectorySearcher(
        entry,
        String.Format("({0}=*)", attribute),
        new string[] { currentRange },
        System.DirectoryServices.SearchScope.Base
        );

    bool lastSearch = false;
    SearchResult sr = null;

    while (true)
    {
        if (!lastSearch)
        {
            ds.PropertiesToLoad.Clear();
            ds.PropertiesToLoad.Add(currentRange);

            sr = ds.FindOne();
        }

        if (sr != null)
        {
            if (sr.Properties.Contains(currentRange))
            {
                foreach (object dn in sr.Properties[currentRange])
                {
                    al.Add(dn);
                    idx++;
                }

                //our exit condition
                if (lastSearch)
                    break;

                currentRange = String.Format(
                    range,
```

```
                        idx,
                        (idx + step)
                        );
            }
            else
            {
                //one more search
                lastSearch = true;
                currentRange = String.Format(range, idx, "*");
            }
        }
        else
            break;
    }
    return al;
}
```

We might call this helper method using some code like this:

```
ArrayList members = RangeExpansion(group, "member");
```

An interesting and possibly confusing aspect to range retrieval with `DirectorySearcher` is that the attribute name in `ResultPropertyValueCollection` includes the range syntax. Thus, we would have to look for `member;range=0-*` and not simply `member`. We should also note that Listing 6.8 works equally well with .NET 1.x and 2.0.

Basics of Writing Attribute Values

Much of the information we have learned about reading attribute data we can also apply to writing. However, there are a few basic rules to understand right off the bat.

- We must use the `DirectoryEntry` family of classes for writing attribute data. The `DirectorySearcher` family is strictly read-only.
- We must use the `LDAP` provider with Active Directory for updates. The global catalog is read-only. Therefore, any object obtained from the global catalog is also read-only, regardless of whether it is a `DirectoryEntry` object.
- If we are using the property cache (which we always recommend), we must call `CommitChanges` to write any changes back to the directory.

All changes are made to the in-memory property cache and will not be written to the server unless this is done.

- The directory will allow us to modify only those attributes that we have permission to modify.
- The directory will allow us to perform only those modifications that the schema allows, and potentially other specific rules governing writes to the attribute that are enforced by the directory.
- The directory will allow us to add only those values of the type defined by the attribute's schema.

The rules may seem obvious by now, but they come up as issues surprisingly often in practice.

`DirectorySearcher` makes it easy to switch to "edit mode" by using the `SearchResult.GetDirectoryEntry` method:

```
//given a SearchResult result that you wish to modify
using (DirectoryEntry entry = result.GetDirectoryEntry())
{
    //now, perform modifications on the DirectoryEntry
}
```

To switch from the GC provider to LDAP, create a new `DirectoryEntry` object with the LDAP provider.

■ NOTE   Switching from GC to LDAP May Require Changing Physical Servers Too

In order to switch from GC to LDAP, we need a domain controller in the domain where the object "lives." The global catalog server we were querying might be from a different domain, so this is not always straightforward.

Setting Initial Values

If an attribute has no value, we can use one of the following two approaches to set an initial value.

- Use the `PropertyValueCollection.Add` method.
- Use the `PropertyValueCollection.Value` method.

For example, to set the description attribute on a `DirectoryEntry` called `entry`, we might do this:

```
entry.Properties["description"].Add("a new description");
//or
entry.Properties["description"].Value = "a new description";
entry.CommitChanges();
```

We recommend avoiding using the array index accessor for setting values in general and especially for setting initial values, as it does not behave exactly the same way against all versions of the .NET Framework and ADSI, and it might cause unexpected problems with routine upgrades and service packs. For example:

```
//don't do this; it might not work as expected
entry.Properties["description"][0] = "a new description";
```

If we wish to set multiple values initially, we can use the `Value` property again, use the `AddRange` method, or call `Add` repeatedly:

```
//Do this
entry.Properties["otherTelephone"].Value =
    new string[] {"222-222-2222", "333-333-3333"};
//or this
entry.Properties["otherTelephone"].AddRange(new string[]
    {"222-222-2222", "333-333-3333"});
//or this
entry.Properties["otherTelephone"].Add("222-222-2222");
entry.Properties["otherTelephone"].Add("333-333-3333"});
entry.CommitChanges();
```

It may seem obvious, but keep in mind that using the `Value` property overwrites the entire attribute, which is why it is appropriate for setting initial values and not for simply adding to the existing values.

Clearing an Attribute

If an attribute is set and we wish to clear it, we can simply call the `Clear` method:

```
entry.Properties["description"].Clear();
entry.CommitChanges();
```

Alternately, the `Value` property can be used to clear an attribute value by setting it to `null` (`Nothing` in Visual Basic), but the `Clear` method seems to convey our intentions better.

Replacing an Existing Attribute Value

If the attribute value is already populated and we want to replace it completely with a different value, the easiest way to do this is with the `Value` property. Using our first example again:

```
entry.Properties["description"].Value =
    "a second description";
entry.CommitChanges();
```

When we set the `Value` property, it has the benefit of completely replacing the existing value with whatever we set in a single LDAP modification operation.

Adding and Removing Values from Multivalued Attributes

If the attribute has multiple values and we wish to modify only parts of it, we should use the `Add`, `AddRange`, and `Remove` methods. This is a very common thing to do when we're modifying membership on a group and we want to add or remove individual members:

```
//given a DirectoryEntry entry bound to a group:
entry.Properties["member"].Add(
    "CN=someuser,CN=Users,DC=domain,DC=com");
entry.Properties["member"].Remove(
    "CN=someotheruser,CN=Users,DC=domain,DC=com");
entry.CommitChanges();
```

If we are careful to check the values in the attribute before modification using the `Contains` method, we can avoid errors caused by adding duplicate entries or removing nonexistent entries.

Attribute Modification Summary

As we have shown, the `Value` property is extremely useful for attribute modifications. We can use it in just about any situation to set single and multiple values. It is also very efficient, as it uses a single `PutEx` call under the hood that results in a single LDAP modification operation. Additionally, the `Add`, `AddRange`, `Remove`, and `Clear` methods are very helpful and efficient under the hood, for similar reasons.

We generally recommend avoiding using array indexers on `Property-ValueCollection` for modifications. At the very least, changing a value using the array index will result in a remove and an add operation under the hood. In some situations, this simply will not work at all. The upcoming sidebar, Caution with Attribute Writing, provides more details about this problem. The other point here is that LDAP does not guarantee that multivalued attributes are stored or read in any specific order, so it is best not to think about them in that way, either.

Caution with Attribute Writing

As we already explained, SDS uses the ADSI `PutEx` method to handle write operations to ADSI objects. `PutEx` supports three types of operations: `Add`, `Delete`, and `Replace`. `Add` and `Delete` allow us to change individual values in an attribute, and `Replace` overwrites the entire value.

The original versions of SDS in .NET 1.0 and 1.1 had a very simple way of calling `PutEx`. Instead of allowing `PropertyValueCollection` to use the `Add` and `Delete` `PutEx` operations, SDS simply did a `Replace` operation on each change to `PropertyValueCollection`. Then, when changes were flushed back to the directory via `CommitChanges`, the entire attribute value was replaced in the directory.

Although this might seem inefficient (and it was in some respects), the simplicity of this model worked pretty well, except with one very important exception.

The Problem

As we covered earlier in this chapter, large multivalued attribute types in Active Directory and ADAM contain a maximum of `MaxValRange` (usually either 1,000 or 1,500) values in `PropertyValueCollection`. The problem, of course, is that doing a `Replace` operation on these types of attributes has the net result of truncating the attribute's value collection, effectively removing all of the values in the attribute that didn't happen to be in `PropertyValueCollection` at the time of the operation. Whoops!

The net result of this was that seemingly innocent edits to these attributes could have large and disastrous impacts. The really bad part of this is that one very commonly used and interesting attribute in Active Directory and ADAM, the `member` attribute that is used to define group memberships, was especially susceptible to this issue. Many developers inadvertently truncated very large Active Directory and ADAM groups, which obviously can be quite disastrous.

The Fix and the Consequences

The Directory Services team at Microsoft decided to fix this issue in .NET 1.0 SP3 and .NET 1.1 SP1 by changing the behavior of `PropertyValue-Collection`. In the current releases (including the 1.x service packs and .NET 2.0), the collection uses all three `PutEx` operations to send only the "deltas" to the directory. This avoids the problem we just described, and improves the efficiency of write operations to the directory, especially on large attribute values.

So, what's the problem? Unfortunately, this change introduced another problem. It seems that not all versions of ADSI allow multiple modification operations on the same attribute between updates to the directory. Essentially this means that we cannot do both a `Delete` and then an `Add` without an intervening call using `CommitChanges`, for example. The last modification would replace the first one and only the `Add` would be performed. Thus, a simple operation like changing a value at a certain index in `PropertyValueCollection` could result in a `Delete` and then an `Add`, which might not work.

To prevent developers from having all sorts of unexpected behavior performing seemingly innocent changes to attributes, SDS uses a new `IADs-OptionOptions` flag (`ADS_OPTION_ACCUMULATIVE_MODIFICATION`) which will determine at runtime whether multiple modifications are supported. If the platform does not support the required ADSI behavior, a `Not-SupportedException` is thrown.

This new behavior was disconcerting to many developers on the platforms that do not support multiple modifications, to say the least! Many developers used the syntax:

```
entry.Properties["someAttribute"][0] =
    "some new value";
```

to initialize or change attribute values and their previously working code suddenly started throwing exceptions when the .NET service packs were applied to their systems. Additionally, since the same code might behave differently on a developer's workstation than on the machine it was deployed to (depending on the version of ADSI), this was even more difficult to troubleshoot.

As of this writing, this issue does not affect Windows XP SP2+ and Windows 2003 SP1, and other versions of Windows require a hotfix (or the next service pack, if available). Thus, we should be especially aware of what code we write and where it will be deployed, taking care to get the latest hotfixes if necessary.

To steer clear of potential issues, one thing we can do that will help is always to use the Value property when intending to replace the current attribute value or to initialize it. For example:

```
entry.Properties["someAttribute"].Value =
    "some new value";
```

This results in only one ADSI PutEx operation, as PropertyValue-Collection is smart enough to treat writes to the Value property as Replace operations. Additionally, using the AddRange method rather than multiple calls to Add can result in more efficient code and fewer problems.

Quite a few Knowledge Base articles related to this issue are available, including 886541, 835763, and 894277. To determine if this new behavior is supported, we can use either IADsObjectOptions with the ADS_OPTION_ACCUMULATIVE_MODIFICATION flag or the new DirectoryEntryConfiguration object in .NET 2.0.

Writing COM Interop Types

We previously covered how to read these types, the special treatment required for handling them, and some of the differences between how `DirectoryEntry` and `DirectorySearcher` marshal the values.

Not much changes when writing these values, except that `Directory-Searcher` is out of the picture now. As we mentioned before, only `DirectoryEntry` can update the directory.

Writing LargeInteger Values

It turns out that it's a little more straightforward to write `LargeInteger` values than it is to read them. Listing 6.9 will produce an `IADsLargeInteger` from a `System.Int64` value.

LISTING 6.9: Converting Int64 Back to IADsLargeInteger

```
using ActiveDs;

public static IADsLargeInteger GetLargeInteger(long val)
{
    IADsLargeInteger largeInt = new LargeInteger();
    largeInt.HighPart = (int)(val >> 32);
    largeInt.LowPart = (int)(val & 0xFFFFFFFF);
    return largeInt;
}
```

For instance, we can use this to set an Active Directory user's account expiration date programmatically, as shown in Listing 6.10.

LISTING 6.10: Setting the Account Expiration Date

```
using System.DirectoryServices;
using ActiveDs;

DirectoryEntry entry;
entry = new DirectoryEntry(
    "LDAP://CN=Kaplan,CN=Users,DC=domain,DC=com",
    null,
    null,
    AuthenticationTypes.Secure
    );
DateTime accExp = DateTime.Now.AddYears(2);
Int64 accExpNum = accExp.ToFileTime();
entry.Properties["accountExpires"].Value =
    GetLargeInteger(accExpNum);
entry.CommitChanges();
```

Note that we are using our semantic knowledge of the accountEx-pires attribute to know that it is best to represent this attribute via a DateTime. We previously covered in this chapter that IADsLargeInteger objects can often be represented by a DateTime or a TimeSpan object. As such, we should use either the ToFileTime (for DateTime) or the ToFile-Ticks (for TimeSpan) method to first convert the value to an Int64 before converting to IADsLargeInteger.

Working with Visual Basic .NET

If we are lucky enough to be using Visual Basic .NET, we instead can use another function similar to that shown in Listing 6.11. In this case, we do not need to resort to the strange syntax with the BitConverter class as we did before when we were reading IADsLargeInteger, because the bit shifting and the conversion classes do what we want them to do.

LISTING 6.11: IADsLargeInteger Conversion in Visual Basic .NET

```
Imports ActiveDs

Function GetLargeInteger(ByVal val As Int64) As IADsLargeInteger
    Dim largeInt As New ActiveDs.LargeIntegerClass

    largeInt.HighPart = CType((val >> 32), Integer)
    val = val << 32
    val = val >> 32
    largeInt.LowPart = (Convert.ToInt32(val))
    return largeInt
End Function
```

However, if we are unlucky enough to still be using .NET 1.0 and we do not have a version of Visual Basic .NET that contains the bit shifting operators, then our best bet is to use the BitConverter class again. This ends up being very similar to the reading example, but in reverse.

Writing DN-With-Binary

Writing DN-With-Binary is a straightforward task. We simply need to create a new IADsDNWithBinary (or use an existing one returned via a read operation), set the two properties, and write the object to the attribute value. Listing 6.12 demonstrates this.

LISTING 6.12: Writing a DN-With-Binary Attribute

```
using System.DirectoryServices;
using ActiveDs;

DirectoryEntry entry;
IADsDNWithBinary dnb = new DNWithBinaryClass();

entry = new DirectoryEntry(
    "LDAP://DC=domain,DC=com",
    null,
    null,
    AuthenticationTypes.Secure
    );

//we would probably never use this example in actual practice...
dnb.BinaryValue = Guid.NewGuid().ToByteArray();
dnb.DNString = "DC=domain,DC=com";

using (entry)
{
    entry.Properties["otherWellKnownObjects"].Value = dnb;
    entry.CommitChanges();
}
```

■ NOTE   DN-With-String Omitted for Brevity Again

We are omitting a sample for the DN-With-String type because the actual approach is very similar to writing with DN-With-Binary, and once again, no actual attributes defined in Active Directory use this syntax. Should we happen to create one, the code is nearly identical.

Writing Security Descriptors

Writing security descriptors is also quite straightforward. Unlike with LargeInteger and DN-With-Binary types, we generally will modify existing security descriptors instead of creating brand-new ones. We should also point out that if we are using .NET 2.0, we will want to use the DirectoryEntry ObjectSecurity property to obtain and modify the ACL in managed code, instead of using COM interop.

We cover working with ObjectSecurity in detail in Chapter 8. However, .NET 1.x developers still need to know this (see Listing 6.13).

LISTING 6.13: Writing a Security Descriptor Using PropertyValueCollection

```
using System.DirectoryServices;
using ActiveDs;

DirectoryEntry entry;
IADsSecurityDescriptor sd;
entry = new DirectoryEntry(
    "LDAP://DC=domain,DC=com",
    null,
    null,
    AuthenticationTypes.Secure
    );

using (entry)
{
    sd = (IADsSecurityDescriptor)
        entry.Properties["ntSecurityDescriptor"].Value;
    //modify the security descriptor here...
    entry.Properties["ntSecurityDescriptor"].Value = sd;
    entry.CommitChanges();
}
```

As we indicated earlier, security descriptors can be quite complex and the subject of a book topic themselves. Finally, we should be aware that the IADsSecurityDescriptor interface has some interesting implications (also called "gotchas"), especially when used with ADAM or when running under a local machine security context. We also discuss these issues, and more, in Chapter 8.

SUMMARY

We now have a complete understanding of how to read and write attribute values to and from the directory using any syntax or data type.

We began with a comparison of the collection classes used by both DirectoryEntry and DirectorySearcher for reading attribute values. We then explored the various types of LDAP data types and explained how they are converted to different types by different layers of the system. We also explained how the schema mapping mechanism performs mappings from LDAP data types to ADSI data types as well as the differences between how these types are marshaled by the DirectorySearcher and DirectoryEntry classes.

After that, we dove into the details of reading all of the different types of attribute values. We focused heavily on the more troublesome types, including `LargeInteger` and security descriptors.

We finished up by describing how to write attribute values and covered the troublesome types again from the writing perspective.

■7■

Active Directory and ADAM Schema

I N THIS CHAPTER, we will provide some high-level guidance on designing schema extensions for Active Directory and ADAM, as well as some information on determining schema information at runtime. This information is meant to complement the schema basics we covered in Chapter 1.

This chapter does not explain every detail of extending the schema. Instead, we try to provide some guidance and tips that may not be easy to get from some other sources, as well as provide some perspective for enterprise developers who are probably coming from a relational database background in data design.

Unlike with relational database development, it is possible for an LDAP programmer never to modify the directory schema at all. In most organizations, getting approval to modify the Active Directory schema requires at least several meetings, and more often divine intervention. With ADAM, however, we are more likely to have the ability and the need to modify the schema.

Schema Extension Best Practices

This set of topics comprises a general list of best practices for designing schema extensions effectively. Some of this we were fortunate enough to learn from others, but some of it comes from our own embarrassing mistakes.

Read All of Microsoft's Documentation Carefully

Unfortunately, we cannot cover all of the intricacies of schema development in this short book, so we recommend a thorough reading of the schema documentation at MSDN[1] in addition to the nuggets of wisdom here. If possible, read the documentation twice (we did).

With that said, this topic is not that scary. Where there used to be some trepidation concerning changing Active Directory's schema (since it was "permanent"), today we can freely mess around with ADAM and even model our schema updates there first, to bring them to Active Directory later.

Register OIDs for New Classes and Attributes

All schema attributes must supply an Object Identifier (OID) to define the attribute or class uniquely across all LDAP directories. When we say "all LDAP directories," we really mean *all* of them, not just the ones internal to our organizations. Every OID used for a schema element should be unique globally. The OID is LDAP's version of the GUID (though the numbers have some meaning), and the LDAP specification requires it.

> ■■ **WARNING**   Do Not Invent OIDs!
>
> This is a bad practice and can lead to trouble. When shipping a product that requires schema extensions, it is imperative to register the OID. Never use a tool like oidgen.exe to create a random OID for a schema extension you might actually deploy. This type of tool might be appropriate for throwaway ADAM instances, but it is inappropriate for any type of production schema extension, shipping or otherwise.

So, where can we get an OID? Probably the easiest method is through Microsoft: It turns out that the company offers a service to do this.[2] An OID registered through this service is rooted in Microsoft's namespace, and in turn is used as the root for our custom OIDs. If the Microsoft OID service does not sound appealing, OIDs are also available from other

---

1. http://msdn.microsoft.com/library/en-us/ad/ad/extending_the_schema.asp
2. http://msdn.microsoft.com/certification/ad-registration.asp

standards bodies, such as the International Organization for Standardization (ISO), at no cost.

Developers planning on shipping a product that extends the Active Directory schema and wishing to get Windows logo certification must register their OID with Microsoft, regardless of where they obtained it originally.

Manage OID Namespaces Thoughtfully

If we had to register a brand-new OID for every single class and attribute we wanted to add to our directory, that process would be quite onerous. Luckily, we typically need to register only one or two OIDs for our entire organization and we are done. Here's how it works.

OIDs are essentially hierarchical naming structures, like the DNS system. Each additional OID suffix adds a new leaf to the tree. When we register to receive an OID from Microsoft, we will likely get a root-level OID similar to this:

```
1.2.840.113556.1.6.1
```

At this point, we will want to create two branches under this OID for attributes and classes (see Table 7.1).

TABLE 7.1: OID Prefixes

OID	Use
1.2.840.113556.1.6.1.1	Application classes
1.2.840.113556.1.6.1.2	Application attributes

Subsequently, we can add attributes sequentially so that our first attribute might be named 1.2.840.113556.1.6.1.2.1, and so on. The whole schema process tends to be centralized, since we seldom want anyone to add to our domain's schema or to ADAM's schema willy-nilly. This turns out to be a good practice, since we want to avoid naming collisions where an OID is duplicated or a random OID is simply made up.

In summary, as long as we have obtained a root-level OID from a valid registrar, we are guaranteed that our OIDs will not collide with another organization's OIDs. After that, as long as our own organization can manage its OID namespace effectively, we won't step on our own toes either.

Practice on ADAM Instances

One thing about LDAP schemas that takes a little getting used to for SQL developers is that schema modifications are more or less permanent in Active Directory and ADAM. While it is possible to set schema objects to a defunct state that prevents them from being used, we cannot actually delete them. Furthermore, a variety of attributes on schema elements can be set only at creation time. We do not have the luxury of simply dropping our tables and starting over.

As such, schema extensions require a little bit more thought than what some developers might typically put into defining SQL schemas. Before ADAM, this process could be a little painful, as many organizations would keep around a "junk" Active Directory on which to test schema extensions. However, today we recommend modeling all of our schema modifications on ADAM first, when possible, since ADAM instances are easy to bring up and tear down. If we make a mistake (which we inevitably will), it is easy enough to simply start over. We don't often have the luxury of starting over with a production Active Directory schema mistake, so be sure to test thoroughly before moving to production.

Set the schemaIDGUID Attribute

There is an additional unique attribute that we can set on classes and attributes, called `schemaIDGUID`, which contains a GUID value. This GUID is typically used in Active Directory and ADAM for applying security settings to individual attributes in access control lists (ACLs). This is how the directory is able to apply such fine-grained access control on directory objects.

We really want to set this value explicitly, because Active Directory and ADAM will create a random GUID for us if we don't specify one. This creates problems when we install the same schema extensions in a development and production environment, because we will need to apply different access control entries in each environment, as each attribute will have a different GUID. However, if we set the GUID explicitly, then we can simply publish this information and make things easier for consumers of our schema. If you examine the MSDN Active Directory Schema reference documentation, you will notice that Microsoft follows this practice.

Use Company-Specific Prefixes on ldapDisplayNames

In practice, we are much more likely to receive a naming collision from the actual name of an attribute than from the OID or even the `linkID` values. For instance, if we were creating a directory-enabled product and we were providing our own schema extension for customers to install, choosing an attribute name like `birthDate`, `ssn`, or `preferredName` might be a bad idea. It is highly likely that someone in our customer base has already used these names in their own schema extensions. Instead, it is common practice to prefix our attributes with our company or organization name to try to keep them unique (e.g., `acmeBirthDate` or `acme-BirthDate`). This rule of thumb applies to both classes and attributes. We have even noticed that Microsoft has begun doing this for some of its newer schema extensions, using the `msds-` prefix.

Choosing an Object Class

LDAP supports three different types of classes, called abstract, structural, and auxiliary. Each one has a different use.

- **Abstract classes**, similar to the object-oriented design principle of the same name, contain a base set of attributes that other objects inherit. No instances of an abstract class can be created in the directory. Instead, they must be subclassed from other abstract, structural, or auxiliary classes. The `top` class is an example of this type of class. Abstract classes can contain auxiliary classes in their definition.
- **Structural classes** are the only type of class that can actually have an instance in the directory. All structural classes derive from at least one abstract class (the `top` abstract class must be defined as the root class for all classes), but they can also derive from another structural class. These classes can contain any number of auxiliary classes in their definition.
- **Auxiliary classes** contain a collection of attributes (usually of a set or similar categorization). These classes can be part of any type of class,

but they must be derived from either another auxiliary class or an abstract class. Auxiliary classes can contain any number of other auxiliary classes as well. We typically use these classes to apply similar characteristics orthogonally to otherwise dissimilar classes. For instance, we would apply the `Security-Principal` auxiliary class to all classes that can represent security principals in Active Directory (users, computers, groups, etc.). Using our object-oriented design analogy again, auxiliary classes are a bit like interface definitions.

Most developers will typically be adding only a few attributes to existing classes. As such, they do not necessarily deal with creating a new class in the directory. However, when extending the schema to accommodate an application or a set of services, it is not a bad idea to group the attributes to be added into one or more auxiliary classes. This way, we can just add the auxiliary class to any type of object should we need to later, and all of our attributes will simply appear as part of the object. It will also serve as a logical grouping and as a single security grouping for the attributes. We can apply the security only to the auxiliary class and have it apply through inheritance to the attributes it contains.

If we are creating a new class where an actual instance will be created in the directory, it is important to give the `objectCategory` attribute some thought as well. In Windows 2000, the `objectClass` was not indexed, though it is indexed today in Windows 2003. This multivalued class holds the complete hierarchy of classes from which our class is derived (not including auxiliary classes). We never actually set this attribute, as it is created automatically when an instance is created and it cannot be changed. The `objectCategory` attribute, however, is a single-valued attribute that is indexed by default in all versions of Active Directory and ADAM. Its value is set to whatever is specified for the `defaultObjectCategory` on the structural class when an instance is created. It is meant to categorize object types across different structural classes and is often used for searching. For instance, the `contact`, `user`, `organizationalPerson`, and `person` classes share the same `objectCategory` attribute of `person`. This allows us to find information about a user across all types of objects that might represent them easily, using the `objectCategory` attribute in the search filter.

If we are to create our own structural class, it is best to set its `default-ObjectCategory` value to a common superclass if it is derived. Otherwise, the `defaultObjectCategory` value should be set to the class itself. For example, if we were to create our own type of user called `specialUser`, derived from the `user` class, we should probably set the `defaultObject-Category` value to be the `person` class in order to have our object returned as part of typical `(objectCategory=person)` types of searches.

Choosing Attribute Syntaxes

Most enterprise application developers and architects have a solid understanding of column data types in SQL repositories. However, LDAP syntaxes can be a bit mysterious at first. One of the most important aspects of LDAP schema design is choosing the appropriate attribute syntax for the data we wish to store. These pointers should help us to understand which attribute syntaxes to select based on the type of data we wish to store.

Throughout this section, we refer to attribute syntaxes by their OIDs and OM syntaxes, as this is how we define an attribute's syntax programmatically. Please refer back to Table 6.1 in Chapter 6 for a full listing of the available syntaxes and their LDAP OID and OM syntax values.

String Data

This is probably the most common data type we will want to store in LDAP. As we see in Table 7.2, there are a few options here.

TABLE 7.2: Various String Attribute Syntaxes

Syntax Name	LDAP Syntax	OM Syntax	Comment
String(Teletex)	2.5.5.4	20	Case insensitive for searching; Teletex characters only
String(Printable)	2.5.5.5	19	Case sensitive for searching; printable characters only
String(IA5)	2.5.5.5	22	Case sensitive for searching; IA5 string

TABLE 7.2: Various String Attribute Syntaxes *(Continued)*

Syntax Name	LDAP Syntax	OM Syntax	Comment
String(Numeric)	2.5.5.6	18	Contains only digits; rarely used in Active Directory
String(Unicode)	2.5.5.12	64	Case insensitive for searching; contains any Unicode character

Our recommendation is to use 2.5.5.12, the Unicode string syntax, for general-purpose string usage. The Unicode string will translate nicely back and forth with the standard System.String data type in .NET, which is also Unicode. The data is also case insensitive for searching, which is really what we want in almost all cases. Very rarely is a case-sensitive search a good or useful thing, and more often than not it will simply bewilder those who are querying the data.

Date/Time Values

The obvious thing to do here is to use 2.5.5.11 (UTC Time or Generalized Time), with either OM syntax 23 or 24 for UTC or Generalized time values, respectively. The major advantage of this approach is that ADSI and System.DirectoryServices (SDS) will marshal the data values in and out as .NET System.DateTime. This is extremely convenient from a programming perspective. The LDAP time formats are also searchable with >= and <= filter types, so there is no disadvantage there. We generally recommend using UTC time values rather than values that contain specific time zones.

The other approach is the one that Microsoft uses in Windows for many date/time values in Active Directory, such as the accountExpires attribute. Because Windows uses 8-byte FILETIME structures internally for so many time values, it was natural to use this format in Active Directory as well. The primary disadvantage of this approach is that data marshaling is so messy in ADSI and SDS (see Chapter 6), so we do not recommend following Microsoft's lead here, unless there is a really compelling scenario that supports this. We also need code to interpret time values stored in this format. We cannot use a normal LDAP search utility to read these values and know what they mean by simply looking at them. This is not the case with the standard UTC and Generalized time formats, which are human readable in their native format.

Numeric Data

For integer data, we almost certainly want to use 2.5.5.9 (`Integer` or `Enumeration`) for 4-byte `Int32` values and 2.5.5.16 (`LargeInteger` or `Interval`) for 8-byte `Int64` values. For floating-point numbers, however, there is no obvious way to proceed. We might consider storing them either as strings in a string syntax attribute or as binary data. The difficulty here is that there is no good way to force the directory to enforce any syntax verification on our numeric data if we use a string or byte array for storage, so this will have to be managed by the application instead.

Binary Data

Octet string, 2.5.5.10, is the obvious choice here. SDS and ADSI marshal this data as raw byte arrays, so that provides the easiest programming model. Alternately, we might consider using a string attribute to store Base64 encoded data, but there is no compelling reason to choose this option.

Boolean Data

Boolean, 2.5.5.8, is the obvious choice here as well. The data is marshaled as `System.Boolean`, so that is by far the easiest programming model. The primary thing to watch out for is that the attribute will likely be nullable, so we must use caution in our conversions. LDAP Booleans are generally "trinary" rather than binary. The `Nullable<T>` type in .NET 2.0 makes this easier to deal with, but it is still something to keep in mind.

Object Identifiers

This one is pretty obvious as well. If we need to store an OID, we should use the 2.5.5.2 syntax. This rarely comes up in typical enterprise data modeling exercises, but it may apply when doing work in cryptography or something similar that makes extensive use of OIDs.

Foreign Keys

Active Directory and ADAM support three different syntaxes for expressing the concept of a foreign key in LDAP: 2.5.5.1 or `Object(DS-DN)`, 2.5.5.7

or `Object(DN-Binary)`, and 2.5.5.14 or `Object(DN-String)`. The attribute types are also known as DN-syntax attributes and they receive special treatment in the directory. LDAP allows us to express relationships between our objects using both the object hierarchy and foreign keys. We should not hesitate to use these features when our data model suggests them.

In choosing among the three options, we essentially have to decide whether we want to express a foreign key relationship or whether we need to express a compound key that associates a foreign object with another piece of data.

In most cases, we will want simple foreign keys and should use the basic `Object(DS-DN)` 2.5.5.1 syntax. The vast majority of these types of attributes in Active Directory and ADAM are built this way. They have the additional benefit of having very simple marshaling to `System.String`. As we saw in Chapter 6, the story with `DN-With-Binary` and `DN-With-String` is not as good.

Several additional best practices are associated specifically with link value attribute design. We cover these in the upcoming section, Modeling One-to-Many and Many-to-Many Relationships.

Other Data Types

When we have a data type that does not fit neatly into one of these buckets, then our best bet is most likely to use either a string or a binary syntax and find a reasonable way to encode our data into one of those attributes.

Modeling One-to-Many and Many-to-Many Relationships

We can use any distinguished name (DN) attribute syntax (2.5.5.1, 2.5.5.7, or 2.5.5.14) to specify the DN of another object in the directory as the value for the attribute. If the other object is moved or renamed, the DN in the attribute value is automatically updated with the change. Any attribute defined with one of the DN syntaxes will have this sort of behavior.

This type of syntax allows us to express a type of foreign-key relationship with any other object in the directory. As anyone who has modeled data for relational databases knows, foreign-key relationships are extremely powerful mechanisms for expressing relationships between entities. However, since DN syntax attributes can be either single- or multivalued, it is much easier to express many-to-many relationships in LDAP than it is in a relational database. As we discussed in Chapter 6, multivalued linked DN syntax attributes also do not have any explicit limitations on the number of members (although there are complications in retrieving all the attribute values if we exceed a certain threshold).

To illustrate this topic, let's create a hypothetical DN syntax attribute called People-Who-Rock (`peopleWhoRock`) that will exist as part of the user object. This will be a multivalued attribute containing the DN for each user object representing people whom we like (they rock!). As the user accounts represented in this attribute are moved or renamed in the directory, their DN is kept up-to-date in our attribute. The system does all of this automatically (like magic). However, if we were one of the lucky people specified in the attribute, wouldn't it be nice to know at a glance who else thinks we rock?

Link Value Pairs

LDAP also allows for the notion of link value paired attributes. Comprising a forward-link and back-link attribute pair, these DN syntax attributes are commonly used in both ADAM and Active Directory. A back link is another DN attribute that the directory calculates to show the opposite relationship to its forward link.

From our previous example, let's suppose we create another attribute called People-Who-Think-We-Rock (`peopleWhoThinkWeRock`) to serve as the back link for our `peopleWhoRock` forward link. These two attributes together will comprise a new link value pair. Every time we add another DN into our `peopleWhoRock` attribute, our own DN will be added automatically to the `peopleWhoThinkWeRock` attribute on our target DN's object. This way, we can see both sides of the relationship. In this case, it is a many-to-many relationship, where the back link tracks all the objects that refer to its containing object in its forward link. If this does not sound familiar yet, a more familiar example of this might be the `member` and `memberOf` linked attributes.

Since the directory maintains back links dynamically, they are never edited directly. Only forward links can be edited. Continuing with our hypothetical attribute, we can update the `peopleWhoRock` attribute, but we cannot change the `peopleWhoThinkWeRock` attribute on any object. That is, we can always specify whom we think rocks, but we cannot force others to recognize our own greatness (too bad!). Another implication of this is that if our own object is renamed or moved in the directory, a change will be recorded for our object, but the subsequent update to the `peopleWhoThinkWeRock` back-link attribute will not result in an actual modification for any other object.

We establish forward links and back links by setting the `linkID` attribute on the `attributeSchema` object *during creation*. The formula for calculation is very simple: A forward link is indicated by an even integer, and its matching back link will be that number plus one. As an example, in Active Directory, `manager` is `linkID` 42 and `directReports` is `linkID` 43. Forward links can be of the 2.5.5.1, 2.5.5.7, or 2.5.5.14 (`DN-DN`, `DN-With-Binary`, or `DN-With-String`) syntax, however back links must have the attribute syntax 2.5.5.1 (`DN-DN`) to use linking.

DN Syntax Attribute Best Practices

When designing DN attributes, we should consider a number of best practices that can potentially save us a lot of pain down the road.

Consider Using Linking for All DN Syntax Attributes

Even if we currently cannot think of a reason to establish a link value pair when creating a new DN attribute, doing so is still generally a good idea. When an object is deleted, it is moved to a special container for deleted objects so that replication partners can also be made aware of the deletion. These deleted objects are collectively referred to as **tombstones**. A tombstone's DN is updated to a special syntax and most of the attributes on the tombstone are removed. For instance, if we were to delete a user's account (named Alice) that we had previously specified in our `peopleWhoRock` attribute, the DN for the deleted user would look something like this:

```
CN=Alice\
DEL:2e17b192-cadc-4eb9-8415-da3d2886ba88,
    CN=Deleted Objects,DC=domain,DC=com
```

The first newline character after `Alice\` is actually part of the DN itself, and the second one is there for formatting purposes only. Alice's user object is now a tombstone in the system that will be persisted for a period of time in the special `Deleted Objects` container until the system removes it.

Tombstones are treated very differently depending on whether a DN syntax attribute is part of a link value pair. If we had created only the `peopleWhoRock` attribute and we never create and link the `peopleWhoThinkWeRock` attribute, then our `peopleWhoRock` attribute will show Alice's tombstone's DN by default. We almost never want this behavior. If, however, we create and link both the `peopleWhoRock` and the `peopleWhoThinkWeRock` attributes, then when Alice's account is deleted, the DN will simply be cleared from the `peopleWhoRock` attribute, which is the behavior most developers would expect.

■■ **WARNING**   linkIDs Must Be Specified When the Schema Is Created

We learned this the hard way. If we fail to specify the `linkID` of an attribute when the schema is created, we have schema that does not behave the way we want and we cannot fix it. We must start over with new attributes (and possibly convert the existing data if this slips into production unnoticed). This is definitely something we will want to avoid.

This surprising behavior can lead to subtle bugs in applications (especially since we cannot read tombstone objects by default and they have almost no data in them), and it is usually not what we want.

■■ **TIP**   Forward Links Do Not Require Back Links

If for some reason, we are dead-set against a back link, we can still specify the `linkID` value for the forward-link attribute and get the other benefits of link value attributes, even though no back-link attribute exists. The behavior does not appear to be documented, but it is supported.

Another feature of linked attributes is that linked multivalued attributes actually behave differently than normal multivalued attributes. In Chapter 6, we discussed enumerating the values of large attributes and mentioned that only linked attributes can have an effectively unlimited size. Regular DN attributes are subject to the size limits that the directory imposes on normal multivalued attributes.

Back Links Are Multivalued and Are Added to the Top Class

When we design an attribute to be a back link to another DN-syntax attribute, it should always be multivalued and it should be added to the top class. If we think about it, this makes perfect sense, for several reasons.

- The directory will allow any class of object to be a value in a DN-syntax attribute. Therefore, the back-link attribute must be placed on a very general class that would be a parent of any object in the directory. The top class is the appropriate LDAP class for this, as it is essentially System.Object in the LDAP world.

- The directory will allow a forward-link attribute on several different objects to contain a link to the same object. As a result, the back-link attribute on the target object will need to contain multiple values. In our hypothetical linked attribute example, if more than one person thought we were awesome, our peopleWhoThinkWeRock attribute must contain multiple values. This is why all back links must be multivalued attributes.

Register linkIDs or Use Auto linkID Generation

The syntax for linkIDs is just a positive integer, as opposed to an OID or a GUID. These linkIDs also have to be unique in the directory, yet obviously, it is much easier to produce collisions with them. As we explained earlier, Microsoft offers a service to register an OID for your organization to use, and it also offers a service to register linkIDs for use within Active Directory. Use this! Do *not* randomly invent linkID values for use in the directory. Let's reinforce this point by way of a true story (the name has been changed to protect the innocent).

An Active Directory administrator—we will call him Steve—bought a vendor product that required a schema extension to Active Directory. This schema extension also introduced several link value attributes. The product installed well and Steve was very happy with its performance. Fast-forward two years: Now Steve wants to install the schema extensions required for

Microsoft's flagship email system, Exchange Server 2003. He runs the installer but gets an error that stops him flat. It seems that the linkIDs Exchange Server 2003 wants to use for its schema are already in use! Steve contacts Microsoft technical support and discovers that his other vendor has used linkID values that Microsoft already registered (correctly) for use with Exchange Server 2003. However, the vendor's schema is already in the directory, preventing Steve from installing the system. So to work around the problem, Microsoft has to create a customized version of the Exchange Server 2003 schema that will install on Steve's directory. As we might imagine, it took a fair amount of time and effort for everyone involved to resolve the issue, and it threw Steve's upgrade plans into a tailspin for a month or so.

The lesson here is that if everyone plays by the rules, no one gets hurt. It's simply too easy to create collisions with linkIDs to allow any laziness. We should always register any linkIDs we create.

One other option is available to us in Windows 2003 Active Directory and ADAM. These directories support a feature called auto link IDs. Instead of hardcoding linkID values, we can specify a special OID value for the forward link, 1.2.840.113556.1.2.50, and specify the ldapDisplayName attribute value of the forward-link attribute for the back link's linkID attribute. Eric Fleischman provides more details on this little-known feature in his blog.[3]

Search Flags and Indexing

We need to consider two more things when adding new attributes to the schema: how they will be indexed, and what other types of behavior we wish them to support. In Active Directory and ADAM, two flags control these behaviors: searchFlags and systemFlags. Both of these attributes represent a set of bitwise flags. Let's try to understand how they work so that we can set them appropriately.

searchFlags

Table 7.3 shows the values for the various searchFlags enumeration members and describes their use.

---

3. http://blogs.technet.com/efleis/archive/2004/10/12/241219.aspx

TABLE 7.3: Active Directory and ADAM searchFlags values

Flag Value	Behavior
1 (bit 0)	The attribute is indexed.
2 (bit 1)	The attribute is indexed and is also indexed in each container, so searches at a specific point in the hierarchy may be optimized. Requires 1 to be set as well.
4 (bit 2)	Add this attribute to the ambiguous name resolution (ANR) set (see Chapter 4). The attribute must also be indexed, so 1 (bit 0) must also be set.
8 (bit 3)	Specifies that the attribute value is preserved when the object is deleted (turned into a tombstone object). By default, most attribute values are cleared on deletion.
16 (bit 4)	Specifies that the attribute will be copied when the object is copied.
32 (bit 5)	Specifies that a tuple index for the attribute will be created. This improves searches where the wildcard appears at the front of the search string—for example, (sn=*mith). Note that this feature requires Windows Server 2003.
64 (bit 6)	Special index value used to enable Virtual List View (VLV) searches (see Chapter 5) on ADAM for versions past Windows Server 2003 SP1.
128 (bit 7)	Marks the attribute as Confidential in Windows Server 2003 SP1+. If this flag is set, the attribute data may be read only by domain administrators (by default), even if the ACL on the object would grant access to the data otherwise.

Unlike the `systemFlags` values, all of the flag values in `searchFlags` are intended for use by "end-user" schema enhancements. Generally, if we will be querying on the attribute, we will want to index it. Note that link value paired attributes are implicitly indexed on Windows Server 2003, so it is not necessary to set this flag in that case.

The flags generally speak for themselves. As with any database indexing, there is an inherent performance and storage implication for indexing, so we should make sure to index judiciously. Multivalued attributes can be especially costly to index.

ANR (see Chapter 4) is not something that is generally used, unless we are building some kind of address book lookup function. Remember that ANR searches can be especially costly, so definitely think twice before setting this value.

From Chapter 4, we learned about substring searches. Tuple indexes are a type of index meant to enhance these types of searches. Tuple indexes are also especially expensive and will provide a real performance benefit only if the substring searched is three characters or longer.

To use VLV searches on ADAM, we should make sure we have Windows Server 2003 SP1, and that we set the 64 value (bit 6) along with the 1 value (bit 0). Otherwise, VLV will not work properly.

The new 128 (bit 7) flag is especially intriguing, as it provides an easy mechanism to hide data in Active Directory without having to use elaborate ACL schemes. We might use this for storing Social Security numbers or something similar, although this data will still be available to domain administrators. As such, we should consider its use carefully.

The MSDN documentation[4] provides more detail on searching behavior and on these flag values.

systemFlags

Unlike `searchFlags`, many of the `systemFlags` values are not intended for general use. For example, Active Directory and ADAM provide no extensibility mechanism for populating constructed attributes, so we probably will not be setting bit 2. In general, we probably should not be setting anything other than bit 0 or 1. Table 7.4 provides the full documentation.

TABLE 7.4: Active Directory and ADAM systemFlags values

Flag Value	Behavior
1 (bit 0)	Prevents an attribute from being replicated.
2 (bit 1)	Adds the attribute to the global catalog in Active Directory only, not in ADAM.
4 (bit 2)	Indicates a constructed attribute.

---

4. www.microsoft.com/technet/prodtechnol/windowsserver2003/library/TechRef/8196d68e-776a-4bbc-99a6-d8c19f36ded4.mspx

TABLE 7.4:   Active Directory and ADAM systemFlags values *(Continued)*

Flag Value	Behavior
16 (bit 4)	Indicates that an attribute is Class 1, which essentially means it is part of the base schema and has special rules applied to it. Generally, only Microsoft uses this, but OEMs who bundle ADAM with their product might use it as well.
32 (bit 5)	Indicates that an attribute is available only via a base-level search.
33554432 (bit 26)	The object is deleted immediately instead of being moved to the Deleted Objects container.
67108864 (bit 27)	The object cannot be moved to a new location in the directory.
134217728 (bit 28)	The object cannot be renamed.
268435456 (bit 29)	Allows an object in the Configuration partition to be moved with restrictions. It is not set by default. Note that this value must be set at creation time and cannot be changed later.
536870912 (bit 30)	Allows an object in the Configuration partition to be moved. It is not set by default. Note that this value must be set at creation time and cannot be changed later.
1073741824 (bit 31)	Allows an object in the Configuration partition to be renamed. It is not set by default. Note that this value must be set at creation time and cannot be changed later.
2147483648 (bit 32)	The object cannot be deleted at all.

We are uncertain what bits 3 and 6–25 do, as Microsoft does not officially document them.

Techniques for Extending the Schema

Creating and updating the directory's schema can be done the same way as any other update to a directory's objects. We discussed how to create and modify objects in Chapters 3 and 6 and these techniques are still valid for schema objects as well. It is possible to use any of the various tools or APIs that can perform these operations. In fact, for .NET version 2.0 users, there is pretty good support for all things schema related using the `ActiveDirectorySchema*` classes in the `System.DirectoryServices.ActiveDirectory` (SDS.AD) namespace.

As such, you might be surprised to hear us recommend *not* using SDS to create or modify schema. After all, it does work, and it is the API this book is primarily about. Why not use it here too?

Instead, we propose to stick with using Lightweight Data Interchange Format (LDIF) scripts, which are standard ASCII-based scripts, for declaratively updating the directory. Both Active Directory and ADAM ship with an LDIF client (called LDIFDE.exe). There are a few reasons for suggesting LDIF as your primary tool for performing schema extensions.

- Schema extensions are performed infrequently and are generally performed by administrators, not developers, especially with Active Directory, which requires high privileges for schema modification.
- LDIF makes it very easy to keep a record of schema modifications so that we can perform them again later, perhaps when moving between a development and a production environment or from ADAM to Active Directory.
- Compiled code is fairly opaque to administrators, who typically prefer LDIF scripts for their readability. Very few administrators will simply trust a compiled program to update their directory, unless they wrote it themselves. LDIF scripts are easy to read, and as such, administrators can view what they are supposed to do.

Is it still possible to extend the schema with SDS? Of course! However, we do not believe this should be done as a general rule. There will always be cases where this is the appropriate thing to and we leave that to your discretion. We will include some samples at the book's web site for performing these operations should we need them.

If we think about it for a moment, we do not often find ourselves building a SQL database with ADO.NET calls, do we? Instead, it is far more prevalent to script out the database design in a set of files that contain DDL statements, and then execute them with a tool such as a query analyzer (or to hand them over to a database administrator!). The same basic theory applies here as well.

We do not attempt to provide a tutorial on LDIF here, but there are a variety of online resources that can help with this, including the Microsoft online documentation we already referenced. The tool and file syntax are very straightforward and developers or administrators should not have any difficulty using them.

Discovering Schema Information at Runtime

SDS and ADSI provide a number of mechanisms to discover schema at runtime. For .NET 2.0 developers, the new SDS.AD namespace provides a nice, strongly typed model for accessing schema information. For .NET 1.x developers, COM interop is required to get this same information. Common to both models are the `IADsClass`, `IADsProperty`, and `IADsSyntax` interfaces, which are commonly referred to as the "abstract schema" since they represent schema information that has been interpreted by ADSI. ADSI also provides a special LDAP path syntax for retrieving these objects. Although this syntax is rarely used, it is available and it looks something like this:

```
LDAP://schema/<schemaobject>
```

In this example, `<schemaobject>` represents the desired schema object. It turns out that SDS.AD uses this same syntax internally to get schema information.

As shown in Listing 7.1, we can determine the schema for an object dynamically at runtime using the `SchemaEntry` property from any `DirectoryEntry`. This particular code is most appropriate when using version 1.x, though it will work for all versions of the framework.

LISTING 7.1: Determining Available Schema at Runtime

```
DirectoryEntry user = new DirectoryEntry(
    "LDAP://DC=domain,DC=com",
    null,
    null,
    AuthenticationTypes.Secure
    );

using (user)
```

```csharp
using (DirectoryEntry schema = user.SchemaEntry)
{
    Type t = schema.NativeObject.GetType();

    object inferiors = t.InvokeMember(
        "Containment",
        BindingFlags.Public | BindingFlags.GetProperty,
        null,
        schema.NativeObject,
        null
        );

    if (inferiors is ICollection)
    {
        Console.WriteLine("Possible Inferiors");
        Console.WriteLine("=====================");
        foreach (string s in ((ICollection) inferiors))
        {
            Console.WriteLine(s);
        }
    }

    object optional = t.InvokeMember(
        "OptionalProperties",
        BindingFlags.Public | BindingFlags.GetProperty,
        null,
        schema.NativeObject,
        null
        );

    if (optional is ICollection)
    {
        foreach (string s in ((ICollection) optional))
        {
            Console.WriteLine("Optional: {0}", s);
        }
    }

    object mand = t.InvokeMember(
        "MandatoryProperties",
        BindingFlags.Public | BindingFlags.GetProperty,
        null,
        schema.NativeObject,
        null
        );

    if (mand is ICollection)
    {
        foreach (string s in ((ICollection) mand))
        {
```

```
                    Console.WriteLine("Mandatory: {0}", s);
                }
            }
        }
```

Things are a bit easier with .NET 2.0 and the new `ActiveDirectory` namespace. As Listing 7.2 shows, not only can we return the same information as Listing 7.1, but also we can easily glean additional information about the attributes, something that we could not do in version 1.x without significantly more code.

LISTING 7.2: Dynamic Schema Information Using Version 2.0

```
using System.DirectoryServices.ActiveDirectory;

ActiveDirectorySchemaClass schema =
ActiveDirectorySchemaClass.FindByName(
        new DirectoryContext(
            DirectoryContextType.DirectoryServer,
            "localhost:389"),
        "organization"
    );

Console.WriteLine("Possible Inferiors");
Console.WriteLine("=============");
foreach (ActiveDirectorySchemaClass adsc in
schema.PossibleInferiors)
{
    Console.WriteLine("{0}",adsc.Name);
}
Console.WriteLine("=============");

foreach (ActiveDirectorySchemaProperty prop in
schema.MandatoryProperties)
{
    Console.WriteLine("=============");
    Console.WriteLine("Attribute {0}",prop.Name);
    Console.WriteLine("Syntax: {0}",prop.Syntax);
    Console.WriteLine("Indexed: {0}",prop.IsIndexed);
    Console.WriteLine("In GC: {0}",prop.IsInGlobalCatalog);
}

foreach (ActiveDirectorySchemaProperty prop in
schema.OptionalProperties)
{
    Console.WriteLine("=============");
    Console.WriteLine("Attribute {0}",prop.Name);
    Console.WriteLine("Syntax: {0}",prop.Syntax);
```

```
        Console.WriteLine("Indexed: {0}",prop.IsIndexed);
        Console.WriteLine("In GC: {0}",prop.IsInGlobalCatalog);
    }
```

Listings 7.1 and 7.2 show similar methods for returning the attributes found on any given class. This is not the only way to determine all of the attributes available in a given class, however. We can also use a few attributes on each object to determine this information dynamically as well.

Using Constructed Attributes

Two constructed attributes, `allowedChildClasses` and `allowedAttributes`, allow us to determine which classes may be children of the current object and which attributes the current object may contain (including constructed attributes), respectively. As we discussed in Chapter 6, constructed attributes require an explicit `RefreshCache` call when using `DirectoryEntry`. Listing 7.3 shows a brief example using these attributes.

LISTING 7.3: Determining Schema Using Constructed Attributes

```
    string adsPath = "LDAP://dc=domain,dc=com";

    DirectoryEntry root = new DirectoryEntry(
        adsPath,
        null,
        null,
        AuthenticationTypes.Secure
        );

    using (root)
    {
        root.RefreshCache(
            new string[]
                {"allowedChildClasses", "allowedAttributes"}
        );

        Console.WriteLine("Possible Inferiors");
        Console.WriteLine("=====================");
        foreach (string s in
            root.Properties["allowedChildClasses"])
        {
            Console.WriteLine(s);
        }
        Console.WriteLine("=====================");

        Console.WriteLine("Available Attributes");
```

```
        Console.WriteLine("=====================");
        foreach (string s in
            root.Properties["allowedAttributes"])
        {
            Console.WriteLine(s);
        }
    }
```

The `allowedAttributes` attribute actually is nothing more than `OptionalProperties` and `MandatoryProperties` combined. If we are not interested in the difference between what is optional and what is mandatory, this attribute is probably easier to use for the same information. The `allowedChildClasses` attribute contains the same information as the `Containment` property from ADSI, and the `PossibleInferiors` property from the `ActiveDirectorySchemaClass` class. Likewise, it can be easier to use than COM interop, or than creating a new class.

However, we might also want to know what attributes we can actually update given our security context. To do so, we need to look to some other attributes that hold this information. Given that this information would be dynamic depending on the client's security context, it makes sense that these should be calculated dynamically by the system and thus that they belong to a constructed attribute. The two attributes we are interested in are `allowed-AttributesEffective` and `allowedChildClassesEffective`. These two attributes contain the names of the classes and attributes that our current security context has permission to update. This is quite useful for developers wishing to dynamically generate a UI and show only the attributes a given user might be able to edit. The code for using these attributes is identical to that in Listing 7.3, but we include in Listing 7.4 for completeness.

LISTING 7.4: Determining Modifiable Attributes and Creatable Classes

```
string adsPath = "LDAP://dc=domain,dc=com";

DirectoryEntry root = new DirectoryEntry(
    adsPath,
    null,
    null,
    AuthenticationTypes.Secure
    );

using (root)
{
```

```
root.RefreshCache(
    new string[]
        {"allowedChildClassesEffective",
         "allowedAttributesEffective"}
);

Console.WriteLine("Effective Child Classes");
Console.WriteLine("=====================");
foreach (string s in
    root.Properties["allowedChildClassesEffective"])
{
    Console.WriteLine(s);
}
Console.WriteLine("=====================");

Console.WriteLine("Effective Attributes");
Console.WriteLine("=====================");
foreach (string s in
    root.Properties["allowedAttributesEffective"])
{
    Console.WriteLine(s);
}
}
```

Reading Schema Objects Directly

Finally, since the LDAP schema for Active Directory and ADAM is stored in the schema naming context, we can always read it directly via LDAP queries. This is a much "closer to the metal" type of approach, since it will be completely up to us to interpret the objects and attributes encountered. As such, it is naturally more complicated to get identical information using this approach than it is using the two other approaches we have shown at this point. However, we should also point out that this is still a very viable approach and is sure to work with all LDAP directories, not just with Active Directory or ADAM. As an example, this technique can be especially helpful if we want to check for possible naming collisions on attributeID, schemaIDGUID, and linkID.

SUMMARY

In this chapter, we tried to cover the important tidbits regarding schema planning and implementation that are relevant to developers. We hope we gave a good flavor of what is available and provided some otherwise hard-to-find guidance. We still recommend reading MSDN's documentation on schema extensions in addition to following the nuggets of wisdom we presented here. The documentation can provide a good starting point, as well as the history and methodology around all things schema related.

8

Security in Directory Services Programming

I N THIS CHAPTER, we take a deeper look at security. We elaborate on the basics introduced in the previous chapters and explore some additional topics we have not yet mentioned.

The first part of the chapter is dedicated to binding and the security context. This is by far one of the most important concepts to understand, as it affects everything we try to do. It is also the primary reason why code fails to perform as expected and is quite often the first thing to investigate when troubleshooting.

The second part of the chapter deals with security settings on individual objects and applies to Active Directory and ADAM. Both Active Directory and ADAM use the standard Windows security descriptor model for securing objects and take advantage of the directory hierarchy to harness the inheritance model supported by security descriptors, much like the Windows file system or registry does. Active Directory and ADAM support security settings all the way down to individual attributes on objects, and we will discuss how to program this model using .NET with version 2.0 and the earlier 1.x release.

Finally, we take a brief but important look at code access security (CAS) and the notion of partially trusted code. This aspect of the .NET security model is often ignored and is not well understood by most developers, but it is critically important at least to know the basics, especially when programming in a partially trusted environment. As Windows itself matures, partial trust scenarios will become increasingly common. We discuss how `System.DirectoryServices` (SDS) and `System.Directory-Services.ActiveDirectory` (SDS.AD) play in this space.

Binding and Delegation

Binding controls the authenticated security context of the client when it performs LDAP operations on the server. Because the server typically performs authorization on every operation requested by the client, establishing an authenticated security context with the server is essential.

A lot of options are involved with binding, especially in Windows, so we devote a significant amount of space in this chapter to explaining the details. As we have suggested previously, binding and security issues are the most common source of problems in .NET directory services programming, so it is well worth the time to try to understand it fully.

In SDS, the `DirectoryEntry` object is responsible for performing all binding operations. The other core object, `DirectorySearcher`, relies completely on `DirectoryEntry` in its `SearchRoot` property to determine its security context. Even if we do not explicitly specify a `SearchRoot`, we should keep in mind that one will be created for us.

Types of Binds

In LDAP terms, there are essentially two types of binds: a **simple bind** and a bind that uses a **Simple Authentication and Security Layer** (SASL) mechanism to perform the authentication. A simple bind requires plaintext credentials and transmits them on the network in clear text. As such, they are certainly simple, but obviously not secure.

SASL is much more interesting. SASL is defined in RFC 2222 and specifies an extensible mechanism where various authentication protocols such as Kerberos, NTLM, and Digest can plug into the SASL structure, providing access to these authentication protocols via LDAP (and any other protocols that use SASL; it is a separate specification that is not part of LDAP).

A directory may support various SASL mechanisms, and it advertises which ones it supports via the `RootDSE` object we discussed in Chapter 3 in the `supportedSASLMechanisms` attribute. Active Directory supports the **GSSAPI**, **GSS-SPNEGO**, **EXTERNAL**, and **DIGEST-MD5** SASL mechanisms.

GSS-SPNEGO is Microsoft's SASL implementation of the Windows **Negotiate** protocol, which is the standard authentication protocol for Windows 2000 and later. The Negotiate protocol is often misunderstood to mean that Kerberos will be attempted first and NTLM will be the fallback protocol. Actually, Negotiate means that the protocol will negotiate with the server which protocol will be used based on its capabilities, and only one is ever tried. This is an important distinction, because certain types of attacks are prevented that could be caused if an attacker could arbitrarily downgrade authentication to NTLM.

GSSAPI is a component that is typically provided with standard Kerberos implementations and is included with Microsoft's Kerberos for standards interoperability. Digest implements the MD5 Message-Digest algorithm (RFC 1321). EXTERNAL is how Microsoft implements client certificate authentication with SSL/LDAP.

From the ADSI and SDS perspectives, we really are interested in two types of binds: the simple bind and the SASL bind with GSS-SPNEGO. These are reflected via the `AuthenticationTypes.None` and `AuthenticationTypes.Secure` enumeration values. ADSI and SDS do not provide access to the other mechanisms.[1] We will refer to GSS-SPNEGO SASL binds as "secure" binds from now on.

Where simple binds always require a username and password to be specified, secure binds can accept credentials or use the credential information from the current Windows security context. This additional feature is extremely powerful and enables a new class of available scenarios for binding. However, this feature also provides no end of trouble when it is not understood fully, due to some of the underlying complexity of Windows security itself.

---

1. This is not completely true, as ADSI does support client certificate authentication with SSL, and ADSI in Windows Server 2003 will attempt Digest authentication if `AuthenticationTypes.Secure` is specified and the server advertises that it supports Digest authentication but not the Negotiate protocol. However, we do not have explicit control over these options and they are rare cases that affect very few scenarios.

LDAP Bind versus ADSI Bind

We use the term "bind" slightly differently when talking about ADSI than we do when talking about the raw LDAP API. When discussing ADSI and SDS, we generally say we are "binding to an object," whereas with LDAP, we say we are "binding to the directory" itself. An LDAP bind changes the state of the persistent connection, but does not access any specific objects in the directory.

So, which is it? As we might expect, since ADSI uses LDAP under the hood, the LDAP bind authenticates the client connection to the directory and does not access a specific object. However, when we do a bind in ADSI, we do specify a specific object to "bind" to, so ADSI actually binds to the directory (if it is not already bound) and then performs a search to locate the object and read its attributes.

Since ADSI and SDS do specify an object when binding in the `Path` property, we will continue to use the words "bind to an object," even if it is not the technically correct definition of a bind in LDAP terms.

Performing a Secure Bind

As we previously stated, secure binds allow for us to bind to the directory with either the current Windows security context or explicitly provided credentials. To perform a secure bind in SDS, we thus have two options with the `DirectoryEntry` constructors.

- Use default credentials (`null`/`Nothing` for the `username` and `password` parameters).
- Supply specific credentials and use the `Authentication-Types.Secure` flag.

Using default credentials might look like this:

```
DirectoryEntry entry = new DirectoryEntry(
    "LDAP://DC=mydomain,DC=com");
```

We can also write code that does the exact same thing, like this:

```
DirectoryEntry entry = new DirectoryEntry(
    "LDAP://DC=mydomain,DC=com",
    null,
    null);
```

To supply explicit credentials, we can write code like this:

```
DirectoryEntry entry = new DirectoryEntry(
    "LDAP://DC=mydomain,DC=com",
    "mydomain\someone",
    "MyBig!Secret88",
    AuthenticationTypes.Secure);
```

Note that we can also use the constructor that just takes the `username` and `password` parameters and rely on the fact that it sets the default value for `AuthenticationTypes` to `AuthenticationTypes.Secure`. However, we generally prefer being explicit to avoid confusion.

It is also possible to combine default credentials with the `AuthenticationTypes.Secure` flag, as we often do in our code examples:

```
DirectoryEntry entry = new DirectoryEntry(
    "LDAP://DC=mydomain,DC=com",
    null,
    null,
    AuthenticationTypes.Secure);
```

We again tend to prefer this syntax, as it is more explicit and makes the intent of our code easier to decipher. We are not relying on any default behaviors that might possibly change or be misunderstood by our successors. See the warning titled Behavior Change in .NET 2.0! for an example of how we can already get into trouble.

The important thing to note here is that if we supply default credentials, a secure bind is always attempted, regardless of our `Authentication-Types`. This seems like a little unintuitive at first and is one of the reasons we always try to be explicit in our code. Even though we tend to use the `AuthenticationTypes.None` flag when we intend to do a simple bind, if we also supply `null` for the `username` and `password` parameters, we will not get a simple bind. We will get a secure bind.

This makes sense when we think about it, as the `Authentication-Types.None` value is equal to zero. It isn't a real value at all for bitwise operations! When this flag is combined with other flags, it does not change the overall value. For example:

```
AuthenticationTypes.None | AuthenticationTypes.Secure =
    AuthenticationTypes.Secure
```

As such, `AuthenticationTypes.None` is useful when supplying specific credentials, but it makes no sense to use it when we are not. When it is combined with other flags, it does not change the overall value. We tend to use it this way only to help convey our intent that we want a simple bind.

Being able to use the current security context is very powerful in that we do not need to hardcode any credentials, or prompt the user who is executing the code to supply them. Unfortunately, this feature gets us into trouble in many cases, as it makes certain assumptions about the current security context that may or may not be true. The rest of this section is dedicated to exploring these issues.

Windows Security Contexts

It is important to have a reasonable understanding of what we mean by Windows security contexts before moving any further. This subject is reasonably large in and of itself and a complete treatment is not possible, so we refer to Keith Brown's book,[2] *The .NET Developer's Guide to Windows Security*, for the full story.

Each thread executing code inside a Windows NT-based process (Windows NT all the way through 2000, XP, 2003, Vista, and beyond) will have a security context represented by a Windows security token that governs the rights and privileges that will be granted to code executing on that thread. In general, the token that will be used by the thread for security purposes is the token that was used to start the underlying process. This is determined by whom and how the process was originally created. Processes launched by an interactive user will use the token associated with that user's log-on session. Processes such as Windows services will use the

---

2. Brown, K. 2004. *The .NET Developer's Guide to Windows Security.* Boston: Addison-Wesley.

> **⬛ WARNING**   Behavior Change in .NET 2.0!
>
> What happens if we do not specify any `AuthenticationTypes` in our constructor? Obviously, the `DirectoryEntry` must have some sort of default behavior, but what? Let's take a simple example:
>
> ```
> //What is the difference between this...
> DirectoryEntry de = new DirectoryEntry(
>     "LDAP://mydomain.com/RootDSE", user, password);
>
> //...and this?
> DirectoryEntry de2 = new DirectoryEntry(
>     "LDAP://mydomain.com/RootDSE");
> de2.Username = user;
> de2.Password = password;
> ```
>
> In .NET 1.x, `AuthenticationTypes` on the `DirectoryEntry` was set to `None` for some constructors and `AuthenticationTypes.Secure` for others. As a result, the two `DirectoryEntry` objects in the preceding code will produce different binds. The first one will produce a secure bind, but the second one will result in a simple bind with credentials passed in plaintext over the network.
>
> Since this behavior is inherently insecure, Microsoft changed in version 2.0 and now always uses `AuthenticationTypes.Secure` as the default if the developer did not specify anything. The result is that the .NET 2.0 `DirectoryEntry` is secure by default, which is a good thing. However, since this behavior is different, it can lead to unexpected breaking changes when migrating 1.x code to 2.0 if the code was counting on a simple bind. This is most likely to cause problems with non-Active Directory directories that do not support Microsoft's GSS-SPNEGO SASL mechanism (all of them, to our knowledge), but it can also cause problems with ADAM where simple and secure binds are used to authenticate two different types of users. It could also break code where firewall rules prevent secure binds from working (e.g., only the LDAP port is open to the domain controller).
>
> The lesson here is one that we have tried to demonstrate consistently throughout this book: Be explicit! If we always specify the `AuthenticationTypes` we want to use, we will never be surprised by default behavior and will have a much better idea of how and why our code works.

token associated with whatever the service was configured to use in the Service Control Manager, and so on.

There is more to the story here, though, because Windows also has a feature known as **impersonation**. Impersonation allows an application to change the security token of a specific thread to a token other than the process token. When a thread is in this state, it is said to be impersonating. Impersonation is often used in server processes where it is useful to execute code on behalf of the various users accessing the system, instead of with the security context of the process itself. The server process can impersonate the user using her credentials and can access local resources with her security context. IIS, with or without ASP.NET, is one such system and will likely be the application that readers of this book are most familiar with and interested in.

In summary, a thread executing code will always have a security context represented by a Windows security token. This token will be either the token that was used to launch the process, or the token that the server created via impersonation by using the client's credentials.

Windows security tokens are very interesting because they can be generated by various mechanisms, such as interactive logins with usernames and passwords, using smart cards, or the exchange of Kerberos tickets. In addition, several different APIs in Windows are used to create and manage tokens.

IIS actually supports several of these mechanisms for generating security tokens for users. It can accept a user's plaintext credentials via Basic authentication and can perform a local login to authenticate the user and create a token. Digest authentication allows IIS to authenticate a user and create a token without exchanging plaintext credentials. IIS can also use Integrated Windows Authentication to create the user's security context via either Kerberos or NTLM (the Negotiate protocol again), without prompting the user. When SSL is used, IIS can use client certificates to create a security token for the user.

Now, let's take this back to SDS. As we stated previously, when using secure binding, we can either specify explicit credentials or use the current security context by specifying null for the Username and Password on the DirectoryEntry. An example of the latter that we have already used extensively throughout this book might be as follows:

```
DirectoryEntry entry = new DirectoryEntry(
    "LDAP://rootDSE",
```

```
null,
null,
AuthenticationTypes.Secure
);
```

Here, since we have specified the `Secure` binding flag and have not specified credentials, the current security context will be used. As we now understand, this security context will be the identity of the current thread, which will be either the process identity or an impersonated identity. The token could have been established in any of the ways that we previously described.

Figure 8.1 demonstrates how the interaction with Active Directory works under the hood during a typical secure bind.

■ TIP   **How Do I Discover the Current Security Context?**

All versions of the .NET Framework offer an easy way to discover the identity of the current security context, regardless of whether impersonation is in effect. The static method `System.Security.Principal.WindowsIdentity.GetCurrent()` will return a `WindowsIdentity` object that essentially wraps the security token. The `Name` property on `WindowsIdentity` will tell us the Windows username associated with it.

Single Hops, Double Hops, and Delegation

Up to this point, we have been discussing security contexts and tokens and how our server applications can impersonate them in order to access local resources on our behalf. What happens when we want our server to use our impersonated context to access a remote resource? In this case, we have to use a feature called **delegation**. Delegation is a security-sensitive operation that is not enabled by default. We will set the basics here and refer again to Keith Brown's security book for the really gritty details.

Prior to Windows 2000, delegation was not supported because of the way NTLM authentication worked. Essentially, NTLM authentication relied on the client to encrypt a unique challenge hash using a key derived from the user's password. This encrypted challenge was called the **response**. The server would subsequently forward the same challenge and the client's response to a domain controller, where it would be validated that it could

1   Client logs in to workstation and authenticates against Active Directory

2   Active Directory authenticates the provided credentials and provides the client with Kerberos ticket

3   Client application performs secure LDAP bind to Active Directory and provides its Kerberos ticket to authenticate

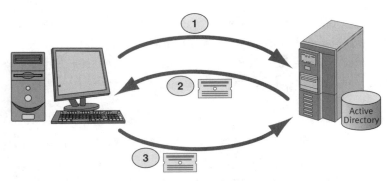

FIGURE 8.1: Active Directory Bind Using Secure Authentication

have come only from our client. The server itself never had access to the client's password nor any key material derived from it. Now, if the server attempted to access a remote resource on the client's behalf, it would in turn be challenged. With no way to encrypt the challenge hash using the client's password (since the server never had it), delegation would fail at that point.

NTLM still works this way today and cannot be used for delegation. Instead, we must use a protocol that supports delegation. For our purposes, we are talking about Kerberos today. The Kerberos protocol supports delegation via the forwarding of a client's Kerberos ticket. This allows a server to use the client's credentials for a limited time to access any remote resources by default. We can constrain what resources our server can access with a client's credentials in Windows 2003 by using a feature called constrained delegation. We will speak more about this feature later. Figure 8.2 illustrates how Kerberos delegation works at a high level. The figure uses a few terms to describe some of these scenarios, so let's define them now.

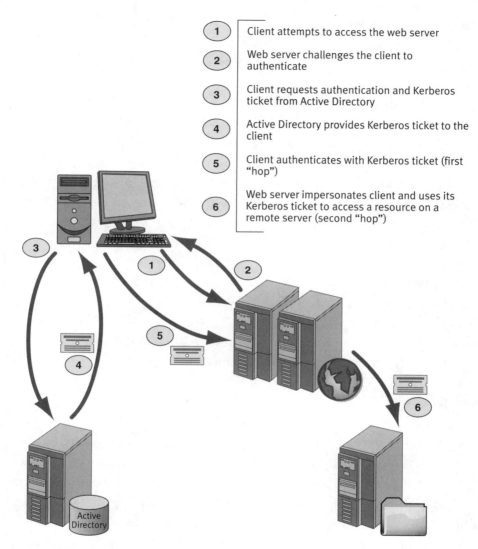

1. Client attempts to access the web server
2. Web server challenges the client to authenticate
3. Client requests authentication and Kerberos ticket from Active Directory
4. Active Directory provides Kerberos ticket to the client
5. Client authenticates with Kerberos ticket (first "hop")
6. Web server impersonates client and uses its Kerberos ticket to access a resource on a remote server (second "hop")

FIGURE 8.2: Kerberos Delegation

Single Hop

A **single hop** occurs when a user sends his security credentials to a single remote network resource. In SDS, this would be equivalent to running a console application on the local machine that accesses the directory on a remote machine and uses Secure binding with default credentials.

Double Hop

A **double hop** occurs when a user sends his security credentials to a remote network service and then that server attempts to forward the user's credentials to a remote resource. In SDS, this occurs frequently in web applications that use Integrated Windows Authentication in IIS. The user's security context on the client machine running the web browser is used to authenticate with IIS. The web application code attempts to use impersonation along with default credentials binding to access the directory on a remote server.

The key with the double hop is that it does not work by default. As we previously stated, delegation is not enabled for an Active Directory account by default. Windows does not allow just any service to forward a user's credentials to another network server resource. In our example, the security context presented by the IIS machine to the directory server will not be accepted and the user will be authenticated as the anonymous user. Since this special account rarely has rights to do anything on the directory, most types of operations will fail. As the IIS scenario we described is quite common, failures due to double-hop issues are some of the most common issues that .NET directory services programmers encounter.

Delegation

Delegation is the feature in Windows that allows a service to access another network service on the user's behalf. When Microsoft changed the native Windows authentication protocol to use Kerberos with Windows 2000, it was able to take advantage of features of the Kerberos protocol to make delegation possible. Because it is a security-sensitive operation, the administrator of the domain must allow the account running the service process to use delegation by marking the account as "trusted for delegation" from the Active Directory Users and Computers (ADUC) MMC. Once this is done, that account can then delegate most other accounts' credentials to other services on the network.

With Kerberos, we do this with tickets. Essentially, once we have set an account as trusted for delegation, any tickets issued for the trusted service to our clients will be marked as "OK to delegate" and they can then be forwarded to remote services. However, this leaves us in a predicament with administrative accounts. Essentially, we have a "trusted" account that can use the credentials of any other account (including domain administrators). A rogue application using an account trusted for delegation could wait for or lure an administrator to use the application and then easily elevate their own privileges or attack other systems. As such, delegation can also be blocked on specific user accounts by marking them as "sensitive and cannot be delegated" from the ADUC MMC. This is often done with highly privileged accounts such as those of domain administrators and account operators, but it can be applied to any account in Active Directory. This prevents the scenario we just discussed, as an administrator's account marked as sensitive cannot be used by an account trusted for delegation.

Constrained Delegation

In Windows 2000, delegation was an all or nothing proposition. If an account was configured for delegation, it could delegate to any and all resources. In Windows Server 2003, a new feature called **constrained delegation** has been added. Constrained delegation is just like it sounds; an account may delegate, but only to specific services. This makes delegation much more appealing to administrators, as they can be very specific about what services an account may access when it is delegating another user's credentials.

Discovering Remote Security Information at Runtime

Often it is useful to know details about the remote security context on the Active Directory server that the bind operation creates. For example, we may wish to know whether we successfully authenticated with Kerberos, as that allows us to determine proactively whether delegation will be possible.

In .NET 2.0, SDS introduces a new class called `DirectoryEntryConfiguration` that provides a mechanism to do just this. The `IsMutuallyAuthenticated` method returns a Boolean based on whether mutual authentication (meaning Kerberos for us today) was used for the bind. An example might look like this:

```
DirectoryEntry entry = new DirectoryEntry(
    "LDAP://DC=mydomain,DC=com",
    null,
    null,
    AuthenticationTypes.Secure
    );

Console.WriteLine(entry.Options.IsMutuallyAuthenticated());
```

In this example, the result would generally be `true` if this was run from a console application and Kerberos authentication was working correctly. However, if we changed `AuthenticationTypes` to `None` and added credentials, the result would be `false`. Note that this method will throw an exception if the bind fails.

Determining mutual authentication status is useful, but the underlying interface that ADSI uses, `IADsObjectOptions`, actually provides detailed information about the remote security context in the form of the return flags from the `InitializeSecurityContext` Windows API function. Also, since .NET 1.1 does not support the new class, it is useful to have our own wrapper that we can use. Listing 8.1 shows an example of one such wrapper.

LISTING 8.1: Retrieving Raw SSPI Result Flags

```
[Flags()]
public enum IscRetFlags
{
    ISC_RET_DELEGATE                 = 0x00000001,
    ISC_RET_MUTUAL_AUTH              = 0x00000002,
    ISC_RET_REPLAY_DETECT            = 0x00000004,
    ISC_RET_SEQUENCE_DETECT          = 0x00000008,
    ISC_RET_CONFIDENTIALITY          = 0x00000010,
    ISC_RET_USE_SESSION_KEY          = 0x00000020,
    ISC_RET_USED_COLLECTED_CREDS     = 0x00000040,
    ISC_RET_USED_SUPPLIED_CREDS      = 0x00000080,
    ISC_RET_ALLOCATED_MEMORY         = 0x00000100,
    ISC_RET_USED_DCE_STYLE           = 0x00000200,
    ISC_RET_DATAGRAM                 = 0x00000400,
    ISC_RET_CONNECTION               = 0x00000800,
    ISC_RET_INTERMEDIATE_RETURN      = 0x00001000,
    ISC_RET_CALL_LEVEL               = 0x00002000,
    ISC_RET_EXTENDED_ERROR           = 0x00004000,
    ISC_RET_STREAM                   = 0x00008000,
    ISC_RET_INTEGRITY                = 0x00010000,
    ISC_RET_IDENTIFY                 = 0x00020000,
    ISC_RET_NULL_SESSION             = 0x00040000,
    ISC_RET_MANUAL_CRED_VALIDATION   = 0x00080000,
    ISC_RET_RESERVED1                = 0x00100000,
    ISC_RET_FRAGMENT_ONLY            = 0x00200000
}

public class AuthenticationStatusChecker
{
    private enum AdsOption
    {
        ADS_OPTION_ACCUMULATIVE_MODIFICATION = 8,
```

```
            ADS_OPTION_MUTUAL_AUTH_STATUS = 4,
            ADS_OPTION_PAGE_SIZE = 2,
            ADS_OPTION_PASSWORD_METHOD = 7,
            ADS_OPTION_PASSWORD_PORTNUMBER = 6,
            ADS_OPTION_QUOTA = 5,
            ADS_OPTION_REFERRALS = 1,
            ADS_OPTION_SECURITY_MASK = 3,
            ADS_OPTION_SERVERNAME = 0
    }
    public static bool
        IsMutuallyAuthenticated(DirectoryEntry entry)
    {
        IscRetFlags authStatus = GetAuthStatus(entry);

        if ((IscRetFlags.ISC_RET_MUTUAL_AUTH & authStatus) ==
            IscRetFlags.ISC_RET_MUTUAL_AUTH)
        {
            return true;
        }
        else
        {
            return false;
        }
    }

    public static IscRetFlags
        GetAuthStatus(DirectoryEntry entry)
    {
        object val = entry.Invoke("GetOption", new object[]
            {AdsOption.ADS_OPTION_MUTUAL_AUTH_STATUS});
        return (IscRetFlags) val;
    }
}
```

One of the benefits of this class is that if we have a problem with delegation and we end up with a null authentication session on the directory server as a result, `GetAuthStatus` will return a value containing the `ISC_RET_NULL_SESSION` flag. This can be a very handy troubleshooting technique.

Guidance for Using SDS with ASP.NET

ASP.NET offers practically every option available to build web applications on the Windows platform, including the full suite of Windows security features and a variety of ASP.NET security features as well as forms authentication and role-based security. Deciding how to build our application may seem overwhelming at first, but it is not difficult if we make a few important decisions up front.

- What type of security architecture will we use for this tier of the application: the **delegated model** or the **trusted subsystem** model?
- What type of authentication will we use?

Trusted Subsystem versus Delegated Model

In a **trusted subsystem** architecture, we use a specific service account to access a remote resource instead of impersonating the user who is accessing the system. We configure the service account with the appropriate rights to access whatever resources we are interested in. Users of the application are authorized to the resources by the application itself.

The **delegated model** is essentially the opposite. The remote resource is accessed using the security context of the authenticated user, not a service account. The application must be able to delegate the user's credentials and act on the user's behalf when accessing the remote resource.

An example of a trusted subsystem scenario might be an outsourced helpdesk application. In this common scenario, we have many changing and unknown helpdesk users providing services such as password resets and group creation to a company. As long as our application can authorize the users as valid helpdesk personnel, we will not have to grant rights to any of these users' accounts directly. Our service account will hold all the rights to reset passwords and create groups, and the application will enforce that only helpdesk personnel can execute these tasks. In this high-turnover type of industry, we will not want to grant these rights directly to the helpdesk users, because the high turnover forces us to be constantly maintaining security on the accounts. Additionally, these privileges could be abused outside the scope of the application if given directly to the users.

An example of a delegated model might be an online user directory where users may update certain parts of their profile (e.g., telephone number, name, etc.). By default, Active Directory allows users to update certain attributes on their own user object. If we provide them with an interface with which to access their own user object, we can delegate their credentials and allow them to make the changes themselves. In this manner, we do not have to worry about a user accessing someone else's user account and making changes. We know that if we use delegation, the only thing the user can accomplish is based on the rights that the user has in the directory (of which updating another user's account is not one).

Both approaches are valid and will be appropriate in different contexts. Some applications make better candidates for one approach versus another. In very large applications with many users, it is often easier to administer a single service account with permission to perform particular actions than it is to try to modify the underlying user's account to give this permission to each user. This is a good candidate for a trusted subsystem approach. In general, if some permission is required for our users in an application that we would not want them to have all the time under all circumstances, we should be using a trusted subsystem model.

Applications where it is imperative that we know and allow our users to perform only what they are allowed to perform are good candidates for delegation models. Administrative tools and web sites are good examples where we have relatively few users that should have the permissions necessary to perform whatever action our application attempts.

Type of Authentication in the Web Application

This is important for any type of web application, but it a much more important decision in a delegated model because we must choose a form of authentication that allows delegation! Essentially two approaches work here.

- Use Kerberos authentication in the web application (done with Integrated Windows authentication in IIS) and configure the web application to use Kerberos delegation.[3]
- Use some type of authentication that supplies explicit credentials, such as ASP.NET forms authentication or HTTP Basic authentication, and use the explicit credentials provided.

---

3. Windows Server 2003 adds a new feature called Protocol Transition or Kerberos Service for User (S4U) that actually allows a server to authenticate a user with one Windows authentication protocol, such as Digest or NTLM, and transition to Kerberos in order to delegate to a remote resource using the new constrained delegation feature.

Both approaches allow us to delegate the user's security context to the directory. Note that with any type of authentication scheme that collects the user's credentials in plaintext, appropriate encryption such as HTTPS/SSL must be used to make the application secure!

Example Approaches for a Trusted Subsystem

Now that we understand what a trusted subsystem is, what are the options for building one in ASP.NET that works with SDS? The first thing to consider is that we need to create a service account in the directory whose credentials will be used. We should give the service account the permissions it needs to perform the tasks the application requires (and no more). Once we have that, there are really two basic approaches here.

- Configure a known identity in IIS or ASP.NET and use default credentials with the `DirectoryEntry`.
- Supply explicit credentials to the `DirectoryEntry`.

Let's take each of these in turn. Configuring the process identity depends on the version of IIS we are using.

Windows Server 2003. With IIS 6 on Windows Server 2003, each application pool may be configured with a specific identity directly. We simply set our application pool identity to our given service account with the proper permissions our application needs. We can then in turn configure our IIS application to use a specific application pool. Since ASP.NET runs in process with our application pool, this means our .NET code will execute with the configured service account's security context. This is by far the easiest of our options to use. We don't have to worry about storing or exposing credentials, and this solution works like a charm. Note that when we are using the process identity as our service account, we must ensure that impersonation is disabled in the web.config file or that we disable impersonation programmatically while performing our SDS tasks.

Windows 2000 Server: A Different Animal. This scenario is not as pretty in IIS 5 on Windows 2000 Server (and in 5.1 in Windows XP). The IIS process (inetinfo.exe) runs as SYSTEM, so any in-process application runs as SYSTEM as well. We are not going to cover what happens when we run in-process as SYSTEM in IIS 5, because it is just a bad idea and it opens up gaping security holes. Most administrators already know this and tend to run their IIS applications out of process.

Out-of-process applications run as IWAM_MACHINE (using dllhost.exe). IIS 5 always impersonates the user first (even the anonymous account, IUSR_MACHINE). This means that although the process might be running as either SYSTEM or IWAM_MACHINE, the identity we see will always be, at a minimum, the anonymous account (IUSR_MACHINE) or the client's identity when using Integrated Windows Authentication (IWA). Since we don't have the option of running the IIS process under another account, we can take advantage of this impersonation and use it to effectively run IIS under another account. We do this by changing the anonymous account from IUSR_MACHINE to our service account configured with the rights we require for our application. Now, that covers only IIS's identity at this point. Since ASP.NET runs in a worker process (not in-process, as IIS 6 does), it is configured with its own identity. We can simply use impersonation in ASP.NET with anonymous allowed and it will impersonate the IIS anonymous account, which in our case will be the service account. This gets around the undesirable situation of storing credentials. It is not as straightforward as using an application pool in Windows 2003, but it accomplishes the same thing.

The problem with this last scenario in Windows 2000 of impersonating the anonymous account is that we may wish to use IWA to identify our users. This is not compatible with our solution. To rectify this, we can instead configure ASP.NET's process account rather than IIS's anonymous account. This identity is configured in the machine.config file under the <processModel> tag. If we set explicit credentials for the userName and password values, we will change the process account that ASP.NET runs under. This is not as desirable as impersonating the anonymous account, because we have the additional complication of storing the credentials securely.

A problem with both of these solutions is that they affect all web applications on the machine. If we are running only a single ASP.NET application per server, it is not a problem to configure everything with the same identity. However, if different applications need to run with different identities, neither of the previous two solutions will work. This usually gives rise to an attempt to configure the identity of the ASP.NET application specifically using the web.config file and the <identity> tag. The syntax looks like this:

```
<identity
    impersonate="true"
    username="domain\user"
    password="password"
/>
```

> **WARNING**   Do Not Put Plaintext Credentials in Configuration Files!
>
> We hope by now that this is relatively obvious, but it is a bad idea to put plaintext credentials in configuration files. If we must store secrets, we should use one of the available technologies for encrypting them appropriately. ASP.NET 2.0 has new configuration encryption features, and .NET 1.x has the aspnet_setreg.exe tool (available as a download from Microsoft) for accomplishing the same goal. If we are storing credentials in our own configuration section, many additional alternatives are available.

We are going to warn developers away from this (most cannot even get it to work). This is not nearly as desirable as impersonating the anonymous account or changing the `<processModel>` tag because of limitations in Windows 2000. Specifically, we essentially need to run our ASP.NET worker process as SYSTEM in order for it to run as our configured identity in web.config. This is because beneath the covers, it is performing a call to LogonUser to create the token for the service account it will impersonate. Windows 2000 requires the "Act as part of the operating system" (SE_TCB_NAME) privilege in order to use LogonUser. This privilege is granted only to the SYSTEM account by default. Also by default, the `<processModel>` tag is set to run as the ASPNET user. We would have to run our ASP.NET process as SYSTEM or grant the TCB privilege to the ASPNET user in order for this to succeed. Most developers never figure this out and just give up after they get errors. It is probably just as well; remember what we said earlier about running in-process with IIS 5? We panned that idea because it required our web applications to run as SYSTEM. It is the same issue here.

Our last approach involves using explicit credentials for a service account and supplying those directly to our DirectoryEntry objects.

Why would we take this approach rather than one of the other approaches? As it turns out, not every web server will be deployed as a domain member server. In some organizations, IT policy restrictions prevent this type of deployment. In this case, we still need a viable solution. Note that in order for a deployment like this to work, the web server will still need appropriate network access to the domain controllers.

The net result of this last approach is that we will store the credentials for the service account somewhere in our configuration system. Again, please heed our warnings and store the credentials securely!

Other Trusted Subsystem Approaches

Another option for building a trusted subsystem is to use COM+—or Enterprise Services, as it is known in .NET. A .NET component that is designed to work as a COM server can be installed in the COM+ catalog and configured to run under a specified identity that represents the service account for the subsystem. The ASP.NET application accesses the COM+ component and all directory services calls are made in that code.

Since the COM+ component runs in a separate process, the thread and process identities of the ASP.NET application do not matter.

We might use the COM+ approach when the directory services calls must use a different identity than the identity that is configured in the web application.

The downside of the COM+ approach is that it is significantly more complicated to build and deploy and it may be more difficult to troubleshoot.

Example Approaches for the Delegation Model

We cited two approaches for using the delegation model. Of these two, the approach using Kerberos delegation is probably the one that web application developers want to use most often as well as the one that gives them the most trouble, so we will focus on it first. There are really four main requirements to get this to work correctly.

- Our IIS web application must be configured to use IWA only and must work with Kerberos authentication (NTLM will not work).
- The process identity in IIS must be configured to allow it to delegate to our domain controllers.
- The ASP.NET application must be configured to impersonate the authenticated user.
- Our `DirectoryEntry` constructors should use default credentials.

Let's take each of these in turn.

Configuring IWA and Kerberos. Configuring our web application to use IWA is not hard, but sometimes getting Kerberos to work can be tricky. IWA actually uses the Negotiate protocol by default to authenticate users, so it can negotiate down to NTLM if Kerberos is not available. We do not want this! However, getting Kerberos authentication to work is usually not a big deal. The thing we forget most often is that if we are accessing the web site with a DNS name that is different from the machine name, we need to set explicit service principal names (SPNs) on our process account in Active Directory that advertise the service as using the additional DNS name. Once again, see *The .NET Developer's Guide to Windows Security* for more details on SPNs.

Configuring the Process Account. Configuring the process account for delegation is typically done by an administrator using the Active Directory Users and Computers (ADUC) MMC. Note that the process account we are using must be a domain account!

If our web applications are configured to run under local accounts (either the `ASPNET` user or `NETWORK SERVICE`, depending on the platform), the computer account for our IIS server must be configured for delegation, instead of a specific service account. If we chose to run the process under a different identity (perhaps by using an application pool identity), then we should configure this account for delegation. Unlike the computer accounts in Active Directory, any service account we create will not have an SPN by default. We must use a tool like SetSPN.exe to create an SPN before Kerberos will work correctly.

Ideally, we would like to use the constrained delegation feature of Windows Server 2003 Active Directory to limit which services our web server account may delegate to (our Active Directory servers in this case).

However, that may not be an option if we are using Windows 2000 Server. In that case, we must use unconstrained delegation.

Configuring ASP.NET Impersonation. This part is definitely easy. We simply need to ensure that our web.config file includes this in the `<system.web>` section:

```
<identity impersonate="true" />
```

This ensures that the current ASP.NET request thread will be impersonating the user we authenticated. Note that we can also impersonate programmatically using the `WindowsIdentity.Impersonate` method if we wish, creating a `WindowsIdentity` object from the `Identity` property of the `HttpContext.User` property. This is more complex, but gives us the flexibility to use impersonation only where needed.

Using Default Credentials. This part is also easy. Here, we are just specifying `null`/`Nothing` for our usernames and passwords and are using `AuthenticationTypes.Secure`, as we have already discussed. Our `DirectoryEntry` will use the impersonated identity of the authenticated user when executing the LDAP bind, and because we have enabled Kerberos delegation correctly, the user's security context will be forwarded successfully to the directory!

The Finer Points of Kerberos Delegation. We have tried to provide a prescriptive recipe to demonstrate how to build a delegated model ASP.NET application to access Active Directory. Because this book is not explicitly about Windows security and Kerberos, we may have glossed over some finer points. However, we have tried to provide a variety of references to other materials to get more information, and we have provided some helpful troubleshooting information.

An Alternate Approach: Delegation with Explicit Credentials. We mentioned that we also can build a delegated model application using explicit credentials. While this approach is not as good from a security standpoint, as it requires that we know the user's plaintext credentials, sometimes we must use it. For example, our web server may not be a domain member server due to IT policy restrictions on how it is deployed. We may also need to delegate to a system that does not use Windows security, such as an ADAM instance that uses ADAM users.

In this case, the delegation is actually fairly straightforward. We must collect the plaintext credentials from the user (typically as part of authentication) and then use the collected credentials in our `DirectoryEntry` constructors when accessing the directory. Here are the key points to remember.

- We are using explicit credentials, so we must protect the web application with HTTPS/SSL to ensure that we are not passing their credentials over the network in plaintext.
- We need a mechanism to securely store the user's credentials for subsequent requests to the application, perhaps via session state or an encrypted cookie.

Because we are not relying on Windows security to protect the user's credentials, the burden is on us to do this well, and we must not take this additional responsibility lightly. We are already dealing in plaintext credentials, which are inherently less secure than their Windows counterparts are, so we are starting at a disadvantage.

Serverless Binding and ASP.NET

If we remember from Chapter 3, serverless binds require a domain security context to work properly. Because of this, serverless binding is appropriate for use only in ASP.NET applications where we are supplying default credentials. We have already discussed the approaches that will use default credentials and will work properly. We should remember that if our chosen approach requires us to supply explicit credentials, it is likely that we will also need to supply some form of server name. Ideally, for Active Directory, we will use the DNS domain name of the domain so that we can still take advantage of the Locator (see Chapters 3 and 9). If we are using another server, such as ADAM or a non-Microsoft LDAP directory, an explicit server name must be specified.

Binding with ADAM

Binding with ADAM is interesting and bears special mention. Unlike Active Directory, where we can bind with a user's credentials using either a simple bind or a secure bind, ADAM only supports simple binds for users in the ADAM store itself.[4]

This seems simple enough, except for one additional fact: ADAM also supports the ability to authenticate Windows users. A Windows user here means a user on the local machine that is hosting ADAM, or a user in any domain with which the server has a trust relationship (Active Directory or a Windows NT4 domain). There are two ways to authenticate a Windows user via a bind to ADAM.

- Use a secure bind to ADAM.
- Use a simple bind to ADAM against an `msDS-bindProxy` object.

"Pass-Through" Authentication to Windows

What does this mean? In the first case, where we do a secure bind to ADAM to authenticate the user, ADAM is using a mechanism called **pass-through authentication**. It essentially just takes the incoming secure bind request and passes it off to the host server to authenticate the user. If that is successful, the user is authenticated. Note that the user in this case does not have a bindable object in the ADAM store representing her. Her actual Windows account was authenticated. The user can be a member of a group in ADAM as a foreign security principal, but she is not an ADAM user (a security principal).

Bind Proxies

The second case involves what is called a **bind proxy** object. Here, a special class of object called a `userProxy` (naturally) is created in ADAM. It has a SID attribute that points to the SID of the Windows principal to be authenticated. The simple bind is accepted by ADAM and is redirected to the server for the actual authentication again. ADAM ships with the `userProxy` class as an optional class in an LDIF file. In actuality, any class that

---

4. This is not actually completely true. The latest version of ADAM also supports Digest authentication for ADAM users. However, SDS does not (currently) have explicit support for Digest authentication, so we are limited to simple binds for SDS. If we use `System.DirectoryServices.Protocols` (SDS.P), then we can specify Digest authentication directly and take advantage of this feature.

contains the msDS-bindProxy auxiliary class can act as a bind proxy. It just happens that it is usually easiest to add the optional userProxy class.

Bind proxies are intended primarily to support applications that cannot do a secure bind. Many non-Microsoft LDAP APIs do not support GSS-SPNEGO, so this mechanism provides some common ground.

The other scenario that bind proxies support is the case where the consuming application requires additional schema on the user object that cannot be added directly to Active Directory for either technical or political reasons. In this case, the bind proxy object has its schema extended to include the additional required attributes. Then the user can authenticate against ADAM using his Active Directory password, but the application can look in ADAM to get the additional data needed.

For more information about bind proxies, we highly recommend reading the ADAM Technical Reference.[5]

Binding and Other Directories

As we already discussed, SDS really exposes two types of binds: the simple bind, specified with AuthenticationTypes.None, and the GSS-SPNEGO SASL bind, supported by AuthenticationTypes.Secure. Since it is unlikely that a non-Windows LDAP directory will support the Windows Negotiate protocol (none of them does, to our knowledge), the simple bind is the way to go.

The only real trick with the simple bind is getting the username in the correct format. The RFC states that the user's distinguished name (DN) must be supported, so that is always a good choice. Some directories may also support other naming mechanisms that may be used with a simple bind (Active Directory supports the User Principal Name [UPN] and NT logon name, for example), so consult your server's reference for more details.

Securing the Simple Bind

In order to secure the bind, we must secure the channel. The only method SDS supports is to use the AuthenticationTypes.SecureSocketsLayer flag. This will use SSL to encrypt the channel, but it requires a valid server

---

5. www.microsoft.com/downloads/details.aspx?FamilyID=96C660F7-D932-4F59-852C-2844B343F3E0&displaylang=en

certificate on the server that the client trusts. This also generally means that we need to use a proper DNS for the server name, as an SSL handshake generally requires that the name requested by the client matches the subject alternative name field of the certificate. We provide some additional troubleshooting tips and details for SSL binds back in Chapter 3 that apply equally to Active Directory and ADAM.

It is also possible to encrypt the channel with some sort of external channel encryption, such as IPSEC, if SSL is not an option.

Client Certificate Authentication

One feature of SSL is that in addition to authenticating the server's identity via its certificate, it can optionally authenticate the client if the client has a certificate and the server is configured to accept certificates. Since LDAP on Windows supports SSL through the same mechanism that other parts of Windows use for SSL (namely, the Schannel SSPI provider), it is natural to wonder how client certificates are supported with LDAP and whether they can be used to authenticate the client.

The good news here is that LDAP fully honors requests for client certificates and will use them if the client code has a valid certificate available (with access to its private key). The question then becomes whether a client certificate authentication can be used as a bind to Active Directory or ADAM.

The answer here is yes for Active Directory. If the client provides a client certificate, the LDAP API will use the EXTERNAL SASL mechanism under the hood to bind the user to Active Directory if an appropriate mapping between the certificate identity and a Windows user can be found. Note that this feature is not documented at all and is rarely used, so there is little practical experience with it. However, if we can get client certificate authentication working with IIS, we should be able to do the same for LDAP. Supposedly, ADAM also supports client certificate authentication, but we were unable to verify that in our own testing, or learn how to configure it.

Binding Features Not Supported by SDS/ADSI

Even though the LDAP API, Active Directory, and ADAM support a variety of SASL mechanisms, the only one currently available for use with ADSI and SDS is GSS-SPNEGO via the `AuthenticationTypes.Secure` flag. If we want to use one of the other methods, such as Digest authentication, we are basically out of luck. Digest is especially tempting for ADAM developers, because it allows a secure binding protocol without the additional trouble of having to secure the channel via SSL.

What is a .NET developer to do? If we absolutely need to have Digest authentication or a different SASL mechanism, we must unfortunately abandon SDS and look at the SDS.P namespace. Because there is no built-in mechanism to interoperate between the two APIs, it is an all or nothing proposition.

Directory Object Permissions in Active Directory and ADAM

In Active Directory and ADAM, the permissions for objects in the directory are determined using Windows security descriptors. These are the same security descriptors used throughout the Windows security model for other objects, such as files and registry keys. In fact, Active Directory and ADAM make some of the most extensive use of the features available in the system to provide such capabilities as read and write permissions on individual attributes.

.NET 2.0 Object Security Model

This is another part of SDS that has received significant improvements in .NET 2.0. .NET 1.x lacked built-in support for working with security descriptors on any type of object, be it a file, a registry key, or a directory object. In order to program security descriptors, developers always had to rely on some sort of interop mechanism, whether they used Windows Management Instrumentation (WMI), one of the ADSI wrappers, or a custom P/Invoke wrapper of the Win32 security APIs.

All of this has changed with version 2.0. Microsoft has introduced a new model for managing security descriptors based on types in the new `System.Security.AccessControl` namespace and on some additions to the `System.Security.Principal` namespace. Because the new model applies to all objects using security descriptors in Windows, developers can use the same familiar set of classes to set security descriptors for files and registry keys, as well as directory objects.

SDS has also been enhanced to support a new mechanism for reading and writing security descriptors based on a new property on the `DirectoryEntry` class, called `ObjectSecurity` (which is also used on objects such as `FileStream` for consistency). A variety of new types and enumerations that support some of the Active Directory-specific settings for access control list (ACL) entries have been added as well.

The central object in the system is the `ActiveDirectorySecurity` class, which is essentially an Active Directory–specific wrapper around the Windows security descriptor structure. This class provides all of the members required to manipulate the discretionary access control list (DACL, for access control), the system access control list (SACL, for auditing), and the other properties of a security descriptor, such as the owner, primary group, and protected status.

A variety of other objects come into play as well.

Access Control Entry Wrappers

An ACL contains a set of access control entries (ACEs). Active Directory and ADAM support some specific types of ACEs, such as the right to create or delete child objects, in addition to more basic functions. In order to make it easier to create these special ACEs, SDS supplies a set of wrapper classes to represent them. Here is a list of the special ACE wrapper classes, with their base class in parentheses:

- `ActiveDirectoryAccessRule` (`ObjectAccessRule`)
- `ActiveDirectoryAuditRule` (`ActiveDirectoryAccessRule`)
- `CreateChildAccessRule` (`ActiveDirectoryAccessRule`)
- `DeleteChildAccessRule` (`ActiveDirectoryAccessRule`)
- `DeleteTreeAccessRule` (`ActiveDirectoryAccessRule`)
- `ExtendedRightAccessRule` (`ActiveDirectoryAccessRule`)
- `PropertyAccessRule` (`ActiveDirectoryAccessRule`)
- `PropertySetAccessRule` (`ActiveDirectoryAccessRule`)

Having these classes makes it much easier to create and manage the special rights the ACEs represent.

Enumerations

These enumeration values represent Active Directory–specific versions of the standard enumerations used in security descriptors:

- ActiveDirectoryRights
- ActiveDirectorySecurityInheritance
- PropertyAccess
- SecurityMasks

The most important is the ActiveDirectoryRights enumeration, which represents the Active Directory version of the Access Mask enumerated constant and contains Active Directory–specific concepts such as "read property" and "write property."

Unlike its ADSI predecessor (IADsSecurityDescriptor), the .NET-based access control model allows developers to decide how security principals will be represented. Using an IdentityReference, either a SecurityIdentifier (SID) type or an NTAccount type can be selected at runtime. Since the security descriptor stores SIDs natively, being able to opt out of conversions to NT account format (domain\principal name) can improve performance dramatically and can even enable some scenarios that were difficult before, such as when the current machine cannot convert the SID into a friendly name, perhaps because it is a workgroup computer.

Reading Security Descriptors

Reading security descriptors is now straightforward. Listing 8.2 shows an example of enumerating the DACL and printing out the owner and group.

LISTING 8.2: Listing the DACL

```
using System;
using System.Collections;
using System.DirectoryServices;
using System.Security.Principal;
using System.Security.AccessControl;
```

```csharp
public class SecurityDescriptors
{
    public static void Main()
    {
        DirectoryEntry entry = new DirectoryEntry(
            "LDAP://dc=mydomain,dc=com",
            null,
            null,
            AuthenticationTypes.Secure
            );

        ActiveDirectorySecurity sec = entry.ObjectSecurity;

        PrintSD(sec);

        AuthorizationRuleCollection rules = null;
        rules = sec.GetAccessRules(
            true, true, typeof(NTAccount));

        foreach (ActiveDirectoryAccessRule rule in rules)
        {
            PrintAce(rule);
        }
    }

    public static void PrintAce(ActiveDirectoryAccessRule rule)
    {
        Console.WriteLine("=====ACE=====");
        Console.Write("    Identity: ");
        Console.WriteLine(rule.IdentityReference.ToString());
        Console.Write("    AccessControlType: ");
        Console.WriteLine(rule.AccessControlType.ToString());
        Console.Write("    ActiveDirectoryRights: ");
        Console.WriteLine(
            rule.ActiveDirectoryRights.ToString());
        Console.Write("    InheritanceType: ");
        Console.WriteLine(rule.InheritanceType.ToString());
        Console.Write("    ObjectType: ");
        if (rule.ObjectType == Guid.Empty)
            Console.WriteLine("<null>");
        else
            Console.WriteLine(rule.ObjectType.ToString());

        Console.Write("    InheritedObjectType: ");
        if (rule.InheritedObjectType == Guid.Empty)
            Console.WriteLine("<null>");
        else
            Console.WriteLine(
                rule.InheritedObjectType.ToString());
```

```
        Console.Write("    ObjectFlags: ");
        Console.WriteLine(rule.ObjectFlags.ToString());
    }

    public static void PrintSD(ActiveDirectorySecurity sd)
    {
        Console.WriteLine("=====Security Descriptor=====");
        Console.Write("    Owner: ");
        Console.WriteLine(sd.GetOwner(typeof(NTAccount)));
        Console.Write("    Group: ");
        Console.WriteLine(sd.GetGroup(typeof(NTAccount)));
    }
}
```

This code may look simple, but it is actually one of the most useful tools for security programmers, because the rules for modifying Active Directory and ADAM security are actually quite complicated. We have found that the best approach is to dump out the original security descriptors, use a GUI tool such as ADUC or ADSI Edit to get the settings we want, and then dump out the resulting security descriptors to see what the difference is. Once we can see the differences, it is usually not too hard to get our desired results.

Changing Security Descriptors

In most cases, we hope there is no reason to need to write security descriptors programmatically. This is generally best left to the administrators of the system to perform. In fact, most directory services programming tasks do not involve security descriptor manipulation at all.

However, we might actually need to build a tool for administrators to use to manage security descriptors, perhaps through a web interface in our case. As such, we cannot skip over this step.

Ideally, this book would provide many examples of the different types of security descriptor manipulations we can perform in order to accomplish even the most esoteric Active Directory security task. Unfortunately, that topic could probably fill another book. We will need to suffice with a brief example.

At the most basic level, writing a security descriptor is a fairly simple task. Listing 8.3 shows one such example using the new `ActiveDirectorySecurity` class from version 2.0.

Why So Complicated?

Windows security descriptors are already somewhat complicated conceptually because of the hierarchy and inheritance support, the combination of Allow and Deny ACEs, and the different types of ACEs that can be created. However, Active Directory and ADAM use the full power of security descriptors to provide the extremely granular level of security offered by the product. In order to provide features such as rights on individual attributes and special extended rights such as administrative password resets, security descriptors in Windows 2000 were enhanced for Active Directory to provide extensibility mechanisms in security descriptors with the `ObjectType`, `InheritedObjectType`, and `ACEFlags` fields. `ObjectType` and `InheritedObjectType` contain arbitrary GUIDs that in the case of Active Directory refer to specific objects in the schema or `Extended Rights` container.

The result is powerful, but also complex and dense in terms of how much information is conveyed in a small structure.

LISTING 8.3: Modifying Security Descriptors

```
DirectoryEntry entry = new DirectoryEntry(
    "LDAP://CN=some object,DC=mydomain,DC=com",
    null,
    null,
    AuthenticationTypes.Secure
    );

ActiveDirectorySecurity sec = entry.ObjectSecurity;
ActiveDirectoryAccessRule rule = new ActiveDirectoryAccessRule(
    new NTAccount("mydomain", "super.user"),
    ActiveDirectoryRights.GenericAll,
    AccessControlType.Allow
    );
sec.AddAccessRule(rule);
entry.CommitChanges();
```

As Listing 8.3 demonstrates, modifications are straightforward. We simply get the security descriptor for the object in question, make the required modifications, and call `CommitChanges`, just like with any other modification to a directory object. The hard part is to know what modifications to make to get the desired results!

Interoperability with SDS.P

One of the great things about the .NET security descriptor classes is that they allow for binary and Security Descriptor Description Language (SDDL) import and export of security descriptors. So, instead of using `DirectoryEntry` and the property cache, we can use other sources, such as `DirectorySearcher`, or perhaps an LDIF export.

One particularly important integration point is with SDS.P. Since it is a lower-level, generic API, it does not include direct support for security descriptors with a property such as `ObjectSecurity`. However, it does allow us to read and write the `ntSecurityDescriptor` attribute on any Active Directory or ADAM object directly as binary. We can then take the resulting byte array and use it to create an `ActiveDirectorySecurity` object and get binary data in and out of it with the `SetSecurityDescriptorBinaryForm` and the `GetSecurityDescriptorBinaryForm` methods.

This allows us to work in our lower-level API for LDAP, but switch to the much more productive .NET-managed ACL for security descriptor work.

Converting between GUIDs and Friendly Names

One of the most difficult tasks in dealing with Active Directory security descriptor esoterica is converting to and from the GUID and friendly name versions of the schema elements and extended rights that are inserted into all of those GUID structures.

Listing 8.4 demonstrates how to convert between the GUID and friendly name of various schema objects and extended rights. It serves as the missing link between the GUIDs used extensively in security descriptors and the way we probably want to work with them. The side benefit is that this sample works well in any version of .NET and we can use it for security descriptor manipulation tasks in .NET 1.x as well.

LISTING 8.4: GUID-to-Friendly-Name Conversion

```
using System;
using System.Collections;
using System.DirectoryServices;
using System.Text;
```

```
public class SchemaGuidConversion
{
    //shows how to use the class...
    public static void Main()
    {
        DirectoryEntry rootDse;
        DirectoryEntry schemaRoot;
        DirectoryEntry extendedRightsRoot;
        string schemaDN;
        string extendedRightsDN = "CN=Extended-Rights,";
        string schemaAtt = "schemaNamingContext";
        string configAtt = "configurationNamingContext";
        Guid samGuid =
            new Guid("3e0abfd0-126a-11d0-a060-00aa006c33ed");
        Guid cpGuid =
            new Guid("ab721a53-1e2f-11d0-9819-00aa0040529b");

        rootDse = new DirectoryEntry("LDAP://rootDSE");
        schemaDN = (string)
            rootDse.Properties[schemaAtt].Value;
        extendedRightsDN += (string)
            rootDse.Properties[configAtt].Value;

        schemaRoot =
            new DirectoryEntry("LDAP://" + schemaDN);
        extendedRightsRoot =
            new DirectoryEntry("LDAP://" + extendedRightsDN);


        Console.WriteLine(
            "cn={0}",
            GetSchemaIDGuid("cn", schemaRoot)
            );
        Console.WriteLine(
            "Validated-SPN={0}",
            GetRightsGuid("Validated-SPN", extendedRightsRoot)
            );
        Console.WriteLine(
            "{0}={1}",
            samGuid.ToString("B"),
            GetNameForSchemaGuid(
                samGuid,
                schemaRoot
                )
            );
        Console.WriteLine(
            "{0}={1}",
            cpGuid.ToString("B"),
            GetNameForRightsGuid(
                cpGuid,
```

```
                    extendedRightsRoot
                    )
                );

        if (rootDse != null)
            rootDse.Dispose();
        if (schemaRoot != null)
            schemaRoot.Dispose();
        Console.ReadLine();
    }

    public static string GetNameForRightsGuid(
        Guid rightsGuid,
        DirectoryEntry extendedRightsRoot
        )
    {
        string filter = String.Format(
            "(rightsGuid={0})",
            rightsGuid.ToString("D")
            );
        return GetNameForGuid(
            filter,
            "cn",
            extendedRightsRoot
            );
    }

    public static string GetNameForSchemaGuid(
        Guid schemaIDGuid,
        DirectoryEntry schemaRoot
        )
    {
        string filter = String.Format(
            "(schemaIDGUID={0})",
            BuildFilterOctetString(
                schemaIDGuid.ToByteArray()
                )
            );
        return GetNameForGuid(
            filter,
            "ldapDisplayName",
            schemaRoot
            );
    }

    public static string GetNameForGuid(
        string filter,
        string targetAttribute,
        DirectoryEntry searchRoot
        )
```

```
{
    string attributeName = null;
    SearchResult result;
    DirectorySearcher searcher =
        new DirectorySearcher(searchRoot);
    searcher.SearchScope = SearchScope.OneLevel;
    searcher.PropertiesToLoad.Add(targetAttribute);
    searcher.Filter = filter;

    using (searcher)
    {
        result = searcher.FindOne();

        if (result != null)
        {
            attributeName = (string)
                result.Properties[targetAttribute][0];
        }
    }

    return attributeName;
}

public static Guid GetRightsGuid(
    string rightsName,
    DirectoryEntry extendedRightsRoot
    )
{
    return GetGuidForName(
        "cn",
        rightsName,
        "rightsGuid",
        extendedRightsRoot
        );
}

public static Guid GetSchemaIDGuid(
    string ldapDisplayName,
    DirectoryEntry schemaRoot
    )
{
    return GetGuidForName(
        "ldapDisplayName",
        ldapDisplayName,
        "schemaIDGUID",
        schemaRoot
        );
}

private static Guid GetGuidForName(
```

```
        string attributeName,
        string attributeValue,
        string targetAttribute,
        DirectoryEntry root
        )
    {
        Guid targetGuid = Guid.Empty;
        SearchResult result;
        object guidValue;
        DirectorySearcher searcher =
            new DirectorySearcher(root);
        searcher.SearchScope = SearchScope.OneLevel;

        searcher.PropertiesToLoad.Add(targetAttribute);
        searcher.Filter = String.Format(
            "({0}={1})",
            attributeName,
            attributeValue
            );

        using (searcher)
        {
            result = searcher.FindOne();

            if (result != null)
            {
                guidValue =
                    result.Properties[targetAttribute][0];
                if (guidValue is string)
                    targetGuid =  new Guid((string) guidValue);
                else
                    targetGuid = new Guid((byte[]) guidValue);
            }
        }

        return targetGuid;
    }

    public static string BuildFilterOctetString(
        //refer to listing 4.2...
    }
}
```

.NET 1.x Interop Model

In .NET 1.x, the story with security descriptors is not nearly as good as it is in .NET 2.0. We do not have managed types or classes for dealing with security descriptors in .NET 1.x, so in order to do the same kind of work, we must use interop. The typical way to do this is to use the ADSI `IADs-SecurityDescriptor` interface, along with its accompanying types for ACLs (`IADsAccessControlList`) and ACEs (`IADsAccessControlEntry`). We could also tackle this problem with some third-party libraries that have been developed, but we will focus on the ADSI approach here. All of the following examples will use COM interop and will assume that we have created the appropriate COM interop assembly with tlbimp.exe or by adding a COM reference to activeds.tlb in Visual Studio .NET.

Reading Security Descriptors in .NET 1.x

There is no `ObjectSecurity` property on `DirectoryEntry`, as there is in .NET 2.0. However, we can get any attribute value that uses security descriptor syntax (2.5.5.15; see Table 6.1 in Chapter 6) from the property cache. For example:

```
//given a DirectoryEntry entry bound to an object
IADsSecurityDescriptor sec;
sec = (IADsSecurityDescriptor)
entry.Properties["ntSecurityDescriptor"].Value;
```

From here, we can access the DACL (and the SACL if we have requested it, as per Chapter 6), as well as the intrinsic properties of the security descriptor itself. Listing 8.5 prints out the trustees and some other values in the DACL.

LISTING 8.5: Examining Security Descriptors in .NET 1.x

```
using ActiveDs;
using System;
using System.Collections;
using System.DirectoryServices;

DirectoryEntry entry = new DirectoryEntry(
    "LDAP://DC=dir,DC=svc,DC=accenture,DC=com",
    null,
    null,
    AuthenticationTypes.Secure
    );
IADsSecurityDescriptor sd = (IADsSecurityDescriptor)
    entry.Properties["ntSecurityDescriptor"].Value;
IADsAccessControlList dacl=
    (IADsAccessControlList) sd.DiscretionaryAcl;
```

```
foreach(IADsAccessControlEntry ace in (IEnumerable) dacl)
{
    Console.WriteLine("Trustee: {0}", ace.Trustee);
    Console.WriteLine("AccessMask: {0}", ace.AccessMask);
    Console.WriteLine("Access Type: {0}", ace.AceType);
    Console.WriteLine("Access Flags: {0}", ace.AceFlags);
}
```

The enumeration values for the members, such as `AccessMask`, `Ace-Type`, and `AceFlags`, are also contained in the `ActiveDs` runtime-callable wrapper (RCW) interop assembly. It is important that we use the values defined there, especially for `AccessMask`, as there are many Active Directory-specific values there. Using the values for filesystem ACLs will get us into trouble!

Notice how we only show the use of `DirectoryEntry` for these samples? This is because it is somewhat complex to retrieve security descriptors from `DirectorySearcher` in .NET 1.x. We discussed this in more detail in Chapters 5 and 6.

■ NOTE   SID-to-Trustee Name Conversion Issues

One interesting aspect of `IADsAccessControlEntry` is that it automatically converts the internal SID structure in the ACE to a friendly trustee name. The SID is a key component of the ACE, as it identifies the principal to which the ACE applies. For example, it will convert the SID `S-1-5-11` to the friendly `NT AUTHORITY\Authenticated Users`. This makes the interface easier to use for developers, especially those programming from scripting languages. However, there is a performance penalty for converting SIDs to friendly names, and it requires a security context in which the names can be resolved. This latter point can cause unexpected problems in some situations, as we will see shortly.

Changing Security Descriptors in .NET 1.x

Writing security descriptors in .NET 1.x is very similar in theory to the .NET 2.0 methods. ACEs on the DACL are added, removed, and modified. The DACL is persisted back to the security descriptor, and the security descriptor is written back to the directory (see Listing 8.6).

LISTING 8.6: Updating a Security Descriptor in .NET 1.x

```
//adding a full control ACE to a test container
using ActiveDS;
using System;
using System.Collections;
using System.DirectoryServices;

DirectoryEntry entry = new DirectoryEntry(
    "LDAP://CN=testcontainer,DC=mydomain,DC=com",
    null,
    null,
    AuthenticationTypes.Secure
    );
IADsAccessControlEntry newAce = new AccessControlEntryClass();
IADsSecurityDescriptor sd = (IADsSecurityDescriptor)
    entry.Properties["ntSecurityDescriptor"].Value;
IADsAccessControlList dacl=
    (IADsAccessControlList) sd.DiscretionaryAcl;
newAce.Trustee = @"mydomain\some user";
newAce.AccessMask = -1;  //all flags
newAce.AceType = 0;  //access allowed
dacl.AddAce(newAce);
sd.DiscretionaryAcl = dacl;
entry.Properties["ntSecurityDescriptor"].Value = sd;
entry.CommitChanges();
```

Obviously, a better coding practice is to use the correct enumerated types to set the values, but we omitted them for the sake of brevity.

Important Caveats

We mentioned earlier in the chapter that the `IADsSecurityDescriptor` class converts the SIDs stored in the DACL and SACL into friendly "trustee" names of the form `domain\principal name` and that a performance penalty is associated with these conversions. Since the interface is designed for a scripting audience that will generally trade performance for productivity most of the time, this is not usually a problem.

However, the conversion of these SIDs into names and then back into SIDs relies on underlying Windows API functions in the Local Security Authority. These APIs in turn rely on RPC calls and domain trust relationships to perform the resolution. If the machine is not a member of the domain or the current security context is a local machine account, calls to resolve domain SIDs may fail.

These failures usually result in timeouts, which can make the time required to read an `IADsSecurityDescriptor` several orders of magnitude greater than normal—more than 1 minute in some cases. More important, though, is that the COM object may be left in some kind of corrupted state that cannot be written back to the directory, even if it has not been modified.

This last issue can make security descriptors very difficult to deal with in some scenarios, such as in ASP.NET applications where no domain membership exists for the machine or where a local machine account is being used. In some deployments, it may be impossible to perform security descriptor manipulation with these interfaces.

With ADAM, there are some additional problems. ADAM uses ADAM-specific SIDs that by default do not work with the `IADsSecurityDe-scriptor` class, as they do not belong to a domain or to the local machine. Essentially, the underlying APIs that are used to look up SID values do not know to look into ADAM instances to resolve them. This culminates in both poor performance characteristics as well as an inability to modify ADAM security descriptors. Hopefully these issues will be addressed in future versions of ADSI and a fix will be released in a future service pack.

Until a fix exists, our best bet is to use .NET 2.0, as the `ActiveDirectorySecurity` class does not suffer from this problem. Another option is to use the `Process` class to invoke the ADAM version of the DSACLs.exe command-line tool, although that is inelegant. Other wrapper classes may also be used (see the next section, Other Approaches).

Other Approaches

Because .NET 1.x did not include any support for security descriptors, a variety of enterprising people implemented libraries to fill this gap. One popular implementation exists as open source on the GotDotNet web site.[6] It is difficult to use from Visual Basic .NET due to its extensive use of unsigned integers, but it is otherwise extremely useful and powerful.

The trick is to get the data into and out of the directory in raw binary format to use as input to these APIs. One approach is to use `Directory-Searcher`, but there are some issues with that, as discussed in Chapter 6.

---

6. www.gotdotnet.com/Community/UserSamples
/Details.aspx?SampleGuid=e6098575-dda0-48b8-9abf-e0705af065d9

Another approach is to use `IADsPropertyList` and `IADsPropertyValue2` to accomplish this via COM interop with SDS. In fact, this is how .NET 2.0 accomplishes the same thing! A sample called "Raw Data Conversion with IADsPropertyList" is available on this book's web site.

Code Access Security

The .NET Framework introduces a new security concept called **code access security,** or CAS. CAS was introduced to solve a particular problem that is unfortunately becoming more common in the hostile computing environment of the Internet-connected age. The essential problem is that a user can often be lured by an attacker to perform an action that he ordinarily would not want to perform. In many cases, a security flaw in an application the user is using allows the attack with no action whatsoever on the user's part. Users often operate with many more privileges than they really need to do their normal tasks, and these extra privileges are exploited to cause additional damage.

.NET tries to address this problem by introducing the concept of restricting what the actual code is allowed to do, independent of what privileges Windows grants the user executing the code. Note that the code cannot perform actions that the current user would not be authorized to perform; CAS only applies further restrictions to the code in question.

A full discussion of CAS is outside the scope of this book, but we once again highly recommend *The .NET Developer's Guide to Windows Security* and LaMacchia *et al.*[7] for greater depth. At a high level, CAS restricts specific actions within code by protecting them with a set of permissions. Code is granted or refused these permissions based on the security policy on the machine executing the code, and on evidence that the code itself supplies about its identity and origin. Evidence can be things such as the location from which the code was run, a strong name signature applied to the assembly, or perhaps an Authenticode signature, to name a few possibilities.

---

7. LaMacchia, B. A., S. Lange, M. Lyons, R. Martin, and K. T. Price. 2002. *.NET Framework Security*. Boston: Addison-Wesley.

Currently, code installed on the local machine will receive by default what is called the `FullTrust` grant set, which essentially means that the code is granted all permissions, even custom ones added to the runtime by third parties through extensibility mechanisms. Because fully trusted code does not fail any permission checks, developers running code from their local machines may not even notice that CAS is at work. This default policy has allowed many developers to simply ignore CAS and learn nothing about it up to now. Only once the code is placed in a "partially trusted" environment does CAS come into play, usually via the dreaded `SecurityException` thrown by the CAS policy system. This often accompanies great surprise and little knowledge of how to contend with the situation!

CAS Encounters of the First Kind

Usually developers will encounter CAS when they execute code that is stored on a network share rather than on the local machine. On a network share, code is generally granted permissions based on the `Intranet` permission set, which is quite a bit more restrictive than the `FullTrust` grant from the local machine.

Other common scenarios for partial trust come with downloadable .NET controls hosted by Internet Explorer, web applications hosted in a SharePoint environment, or code executed in the Visual Studio Tools for Office (VSTO) environment. All of these have default policies that restrict the trust given to the executing code. Since the security policy is configurable, any environment could potentially have full trust or partial trust, but these are some of the more common examples.

As .NET 2.x and the next version of Windows become common on users' workstations, technologies like ClickOnce will make partial trust even more common for developers—and will make it something that all of us will need to have a basic understanding of in order to be effective developers and architects.

The Relevance to SDS

This whole discussion is relevant to SDS, SDS.AD, and SDS.P because most operations in all three namespaces will end up demanding certain

permissions of the caller. Specifically, all three use the `Directory-`
`ServicesPermission` class in `System.DirectoryServices` for CAS
purposes. Incidentally, this is the only dependency between SDS and
SDS.P. They are otherwise completely separate.

The `DirectoryServicesPermission` class has some additional supporting classes associated with it. Specifically, the `DirectoryServicesPermis-`
`sionAttribute` class provides an attribute for declarative use of the
`DirectoryServicesPermission` class. Additionally, the `DirectorySer-`
`vicesPermissionAccess` enumeration, `DirectoryServicesPermission-`
`Entry` class, and `DirectoryServicesPermissionEntryCollection` class
can be used with the main permission and attribute classes. However, we can
safely ignore these other types for reasons we will explain shortly.

> **■ NOTE** **DirectoryServicesPermission Is Not Used for Security Descriptors**
>
> The `DirectoryServicesPermission` classes we are describing now
> are not used for security purposes related to binding or to changing
> ACLs on directory objects in Active Directory and ADAM. They are
> used only for CAS. Hopefully, you have already gathered this if you
> read the earlier part of this chapter. We mention this because this was
> a point of confusion with .NET 1.x users who were looking for built-in
> .NET types to manage security descriptors and did not find them.

SDS in Partial Trust Scenarios in .NET 2.0

Now that we know the high-level basics, let's take a quick look at partial
trust programming with directory services. We start with .NET 2.0, where
the story is a bit more straightforward.

There are two important points to know right off the bat about CAS that
are different in .NET 2.0.

- In this release of the framework, the System.DirectoryServices.dll
  assembly and the System.DirectoryServices.Protocols.dll assembly
  allow "partially trusted callers."
- Microsoft has significantly reduced the complexity of using the
  `DirectoryServicesPermission` class by moving away from the

use of path- and access-level variations. Most methods simply demand `Unrestricted` access to `DirectoryServicesPermission` now.

Allowing Partially Trusted Callers

The first point is subtle, but critically important. Without going into a lengthy explanation again, there are essentially two types of assemblies in .NET with respect to CAS: those that allow partially trusted callers and those that do not. This is defined by whether the `AllowPartiallyTrust-edCallersAttribute` (APTCA, for short) is applied to the assembly.

If an assembly is marked with APTCA, then an immediate caller that does not have `FullTrust` can access the types in the assembly. However, any assembly that does not have APTCA on it will allow only immediate callers that have `FullTrust`.

For example, if Assembly A (a framework assembly, for example) has APTCA, and code in our assembly, Assembly B, calls it, the framework will allow Assembly B to link to Assembly A at runtime, even if Assembly B does not have `FullTrust` where it is running. However, if Assembly A did not have APTCA and Assembly B did not have `FullTrust`, the runtime would not allow Assembly B to access Assembly A, regardless of whether Assembly B had the permissions that Assembly A was going to demand.

Note that APTCA does not necessarily mean that permission demands will succeed. It is just a necessary precondition for anything to be allowed to work if the immediate caller has partial trust.

The bottom line here is that in .NET 2.0, the directory services assemblies can be called directly from partially trusted code. In .NET 1.x, they could not. This severely limited the options for .NET 1.x developers.

A Simplified Model

.NET 1.x featured a fairly complicated CAS permission system for SDS. `DirectoryServicesPermission` could be configured to place different restrictions on reading versus modifying the directory, and provided the ability to scope the access levels to different directory paths.

While this flexibility might sound interesting, in practice it turned out to be too complex and cumbersome in most situations. Based on our highly scientific study, exactly three developers ever tried it and actually used it. That might be overstating its use somewhat, but the point is that it was not really taken advantage of by many developers.

In .NET 2.0, Microsoft has opted not to use the complex model of paths and access levels. Instead, whenever `DirectoryServicesPermission` is checked, it simply checks the `PermissionState.Unrestricted` permission state. The other supporting classes have not been officially obsoleted, but they are no longer checked. Do not bother trying to use them!

The Problem

So, now that we have reported a little bit of good news on the changes in .NET 2.0 that make CAS easier to use with directory services programming, we must report the bad news as well. The problem for developers working under partial trust in .NET 2.0 is that `DirectoryServicesPermission` is not included in any of the default permission sets included with the framework.

What does this mean? The default CAS policy on a machine will place any code running on the machine in a specific code group based on its zone. The zone is determined by the location from which the code was executed, much like the way Internet Explorer's security zones work. The code groups are even named similarly, such as `Intranet` and `Internet`.

Since `DirectoryServicesPermission` is not part of any of the permission sets assigned to these code groups, except for the `FullTrust` permission set given to code running on the local machine, no code falling into one of the default code groups will have `DirectoryServicesPermission`! This is a little disappointing, as we do not have any default scenarios in which our partially trusted directory services code will run.

For example, if our code is located on a network share, it will receive the `Intranet` permission set by default because the network share membership condition matches the `LocalIntranet` code group. Since this permission set does not contain `DirectoryServicesPermission`, any directory services code will not be permitted to run.

However, we can make local security policy changes to address this.

Configuring DirectoryServicesPermission for Use with Partial Trust

Our goal is to get our code to have a membership condition that will match a code group with a permission set that contains `DirectoryServices-Permission` with the `Unrestricted` flag set to `true`. This seems simple enough. There are a couple of approaches we might use.

- Modify the local policy so that a permission set that matches a code group that matches our code contains the required `DirectoryServicesPermission`.
- Create a new permission set, code group, and membership condition that contain the required permission(s) and will match our code specifically.

The first approach is less desirable from a security perspective, because modifying an existing permission set will grant this permission to all of the other code that matches it. Unless you really want to do this in your environment, we recommend applying the principle of least privilege instead.

Creating a separate permission set is not really a big deal and it allows us to fine-tune the permissions to what we really need. We can do this quite easily using caspol.exe or via the .NET Framework Configuration MMC snap-in.

The next thing to decide is what membership condition to use to get our new permission set to match our code. There are also a few ways we can do this.

- Use a strong name key to sign our assembly and use the strong name membership condition.
- Use a URL membership condition to match the code to the location from which it loads.

There are other possible membership conditions as well, but for the purposes of this discussion, we will keep it simple.

Generally speaking, the strong name membership condition is the way to go in this situation. It allows fine-grained control over the match between the target assemblies and the security policy to be applied based on which assemblies are signed with the strong name key.

There are some additional points to consider as well, such as whether all applications in the call stack will have the required `DirectoryServicesPermission` or whether only a specific assembly will have it, and whether it will use the `Assert` method to block demands for the permission from propagating up the call stack. Additionally, we may need to consider whether our code using `DirectoryServicesPermission` will also be called by partially trusted code and will in turn need the `AllowPartiallyTrustedCallersAttribute` applied to it. Since these questions will vary depending on the exact circumstances of the deployment, we don't have exact prescriptive guidance here.

Partial Trust in .NET 1.x

Partial trust scenarios in .NET version 1.x are similar to those in .NET 2.0, with the following important differences.

- SDS does not have the `AllowPartiallyTrustedCallersAttribute` in .NET 1.x.
- SDS does attempt to enforce the more complicated logic allowed by the `DirectoryServicesPermission` class.

The first point is much more important because it completely changes how we have to use SDS in a partial trust scenario. Because the APTCA attribute is not present in this version, any assembly wishing to use SDS in partial trust must itself have `FullTrust`. Thus, it is not possible to grant a minimum set of permissions to our assembly, as we would prefer from a security perspective.

The reason for this is basically historical. When Microsoft released the original version of the .NET Framework, it was conservative in granting APTCA to the various assemblies shipped with it. Because SDS is so close to the ADSI COM layer and requires some interop for certain tasks, Microsoft did not include SDS in the original list.

We can still apply much of the same logic to our process for .NET 1.x as we did for .NET 2.0. However, instead of creating a specific permission set with `DirectoryServicesPermission` and any other permissions we require, we must apply `FullTrust` to the membership condition we are using to identify our assemblies.

What Use Is DirectoryServicesPermission in .NET 1.x?

We just explained how SDS in .NET 1.x does not allow partially trusted callers. If this is the case, then why have DirectoryServicesPermission? How would it be used if the calling assembly must have FullTrust anyway?

There actually is a scenario where DirectoryServicesPermission might be useful in .NET 1.x, although it is probably not common. Even though the immediate caller must have FullTrust, the permission Demand for DirectoryServicesPermission will propagate up the call stack. If there are partially trusted callers above the fully trusted assembly on the call stack and the intermediate FullTrust assembly allows partially trusted callers and does not block the Demand for the permission via an Assert, then the callers up the call stack will require DirectoryServicesPermission. In this case, the partially trusted assemblies will need to have a membership condition that matches a code group and permission set with DirectoryServicesPermission in it. This scenario is a little obscure, but it could happen. Whether it has ever happened in real life is a good question, though.

It is also important in this circumstance to consider whether our assemblies that call SDS will need the APTCA attribute themselves, and whether they will need to use the Assert method to block the stack walk caused by the Demand for DirectoryServicesPermission from SDS. These factors will depend somewhat on our specific deployment.

Previously we mentioned that DirectoryServicesPermission allows a variety of different configurable options, including allowing different types of access to different directory entry paths. Given that this option is no longer being used in .NET 2.0, we recommend avoiding these features and simply using the Unrestricted option.

SUMMARY

In this chapter, we touched upon some of the more important security topics that SDS developers will face. Binding and the security context is probably the biggest challenge that a developer will encounter. A failure to understand the security context of SDS code is the leading cause of seemingly "random" or "hard-to-diagnose" errors. If we had to recommend one area where we should focus our attention, it is to understand where and in what context our code will be executing.

While writing or reading security descriptors is not as common a task as might be envisioned, it is extremely helpful to understand the basics of how these mechanisms work and are manipulated in SDS. It is also important to understand the differences between versions 1.x and 2.0 of the .NET Framework in this space, as they are definitely not the same.

Finally, a basic understanding of CAS as it relates to SDS will ensure that our code can be deployed across environments. Using .NET, we have some exciting options for deploying our code where it may be partially trusted. Increasingly, a solid understanding of how CAS will affect our deployment options is becoming necessary. While .NET version 1.x made CAS in directory services programming nearly unusable, version 2.0 has made great strides toward providing an easy and consistent model that we can actually use.

■ 9 ■
Introduction to the ActiveDirectory Namespace

I N CHAPTER 2, we briefly outlined a new namespace in version 2.0 of the .NET· Framework, `System.DirectoryServices.ActiveDirectory` (SDS.AD). SDS.AD adds a large number of new classes to the .NET directory services programming landscape that make managing Active Directory and ADAM significantly easier.

We already jumped into some of the features of SDS.AD in Chapter 7, when we demonstrated its new schema management features. Because the namespace is so large, we could probably spend an entire book discussing all of the features available to us. However, since we have limited space and time here, we have decided to focus this chapter on the parts of the namespace that we believe will be most useful for enterprise developers.

We start with the `DirectoryContext` class. `DirectoryContext` is used to initialize many of the other classes in the namespace. As such, it is the key to understanding how to use everything else.

We then move on to a discussion of locating domain controllers. This is probably the most useful feature for enterprise developers in SDS.AD, and the one we use the most often in our work.

We spend a little bit of time discussing how SDS.AD works its magic by marrying together the ADSI-based functionality of `System.DirectoryServices` (SDS) with some Windows APIs used to manage Active Directory.

Understanding the underpinnings helps developers using .NET Framework version 1.x know how to accomplish similar things on their own, without SDS.AD, and gives all of us a better understanding of how things work.

We wrap up with some samples demonstrating our favorite nuggets and gems included in the new namespace that can make our normal SDS programming easier.

Working with the DirectoryContext Class

At the center of SDS.AD is a class called `DirectoryContext`. `DirectoryContext` gathers the information needed to specify which directory to connect to and what credentials to use for the connection, in addition to the type of object that we wish to create. As we glance through the rest of the SDS.AD classes, we notice that nearly all of them seem to take a `DirectoryContext` object as an argument for their methods and constructors.

General Usage

To learn more about how `DirectoryContext` works, let's first look in Listing 9.1 at the class in terms of its public constructors and properties and its key supporting enumeration, `DirectoryContextType`.

LISTING 9.1: The DirectoryContext and DirectoryContextType Public Members

```
public class DirectoryContext
{
    // Constructors
    public DirectoryContext(DirectoryContextType cType);
    public DirectoryContext(
        DirectoryContextType cType,
        string name);
    public DirectoryContext(
        DirectoryContextType cType,
        string username,
        string password);
    public DirectoryContext(
        DirectoryContextType cType,
        string name,
        string username,
        string password);

    // Properties
```

```
    public DirectoryContextType ContextType { get; }
    public string Name { get; }
    public string UserName { get; }
}

public enum DirectoryContextType
{
    Domain,
    Forest,
    DirectoryServer,
    ConfigurationSet,
    ApplicationPartition
}
```

We see right away that each constructor requires us to specify a `DirectoryContextType` enumeration value. This value helps SDS.AD decide how to use the other parameters we have specified to build the object that uses `DirectoryContext` for initialization.

The first constructor requires only a single `DirectoryContextType` parameter. It is intended for creating only `Domain` and `Forest` objects, as the other types of objects, which correspond to the `DirectoryServer`, `ConfigurationSet`, and `ApplicationPartition` enumeration values, require the `name` parameter to be set in order to provide enough information to build the object.

The other three constructors also allow us to provide a `name`, a `username` and `password` combination, or all three additional parameters.

The `name` parameter is used for determining to which directory to connect. This might be the DNS domain name of a domain for an Active Directory domain, or it might be the DNS domain name of a specific ADAM server with its LDAP port included. It depends, again, on what type of context we are creating.

The `username` and `password` parameters are used for supplying alternate security credentials for the connection. This works in much the same way as with the `username` and `password` parameters on the `DirectoryEntry` class that we described in Chapters 3 and 8. If we do not use one of the constructors that take a `username` and `password` parameter, then the current security context is used to make the connection. This is also just like the behavior we already described with the `DirectoryEntry` class. As usual, we generally recommend avoiding the use of specific credentials, but we covered the scenarios where we consider that valid in Chapter 8, and we will not rehash it here.

As we might guess, the `Domain` and `Forest` enumeration values are relevant only when working with Active Directory. After all, ADAM does not have domains and forests! The `ConfigurationSet` value is relevant only when working with ADAM, as configuration sets are exclusively an ADAM concept. On the other hand, `DirectoryServer` and `ApplicationPartition` are relevant for both directories.

■ NOTE DirectoryContext Cannot Be Used with ADAM Users

For whatever reason, Microsoft designed `DirectoryContext` to work exclusively with Windows users. Currently we cannot supply the credentials of an ADAM user, and use them to create any kind of SDS.AD class that references ADAM. Perhaps Microsoft did this because most management of ADAM instances is still done with Windows users. Perhaps it was difficult to make some of the APIs work together, or perhaps Microsoft was concerned about the potential security issues around simple LDAP binds that we described in Chapter 8. In any event, make sure you always use a Windows user when specifying explicit credentials.

The upside of this limitation is that when SDS.AD uses LDAP, it always does a secure LDAP bind (with `Signing` and `Sealing` as well). We never have to worry about SDS.AD passing our credentials on the network in plaintext.

Examples of Using DirectoryContext

Perhaps the easiest way to get the hang of the `DirectoryContext` class is to use it in several examples to build specific types of other SDS.AD objects. In each example, we show what we are trying to do and what our various assumptions and constraints are for doing it.

In Listing 9.2, we show three approaches for building a `Forest` object. The first uses a `DirectoryContext` with only the `DirectoryContextType` supplied. This assumes that we want to use our current security context to build a `Forest` object for the current user's Active Directory forest. The second uses a shortcut on the `Forest` class to do the exact same thing, without actually creating an explicit `DirectoryContext` object. The third

> **▪ NOTE** **Watch Out for IDisposable Again in SDS.AD**
>
> As with our core classes in SDS, many of the classes in SDS.AD implement `IDisposable` as well. While we are not aware of any bugs related to object cleanup in SDS.AD, as there are in SDS in .NET Framework version 1.x, we still recommend proper cleanup of these objects using the standard patterns we showed in Chapter 3.

uses both a forest name in the `name` parameter and alternate credentials to access an Active Directory forest that our current security context might not trust.

LISTING 9.2: Using DirectoryContexts to Create Forest Objects

```
//using System.DirectoryServices.ActiveDirectory;

Forest currentForest = null;
Forest alternateCurrentForest = null;
Forest otherForest = null;

//create a new DirectoryContext for a Forest
//using defaults for name and credentials
DirectoryContext context = new DirectoryContext(
    DirectoryContextType.Forest);

using (currentForest = Forest.GetForest(context))
{
    Console.WriteLine(currentForest.Name);
}

//Use the shortcut static method on the Forest class to
//do the same thing as above
using (alternateCurrentForest = Forest.GetCurrentForest())
{
    Console.WriteLine(alternateCurrentForest.Name);
}

//Now, connect to a completely different forest
//specifying its name and the credentials we need to
//access it
DirectoryContext otherContext = new DirectoryContext(
    DirectoryContextType.Forest,
    "other.yourforest.com",
    @"other\someone",
    "MySecret!0");
```

```
using (otherForest = Forest.GetForest(otherContext))
{
    Console.WriteLine(otherForest.Name);
}
//OUT:
//main.myforest.com
//main.myforest.com
//other.yourforest.com
```

We can use very similar logic to create a `Domain` object, so we will not bother to show that. Essentially, we just need to supply the name of the domain we wish to access and specify the `DirectoryContext-Type.Domain` enumeration value where appropriate. Note, however, that we might also access other domains in the same forest this way instead of completely unrelated domains outside of our forest. Depending on what we are doing, alternate credentials may or may not be required.

Now, let's access a specific server. Listing 9.3 shows an example of accessing an Active Directory domain controller by its DNS name and then an example of accessing an ADAM instance on our local machine using the local administrator account.

LISTING 9.3: Using DirectoryContext to Access Specific Servers

```
//using System.DirectoryServices.ActiveDirectory;
DomainController dc = null;
AdamInstance adam = null;

//create a new DirectoryContext for a
//domain controller using a name and
//default credentials
DirectoryContext dcContext = new DirectoryContext(
    DirectoryContextType.DirectoryServer,
    "mydc.mydomain.com");

using (dc = DomainController.GetDomainController(dcContext))
{
    Console.WriteLine(dc.Name);
}

//Now, connect to a local ADAM instance
//specifying a port and local admin credentials
DirectoryContext adamContext = new DirectoryContext(
    DirectoryContextType.DirectoryServer,
    "127.0.0.1:50000",
```

```
    @"MYMACHINE\administrator",
    "MySecret!0");

using (adam = AdamInstance.GetAdamInstance(adamContext))
{
    Console.WriteLine(adam.Name);
}
//OUT:
//mydc.mydomain.com
//myadaminstance.mydomain.com
```

We can use the `DirectoryServer` enumeration value to build both `DomainController` and `AdamInstance` objects, as they both derive from the same base class, `DirectoryServer`. In each case, we have the option of specifying credentials and may specify the server name in various formats, including DNS domain names and IP addresses. We may also include the port to use if needed, as we might with ADAM. The rules governing the available syntaxes are the same as what we spelled out in detail in Chapter 3 for specifying servers and usernames. Given that the same set of technologies is used under the hood, this should come as no surprise.

If we have an ADAM configuration set, we may use similar logic to the `AdamInstance` part of Listing 9.3 to create a `ConfigurationSet` object by changing our `DirectoryContext` to use the `ConfigurationSet` enumeration value and changing our other classes to use the appropriate `ConfigurationSet` class. Note that we cannot use our normal `using` statement here to take care of object cleanup because for some reason, `ConfigurationSet` does not support `IDisposable`, even though it has a `Dispose` method! We assume that this is just a small glitch that will be cleaned up in a future service pack. Given that this is all new functionality, there's bound to be a rough edge here or there.

Unfortunately, we cannot show every possible example of using a `DirectoryContext` object to build every imaginable type of SDS.AD object, but we hope that by now we've established the ground rules that we can use for building the other types. The key is to understand which values of the `DirectoryContextType` enumeration we can combine with values of the `name` parameter (potentially including a null value) to achieve our goal. We also have most of the same flexibility with the credentials that we have with SDS.

Locating Domain Controllers

We have mentioned the Locator previously throughout the book, especially in Chapter 3 when we were discussing serverless binding. However, until now we have not really taken the time to explain what it is or what we can do with it. For example, when we use an `ADsPath` like `LDAP://DC=mydomain,DC=com` that contains no server name, we are in fact using the Locator service to find a domain controller from the `mydomain.com` domain. Most of the samples we find that demonstrate LDAP programming with Active Directory show the use of serverless binding, but rarely is any mention made about how it actually works.

When we speak of the Locator, we are talking about the Domain Controller Locator as implemented by the local Netlogon service. It is used by various parts of Windows, including LDAP, to automatically find the most appropriate domain controller to contact. The Domain Controller Locator, or simply Locator here, is responsible for making sure that network clients contact the servers that the domain administrators have designated for them to use based on the network topology of the organization. Without it, network clients would have no way to determine which domain controllers to use, so it is a fundamental underpinning of the Active Directory infrastructure.

How the Domain Controller Locator Works

Each domain controller in the domain registers itself in DNS along with the Active Directory site it is in and the sites that it includes. The Locator is called via a remote procedure call (RPC) to the Netlogon service using the `DsGetDcName` API. Once contacted, the client passes some information to the Locator, which in turn looks up a name and then sends a datagram (like a ping) to the domain controller to see if it is alive. For NetBIOS-style names, this datagram is in the form of a mailslot message. For DNS-style names, it is an LDAP search using UDP rather than TCP. Starting with the domain controllers that are in the site closest to the caller (as determined by looking up the client's site) the Locator sends a datagram to each domain controller and returns when the first one responds. Information about the "winning" domain controller is then cached such that subsequent uses of the Locator will return the cached information. However, eventually the cache will expire, or another process on the machine might force a refresh, and the Locator will initiate this process again. This last point is important to understand. We should not code any application to expect that the Locator will always return the same information. There is no guarantee that the same domain controller will always be contacted.

Finally, it may seem obvious, but the Locator is used only with Active Directory. ADAM requires a server name to be specified when constructing an LDAP string, as is the case with many other pure LDAP directories.

Using the Locator Service

The Locator can be accessed from the `Domain`, `Forest`, `ApplicationPartition`, `DomainController`, and `GlobalCatalog` classes. All of these classes contain methods used to find a single domain controller or to enumerate all domain controllers. Each method uses the Locator to accomplish this. Listing 9.4 demonstrates how to use the Locator to find a single domain controller.

LISTING 9.4: Finding a Single Domain Controller

```
DirectoryContext ctx = new DirectoryContext(
    DirectoryContextType.Domain,
    "mydomain.org",
    );

using (DomainController dc = DomainController.FindOne(ctx))
{
    Console.WriteLine(dc.Name);
    Console.WriteLine(dc.OSVersion);
    Console.WriteLine(dc.SiteName);
    Console.WriteLine(dc.IPAddress);
    Console.WriteLine(dc.Forest);
    Console.WriteLine(dc.CurrentTime);
}
```

Under the hood, SDS.AD calls the `DsGetDcName` API to accomplish this. SDS.AD internally uses this function to get the name of a domain controller in the domain we specify. It then calls another function, called `DsGetDomainControllerInfo`, and it performs an LDAP search to pull all the information together about a particular domain controller.

Enumerating All Domain Controllers

In addition to returning information about a domain controller, we can use the Locator to enumerate all the domain controllers in the domain. Listing 9.5 shows one such example using the Domain class.

LISTING 9.5: Enumerating All Domain Controllers

```
Domain domain = Domain.GetCurrentDomain();

using (domain)
{
    foreach (DomainController dc in
        domain.FindAllDiscoverableDomainControllers())
    {
        using (dc)
        {
            Console.WriteLine(dc.Name);
            Console.WriteLine(dc.OSVersion);
            Console.WriteLine(dc.SiteName);
            Console.WriteLine(dc.IPAddress);
            Console.WriteLine(dc.Forest);
            Console.WriteLine(dc.CurrentTime);
        }
    }
}
```

Advanced Locator Features

This is nice, but so far, we haven't shown much that we cannot accomplish with a simple serverless bind, a bind using a DNS domain name, or some basic LDAP searches to find all of the domain controllers in a domain. However, serverless binding does not allow us to harness the full power of the Locator. In fact, the underlying API, DsGetDcName, allows us to specify a variety of options that change its behavior. In SDS.AD, these are expressed in the LocatorOptions enumeration. The option that we think is most interesting is the ForceRediscovery value, as it can be used to purge the internal cache and locate a domain controller again. If we suspect that our domain controller has suddenly stopped responding, we can now proactively try to find a new one. Let's modify Listing 9.4 to show how easy this is. Listing 9.6 now forces a rediscovery.

LISTING 9.6: Forcing Rediscovery

```
DirectoryContext ctx = new DirectoryContext(
    DirectoryContextType.Domain,
    "mydomain.org",
    );

//Notice the extra parameter here...
using (DomainController dc = DomainController.FindOne(
    ctx,
    LocatorOptions.ForceRediscovery)
)
{
    Console.WriteLine(dc.Name);
    Console.WriteLine(dc.OSVersion);
    Console.WriteLine(dc.SiteName);
    Console.WriteLine(dc.IPAddress);
    Console.WriteLine(dc.Forest);
    Console.WriteLine(dc.CurrentTime);
}
```

All we did was use the overloaded `FindOne` method that takes a `LocatorOptions` parameter, and then specify `ForceRediscovery`. Now, if our previous domain controller were truly down, we would get a brand-new result. Perhaps we can take the new server information and use that to recover gracefully from whatever problems our other code might have encountered when the previous domain controller went offline. Obviously, this depends on what we were doing and how we built our application, but at least we have some control!

In addition to specifying `LocatorOptions`, we can also use the feature in `DsGetDcName` that allows us to specify a specific Active Directory site name so that we can locate a domain controller in an arbitrary site. Serverless binding will always use the current site, so we don't have this kind of flexibility with it. Let's modify Listing 9.4 one more time to demonstrate this. Listing 9.7 shows how we specify a site to use.

LISTING 9.7: Finding a Domain Controller by Site Name

```
DirectoryContext ctx = new DirectoryContext(
    DirectoryContextType.Domain,
    "mydomain.org",
    );
```

```
//Now we are specifying a site name
using (DomainController dc = DomainController.FindOne(
    ctx,
    "othersite")
)
{
    Console.WriteLine(dc.Name);
    Console.WriteLine(dc.OSVersion);
    Console.WriteLine(dc.SiteName);
    Console.WriteLine(dc.IPAddress);
    Console.WriteLine(dc.Forest);
    Console.WriteLine(dc.CurrentTime);
}
```

While our sample does not show this, we can also specify `LocatorOptions` in addition to a site name, as the `FindOne` method actually has four overloads that allow all of the combinations.

In addition to that, the `Domain`, `Forest`, `GlobalCatalog`, and `ApplicationPartition` classes all have similar methods that tie into the same infrastructure. No matter where we start or what we are looking for, we now have the full power of the Locator to find any kind of domain controller, global catalog server, or set of servers that we need.

DsGetDcName under the Hood

To replicate finding a single domain controller in .NET 1.1, we would need to wrap many of these API calls ourselves. In order to understand better what SDS.AD is doing, let's look more closely at the `DsGetDcName` C++ API declaration and its parameters:

```
DWORD DsGetDcName(
  LPCTSTR ComputerName,
  LPCTSTR DomainName,
  GUID* DomainGuid,
  LPCTSTR SiteName,
  ULONG Flags,
  PDOMAIN_CONTROLLER_INFO* DomainControllerInfo
);
```

`DsGetDcName` is the core function used to invoke the Locator. We can call it using P/Invoke and return domain controllers by domain, site, or computer (the domain associated with a particular member server). Using some flags that we already described in the context of the `LocatorOptions` enumeration, we can additionally require that the returned domain controller have some specific characteristics. The output of this API is a DOMAIN_CONTROLLER_INFO structure. Listing 9.8 is a sample C# P/Invoke declaration for this structure and shows all of the useful information returned in it.

LISTING 9.8: DOMAIN_CONTROLLER_INFO Structure

```
using LPTSTR = System.String;
using BOOL = System.Int32;
using GUID = System.Guid;
using DWORD = System.Uint32;

[StructLayout(LayoutKind.Sequential, CharSet = CharSet.Auto)]
internal struct DOMAIN_CONTROLLER_INFO
{
    internal LPTSTR DomainControllerName;
    internal LPTSTR DomainControllerAddress;
    internal DWORD DomainControllerAddressType;
    internal GUID DomainGuid;
    internal LPTSTR DomainName;
    internal LPTSTR DnsForestName;
    internal DWORD Flags;
    internal LPTSTR DcSiteName;
    internal LPTSTR ClientSiteName;
}
```

Just as SDS.AD does under the hood, once we have the name of a domain controller, we can use DsGetDomainControllerInfo to return more information about the domain controller itself. Listing 9.9 shows another C# declaration for the returned structure.

LISTING 9.9: C# Declaration of Structure Returned by DsGetDomainControllerInfo

```
using LPTSTR = System.String;
using BOOL = System.Int32;
using GUID = System.Guid;

[StructLayout(LayoutKind.Sequential, CharSet = CharSet.Auto)]
internal struct DOMAIN_CONTROLLER_INFO_2
{
    internal LPTSTR NetbiosName;
    internal LPTSTR DnsHostName;
    internal LPTSTR SiteName;
    internal LPTSTR SiteObjectName;
    internal LPTSTR ComputerObjectName;
    internal LPTSTR ServerObjectName;
    internal LPTSTR NtdsDsaObjectName;
    internal BOOL fIsPdc;
```

```
    internal BOOL fDsEnabled;
    internal BOOL fIsGc;
    internal GUID SiteObjectGuid;
    internal GUID ComputerObjectGuid;
    internal GUID ServerObjectGuid;
    internal GUID NtdsDsaObjectGuid;
}
```

One thing to note about the `DsGetDomainControllerInfo` function is that it actually returns an array of structures shown in Listing 9.9. We need to iterate through the returned structures to find the one in which we are interested.

To enumerate multiple domain controllers, SDS.AD is using the `DsGetDcOpen` method to get a handle (pointer) to an enumeration context. When used in conjunction with `DsGetDcNext` and `DsGetDcClose`, these three API functions enumerate all of the available domain controllers. To replicate this functionality in .NET 1.1, not only would we need to wrap these three methods, but we would also need to ensure that our code was used only on the Windows XP platform or later. Some of these functions do not exist in previous versions of Windows. Internally, SDS.AD is making this decision for us and is using the DNS to generate the same information if our code executes on Windows 2000 or Windows NT4. Obviously, it would take considerable effort to build something this easy to use in version 1.x of the .NET Framework, so we are glad to have SDS.AD these days!

Applications for Locating Domain Controllers

So, why do we need this? We already discussed some of the applications for `LocatorOptions` for forcing rediscovery and we demonstrated how we could locate domain controllers in other sites. Sometimes we need to enumerate the domain controllers in the domain to inspect nonreplicated attribute values that will be different on every server. As an example, in order to accurately find the last time a user has logged into the domain, we need to inspect the nonreplicated `lastLogon` attribute. We demonstrate this in Chapter 10. Obviously, there are many other possible uses for the Locator than what we've demonstrated, but these are a few of our favorite applications.

Understanding the Active Directory RPC APIs

Before SDS.AD, Active Directory programmers were forced into different camps based on the programming language they used. The original design of the directory services APIs had some features of Active Directory available via LDAP, and others were available only by RPC calls. The LDAP features were (for the most part) available to the higher-level languages because they could use ADSI with the `LDAP` provider. However, the RPC calls were designed for C++ users only. While some of these APIs got explicit ADSI wrappers (for example, `DsCrackNames` and `IADsNameTranslate`), many did not.

As such, the high-level languages were second-class citizens. This tradition continued with .NET Framework version 1.x, as SDS really just wrapped ADSI functionality. While we had the ability to access the other APIs via P/Invoke, they were not packaged neatly for us.

The key design challenge for the SDS.AD namespace was to find a way to marry the LDAP and RPC functionality together into a cohesive design. In our opinion, this design is quite successful and is leaps and bounds better than what we had before or what we would likely have cobbled together on our own with a bunch of P/Invoke statements.

The purpose of this section is to briefly overview some of the other Active Directory RPC APIs to get a better feel for what they do. Table 9.1 breaks down most of them and categorizes them by use. We also show which ones SDS.AD uses directly.

As Table 9.1 shows, SDS.AD uses quite a few of these API calls. We would need to wrap each method ourselves in order to achieve similar functionality. Since we know that this is a lot of work, we have created wrappers for a number of the methods listed in Table 9.1 for you and we included them on this book's web site for download.

Useful Shortcuts for Developers

In addition to the methods we have already discussed for creating different SDS.AD objects with the `DirectoryContext` class and locating and enumerating domain controllers, a number of shortcuts are exposed by SDS.AD that make normal SDS programming easier too. The following is a grab bag of our favorites.

TABLE 9.1: Active Directory RPC API Functions

Purpose	RPC function	Wrapped in SDS.AD
These APIs are used to access the Locator services. With them, we can find the current domain, forest, global catalog servers, and all domain controllers. All of these methods allow anonymous credentials.	`DsGetDcName`	Yes
	`DsGetDcOpen`	Yes
	`DsGetDcNext`	Yes
	`DsGetSiteName`	No
	`DsGetDcSiteCoverage`	No
	`DsGetDcClose`	Yes
	`NetApiBufferFree`	Yes
In order to use a number of the other Ds* APIs, we must have a handle to an RPC session with a domain controller. These APIs are used to bind to the directory and obtain the handle necessary for further Ds* API calls.	`DsBind`	No
	`DsBindWithCred`	Yes
	`DsBindWithSpn`	No
	`DsBindWithSpnEx`	No
	`DsMakePasswordCredentials`	Yes
	`DsUnBind`	Yes
	`DsFreePasswordCredentials`	Yes
Once we have an established RPC session, we can use the handle we obtained to query for more information or to use utility functions. These methods use an authenticated session and return information that would be difficult to obtain without fairly complicated directory searches.	`DsGetDomainControllerInfo`	Yes
	`DsListDomainsInSite`	Yes
	`DsListInfoForServer`	No
	`DsListRoles`	Yes
	`DsListSites`	Yes
	`DsListServersInSite`	No
	`DsListServersForDomainInSite`	No
	`DsCrackNames`	Yes
	`DsFreeDomainControllerInfo`	Yes
	`DsFreeNameResult`	Yes

Active Directory Shortcuts

Throughout this book, we have shown quite a few examples of how we can bind to the `RootDSE` object to obtain the distinguished name (DN) values for our directory partitions. We subsequently use those DN values to create `DirectoryEntry` objects bound to those root partitions. Listing 9.10 shows how this typically looks.

LISTING 9.10: Binding to the Default Naming Context

```
DirectoryEntry root = new DirectoryEntry(
    "LDAP://RootDSE",
    null,
    null,
    AuthenticationTypes.Secure
    );

using (root)
{
    string attr = "defaultNamingContext";
    string dnc = root.Properties[attr][0].ToString();
}

DirectoryEntry entry = new DirectoryEntry(
    "LDAP:// + dnc",
    null,
    null,
    AuthenticationTypes.Secure
    );

using (entry)
{
    //now we are bound to default context
}
```

SDS.AD has something much easier. We can simply use the `Domain` class to accomplish the same thing in a few lines of code. Listing 9.11 shows a revised example that demonstrates how this would work.

LISTING 9.11: Binding to the Default Naming Context, Revised

```
Domain domain = Domain.GetCurrentDomain();

using (domain)
using (DirectoryEntry entry = domain.GetDirectoryEntry())
{
    //now we are bound to default context
}
```

The second method is obviously easier to use. Additionally, we can still use the `DirectoryContext` class and the other methods on the `Domain` class to control which domain to use and what security context we want to establish. We have not lost any crucial flexibility in this simplification.

Several other classes give us similar shortcuts to the other key partitions that we use frequently. Using the `ActiveDirectorySchema` class, for instance, we can get a `DirectoryEntry` bound to the schema partition (see Listing 9.12).

LISTING 9.12: **Getting the Schema Container**

```
ActiveDirectorySchema ads = ActiveDirectorySchema.GetCurrentSchema();

using (ads)
using (DirectoryEntry entry = ads.GetDirectoryEntry())
{
    //bound to schema partition
}
```

Finally, the `Forest` and `Domain` classes now make quick work of locating those pesky FSMO role holder servers that we occasionally care about. It is so easy that it isn't worth showing a code sample, but check out the `SchemaRoleOwner` and `NamingRoleOwner` properties on the `Forest` class and the `InfrastructureRoleOwner`, `PdcRoleOwner`, and `RidRoleOwner` properties on the `Domain` class.

ADAM Shortcuts

For ADAM, we always need to know the name of the server where our ADAM instance resides. Since a server could host more than one instance of ADAM, the only difference would be the port number on which each instance was listening.

Using SDS.AD, we can easily enumerate our ADAM instances, and even set the `defaultNamingContext` attribute for easy default partition binds later. Listing 9.13 shows an example of how to perform the enumeration.

LISTING 9.13: **Enumerating ADAM Instances**

```
DirectoryContext ctx = new DirectoryContext(
    DirectoryContextType.DirectoryServer,
    "servername"
    );
```

```
ConfigurationSet cs = ConfigurationSet.GetConfigurationSet(ctx);

foreach (AdamInstance ai in cs.AdamInstances)
{
    Console.WriteLine(ai.DefaultPartition);
}
```

Unlike the previous Active Directory examples, using `GetDirectory-Entry` from the `AdamInstance` will not return us an entry bound to the default partition. By default, ADAM does not have a value set for the `defaultNamingContext` attribute.

However, we can set a `defaultNamingContext` attribute by setting the `DefaultPartition` property on our `AdamInstance` and calling the `Save` method. Listing 9.14 demonstrates.

LISTING 9.14: Setting the defaultNamingContext Attribute in ADAM

```
AdamInstance adam;
DirectoryContext ctx = new DirectoryContext(
    DirectoryContextType.DirectoryServer,
    "localhost:389");

using (adam = AdamInstance.GetAdamInstance(ctx))
{
    adam.DefaultPartition = "O=My,C=Adam";
    adam.Save();
}
```

Once we do this, a `defaultNamingContext` attribute will be set and published in the `RootDSE` object. We can then use it to form a DN and bind to the default partition, as we are used to doing with Active Directory.

SUMMARY

At this point, we know just enough about `System.DirectorySer-vices.ActiveDirectory` to be dangerous. Instead of an exhaustive study of the entire namespace, we took the approach of focusing on the features most relevant to enterprise developers.

The `DirectoryContext` class is the starting point for nearly everything else in SDS.AD. We demonstrated how to use it correctly to build some of the core objects such as the `Forest`, `Domain`, and `DirectoryServer` classes. We also discussed how its parameters determine what type of object will be built, what directory we will connect to, and what security context we'll use.

Our favorite feature of SDS.AD is the integration of the Domain Controller Locator. We showed how we can locate domain controllers in Active Directory using a variety of options and demonstrated how to enumerate domain controllers. We got under the hood a little bit and discussed how the Active Directory RPC APIs are used to make all of this work.

We then continued with our discussion of the Active Directory RPC APIs with a listing of what they do and which ones are used in SDS.AD. This deeper understanding helps us to know how SDS.AD does its magic.

We wrapped up with some of our favorite little features in SDS.AD that make our lives easier when programming in plain-old SDS.

PART II
Practical Applications

■ 10 ■
User Management

I N THIS SECTION, we take many of the abstract concepts we learned in the first part of the book and begin to apply them to real-world problems. One of the most common programming activities that most developers will perform against Active Directory and ADAM is user account management.

Active Directory user management is fairly straightforward once we know all of the basic rules. However, there are many interesting rules and behaviors concerning how attribute values in Active Directory are used to determine how user objects behave in Windows. In order to get the results we want, it is important to learn these rules and behaviors. We try to demonstrate most of them in this chapter.

To a lesser extent, we also investigate user account management in ADAM. ADAM is very similar to Active Directory in most respects, but it has a few significant differences worth pointing out.

Finding Users

When we speak of user objects for the remainder of this chapter, we are really talking about the user class in both Active Directory and ADAM. This is the class that acts as a security principal for Active Directory (and often, for ADAM). It is typically the class that we care the most about. The first thing we are likely to want to do with user accounts in Active Directory is find them. Given all that we know about searching from Chapters 4 and 5, this should be easy. Essentially, we just need to know where we want to search and what filter to use to find users.

Let's start with the LDAP filter. Our goal is to build an LDAP filter that will find exactly what we want and that will be as efficient as possible. A few attributes in Active Directory distinguish `user` objects from other object types that we can use to build a filter:

- `objectCategory`
- `objectClass`
- `sAMAccountName`
- `sAMAccountType`

The `objectCategory` attribute has the advantage of being single-valued and indexed by default on all versions of Active Directory. This attribute is meant to be used to group common types of objects together so that we can search across all of them. Many of the schema classes related to users share the same value of `person` as their object category. While this is useful for searches in which we want to find information across many different types of user-related objects, it is not as useful for finding the `user` objects we typically care about (which are usually security principals). For example, in Active Directory, since both `user` and `contact` classes share the same `objectCategory` value of `person`, it alone will not tell them apart.

The `objectClass` attribute seems like a no-brainer, as `(object-Class=user)` will always find `user` objects exclusively. The problem here is that in many forests, the `objectClass` attribute is not indexed and it is always multivalued. As we know from the section titled Optimizing Search Performance, in Chapter 5, we generally want to try to avoid searches on nonindexed attributes, so using `objectClass` alone in a filter might not be the most efficient solution. This is why we see a lot of samples that search for `user` objects using an indexed filter like this:

```
(&(objectCategory=person)(objectClass=user))
```

This will get the job done, but we can do even better than this.

> **▪ NOTE**   Behavior Change in Windows Server 2003
>
> Windows Server 2003 Active Directory indexes the `objectClass` attribute by default, so this rule really only applies to Windows 2000 Active Directory now. Additionally, the schema administrators for your domain may have already indexed it, so check the schema before making assumptions.

One key difference between `contact` objects and `user` objects in Active Directory is that `user` objects have a `sAMAccountName` attribute that is indexed by default. Thus, we could build a filter like this:

```
(&(objectCategory=person)(sAMAccountName=*))
```

This will separate the contacts from the users effectively. However, another approach is available that can find `user` objects directly, and it may be the most efficient technique for Active Directory:

```
(sAMAccountType=805306368)
```

Using the `sAMAccountType` attribute with a value of `805306368` accesses a single-valued, indexed attribute that uniquely defines `user` objects. The only downside here is that this attribute is not well documented, so it may not be recommended by Microsoft. However, in our investigations, it is effective.

One piece of good news is that all of these attributes are included in the global catalog, so we can use all of these filters there as well.

This should provide a foundation to build on for various `user` object searches. We may also wish to combine these filters with other attributes to find different subsets of `user` objects matching specific criteria. We will see some examples of that in the rest of this section.

Finding Users in ADAM

Things change a little bit for ADAM, because we don't have things like `sAMAccountName` or `sAMAccountType` on an ADAM user. These attributes are actually from the auxiliary class called `securityPrincipal`. This class happens to be slightly different depending on whether it comes from

Active Directory or ADAM. In this case, the securityPrincipal class does not contain sAMAccountName or related attributes in ADAM.

This means that we need to adjust our filters slightly to find our users in ADAM. It turns out that we can use some other indexed attributes, such as userPrincipalName, to find our users. However, since this attribute is not required, we have to be careful and ensure that all of our user objects have set a value for userPrincipalName.

As mentioned in Chapter 8, ADAM also includes the idea of a user-Proxy object that we often will want to return as well. To do so, we should look for common attributes found on both classes that would filter them for our needs. In this case, we know that both the user and userProxy classes contain userPrincipalName, so it is a good candidate for this purpose. We could use a simple filter such as (userPrincipalName=*) if we knew that all of our objects would have a value set for this attribute. However, since not all user or userProxy objects might have a value set for userPrincipalName, we would have to use objectCategory to be safe. For example:

```
(|(objectCategory=person)(objectCategory=userProxy))
```

The implications here are that if any other class in the directory also shared the same objectCategory of person or userProxy, they would also be returned. In default ADAM instances, this does not occur, but we should always check with our particular ADAM instance. Now, if we want to separate the two classes and treat them differently, we can use object-Class, as the classes are different for each type:

```
(&(objectClass=user)(objectCategory=person))
```

```
(&(objectClass=userProxy)(objectCategory=userProxy))
```

The first filter will return only user objects using objectCategory as an index, and the second will return only userProxy objects in the same manner. It is important to remember that we can customize ADAM heavily with application-specific classes. We should never rely on the fact that any particular class will be there or even be indexed. As such, these are only guidelines, and we really need to check the particular ADAM instance's schema ourselves to determine what is there.

> **■ NOTE** **New Versions of ADAM Include the userProxyFull Class**
>
> With later versions of ADAM, a new class called `userProxyFull` can be found that essentially mirrors the `user` class with the addition of the `msDS-BindProxy` auxiliary class. This means that we cannot use `objectCategory` to distinguish between `user` and `userProxyFull` classes as we can with `userProxy` classes. We must instead rely upon the `objectClass` to distinguish between the two. This is another example of where we need to be cognizant of what our schema is for ADAM.

Creating Users

Creating users in Active Directory is actually just like creating any other object in the directory. We simply create an instance of the class we want and set any required attributes on the object. However, to get a fully functional user object that is "enabled," has a password, and has other useful attributes takes a bit more work.

But first, the basics! Let's create a `user` object in an organizational unit called `people` that exists in the root of our domain (see Listing 10.1).

LISTING 10.1: Creating an Active Directory or ADAM User

```
DirectoryEntry parent = new DirectoryEntry(
    "LDAP://OU=people,DC=mydomain,DC=com",
    null,
    null,
    AuthenticationTypes.Secure
    );

DirectoryEntry user =
    parent.Children.Add("CN=test.user", "user");

using (user)
{
    //sAMAccountName is required for W2k AD, we would not use
    //this for ADAM, however.
    user.Properties["sAMAccountName"].Value = "test.user";

    //userPrincipalName is not required, but recommended
    //for ADAM. AD also contains this, so we can use it.
    user.Properties["userPrincipalName"].Value = "test.user";
    user.CommitChanges();
}
```

As Listing 10.1 demonstrates, creating a user is pretty simple. We just need to know the distinguished name (DN) of the object that will serve as the user's parent container. This is typically an organizational unit, but it could be a container or a lot of different things in ADAM. We should also note that ADAM is slightly different from Active Directory in that sAMAccountName does not exist in ADAM, so there are actually no required attributes! Instead, we chose to populate userPrincipal-Name (which is a good idea in both Active Directory and ADAM). The userPrincipalName attribute is one of the accepted names used for binding to the directory.

If we remember from Chapter 3, we know that creating an object requires supplying a relative distinguished name (RDN) value. The prefix that we should use is defined in the schema by the rDNAttId attribute on the class. Active Directory and ADAM tend to use the CN RDN prefix for a number of object types; however, it is not uncommon for third-party LDAP directories from other vendors to use something different (e.g., UID). The RDN prefix (e.g., CN, OU, O, etc.) will differ slightly by object, but for user objects, we should generally choose the CN prefix. Essentially, we must always supply the name using the correct RDN attribute name for the class being created.

In Listing 10.1, we set the sAMAccountName attribute. This is not strictly required in the Windows 2003 version of Active Directory, but it is in the Windows 2000 version. Windows 2003 Active Directory will pick a random name for us, though, so it is probably a good idea to set one intentionally, especially since this is the user's login name in the Windows NT format (domain\login).

While the code in Listing 10.1 will create a user object in Active Directory (and with slight modification, in ADAM) it will not be very useful. The user account will not have a password, it will contain very few attributes, and it will not even be enabled by default. While some of these attributes are simple strings that do not require anything particularly complicated to set, passwords and account properties are more complicated. The sections that follow detail how to deal with them and make user accounts behave like the user accounts we have come to expect.

Managing User Account Features

Creating user objects in Active Directory is not difficult. As we have seen, with the right permissions, we can create a basic user account in just a few lines of code.

However, getting user objects to behave like Windows user accounts is a bit more challenging. Windows accounts have many features, such as enabled/disabled status, names and identifications used for security and email, password management, and expiration and lockout status, all of which require more-intimate knowledge of how things work under the hood. The next several sections explore this in detail.

Managing Basic User Account Properties in Active Directory

Many of the important behaviors associated with a Windows account in Active Directory, such as enabled/disabled status, are controlled by an attribute called userAccountControl. This attribute contains a 32-bit integer that represents a bitwise enumeration of various flags that control account behavior.

These flags are represented in ADSI by an enumerated constant called ADS_USER_FLAG. Because this enumeration is so important in terms of working with user objects in System.DirectoryServices (SDS), we will convert the ADSI enumeration into a .NET-style enumeration, as shown in Listing 10.2.

LISTING 10.2: User Account Control Flags

```
[Flags]
public enum AdsUserFlags
{
    Script = 1,                                   // 0x1
    AccountDisabled = 2,                          // 0x2
    HomeDirectoryRequired = 8,                    // 0x8
    AccountLockedOut = 16,                        // 0x10
    PasswordNotRequired = 32,                     // 0x20
    PasswordCannotChange = 64,                    // 0x40
    EncryptedTextPasswordAllowed = 128,           // 0x80
    TempDuplicateAccount = 256,                   // 0x100
    NormalAccount = 512,                          // 0x200
    InterDomainTrustAccount = 2048,               // 0x800
    WorkstationTrustAccount = 4096,               // 0x1000
    ServerTrustAccount = 8192,                    // 0x2000
    PasswordDoesNotExpire = 65536,                // 0x10000
```

```
        MnsLogonAccount = 131072,                               // 0x20000
        SmartCardRequired = 262144,                             // 0x40000
        TrustedForDelegation = 524288,                          // 0x80000
        AccountNotDelegated = 1048576,                          // 0x100000
        UseDesKeyOnly= 2097152,                                 // 0x200000
        DontRequirePreauth= 4194304,                            // 0x400000
        PasswordExpired = 8388608,                              // 0x800000
        TrustedToAuthenticateForDelegation = 16777216,  // 0x1000000
        NoAuthDataRequired = 33554432                           // 0x2000000
    }
```

As we look through the members of this enumeration, we see a variety of words we associate with Windows accounts, such as `AccountDisabled` and `PasswordNotRequired` (the last one we hope you never use!). We also see some flags that we probably do not recognize, such as `MnsLogonAccount` and `UseDesKeyOnly`. For the most part, the esoteric flags are not important in daily account management tasks, so we can ignore them. Chances are, if we need these flags we are probably quite aware of them already.

The important thing to note is that even though 21 flags are currently defined for use with the `userAccountControl` attribute, Active Directory does not actually use all of them! Specifically, the ones that are not meaningful to Active Directory are

- `AccountLockedOut`
- `PasswordCannotChange`
- `PasswordExpired`

Active Directory actually uses different mechanisms to control these account properties, so do not try to read them from `userAccountControl`! We discuss how to deal with the special cases in the upcoming sections.

Reading User Account Properties

Reading the `userAccountControl` attribute is simple. Listing 10.3 uses an enumeration we defined in Listing 10.2.

LISTING 10.3: Reading the userAccountControl Attribute

```
DirectoryEntry user = new DirectoryEntry(
    "LDAP://CN=User1,CN=users,DC=domain,DC=com",
    null,
```

```
    null,
    AuthenticationTypes.Secure
    );

AdsUserFlags userFlags = (AdsUserFlags)
    user.Properties["userAccountControl"].Value;

Console.WriteLine(
    "AdsUserFlags for {0}: {1}",
    user.Path,
    userFlags
    );
```

This will generally write `NormalAccount` to the console for a typical user and may include other flags as well, depending on our specific deployment. If the account is disabled, `AccountDisabled` will be displayed in addition.

For Windows Server 2003 Active Directory, we could also use the `msDS-User-Account-Control-Computed` attribute in place of `userAccountControl`. Since it is constructed, we would need to use our `RefreshCache` technique from Chapter 3. However, the one benefit of using this attribute is that the three flags we previously mentioned as not being used with `userAccountControl` would actually be used and be accurate. This is not an option with Windows 2000 Server Active Directory installations—they will always need to use `userAccountControl` for reading user account properties.

Writing User Account Properties

Writing values is equally as easy as reading them. We just create an integer value representing the proper combination of flags and overwrite the existing `userAccountControl` value, as shown in Listing 10.4.

LISTING 10.4: Writing Account Values

```
DirectoryEntry entry = new DirectoryEntry(
    "LDAP://CN=some user,CN=users,DC=mydomain,DC=com",
    null,
    null,
    AuthenticationTypes.Secure
    );

AdsUserFlags newValue = AdsUserFlags.NormalAccount
```

```
 | AdsUserFlags.DontExpirePassword;

entry.Properties["userAccountControl"].Value = newValue;
entry.CommitChanges()
```

The trick here is that we must use valid combinations of flag values. In addition, other aspects of the account or the policies in effect may prevent certain values from being set.

A classic example that can trip up new developers happens when enabling an account by "unsetting" the `AccountDisabled` flag. In many domains, a minimum password length is required for all user accounts (and hopefully this is what you use as well). An account cannot be enabled unless it has a password. Therefore, we must set a valid password before enabling the account.

As a result, many typical provisioning processes that create accounts follow this protocol.

1. Create the account with initial values and commit changes.
2. Use the `SetPassword` operation to set an initial password.
3. Enable the account and commit changes again.

Keep this in mind when creating and provisioning user accounts if errors occur.

Delegation Settings

Three flags in the enumeration relate to delegation, which we discussed in Chapter 8. Specifically, `TrustedForDelegation` and `TrustedToAuthenticateForDelegation` are used by service accounts that will be allowed to delegate users' credentials to other machines. The difference between them is that `TrustedForDelegation` is the "unconstrained" delegation setting that works with Windows 2000 Server, and it represents the flag used when only Kerberos authentication is allowed in constrained delegation. `TrustedToAuthenticateForDelegation` is new with Windows Server 2003 and is used when delegation from any protocol is allowed. This is known as the "Protocol Transition" setting.

Finally, `AccountNotDelegated` is used to flag an account as "sensitive and cannot be delegated." This is typically used on highly privileged accounts such as those used by directory administrators, where we would probably not want their account to be delegated by another service due to the security risk it poses.

Managing Basic User Account Properties in ADAM

ADAM works differently than Active Directory in that it does not rely on the `userAccountControl` attribute to maintain important account properties. Instead, Microsoft introduced a number of attributes prefixed with `ms-DS-` or `msDS` to hold this information:

- `ms-DS-UserAccountAutoLocked`*
- `msDS-User-Account-Control-Computed`*
- `msDS-UserAccountDisabled`
- `msDS-UserDontExpirePassword`
- `ms-DS-UserEncryptedTextPasswordAllowed`
- `msDS-UserPasswordExpired`*
- `ms-DS-UserPasswordNotRequired`

The * in the preceding list indicates that the attribute is constructed.

With the exception of the integer-valued `msDS-User-Account-Control-Computed`, these attributes are Boolean values in the directory. Some of these attributes are also constructed attributes and as such, they cannot be written. We wish we could say there was some method behind the slightly different `ldapDisplayName` prefix values, but it just appears that it was overlooked.

Reading User Account Properties

The constructed attribute called `msDS-User-Account-Control-Computed` takes the place of `userAccountControl` in ADAM. This attribute is new to Windows Server 2003 Active Directory and ADAM and we can use it rather than `userAccountControl` to read account properties. However, given that this is a constructed attribute, we can neither search on any values held within it nor set any values on this attribute. Listing 10.5 demonstrates how similar it is to read this attribute compared to using the userAccountCon-trol attribute in Listing 10.3.

LISTING 10.5: Reading the msDS-User-Account-Control-Computed Attribute

```
DirectoryEntry user = new DirectoryEntry(
    "LDAP://CN=User1,CN=users,DC=domain,DC=com",
    null,
    null,
    AuthenticationTypes.Secure
    );

//this is a pain to type a lot :)
string msDS = "msDS-User-Account-Control-Computed";

using (user)
{
    //this is constructed attribute
    user.RefreshCache(
        new string[]{msDS}
        );

    AdsUserFlags userFlags =
        (AdsUserFlags)user.Properties[msDS].Value;

    Console.WriteLine(
        "AdsUserFlags for {0}: {1}",
        user.Path,
        userFlags
        );
}
```

We should note that the msDS-User-Account-Control-Computed attribute will accurately hold values like AccountLockedOut, Password-CannotChange, and PasswordExpired. This departs from the user-AccountControl attribute, where these values are not represented accurately because the flags are not used. We also have the option of using the special "alias" attributes such as ms-DS-UserAccountAutoLocked here. We simply read the Boolean value they return. In many cases, this may be more straightforward.

Writing User Account Properties

Since the `userAccountControl` attribute is not used with ADAM, and its equivalent but constructed attribute cannot be written, we need to use the other `msDS` and `ms-DS` attributes to actually set values. Listing 10.6 shows one such example where we can enable or disable an ADAM account.

LISTING 10.6: Writing Account Values

```
string adsPath =
    "LDAP://localhost:389/"
    + "CN=User1,OU=Users,O=dunnry,C=US";

DirectoryEntry user = new DirectoryEntry(
    adsPath,
    null,
    null,
    AuthenticationTypes.Secure
    );

string attrib = "msDS-UserAccountDisabled";

using (user)
{
    //disable the account
    user.Properties[attrib].Value = true;
    user.CommitChanges();
}
```

As writing each of the other nonconstructed Boolean account properties is exactly the same, we will not demonstrate further examples. The key point to take away here is that we need to look to these attributes in lieu of using the `userAccountControl` attribute for ADAM.

■ **NOTE**   Boolean Attributes Can Accept String Values as Well

Boolean syntax attributes can accept both the .NET Boolean `true` and `false` as well as the LDAP string equivalent `TRUE` and `FALSE` (note the case). This is because the underlying value is held as a string in the LDAP directory and only marshaled as a Boolean for us to use in .NET. If we remember that searching for Boolean attributes requires using `TRUE` and `FALSE`, all of this stuff starts to make sense. Since using the actual Boolean type in .NET tends to be easier, we only mention it in passing as a fun factoid.

Determining Domain-Wide Account Policies

When working with user accounts in Active Directory, it is common to need to refer to domain-wide account policies. For example, policies such as the minimum and maximum password age and the minimum password length, as well as lockout policy, are determined at the domain level and apply to each `user` object in the domain.

All of the values are stored directly in the domain root object (not in `RootDSE`, but in the object pointed to by the `defaultNamingContext` attribute in `RootDSE`) as a set of attributes such as `maxPwdAge`, `min-PwdLength`, and `lockoutThreshold`. Additionally, the password complexity rules are encoded in an enumerated value in the `pwdProperties` attribute.

These values tend to be quite static in most domains, so we would typically want to read these values only once per program execution. To make the policy values easy to consume, we show in Listing 10.7 a wrapper class for the domain account policies that converts all of the values into convenient .NET data types, such as `TimeSpan`. A special .NET enumeration type for the types of the password policy is also included. We won't be able to include all of the class properties in the book, as that would take too much space, but we will have the full class available on the book's web site.

We will refer to this sample in future discussions when demonstrating how to determine an account's lockout status and for finding accounts with expiring passwords. It is also worthy to note that any `LargeInteger` values in these policy attributes are stored as negative values. We chose to invert them back to positive values because it is easier to think about them in this way. Developers choosing to use these attributes should keep this in mind, as it will throw off calculations later if not accounted for.

LISTING 10.7: Determining Domain Policies

```
[Flags]
public enum PasswordPolicy
{
    DOMAIN_PASSWORD_COMPLEX=1,
    DOMAIN_PASSWORD_NO_ANON_CHANGE=2,
    DOMAIN_PASSWORD_NO_CLEAR_CHANGE=4,
    DOMAIN_LOCKOUT_ADMINS=8,
    DOMAIN_PASSWORD_STORE_CLEARTEXT=16,
    DOMAIN_REFUSE_PASSWORD_CHANGE=32
}
```

```
public class DomainPolicy
{
    ResultPropertyCollection attribs;

    public DomainPolicy(DirectoryEntry domainRoot)
    {
        string[] policyAttributes = new string[] {
            "maxPwdAge", "minPwdAge", "minPwdLength",
            "lockoutDuration", "lockOutObservationWindow",
            "lockoutThreshold", "pwdProperties",
            "pwdHistoryLength", "objectClass",
            "distinguishedName"
            };

        //we take advantage of the marshaling with
        //DirectorySearcher for LargeInteger values...
        DirectorySearcher ds = new DirectorySearcher(
            domainRoot,
            "(objectClass=domainDNS)",
            policyAttributes,
            SearchScope.Base
            );

        SearchResult result = ds.FindOne();

        //do some quick validation...
        if (result == null)
        {
            throw new ArgumentException(
                "domainRoot is not a domainDNS object."
                );
        }

        this.attribs = result.Properties;
    }

    //for some odd reason, the intervals are all stored
    //as negative numbers.  We use this to "invert" them
    private long GetAbsValue(object longInt)
    {
        return Math.Abs((long)longInt);
    }

    public TimeSpan MaxPasswordAge
    {
        get
        {
            string val = "maxPwdAge";
            if (this.attribs.Contains(val))
            {
```

```
                    long ticks = GetAbsValue(
                        this.attribs[val][0]
                        );

                    if (ticks > 0)
                        return TimeSpan.FromTicks(ticks);
                }

                return TimeSpan.MaxValue;
            }
        }

        public PasswordPolicy PasswordProperties
        {
            get
            {
                string val = "pwdProperties";
                //this should fail if not found
                return (PasswordPolicy)this.attribs[val][0];
            }
        }

        //truncated for book space
    }
```

Listing 10.7 is meant to run on an Active Directory domain. Where does this leave ADAM instances? By default, ADAM will assume any local or domain policies on the Windows 2003 server where it is running. This means that if our Windows 2003 server is a member of the domain, we can simply use code similar to that in Listing 10.7. If, however, the server is running in a workgroup configuration, the policy will be determined locally. Therefore, Listing 10.7 would not be appropriate. Instead, we would need to know our local policy or attempt to discover it using Windows Management Instrumentation (WMI) classes.

Determining Password Expiration

Earlier in this chapter, we mentioned that accounts could have passwords that expire. Most Active Directory domains and many ADAM instances force passwords to expire periodically to improve security. As such, we often need to know when a user's password will expire.

Determining password expiration on user accounts in Active Directory and ADAM might appear tricky, but really, it is a simple matter of calculation.

Password expiration is determined based on when an individual password was last changed, and on the domain-wide password expiration policy, which we detailed in the previous section. The algorithm is essentially this:

```
if "password change date" + "max password age" >= "now"
    "password is expired"
```

Typically, Windows monitors password expiration and will inform a user that her password is expiring soon when she logs on locally to Windows. It then provides a mechanism to change the password. As long as the user changes her password before it expires, she can continue to log in to the domain and all is good. However, if the password expires, then the user cannot log in again until an administrator resets it.

This situation is not as straightforward for ADAM users, as there is no natural "login" process that informs users of pending password expiration and prompts them for a password change. Instead, it is completely up to the developer to supply both a notification and a means by which to change a password when using ADAM.

Programmatic LDAP binds to either directory must be handled explicitly by the developer, as we will not be warned of pending password expiration. Once a password has expired, all LDAP binds will fail until the password is reset by the user or an administrator.

How Password Modification Dates Are Stored

Active Directory and ADAM use the `pwdLastSet` attribute to record when a password was last changed, via either an end-user password change or an administrative reset. Like most time-based Windows data in the directory, the attribute uses the 2.5.5.16 `LargeInteger` attribute syntax, which essentially holds a Windows `FILETIME` structure as an 8-byte integer. We already discussed how to read and write these attributes in Chapter 6, as well as build LDAP search filters based on them in Chapter 4, so that knowledge should be easy to apply to this problem.

There is one edge case that developers should be aware of when dealing with this attribute. Namely, the `pwdLastSet` attribute can be set to zero (0), which implies that the password is automatically expired and must be changed at next login.

> ▪▪ **NOTE**　Zero Is Not a Valid FILETIME Value in .NET
>
> The 0 value for pwdLastSet is especially important to remember because it is not a valid FILETIME value. If we pass it to a .NET function that converts between .NET DateTime structures and FILETIME, it will throw an error. Additionally, if pwdLastSet is 0, the user cannot bind to the directory via LDAP. This makes it impossible to do programmatic password changes via LDAP. Only administrative resets with different credentials are possible in this state.

Determining a Single User's Password Expiration Date

Now that we know the details on how this mechanism works, we are ready to write some code to check this. The first thing we need is a user's pwdLastSet value as a .NET Int64, or long integer. As per Chapter 6, we can do this using DirectorySearcher and its built-in marshaling of the data, or we can use one of the conversion functions we described for use with DirectoryEntry. For our purposes, we will use DirectorySearcher for converting the LargeInteger values in conjunction with Listing 10.7 to obtain domain policies.

We will step through a larger class we have chosen to name Password-Expires, explaining as we go the thought process that surrounds what we are trying to accomplish. As such, we might have to refer to previous listings to see any member variables. This is a complete class and it requires a number of lines, but don't worry about needing to copy it verbatim. We will include it as a sample on the book's web site under its listing number.

The first part of determining password expiration is to determine our domain policy for the maximum password age (MaxPwdAge). Listing 10.8 shows how we can easily accomplish this using the DomainPolicy class we introduced in Listing 10.7 along with some tricks we learned in Chapter 9 using System.DirectoryServices.ActiveDirectory (SDS.AD) classes.

LISTING 10.8: PasswordExpires, Part I

```
public class PasswordExpires
{
    DomainPolicy policy;

    const int UF_DONT_EXPIRE_PASSWD = 0x10000;
```

```
public PasswordExpires()
{
    //get our current domain policy
    Domain domain = Domain.GetCurrentDomain();
    DirectoryEntry root = domain.GetDirectoryEntry();

    using (domain)
    using (root)
    {
        this.policy = new DomainPolicy(root);
    }
}
```

In Listing 10.8, we are simply using the `Domain` class from SDS.AD to get a `DirectoryEntry` object bound to the current domain's default naming context. We need the root partition of the domain in order to determine our domain policies. At this point, we simply load our `DomainPolicy` object with our root `domainDNS` object. Next, we need to calculate the actual `DateTime` when a user's password would expire. Listing 10.9 shows how we can accomplish this.

LISTING 10.9: PasswordExpires, Part II

```
public DateTime GetExpiration(DirectoryEntry user)
{
    int flags =
        (int)user.Properties["userAccountControl"][0];

    //check to see if password is set to expire
    if(Convert.ToBoolean(flags & UF_DONT_EXPIRE_PASSWD))
    {
        //the user's password will never expire
        return DateTime.MaxValue;
    }

    long ticks = GetInt64(user, "pwdLastSet");

    //user must change password at next login
    if (ticks == 0)
        return DateTime.MinValue;

    //password has never been set
    if (ticks == -1)
    {
        throw new InvalidOperationException(
            "User does not have a password"
            );
    }
```

```
//get when the user last set their password;
DateTime pwdLastSet = DateTime.FromFileTime(
    ticks
    );

//use our policy class to determine when
//it will expire
return pwdLastSet.Add(
    this.policy.MaxPasswordAge
    );
}
```

The first thing we do in Listing 10.9 is check to see if the user's account is set so that the password never expires. We will use the convention that `DateTime.MaxValue` means it will never expire. Next, we are using a helper function called `GetInt64` (see Listing 10.10). This function marshals the user's `pwdLastSet` attribute into an `Int64` for us using a `DirectorySearcher` object. Notice that one of three conditions can arise out of this check. First, the `pwdLastSet` attribute might be `null` (if it is not set on the object), in which case the user account has no password. We chose to treat the situation where a user does not have a password as an error condition, but this can differ by application. Second, the attribute might be `0`, which means that the user must change her password at the next logon. We chose to use the convention that `DateTime.MinValue` meant that the password must be changed at next log on. Lastly, the attribute might contain some value that we can interpret as a `FILETIME` structure and can convert using `DateTime.FromFileTime`. The calculation for determining when a user's password will expire is simple. We just add the `DateTime` value of when the user last changed her password to the `TimeSpan` value of the domain's `MaxPwdAge` policy. If the user's password has already expired, we will still get a `DateTime` value, but it will be in the past.

Knowing the date a user's password has expired is nice, but we might actually want to know how much time is left before the user's password expires. That is a very easy calculation, as Listing 10.10 demonstrates.

LISTING 10.10:   PasswordExpires, Part III

```
public TimeSpan GetTimeLeft(DirectoryEntry user)
{
    DateTime willExpire = GetExpiration(user);
```

```
        if (willExpire == DateTime.MaxValue)
            return TimeSpan.MaxValue;

        if (willExpire == DateTime.MinValue)
            return TimeSpan.MinValue;

        if (willExpire.CompareTo(DateTime.Now) > 0)
        {
            //the password has not expired
            //(pwdLast + MaxPwdAge)- Now = Time Left
            return willExpire.Subtract(DateTime.Now);
        }

        //the password has already expired
        return TimeSpan.MinValue;
    }

    private Int64 GetInt64(DirectoryEntry entry, string attr)
    {
        //we will use the marshaling behavior of
        //the searcher
        DirectorySearcher ds = new DirectorySearcher(
            entry,
            String.Format("({0}=*)", attr),
            new string[] { attr },
            SearchScope.Base
            );

        SearchResult sr = ds.FindOne();

        if (sr != null)
        {
            if (sr.Properties.Contains(attr))
            {
                return (Int64)sr.Properties[attr][0];
            }
        }
        return -1;
    }
```

We chose to return a TimeSpan value representing the time left before a user's password would expire in Listing 10.10. If either TimeSpan.Max-Value or TimeSpan.MinValue is returned, it is meant to indicate that the user's password does not expire or has already expired, respectively. For completeness, we have also included our helper GetInt64 in Listing 10.10, though by now we know that everyone is probably aware of how to marshal LargeInteger values from Chapter 6.

We typically want to do something based on when a password will expire, so it is important to know how much time is left. However, if we just want to know whether an account has expired, we can use the previously mentioned `msDS-User-Account-Control-Computed` attribute for Windows 2003 Active Directory and ADAM, or the aptly named `msDS-UserPasswordExpired` attribute for ADAM, to just give us a yes/no answer. Listing 10.11 shows one such example.

LISTING 10.11: Checking Password Expiration

```
string adsPath = "LDAP://CN=User1,OU=Users,DC=domain,DC=com";

DirectoryEntry user = new DirectoryEntry(
    adsPath,
    null,
    null,
    AuthenticationTypes.Secure
    );

string attrib = "msDS-User-Account-Control-Computed";

using (user)
{
    user.RefreshCache(new string[] { attrib });

    int flags = (int)user.Properties[attrib].Value
        & (int)AdsUserFlags.PasswordExpired);

    if (Convert.ToBoolean(flags)
    {
        //password has expired
        Console.WriteLine("Expired");
    }
}
```

Of course, the problem with something like Listing 10.11 is that we don't know when the password actually expired or how much time is left before it does expire. Additionally, as we previously mentioned, a solution like this will work with only Windows 2003 Active Directory and ADAM. Windows 2000 Active Directory users must use a solution such as that shown in Listing 10.8.

Searching for Accounts with Expiring Passwords

Another thing we may wish to do is find all of the accounts with passwords expiring within a certain time range, perhaps to send an email notification directing users to a web-based portal where they can change their passwords. This is important for ADAM users and any Active Directory users that do not typically log in to Windows via the workstation.

The crux of this search is based on creating a search filter with the correct values. Let's say we want to find user accounts with passwords expiring between two dates. Since password expiration is based on the date the password was last changed and the maximum password age domain policy, we subtract the maximum password age from the two dates to get the values of `pwdLastSet` that will match. The code might look like that shown in Listing 10.12.

LISTING 10.12: Finding Expiring Passwords

```
public static string GetExpirationFilter(
    DateTime startDate,
    DateTime endDate,
    TimeSpan maxPwdAge
    )
{
    Int64 lowDate;
    Int64 highDate;
    string filterPattern = "(&(sAMAccountType=805306368)" +
        "(pwdLastSet>={0})(pwdLastSet<={1}))"

    lowDate = startDate.Subtract(maxPwdAge).ToFileTime();
    highDate = endDate.Subtract(maxPwdAge).ToFileTime();

    return String.Format(
        filterPattern,
        lowDate,
        highDate
        );
}
```

A complete sample that enumerates users with expiring passwords between two dates is available on this book's web site.

In both examples, we see that .NET makes this especially easy. The built-in support for dates, time spans, and Windows FILETIME structures simplifies much of the work. We can also easily construct variations on this, using similar techniques, to find accounts whose passwords have already expired, or to find all accounts that will expire before or after a certain date.

■ NOTE   Performance Implications of Using pwdLastSet

The `pwdLastSet` attribute is not indexed, nor is it stored in the global catalog in Active Directory by default. As such, this search cannot be performed across an entire forest, and it can be slow, introducing the possibility of timeouts. Using a small page size for our `Directory-Searcher`, our results will be returned more quickly and we can help mitigate some of these risks. It is definitely much faster than enumerating all of the users in the domain and looking at each individual attribute value on the client side.

Determining Last Logon

The last time a user has logged onto the domain is held in an attribute on the user object. Called `lastLogon`, this attribute is a nonreplicated attribute, which means that each domain controller holds its own copy of the attribute, likely with different values. Checking the last time a user has logged onto the domain requires us to visit each domain controller and read the attribute. The value found for the latest `lastLogon` is the value we are after.

We covered in Chapter 9 how to use the Locator to enumerate all the domain controllers. We will use this technique again to iterate through each controller and retrieve the `lastLogon` attribute for each user. Listing 10.13 demonstrates how to accurately determine the last time a user has logged into the domain.

LISTING 10.13: Finding a User's Last Logon

```
string username = "user1";
string domain = "mydomain.com";

public static void LastLogon(string username, string domain)
{
    DirectoryContext context = new DirectoryContext(
        DirectoryContextType.Domain,
        domain
        );
```

```
DateTime latestLogon = DateTime.MinValue;
string servername = null;

DomainControllerCollection dcc =
    DomainController.FindAll(context);

foreach (DomainController dc in dcc)
{
    DirectorySearcher ds;

    using (dc)
    using (ds = dc.GetDirectorySearcher())
    {
        ds.Filter = String.Format(
            "(sAMAccountName={0})",
            username
            );
        ds.PropertiesToLoad.Add("lastLogon");
        ds.SizeLimit = 1;

        SearchResult sr = ds.FindOne();

        if (sr != null)
        {
            DateTime lastLogon = DateTime.MinValue;
            if (sr.Properties.Contains("lastLogon"))
            {
                lastLogon = DateTime.FromFileTime(
                    (long)sr.Properties["lastLogon"][0]
                    );
            }

            if (DateTime.Compare(lastLogon,latestLogon) > 0)
            {
                latestLogon = lastLogon;
                servername = dc.Name;
            }
        }
    }
}

Console.WriteLine(
    "Last Logon: {0} at {1}",
    servername,
    latestLogon.ToString()
    );
}
```

We are using the SDS.AD namespace here to enumerate all of our domain controllers, and then we are using `DirectorySearcher` and `SearchResult` to marshal the `LargeInteger` syntax `lastLogon` attribute more easily. In domains with widely distributed domain controllers, we should be aware that network latency can slow this technique dramatically.

We should further keep in mind that this technique is relatively slow because it must bind to each domain controller in turn to find the user account and retrieve the `lastLogon` value. However, it is accurate, as each domain controller is searched and the latest logon is found.

Finding Stale Accounts

There is one more method we can use for finding old or unused accounts if we're running Windows Server 2003 Active Directory in full Windows 2003 mode. The `user` class schema has been updated to add a new attribute called `lastLogonTimestamp`. This is a replicated value that is updated periodically. How often the attribute is updated depends on a new domain policy attribute named `msDS-LogonTimeSyncInterval`. By default, this value is 14 days, but it is configurable. As such, this attribute is not accurate for purposes of determining exactly the last time a user logged into the domain. We must use the `lastLogon` attribute when accuracy matters.

The syntax of this attribute is `LargeInteger`, so it is similar to other techniques we have already demonstrated. We can simply create a filter using the `DateTime.ToFileTime` method appropriately:

```
//find all users and computers that
//have not been used in 30 days
String filter = String.Format(
    "(&(objectClass=user)(lastLogonTimestamp<={0}))",
    DateTime.Now.Subtract(TimeSpan.FromDays(30)).ToFileTime()
    );
```

At first blush, this seems like a pretty easy thing to do. Indeed it is, if we can live with the following limitations.

- It is inaccurate up to the value of `msDS-LogonTimeSyncInterval` (14 days by default). This means we can be no better than the resolution of this attribute in terms of our accuracy in finding accounts.

- This is a Windows 2003 Active Directory–only feature, and even then, only when running in Windows 2003 mode.

Only NTLM and Kerberos logins update this attribute. Service Pack 1 must be applied to correct problems with NTLM as well. This means that any other type of operation that generates a login—certificates, custom Security Support Provider Interface (SSPI), Kerberos Service for User (S4U), and so on—will not update this attribute.

Additional caveats that depend on when the domain functional level was increased also affect the accuracy of this attribute. You can find further information about all the caveats at www.microsoft.com/technet/ prodtechnol/windowsserver2003/library/TechRef/54094485-71f6-4be8- 8ebf-faa45bc5db4c.mspx.

Determining Account Lockout

Determining whether an account is locked out is a strange odyssey. On the surface, it appears simple enough: We have a flag on `userAccountControl` called `UF_LOCKOUT`. Surely, that would mean that checking to see if the flag was flipped would tell us whether an account was locked out, right? Well, that really depends on which provider we use. As we mentioned earlier in this chapter, the `userAccountControl` attribute is inaccurate in terms of determining an account's lockout status for the `LDAP` provider. The situation is somewhat better if we use the `WinNT` provider, as this version of the `userAccountControl` attribute accurately reflects lockout status. Microsoft was aware of this flakey implementation and fixed it on Windows 2003 Active Directory and ADAM with the `msDS-User-Account-Control-Computed` attribute. This constructed attribute will accurately reflect the `UF_LOCKOUT` flag for the `LDAP` provider. Listing 10.14 shows a sample of how this would work.

LISTING 10.14: Determining Account Lockout

```
//user is a DirectoryEntry for our user account

string attrib = "msDS-User-Account-Control-Computed";

//this is a constructed attrib
user.RefreshCache(new string[]{attrib});
```

```
const int UF_LOCKOUT = 0x0010;

int flags =
    (int)user.Properties[attrib].Value;

if (Convert.ToBoolean(flags & UF_LOCKOUT))
{
    Console.WriteLine(
        "{0} is locked out",
        user.Name
        );
}
```

There are a couple problems with this method, of course.

- This works only for Windows 2003 Active Directory and ADAM, not for Windows 2000 Active Directory.
- Since msDS-User-Account-Control-Computed is a constructed attribute, it cannot be used in an LDAP search filter.

Unfortunately, since this attribute cannot be used in a search filter, we really cannot use this method to find locked accounts proactively. Luckily, we can actually compute whether an account is locked out fairly accurately, and search for it. Previously in this chapter, we showed how we could determine the domain's lockout duration policy. Used in conjunction with the lockoutTime attribute, we can accurately predict whether an account is locked out, and search for it. Listing 10.15 shows one such example.

LISTING 10.15: Searching for Locked-Out Accounts

```
class Lockout : IDisposable
{
    DirectoryContext context;
    DirectoryEntry root;
    DomainPolicy policy;

    public Lockout(string domainName)
    {
        this.context = new DirectoryContext(
            DirectoryContextType.Domain,
            domainName
            );

        //get our current domain policy
        Domain domain = Domain.GetDomain(this.context);
```

```
        this.root = domain.GetDirectoryEntry();
        this.policy = new DomainPolicy(this.root);
    }

    public void FindLockedAccounts()
    {
        //default for when accounts stay locked indefinitely
        string qry = "(lockoutTime>=1)";

        TimeSpan duration = this.policy.LockoutDuration;

        if (duration != TimeSpan.MaxValue)
        {
            DateTime lockoutThreshold =
                DateTime.Now.Subtract(duration);

            qry = String.Format(
                "(lockoutTime>={0})",
                lockoutThreshold.ToFileTime()
                );
        }

        DirectorySearcher ds = new DirectorySearcher(
            this.root,
            qry
            );

        using (SearchResultCollection src = ds.FindAll())
        {
            foreach (SearchResult sr in src)
            {
                long ticks =
                    (long)sr.Properties["lockoutTime"][0];

                Console.WriteLine(
                    "{0} locked out at {1}",
                    sr.Properties["name"][0],
                    DateTime.FromFileTime(ticks)
                    );
            }
        }
    }

    public void Dispose()
    {
        if (this.root != null)
        {
            this.root.Dispose();
        }
    }
}
```

Listing 10.15 gives us a fairly simple way of finding accounts that have been locked. We are using the `DomainPolicy` helper class we introduced earlier in this chapter to read the `lockoutDuration` attribute on the root domain. If the attribute is set to `TimeSpan.MaxValue`, it means that an account is to stay locked until an administrator unlocks it. We are accounting for this policy possibly by setting our search filter to designate that any account with a `lockoutTime` with a nonzero value is locked out. This filter is appropriate only when our domain policy tells us that accounts are to be locked out indefinitely, until an administrator unlocks them.

Managing Passwords for Active Directory Users

Unlike most Active Directory and ADAM user-management tasks, which we perform through simple manipulation of Active Directory objects and attributes via LDAP, managing passwords is a bit complex. Password changes require very special semantics that are enforced by the server, and developers need to understand these semantics for password management applications to be successful.

In order to try to facilitate the password management process, ADSI exposes two methods on the `IADsUser` interface: `SetPassword` and `ChangePassword`. `SetPassword` is used to perform an administrative reset of a user's password and is typically performed by an administrator. Knowledge of the previous password is not required. `ChangePassword` is used simply to change the password from one value to another and is typically performed only by the user represented by the directory object. It does require knowledge of the previous password, and thus it takes the old and new passwords as arguments.

Since the `DirectoryEntry` object does not directly expose the `IADsUser` ADSI interface, this is one case where we must use the `DirectoryEntry.Invoke` method to call these ADSI methods via late-bound reflection:

```
//given a DirectoryEntry "entry" that points to a user object
//this will reset the user's password
entry.Invoke("SetPassword", new object[] {"newpassword"});

//this will change the user's password
entry.Invoke("ChangePassword",
    new object[] {"oldpassword", "newpassword"});
```

Note that the parameters to the `SetPassword` and `ChangePassword` methods are passed in as an array of objects that contain strings.

Password Management Complications

This seems simple enough; just call the right method and pass in the right arguments. Unfortunately, in practice this turns out not to be the case, as password management functions tend to be the most troublesome aspect of programmatic user management beyond the normal issues related to security that we discussed in Chapter 8.

Password management can be hard, for a variety of reasons.

- Password policy and security can be complicated and must be understood.
- The underlying ADSI methods actually try a complicated series of different approaches to set or change the password, and all of them use different protocols and have different requirements and failure modes.
- The errors returned by ADSI are often not helpful and the resulting exception in .NET needs other special care.

Developers who have issues reliably using `SetPassword` and `Change-Password` in all environments are unfortunately not in the minority. However, the following exploration of these three points will be immensely helpful.

Understanding Password Policy and Security

Active Directory enforces password policy at the domain level. Password policies that can be set include:

- The minimum allowed length
- The maximum allowed age
- The minimum allowed age (how often we can change passwords)
- Password complexity
- Password history (determines when we can reuse an old password)

Complex passwords are just passwords that require some mix of upper- and lowercase letters, numbers, and special characters. All of these policies are exposed via attributes set in the domain root object, which can easily be found via the `defaultNamingContext` attribute on `RootDSE`. We discussed how to find these domain-wide policy settings earlier in this chapter.

Knowing what these values are will help us predict how the server will behave when asked to modify any given password. All of the policies that are enabled are enforced for each password modification; however, administrative password resets (as opposed to end-user password changes) ignore all of them except for length and complexity. This makes sense, since an administrator who (presumably) has no knowledge of the user's previous passwords performs the reset.

Password security is relatively straightforward. Essentially, administrative users have rights to reset any account's password, and normal users have rights to change only their own passwords. The only trick here is that the right to reset passwords can be delegated beyond the scope of the default groups, such as `Domain Admins` and `Account Operators`, so it is possible that users outside of those groups have this right.

From the application developer's perspective, our job is to know which of the two tasks we are trying to perform and to make sure that we have the correct credentials to do so. This is pretty easy when building applications to change passwords, as the user has to give us her old password to make the change, so it is relatively easy to bind to the directory with her credentials directly and avoid any tricky impersonation scenarios (see Chapter 8). For password reset operations, our options can equally vary between using the current user's security context (if it's an admin application), to using a trusted service account (this is often done with helpdesk-type applications). There is not a clear-cut answer of which method to use here, and it will often depend on the type of application we are trying to build. Chapter 8 explains these scenarios in detail, especially for web applications.

Understanding the Underlying ADSI Methods

The `SetPassword` and `ChangePassword` methods may seem simple on the outside, but under the hood, it is just the opposite. There is a variety of different ways to modify passwords against Active Directory, and these methods pretty much try all of them. On the one hand, this is great for developers, as this approach gives developers the best possible chance that their operation will succeed. The downside of this approach is that each technique has different requirements and different ways to fail, so figuring out why things are not working can be especially difficult.

`SetPassword` and `ChangePassword` attempt password modifications using the following methods, in order:

- LDAP password modification over an SSL channel
- The Kerberos set password protocol over the Kerberos password port (`SetPassword` only)
- A Net* API remote procedure call (RPC)

As noted in the list, the Kerberos set password protocol is used only for `SetPassword`. `ChangePassword` does not seem to have an equivalent Kerberos protocol implementation. Let's take each technique in turn.

LDAP Password Modification

The first technique that is always attempted is an LDAP-based password modification. The core of this technique involves modifying the `unicodePwd` attribute directly. `SetPassword` does one modification with the `Replace` modification type specified, and `ChangePassword` does two modifications with a `Delete` and an `Add` specified, in that order. Active Directory enforces a restriction that any modification to the `unicodePwd` attribute must be made over an encrypted channel with a cipher strength of 128 bits. Otherwise, the server will reject the attempted modification. This helps ensure that the plaintext password is not intercepted on the network.

This is where SSL comes in. If we recall from Chapter 3, Active Directory supports two mechanisms for channel encryption: SSL and Kerberos. However, only SSL supports the minimum 128-bit cipher strength on all Active Directory platforms. Kerberos-based encryption has been strengthened to meet this requirement on Windows Server 2003, but not on Windows 2000 Server. Because the function attempts to work with either version of Active Directory, it always selects only SSL for the channel encryption technique.

This is unfortunate, because Kerberos-based encryption works out of the box with Active Directory, but SSL requires additional configuration steps including the acquisition of proper SSL certificates for each participating domain controller. Since SSL/LDAP is not required for normal Active Directory operation, many administrators do not bother to configure it. As a result, SSL is often not available for performing password modifications with `SetPassword` and `ChangePassword`.

Additionally, for an SSL/LDAP bind to succeed, proper DNS names must be used to connect to the domain controller. Typically, the server authentication aspect of the SSL handshake requires that the name used to access the server match the name of the server in the certificate, which is typically a DNS name. Therefore, it is important to remember to avoid using IP addresses and NetBIOS names when accessing a domain controller if SSL support is required.

A final thing to remember is that SSL/LDAP uses TCP port 636, not port 389, like typical LDAP traffic does. We must take this into account with any network firewall restrictions to make sure the proper ports are open.

Kerberos Set Password Protocol

The Kerberos specification includes a facility for setting user passwords. This facility does not use the original user's password, so it is used only for administrative resets (`SetPassword`) and not for end-user password changes using `ChangePassword`.

The Kerberos set password protocol also uses a different network port (TCP 441) than normal Kerberos traffic, which goes over port 88 UDP and TCP. Once again, we must consider potential firewall issues if we wish to use this protocol.

Kerberos set password is available when a secure bind was requested and the secure bind negotiates to Kerberos rather than to NTLM. Chapter 8 contains more information about this, including some sample code we can use to verify secure bind status on the server side.

Net* API RPCs

The final method attempted by the password modification methods are one of two RPC functions from the Net* family: `NetUserSetInfo` and `NetUser-ChangePassword`. They are used for `SetPassword` and `ChangePassword`, respectively.

The key thing to remember with these RPC functions is that they must use the current thread's security context. They do not directly support plaintext credentials to establish a security context, as LDAP does. With Windows 2000, this had the surprising effect of ignoring any credentials supplied to `DirectoryEntry` for `SetPassword` privileges. Developers found that if they switched environmental factors, identical code that previously worked would fail. There was also no way to know which of the three methods was being selected. So, if the test environment had SSL certificates installed correctly, `SetPassword` and `ChangePassword` would work just fine. Moving the identical code to production, where perhaps the SSL certificate was not installed correctly, would fail because unbeknownst to the developer, `SetPassword` had actually used `NetUserSetInfo` under the covers. This violated most developers' idea of obvious behavior. After all, if the previous two methods can use the credentials supplied to `Directory-Entry` to affect password modifications with identical code, why wouldn't this one? Microsoft decided to fix this unexpected behavior with Windows 2003. Now, if the code specifies plaintext credentials in `DirectoryEntry`, these methods will use another API, `LogonUser`, to create a Windows login token for the code to impersonate while making the RPC function call. This has the effect of keeping the outward behavior of all three methods the same.

For Windows 2000 users, the only way to get this third method working correctly is to make sure our current thread's credentials are those of an account that has the proper privileges. From Chapter 8, we know this means that either our code must run under a trusted subsystem that holds these rights, or we must impersonate an account that holds these rights for the duration of the call. Please refer back to Chapter 8 for more details, and for additional references.

Finally, remember that a Windows RPC requires TCP port 135 (and potentially, other ports) to be open to the domain controller.

Error Handling with the Invoke Method in .NET

So far, all of the issues we have discussed apply to any API that calls `Set-Password` or `ChangePassword`. While error handling for these two methods is certainly relevant, it is a larger .NET topic that affects any code that uses reflection via the `Invoke` method. When the `Invoke` method is used to call any ADSI interface method, any exception thrown by the target method, including a COM error triggered via COM interop, will be wrapped in a `System.Reflection.TargetInvocationException` exception, with the actual exception in the `InnerException` property. Therefore, we will need to use a pattern like this with the `Invoke` method:

```
//given a DirectoryEntry "entry" that points to a user object
//this will reset the user's password
try
{
    entry.Invoke("SetPassword", new object[] {"newpassword"});
}
catch (TargetInvocationException ex)
{
    throw ex.InnerException;
}
```

Obviously, we may wish to do something different from simply rethrowing the `InnerException` property. The point here is that `InnerException` contains the information we are interested in.

The other issue here is that the exceptions coming back from ADSI vary, from the vaguely helpful to the truly bewildering. We will not attempt to list all of them here, but here are a few hints.

- `System.UnauthorizedAccessException` always indicates a permissions problem.
- A `System.Runtime.InteropServices.COMException` exception with `ErrorCode 0x80072035` `"Unwilling to perform"` generally means that an LDAP password modification failed due to a password policy issue.
- A `System.Runtime.InteropServices.COMException` exception from one of the Net*APIs is usually pretty specific about what the problem was.

Recommendations for Successful Password Modification Operations

In our experience, it is possible to get `SetPassword` and `ChangePassword` to work in just about any environment, as long as we understand what they are doing under the hood and we recognize any dependencies involved in each technique. However, the approach that yields the most consistent results is to enable SSL on our domain controllers so that LDAP password modifications will be used.

Administrators may complain that they do not want to enable SSL due to the potential expense and complexity of obtaining third-party certificates or configuring an internal Windows certificate authority. Given that this is not required for general-purpose Active Directory operation, they may regard this as a nice-to-have feature and try to insist that you find another way to get this to work. We suggest you do your best to try to convince them otherwise!

Why Can't We Do LDAP Password Modifications Directly in SDS?

You may be wondering why we cannot use SDS to modify the `unicodePwd` attribute directly. After all, it seems like this should be possible. However, even though we can create the correct value syntax to set `unicodePwd` correctly, the ADSI property cache prevents this from working. The fact that `unicodePwd` is a "write-only" attribute seems to interfere with our ability to modify it. It may be possible to reset passwords (depending on the version of the .NET Framework we are using), but it is definitely not possible to change passwords.

SDS.P to the Rescue

This is one area where we can do something with `System.Directory-Services.Protocols` (SDS.P) that we cannot do with SDS. The lower-level access to direct LDAP modification operations available in SDS.P allows us to perform LDAP password modifications. There are three keys to this approach.

- A 128-bit encrypted channel must be established, either by SSL or by secure bind channel encryption.

- The `unicodePwd` attribute value is actually submitted as an octet string (byte array) that contains the Unicode encoding of the password value surrounded by double quotes (see Listing 10.16).

- The reset password takes a single modification operation with the `Replace` operation type, and the change password operation takes a `Delete` operation of the old value followed by an `Add` of the new value.

One interesting thing here is the secure channel requirement. If we have both client and server with operating systems more recent than Windows 2000, we can use the built-in Kerberos-based channel encryption that is available with a typical secure bind and we do not need SSL. This gives us some options that are not available with the ADSI methods.

Listing 10.16 demonstrates how we might apply SDS.P to password modification operations. It is implemented to allow both password changes and resets and it works with either type of channel encryption, although only one set of options is demonstrated.

LISTING 10.16: Using .Protocols for Password Ops

```
using System;
using System.DirectoryServices.Protocols;
using System.Net;
using System.Text;

public class PasswordModifier
{
    public static void Main()
    {
        NetworkCredential credential = new NetworkCredential(
            "someuser",
            "Password1",
            "domain"
            );
        DirectoryConnection connection;

        try
        {
            //change these options to use Kerberos encryption
            connection = GetConnection(
                "domain.com:636",
                credential,
                true
                );

            ChangePassword(
                connection,
                "CN=someuser,CN=users,DC=domain,DC=com",
                "Password1",
                "Password2"
                );

            Console.WriteLine("Password modified!");
            IDisposable disposable = connection as IDisposable;
```

```
            if (disposable != null)
                disposable.Dispose();
        }
        catch (Exception ex)
        {
            Console.WriteLine(ex.ToString());
        }
    }

    private static DirectoryConnection GetConnection(
        string server,
        NetworkCredential credential,
        bool useSsl
        )
    {

        LdapConnection connection =
            new LdapConnection(server);

        if (useSsl)
        {
            connection.SessionOptions.SecureSocketLayer = true;
        }
        else
        {
            connection.SessionOptions.Sealing = true;
        }

        connection.Bind(credential);
        return connection;
    }

    private static void ChangePassword(
        DirectoryConnection connection,
        string userDN,
        string oldPassword,
        string newPassword
        )
    {

        DirectoryAttributeModification deleteMod =
            new DirectoryAttributeModification();
        deleteMod.Name = "unicodePwd";
        deleteMod.Add(GetPasswordData(oldPassword));
        deleteMod.Operation= DirectoryAttributeOperation.Delete;

        DirectoryAttributeModification addMod =
            new DirectoryAttributeModification();
        addMod.Name = "unicodePwd";
        addMod.Add(GetPasswordData(newPassword));
        addMod.Operation = DirectoryAttributeOperation.Add;
```

```
        ModifyRequest request = new ModifyRequest(
            userDN,
            deleteMod,
            addMod
            );

    DirectoryResponse response =
        connection.SendRequest(request);
}

private static void SetPassword(
    DirectoryConnection connection,
    string userDN,
    string password
    )
{
    DirectoryAttributeModification pwdMod =
        new DirectoryAttributeModification();
    pwdMod.Name = "unicodePwd";
    pwdMod.Add(GetPasswordData(password));
    pwdMod.Operation = DirectoryAttributeOperation.Replace;

    ModifyRequest request = new ModifyRequest(
        userDN,
        pwdMod
        );

    DirectoryResponse response =
        connection.SendRequest(request);
}

private static byte[] GetPasswordData(string password)
{
    string formattedPassword;
    formattedPassword = String.Format("\"{0}\"", password);
    return (Encoding.Unicode.GetBytes(formattedPassword));
}
}
```

Managing Passwords for ADAM Users

Managing passwords in ADAM is similar to managing passwords in Active Directory. However, there are a few important differences to be aware of. The primary difference is that the Kerberos password change protocol and the Net* APIs are not available for ADAM. This is because ADAM does not function as a Kerberos ticket granting service, nor does it expose the security account manager RPC interfaces that Active Directory does.

Because of this, the only technique available for modifying passwords on ADAM users is LDAP. None of the other techniques that the ADSI `IADsUser.SetPassword` and `ChangePassword` methods implement applies.

The other key difference is that ADAM allows us to relax the requirement on having a 128-bit secure channel for password modifications. This is helpful, because SSL is the only binding option available for ADAM users that allows encryption, and once again, SSL is not always an attractive option for administrators. SSL is notoriously more difficult to configure on ADAM than it is on Active Directory because of the extra complexity of associating the certificate with the correct service account.

To disable the requirement for a secure channel to be used for password modification operations, the thirteenth bit of the `dsHeuristics` attribute must be changed. The ADAM documentation contains more details on this. We mention this only because ADAM is often used for prototyping due to its portability and ease of deployment. For testing and development purposes, we often disable this requirement ourselves instead of wading through all the SSL muck. However, in production applications, we would never recommend to relax the security requirements around password management.

Programming Differences When Setting ADAM Passwords

When we relax the secure channel password requirements with ADAM, we need a way to specify that we will be sending plaintext passwords on the normal LDAP port instead of ciphertext on the SSL port. We use the `IADsObject-Options` interface for this, using the `ADS_OPTION_PASSWORD_PORT_NUMBER` and `ADS_OPTION_PASSWORD_METHOD` flags in conjunction with the `SetOp-tion` method. We have two ways to do this. In .NET 2.0, a new wrapper class, `DirectoryEntryConfiguration`, has strongly typed methods for setting these options. Listing 10.17 shows how we can accomplish this.

LISTING 10.17: Using DirectoryEntryConfiguration for ADAM

```
//.NET 2.0 sample for ADAM password changes
DirectoryEntry entry = new DirectoryEntry(
    "LDAP://adamserver.com/CN=someuser,OU=users,O=adamsample",
    "someuser@adam",
    "UserPassword1",
    AuthenticationTypes.None
    );
```

```
entry.Options.PasswordPort = 389;
entry.Options.PasswordEncoding =
    PasswordEncodingMethod.PasswordEncodingClear;

entry.Invoke(
    "ChangePassword",
    new object[] {"UserPassword1", "UserPassword2"}
    );
```

In .NET 1.x, we do not have the handy wrapper class for `IADsObjectOp-tions`, so instead we will use the `Invoke` method via reflection to accomplish the same thing. Listing 10.18 demonstrates the necessary operations.

LISTING 10.18: Setting IADsObjectOptions via Reflection

```
//.NET 1.x sample
const int ADS_OPTION_PASSWORD_PORTNUMBER = 6;
const int ADS_OPTION_PASSWORD_METHOD = 7;
const int ADS_PASSWORD_ENCODE_CLEAR = 1;

DirectoryEntry entry = new DirectoryEntry(
    "LDAP://adamserver.com/CN=someuser,OU=users,O=adamsample",
    "someuser@adam",
    "UserPassword1",
    AuthenticationTypes.None
    );
entry.Invoke(
    "SetOption",
    new object[] {ADS_OPTION_PASSWORD_PORTNUMBER, 389}
    );
entry.Invoke(
    "SetOption",
    new object[] {
    ADS_OPTION_PASSWORD_METHOD,
    ADS_PASSWORD_ENCODE_CLEAR
    }
    );
entry.Invoke(
    "ChangePassword",
    new object[] {"UserPassword1", "UserPassword2"}
    );
```

Even if we do not relax the secure channel password requirement for ADAM, it may still be necessary to change the password port number if our ADAM instance uses a different port for SSL traffic than the standard 636. Consequently, both of the techniques shown in Listings 10.17 and

10.18 still apply, though we will want to use the SSL password encoding option instead.

Additionally, it is possible to apply the LDAP password modification sample using SDS.P from the previous section on Active Directory password modification. There are two caveats.

- We may need to change the encryption method and port number as appropriate.
- When we are modifying passwords of ADAM users with an ADAM account, it will not be possible to use Kerberos channel encryption, as ADAM users cannot do Kerberos-based secure binds. That approach is not appropriate here. It is still possible to use this approach when using pass-through binding as a Windows user with a secure bind.

Sadly, all of this seems more complicated than it really needs to be, and it probably is. We hope that we have at least explained the topic thoroughly and have given you the tools you need to get the work done.

Determining User Group Membership in Active Directory and ADAM

We often need to know a user's group membership, especially when building applications that require role-based security. There are many cases when we cannot simply rely on Windows to do this expansion for us, and we need an LDAP-based approach instead. Unfortunately, many samples that attempt to show how to do this miss important details or make key mistakes that can lead to compromised security in our applications. We attempt to right these wrongs and show some proven techniques that have been effective for us.

Two linked multivalued attributes, called `member` and `memberOf`, control group membership. The group object always holds the `member` attribute. The `memberOf` attribute is a calculated back link held on the group member object itself. As such, group membership is always managed from the group object side (the forward link) of the relationship and the back link is updated by the system automatically. That is, we can read the memberOf attribute, but we cannot modify it directly. This multivalued attribute contains the user's direct group membership, with one exception: It does not contain what is called the primary group. This group receives special treatment, and we cover how to read it in the next chapter.

When we say that the memberOf attribute contains the user's direct membership, we mean that while we can view groups that directly contain the user object, we cannot view any group membership that is derived from the nesting of group memberships. We will have to use either a recursive technique or the tokenGroups attribute to expand a user's membership fully.

It turns out that using the tokenGroups attribute is typically what we are after. This attribute holds a security identifier (SID) for each security group (including the aforementioned primary group) for which the user is a member, including nested group membership. Recursive solutions can often be a little messy. As such, the only advantage that the recursive technique holds is that it will expand group membership in distribution lists, while the tokenGroups attribute contains only security group membership.

We will cover three techniques for reading group membership using the tokenGroups attribute. The first technique will use an LDAP search to find each SID in the tokenGroups attribute, and the second technique will use the DsCrackNames API to convert them in a single batch. The third technique will be a .NET 2.0-only solution using the new IdentityReference-based classes.

Our ultimate goal will be to convert the tokenGroups attribute into a collection of human-readable group names. A typical example of this is to build a GenericPrincipal object and fill it with roles for a custom ASP.NET Forms authentication mechanism.

Retrieving the User's Token Groups

Regardless of the technique we choose to decode the tokenGroups attribute, we must first retrieve it. Since this is a constructed attribute, we must use the RefreshCache technique shown in Chapter 3 to first load the attribute into the property cache in a DirectoryEntry object. This is one of the few attributes that requires a Base search scope with Directory-Searcher, so we will generally choose to use a DirectoryEntry instance for this work instead:

```
//user is a DirectoryEntry
user.RefreshCache(
    new string[] {"tokenGroups"}
    );

//now the attribute will be available
int count = user.Properties["tokenGroups"].Count;

Console.WriteLine(
    "Found {0} Token Groups",
    count
    );
```

Technique #1: Using an LDAP Search

The big upshot to this approach is that this technique is pretty fast and we don't have to worry about using any P/Invoke code that can be intimidating to less-experienced developers. We simply iterate through the returned attribute and build a large LDAP filter that represents each security group. Once we build the filter, we can easily search the domain for the groups and return each one. Listing 10.19 shows how we can accomplish this.

LISTING 10.19: Retrieving Token Groups with an LDAP Search

```
StringBuilder sb = new StringBuilder();

//we are building an '|' clause
sb.Append("(|");

foreach (byte[] sid in user.Properties["tokenGroups"])
{
    //append each member into the filter
    sb.AppendFormat(
        "(objectSid={0})", BuildFilterOctetString(sid));
}

//end our initial filter
sb.Append(")");

DirectoryEntry searchRoot = new DirectoryEntry(
    "LDAP://DC=domain,DC=com",
    null,
    null,
    AuthenticationTypes.Secure
    );

using (searchRoot)
{
```

```
//we now have our filter, we can just search for the groups
DirectorySearcher ds = new DirectorySearcher(
    searchRoot,
    sb.ToString() //our filter
    );

using (SearchResultCollection src = ds.FindAll())
{
    foreach (SearchResult sr in src)
    {
        //Here is each group now...
        Console.WriteLine(
            sr.Properties["samAccountName"][0]);
    }
}
}

private string BuildFilterOctetString(byte[] bytes)
{
    //see listing 4.2 for the complete code
}
```

We rely on the helper method called BuildFilterOctetString from Listing 4.2 in Chapter 4 to format the binary SID correctly into a format we can use for our filter. This technique is fairly simple and relatively elegant. It is a great solution when we want to get more information about each group than just the name. The downside is that we don't directly have access to the DOMAIN\GroupName format from SearchResult. That would require string parsing, an additional search to find the NetBIOS name of the domain from the configuration partition, or a call to DsCrackNames to convert the name appropriately into our chosen format. Since DOMAIN\GroupName happens to be one of the most widely used formats, this tends to be its major drawback.

Notice that we use the sAMAccountName attribute to identify the group. This is important, as the sAMAccountName is used for security purposes and is unique in the domain. We often see samples that parse the DN to retrieve the group's CN. However, a CN can be duplicated in different containers in the same domain, so we can accidentally introduce security flaws by assuming it is unique. Always use a unique identifier intended for security purposes when making security decisions!

Technique #2: Using DsCrackNames

A more advanced technique exists that relies on the `DsCrackNames` API and forgoes searching the directory completely. The basic premise is that we will convert all of the byte-format SIDs into their string-readable Security Descriptor Description Language (SDDL)–format equivalents and pass an entire array of them into the `DsCrackNames` API, which can convert them into another format of our choosing (DN, NT Account format, etc.).

For .NET version 1.1, this requires using P/Invoke in order to convert the SID into SDDL format. It also involves wrapping the `DsCrackNames` API. Getting everything set up requires a bit of work, but it works well once it is done.

We have included all of the P/Invoke code and wrappers needed to use this functionality in the sample code included on this book's web site. For reference purposes, Listing 10.20 includes some of the important bits.

LISTING 10.20: Using DsCrackNames to Convert TokenGroups

```
//convert to array of string SIDs
int size = this.Properties["tokenGroups"].Count;
PropertyValueCollection pvc = this.Properties["tokenGroups"];

string[] sids = new string[size];

for (int i=0; i < size; i++)
{
    sids[i] = AdUtils.ConvertSidToSidString((byte[])pvc[i]);
}

//we want to pass in the SID format and retrieve
//the NT Format names.  This utility class is
//included in our web site library samples
//groupNames contains all the converted groups now
string[] groupNames = AdUtils.DsCrackNamesWrapper(
    sids,
    this.Context.Handle,
    DS_NAME_FORMAT.DS_SID_OR_SID_HISTORY_NAME,
    DS_NAME_FORMAT.DS_NT4_ACCOUNT_NAME
    );
```

Listing 10.20 uses two wrapper classes that help us convert a binary SID to the SDDL-format SID, and wraps our call to `DsCrackNames`. We are omitting this wrapper code because it would take several pages to present and it contains mostly P/Invoke declarations. We are also going to gloss over how we came to get the RPC handle necessary for DsCrackNames, for similar reasons. We wish we could dive into this code, as it is interesting, but it just takes too much book space and is irrelevant for this discussion. As usual, the complete listing is available on the book's web site. We should also note that developers more familiar with the IADsNameTranslate ADSI interface are free to substitute this method for DsCrackNames. They are actually one and the same.

For version 2.0, we no longer need to use P/Invoke for converting the SID, as we can do this using the SecurityIdentifier class. However, if we are already using version 2.0, then we should use technique #3 instead.

Technique #3: Using the SidIdentifier and IdentityReference Classes

This last technique uses the SidIdentifier and IdentityReference classes to convert between any of the IdentityReference-derived formats. These classes are available only in .NET 2.0. As demonstrated in Listing 10.21, this is the cleanest and simplest solution out of the three. As long as we are after only one of the IdentityReference formats (of which the widely used NTAccount format is one), we are in pretty good shape.

LISTING 10.21: Using SidIdentifier and IdentityReference

```
//we use the collection in order to
//batch the request for translation
IdentityReferenceCollection irc
    = ExpandTokenGroups(user).Translate(typeof(NTAccount));

foreach (NTAccount account in irc)
{
    Console.WriteLine(account);
}

//Sample Helper Function
private IdentityReferenceCollection ExpandTokenGroups(
    DirectoryEntry user)
{
    user.RefreshCache(new string[]{"tokenGroups"});

    IdentityReferenceCollection irc =
        new IdentityReferenceCollection();

    foreach (byte[] sidBytes in user.Properties["tokenGroups"])
    {
```

```
        irc.Add(new SecurityIdentifier(sidBytes, 0));
    }
    return irc;
}
```

Each technique we presented has its own advantages and disadvantages. Depending on what information we require, we might choose one or more of the options. For instance, it is entirely plausible that we will want more information about each group, yet we also will want the group's NT format name. In this case, we might combine techniques #1 and #2 or #1 and #3.

Retrieving tokenGroups from ADAM

So far, the techniques we have described have applied to Active Directory. However, we may wish to expand an ADAM user's group membership as well. Additionally, if we are using ADAM in a pass-through authentication scenario where we are authenticating Windows users, we might like to know both their Windows and ADAM group memberships.

It turns out that ADAM also supports the `tokenGroups` attribute for ADAM users and bind proxy objects. We can use the same techniques we just described for them as well. The only caveat is that we cannot refer to ADAM groups by their `sAMAccountName`, as they do not have one. We also cannot use any Windows-based techniques for resolving SIDs into names, such as techniques #2 and #3 that we just described. We must use an LDAP search, as shown with technique #1.

ADAM has an additional trick up its sleeve, though. The `RootDSE` object supports the `tokenGroups` attribute as well and will provide both the Windows and ADAM group SIDs for the currently bound user. This is especially helpful with pass-through authentication, as there is no actual object representing the user in ADAM in this scenario. What object would we query to read the `tokenGroups` attribute? The code looks approximately like this:

```
DirectoryEntry entry = new DirectoryEntry(
    "GC://localhost:389",
    null,
    null,
    AuthenticationTypes.Secure);

entry.RefreshCache(new string[] {"tokenGroups"});
```

We should instantly notice that something is strange here. We are using the `GC` provider with ADAM and specifying a port of 389 (our ADAM instance's LDAP port in this case). What gives?

For some reason, the `LDAP` provider in ADSI cannot retrieve constructed attributes off of the `RootDSE` object, but the `GC` provider can. We also do not specify the `RootDSE` object name in the `ADsPath` in this case. We are uncertain of the reason, but we know this works.

At this point, the list of group SIDs we read from the `tokenGroups` attribute may contain both Windows and ADAM SIDs, so we may need to do two passes to resolve them into friendly names. However, we can still use techniques #1, #2, and #3 to do this.

SUMMARY

All of the topics in this chapter center on how to manage user objects in either Active Directory or ADAM. This tends to be the most common task that developers are asked to perform. We have covered how we can efficiently find our user objects and set account properties in conjunction with domain-wide policies.

We also touched upon some of the more difficult tasks of setting passwords, as well as determining last logons and password expirations. Finally, we covered how to determine a user's group membership. While we have covered some of the most common, yet troublesome, tasks in user management, we have not exhaustively covered every possible user management scenario. Unfortunately, there are far too many to do them justice. We hope that because we showed the most irksome of the tasks, developers can extrapolate from the examples and use previous chapters as leaping points to figure out each unique scenario.

■ 11 ■

Group Management

S ECURITY AND DISTRIBUTION GROUPS play an important role in managing objects within any Active Directory and ADAM installation. While security groups are critical to Windows resources that are managed by access control lists (ACLs), it is not uncommon to use security groups as a basis for authorization roles within our own applications as well. As such, creating and managing security groups within Active Directory and ADAM becomes important from beyond the simple administrative detail of placing a user into a specific group. We often need to automate the management of group membership from within the application to drive the functionality. This chapter deals with the most common tasks for managing groups and their memberships. We will be building on the techniques and concepts presented in the first sections of this book to apply them to real-world tasks and scenarios.

We will start by looking at how we can create security groups, and then how we add and remove users from them. Finally, we will wrap up with how we can inspect groups to determine their membership, including both normal groups and primary groups.

Creating Groups in Active Directory and ADAM

Creating groups in Active Directory and ADAM is actually a straightforward process. The tricky part comes later, when we need to manage their members! Only two attributes really matter when creating a group in Active Directory: They are sAMAccountName and groupType.[1]

The sAMAccountName attribute contains the pre-Windows 2000 NT-compatible name for the group object. It must be unique within the domain. When we see a group name appear in the format domain\some group, the some group part is the sAMAccountName. As such, it is important for security purposes.

The groupType attribute controls which type and scope of group is created: security or distribution, and universal, global, or local scoped. We can create any of these group types with just a few combinations of constants, as shown in Listing 11.1.

LISTING 11.1: Group Constants

```
//Group Constants (uint)
ADS_GROUP_TYPE_BUILTIN_LOCAL_GROUP    = 0x00000001;
ADS_GROUP_TYPE_GLOBAL_GROUP           = 0x00000002;
ADS_GROUP_TYPE_DOMAIN_LOCAL_GROUP     = 0x00000004;
ADS_GROUP_TYPE_SECURITY_ENABLED       = 0x80000000;
ADS_GROUP_TYPE_UNIVERSAL_GROUP        = 0x00000008;
```

Using these constants, we can construct an enumeration that represents the typical valid combinations we might want to create. One such enumeration is shown in Listing 11.2.

LISTING 11.2: Valid Group Type Combinations

```
[Flags]
public enum GroupType : uint
{
    LocalDistribution = ADS_GROUP_TYPE_DOMAIN_LOCAL_GROUP,

    LocalSecurity = ADS_GROUP_TYPE_DOMAIN_LOCAL_GROUP
      | ADS_GROUP_TYPE_SECURITY_ENABLED,

    GlobalDistribution = ADS_GROUP_TYPE_GLOBAL_GROUP,
```

---

1. Back in Chapter 3, we mentioned that Windows Server 2003 will provide a default value for sAMAccountName if we do not provide one. This rule applies to both user and group objects. As such, only Window 2000 Server requires that sAMAccountName be set explicitly. However, as we suggested in Chapter 3, it is generally better to provide an explicit value, as the randomly generated default is generally not what we want. On the other hand, all versions of Active Directory will default the value of groupType to make the group a global security group. However, creating anything other than a global security group requires changing this attribute. Once again, we recommend being explicit for code clarity.

```
GlobalSecurity = ADS_GROUP_TYPE_GLOBAL_GROUP
  | ADS_GROUP_TYPE_SECURITY_ENABLED,

UniversalDistribution = ADS_GROUP_TYPE_UNIVERSAL_GROUP,

UniversalSecurity = ADS_GROUP_TYPE_UNIVERSAL_GROUP
  | ADS_GROUP_TYPE_SECURITY_ENABLED
}
```

Once we have our `sAMAccountName` and `groupType` attributes, it is a simple matter to create the group. In Listing 11.3, we will use the technique we learned in Chapter 3 to create the security group. We will specify three things: a common name (CN), the `sAMAccountName` attribute, and the `groupType` attribute. Once this is done, we can commit it to the directory using `CommitChanges`.

LISTING 11.3: Creating a Security Group

```csharp
string groupOU = "LDAP://OU=Groups,DC=domain,DC=com";
string groupName = "Group1";

//this is where the group will be created
DirectoryEntry parent = new DirectoryEntry(
    groupOU,
    null,
    null,
    AuthenticationTypes.Secure
    );

using (parent)
{
    DirectoryEntry group = parent.Children.Add(
        String.Format("CN={0}", groupName),
        "group"
        );

    using (group)
    {
        //this is the default if not specified
        GroupType type = GroupType.GlobalSecurity;

        group.Properties["sAMAccountName"].Add(groupName);
        group.Properties["groupType"].Add((int)type);
        group.CommitChanges();
    }
}
```

Note that we may wish to do a search to verify whether a group with this sAMAccountName already exists in the domain before attempting to add it. We can use the techniques for searching that we covered in Chapter 4 to check this easily. If we attempt to add a group whose sAMAccountName is already in use, we will receive a COMException.

Things do not change much when creating a group using ADAM. The biggest difference is that there are no required attributes. This is because similar to user objects (see Chapter 10), the sAMAccountName attribute is not used with ADAM. Additionally, although ADAM supports setting different groupType values, they do not control any behavior in ADAM. This is because ADAM does not support the concept of domains, so setting the scope to local, universal, or global does not make sense. In practice, as long as groupType has the ADS_GROUP_TYPE_SECURITY_ENABLED flag set, there are no differences between any of the group types in ADAM. Given this behavior, we should typically accept the default groupType that corresponds to GroupType.GlobalSecurity from Listing 11.2 and not bother trying to set it explicitly.

Manipulating Group Membership

As we mentioned in the last chapter, two linked attributes—called member and memberOf—control group membership. The group object always holds the forward-linked member attribute; the memberOf attribute is a calculated back link held on the group member object itself. As such, group membership is always managed from the group object side of the relationship and the back link is updated by the system automatically.

We have a couple of options for adding and removing group members. We can use the IADsGroup.Add and IADsGroup.Remove methods using the Invoke syntax, or we can directly manipulate the member attribute. The only situation we really need to worry about is an error condition that can arise when adding a user that is already a member, or removing a user that is not already a member of the group. To avoid this error condition, we should either check the target object's membership or catch this error explicitly.

We can use the IADsGroup.IsMember method to check group membership instead of relying on the PropertyValueCollection.Contains method. We will typically prefer to use the former method because as we learned in Chapter 6, the member attribute can often be quite large and will require range retrieval to return all the values. The Contains method is inadequate for large groups, as the collection will not contain all of the member values.

Listing 11.4 demonstrates a simple class that inherits from Directory-Entry and provides two new methods to add and remove memberships. This example is taken from a much larger class that is more comprehensive, but has been pared down to fit in this book. The full implementation will be available with the sample code on this book's web site.

LISTING 11.4: **Strongly Typing the Group Membership**

```
public Group : DirectoryEntry
{
    public bool Remove(DirectoryEntry obj)
    {
        if (IsMember(obj))
        {
            this.Invoke(
                "Remove",
                new object[]{ obj.Path }
                );
            return true;
        }
        return false;
    }

    public bool Add(DirectoryEntry obj)
    {
        if (!IsMember(obj))
        {
            this.Invoke(
                "Add",
                new object[]{ obj.Path }
                );
            return true;
        }
        return false;
    }

    public bool IsMember(DirectoryEntry obj)
    {
        return (bool) this.Invoke(
            "IsMember",
            new object[]{ obj.Path }
            );
    }
}
```

Using this class is as simple as creating something like this:

```
//group represents a Group object for the group
//and user represents a DirectoryEntry object for the user
if (group.Add(user))
{
    Console.WriteLine(
        "{0} added successfully",
        user.Name
        );
}
```

Of course, we can always directly update the group's member attribute to add or remove membership. For completeness, Listing 11.5 shows an example of directly adding to the member attribute.

LISTING 11.5: Using the member Attribute to Manage Membership

```
class Group : DirectoryEntry
{
    const int ERR_DS_ATTRIBUTE_OR_VALUE_EXISTS = -2147016691;
    const int ERR_DS_NO_ATTRIBUTE_OR_VALUE = -2147016694;

    private bool Add(string memberDN)
    {
        try
        {
            this.Properties["member"].Add(memberDN);
            this.CommitChanges();
        }
        catch (System.Runtime.InteropServices.COMException ex)
        {
            if (ex.ErrorCode !=
                ERR_DS_ATTRIBUTE_OR_VALUE_EXISTS)
                throw;

            return false; //already a member
        }

        return true;
    }

    private bool Remove(string memberDN)
    {
        try
        {
            this.Properties["member"].Remove(memberDN);
            this.CommitChanges();
```

```
        }
        catch (System.Runtime.InteropServices.COMException ex)
        {
            if (ex.ErrorCode != ERR_DS_NO_ATTRIBUTE_OR_VALUE)
                throw;

            return false; //not a member
        }

        return true;
    }
}
```

Listing 11.5 demonstrates how to catch the error that will occur when we add a duplicate member. Similarly, we need to catch the error that will occur when we try to remove a member that does not exist. These two new method overloads in Listing 11.5 would complement the methods shown in 11.4.

The question that naturally arises is which one should I use? Choosing between the two methods is a bit of a balancing act. In a number of circumstances, it is actually easier to revert to invoking the IADsGroup methods. This is especially true when determining group membership. The thing we need to keep in mind is that using the IsMember method and then adding the member requires two network trips. Manipulating the member attribute directly will save us one network trip by skipping the membership check. However, depending on our usage, we could also end up throwing a lot of exceptions that might offset this advantage.

If we are rebuilding group membership from the ground up, it is generally going to be faster to just add directly to the member attribute and call CommitChanges one time. We will be able to do this because we know that duplicates won't exist. In any other scenario, we should choose between the two methods shown in Listings 11.4 and 11.5 as our data demands.

Expanding Group Membership

A common issue that developers face is how to unroll or expand the group membership of a given group. Given that groups can contain a variety of objects, such as users, computers, or other groups, what appears to be a very simple idea can quickly grow complex. Compounding this issue is the

> **■ WARNING**   ADsPath Is Not the Same As DN
>
> A subtle point that developers often overlook when using the `IsMember` method or the `PropertyValueCollection.Contains` method is the format that must be presented as an argument. For adding directly to the `member` attribute, this format is the DN format. When invoking the `IADsGroup` methods, the format used is the `ADsPath` format, which includes `"LDAP://"` (`DirectoryEntry.Path` is this format). Often we see developers switch between the two formats and become frustrated when it won't work. We should also note that using the `Invoke` method does not require an explicit `CommitChanges` call, but that adding to the `member` attribute naturally does.

fact that since groups can contain other groups, membership often can be duplicated when fully expanded, and even circular. These particular problems lend themselves well to a recursive solution. We will tackle this problem slightly differently, depending on the version of the framework that is being used, but the general algorithm will remain the same.

1. Create a `Hashtable` to track unique members and groups.
2. Starting with the first group, expand the direct membership.
3. Determine which members are groups.
4. Recurse each group member with the previous algorithm, starting at step #2.
5. Add all nongroup members into a collection.

This approach leads us to two implementations of group expansion: one for version 1.1 and one for version 2.0 of the .NET Framework.

Using .NET Version 2.0

Using attribute scope queries (ASQs) allows us to shorten the amount of code we would otherwise need to employ. Since the `member` attribute is a DN-format attribute, it naturally lends itself to using this type of query. A nice side effect of using ASQs is that the method avoids the need to use range retrieval for large groups. Listing 11.6 shows an example of a class that uses this technique to recursively unroll a group and retrieve all the members. The entire class is available on the book's web site.

LISTING 11.6: Expanding Membership in Version 2.0

```
public class GroupExpander2
{
    DirectoryEntry group;
    ArrayList members;
    Hashtable processed;

    public GroupExpander2(DirectoryEntry group)
    {
        if (group == null)
            throw new ArgumentNullException("group");

        this.group = group;
        this.processed = new Hashtable();
        this.processed.Add(
            this.group.Properties[
                "distinguishedName"][0].ToString(),
            null
            );

        this.members = Expand(this.group);
    }

    public ArrayList Members
    {
        get { return this.members; }
    }

    private ArrayList Expand(DirectoryEntry group)
    {
        ArrayList al = new ArrayList(5000);
        string oc = "objectClass";

        DirectorySearcher ds = new DirectorySearcher(
            group,
            "(objectClass=*)",
            new string[] {
                "member",
                "distinguishedName",
                "objectClass" },
            SearchScope.Base
            );

        ds.AttributeScopeQuery = "member";
        ds.PageSize = 1000;

        using (SearchResultCollection src = ds.FindAll())
        {
            string dn = null;
```

```
        foreach (SearchResult sr in src)
        {
            dn = (string)
                sr.Properties["distinguishedName"][0];

            if (!this.processed.ContainsKey(dn))
            {
                this.processed.Add(dn, null);

                //oc == "objectClass", we had to
                //truncate to fit in book.
                //if it is a group, do this recursively
                if (sr.Properties[oc].Contains("group"))
                {
                    SetNewPath(this.group, dn);
                    al.AddRange(Expand(this.group));
                }
                else
                    al.Add(dn);
            }
        }
    }
    return al;
}

//we will use IADsPathName utility function instead
//of parsing string values.  This particular function
//allows us to replace only the DN portion of a path
//and leave the server and port information intact
private void SetNewPath(DirectoryEntry entry, string dn)
{
    IAdsPathname pathCracker = (IAdsPathname)new Pathname();

    pathCracker.Set(entry.Path, 1);
    pathCracker.Set(dn, 4);

    entry.Path = pathCracker.Retrieve(5);
}
}
```

We can determine which members are groups by inspecting the objectClass attribute for the group class. This also has the nice side effect that any custom classes that have been derived from the group class will be handled as well.

We are also using the IADsPathName utility interface in Listing 11.6. This interface is a handy way to parse and manipulate paths in LDAP. While we do not explicitly show the COM interop declarations needed to use this interface, they will be included as part of the downloadable code on this book's web site.

Using .NET Version 1.1

Since we do not have the option of using ASQ searches in this version, we must rely on using a `DirectorySearcher` instance to find our objects by membership. Listing 11.7 shows one such class that has been abbreviated to fit in this book.

LISTING 11.7: Expanding Membership in Version 1.1

```
public class GroupExpander
{
    DirectoryEntry searchRoot;
    ArrayList members;
    Hashtable processed;

    const string DN_ATTRIB = "distinguishedName";

    public GroupExpander(
        DirectoryEntry group,
        DirectoryEntry searchRoot)
    {
        if (group == null)
            throw new ArgumentNullException("group");

        //a null searchRoot can lead to unexpected
        //behavior, especially with ADAM
        if (searchRoot == null)
            throw new ArgumentNullException("group");

        this.searchRoot = searchRoot;
        this.processed = new Hashtable();

        this.members = Expand(group);
    }

    public ArrayList Members
    {
        get{ return this.members; }
    }

    public static ArrayList RangeExpansion(
        DirectoryEntry entry,
        string attribute)
    {
        //RangeExpansion method as shown in Chapter 6
```

```
    }


    private ArrayList Expand(DirectoryEntry group)
    {
        ArrayList al = new ArrayList(5000);
        string dn = group.Properties[DN_ATTRIB][0].ToString();

        if (!this.processed.ContainsKey(dn))
        {
            this.processed.Add(dn,null);
        }

        //first we find all members of nested
        //groups, then the direct members
        string filter = String.Format(
            "(&(objectClass=group)(memberOf={0}))",
            dn
            );

        DirectorySearcher ds = new DirectorySearcher(
            this.searchRoot,
            filter
            );

        using (SearchResultCollection src = ds.FindAll())
        {
            string srDN = null;
            foreach (SearchResult sr in src)
            {
                srDN = (string)sr.Properties[DN_ATTRIB][0];

                if (!this.processed.ContainsKey(srDN))
                {
                    using (DirectoryEntry grp =
                        sr.GetDirectoryEntry())
                    {
                        al.AddRange(Expand(grp));
                    }
                }
            }
        }

        foreach(string member in RangeExpansion(group,"member"))
        {
            //in case our nested groups contained the
            //same members, we need to check for uniqueness
            if (!this.processed.ContainsKey(member))
            {
                this.processed.Add(member, null);
```

```
                al.Add(member);
            }
        }

        return al;
    }
}
```

Listing 11.7 detects nested groups by searching for `group` objects that have direct membership to the inspected group via the `memberOf` attribute. Since we are performing this task recursively, we can get deeply nested and even circular-referenced groups. Other than not using ASQ, the big difference between Listings 11.6 and 11.7 is that we are passing in a reference to the `SearchRoot` we should use to find other nested groups. Typically, we will use the root of the partition, but it could be anywhere. Passing in the `SearchRoot` is necessary in order to avoid all sorts of nasty and fragile code to detect where a search should be rooted. Finally, as Listing 11.7 demonstrates, we must use range retrieval to expand the member attribute for large groups. We have omitted the code implementation for the `RangeExpansion` method, but it is identical to that shown in Listing 6.8, in Chapter 6.

It turns out that both of these methods are fairly fast when performed on small to mid-size (less than 20,000 members) groups. For unknown reasons at the time of this writing, the version 2.0 method had difficulty scaling to very large groups (more than 20,000 members) and will perform badly. Given that it is generally regarded as a bad practice to have groups that contain this many direct members, we are hopeful that none of our readers will actually be affected by this.

Primary Group Membership

Primary groups are an artifact of POSIX compliance for Windows NT. Unless we are using POSIX-compliant applications or Services for Macintosh, we typically do not change this value from its default of `Domain Users`.

Unlike normal group membership where the `member` attribute holds the group membership, primary group membership is held on the member's side rather than the group's side in the form of the `primaryGroupID` attribute. This attribute holds the significant and unique part of the primary group's security identifier (SID), known as the relative identifier (RID). It is only through calculation that we can determine the user's membership in a particular primary group. It is important to note that a user can be part of only one primary group at a time.

The difficulty with using the primary group starts with the inconsistency of how different ADSI providers treat it. Using the WinNT provider, we can enumerate all groups using the IADsUser.Groups property. This enumeration will include all groups including the primary group, but we have no indication as to which group is the primary group. Just to be contrary, the LDAP provider will enumerate all groups except for the primary group using the same ADSI interface. In order to include the primary group using the LDAP provider, we have to enumerate all the security groups held in the tokenGroups attribute, but again we have no indication as to which one is the primary group.

In these scenarios, we can see a couple of methods by which to determine which group is the primary group.

- We can enumerate membership using both the LDAP and WinNT providers using the IADsUser.Groups property, and figure out which group is missing, and we will have found our primary group. This works fine, but it seems rather clunky, as we have to use both providers to get this information, not to mention we are relying on an aberration for an implementation.

- We could also search for all of the groups in the domain and return their primaryGroupToken attribute. This constructed attribute is the RID of the group. We can then compare this RID to the user's primaryGroupID attribute and see if they match. When they match, we have found our primary group. The major downside is that since primaryGroupToken is a constructed attribute, we cannot search for it directly. Furthermore, the search is relatively slow on domains with a large number of groups, since we would have to inspect them all.

- Knowing the user's SID and the group's RID we can construct the primary group's SID and directly bind to the primary group.

It turns out that the last technique is the easiest to do in .NET, as we can easily handle the resulting byte array and determine the primary group. The steps to perform this are simple.

1. Retrieve the user's SID in byte array format:

```
byte[] userSID = user.Properties["objectSid"][0] as byte[];
```

2. Retrieve the user's `primaryGroupId` RID:

```
int primaryGroupID =
    (int)user.Properties["primaryGroupId"][0];
```

3. Overwrite the user's RID with the primary group RID:

```
//Create the Primary Group SID
byte[] sidBytes = CreatePrimaryGroupSID(userSID, primaryGroupID);

private byte[] CreatePrimaryGroupSID(
    byte[] userSid,
    int primaryGroupID)
{
    //convert the int into a byte array
    byte[] rid = BitConverter.GetBytes(primaryGroupID);

    //place the bytes into the user's SID byte array
    //overwriting them as necessary
    for (int i=0; i < rid.Length; i++)
    {
        userSid.SetValue(
            rid[i],
            new long[]{userSid.Length - (rid.Length - i)}
            );
    }
    return userSid;
}
```

4. Construct a SID binding string and bind to the primary group:

```
adsPath = String.Format(
    "LDAP://<SID={0}>",
    BuildOctetString(sidBytes)
    );

DirectoryEntry primaryGroup = new DirectoryEntry(
    adsPath,
```

```
        null,
        null,
        AuthenticationTypes.Secure
        );

    //we now have our primary group
    using (primaryGroup)
    {
        Console.WriteLine(
            "Primary Group: {0}",
            primaryGroup.Name
            );
    }

    //From Listing 3.5 in Chapter 3
    private string BuildOctetString(byte[] bytes)
    {
        StringBuilder sb = new StringBuilder();
        for(int i=0; i < bytes.Length; i++)
        {
            sb.Append(bytes[i].ToString("X2"));
        }
        return sb.ToString();
    }
```

We will typically use this technique when we need to determine the primary group directly. Otherwise, if we only want to obtain an enumeration of our security groups, including the primary group, we should rely upon using the `tokenGroups` attribute, as shown in Chapter 10.

Some developers might be wondering how to set the primary group for a user to something other than the default value of `Domain Users`. As we mentioned earlier, unless we are specifically dealing with POSIX applications or Macintosh clients, there is no reason to attempt this. However, throwing caution to the wind, we will show you how to accomplish this even if we don't think you will generally ever need to do this:

```
    //group is DirectoryEntry for primary group
    group.RefreshCache(new string[]{"primaryGroupToken"});

    //this is our user DirectoryEntry that will have
    //its primary group set to 'group'.
    user.Properties["primaryGroupID"].Value =
        group.Properties["primaryGroupToken"].Value;

    user.CommitChanges();
```

The code seems pretty simple, and for the most part, it is. Just be aware that the user must already be a member of the group that is to be set as the primary group. That might seem strange or possibly redundant, but if we consider that it would be a major security violation if just anyone could change their primary group to `Domain Admins` just because they had the ability to write to the `primaryGroupID` attribute, we can see why this limitation exists. Once the primary group is set, we can remove the direct group membership from the group itself and the user will still be a member.

Foreign Security Principals

Foreign security principals (FSPs) are created anytime we add a security principal from a trusted domain or machine to the local domain or ADAM instance. Represented in the directory by the `foreignSecurityPrincipal` class, FSPs can also include the intrinsic Windows SIDs such as `Authenticated Users` and even `Everyone`. FSPs are created in the special `ForeignSecurityPrincipals` container, which is normally hidden without using the Advanced view option in the Active Directory Users and Computers (ADUC) MMC. The FSP serves as the local representation of a foreign user that can then be added to security groups or used as a local security principal. What makes the treatment of FSPs special is that we don't have to do a thing to use them. The system (either Active Directory or ADAM) takes care of creating and using the FSP automatically.

For instance, suppose we wish to add a Windows user account as a member of an ADAM group. Since the Windows user account does not reside locally in ADAM, we might wonder how we can add a foreign object to an ADAM group. We can accomplish this with code similar to that shown in Listing 11.8. Essentially, we create a reference to the Windows object using the account's SID. When we add this SID to the ADAM group, the system determines that the object does not reside locally in the directory. Subsequently, an FSP representing the Windows account is created automatically and is set as the member of the group. The FSP is a local reference to the Windows account in this case. Most importantly, the developer doesn't need to do anything to create the FSP in the proper container or to add it to the group. The system does all of this automatically.

LISTING 11.8: Foreign Security Principals

```
DirectoryEntry entry = new DirectoryEntry(
    "LDAP://localhost:389/O=Dunnry,C=US",
    null,
    null,
    AuthenticationTypes.Secure
    );

//This is the user we wish to add
NTAccount account = new NTAccount("ASPNET");

SecurityIdentifier sid = (SecurityIdentifier)
    account.Translate(typeof(SecurityIdentifier));

//this is how we reference local users as well
string userPath = String.Format("LDAP://<SID={0}>", sid);

using (entry)
{
    DirectorySearcher ds = new DirectorySearcher(
        entry,
        "(cn=Readers)"
        );

    SearchResult sr = ds.FindOne();

    if (sr != null)
    {
        using (DirectoryEntry group = sr.GetDirectoryEntry())
        {
            Console.WriteLine(
                "Add {0}",
                userPath
                );

            group.Invoke("Add", new object[]{userPath});

            foreach (object o in group.Properties["member"])
            {
                Console.WriteLine(
                    "{0} was added",
                    o
                    );
            }
        }
    }
}
Output:
```

```
Add LDAP://<SID=S-1-5-21-1333191943-1296836545-315636210-
CN=S-1-5-21-1333191943-1296836545-315636210-
1009,CN=ForeignSecurityPrincipals,O=Dunnry,C=US was added
```

As the output from Listing 11.8 shows, the distinguished ......
the FSP object is shown when we enumerate the group membership. FSPs are somewhat annoying in that we often have no idea what the SID in the CN refers to and would like to convert this back to NT Account format instead.

We can do this very easily if we are using ADAM. It turns out in ADAM that the `foreignSecurityPrincipal` class has the `msDS-BindProxy` class set as one of its auxiliary classes. This latter class includes a constructed attribute called `msDS-PrincipalName` that holds the NT Account name for us. Using the `RefreshCache` technique from Chapter 3, or specifically including it as an attribute to be returned from a search, will show us the NT Account format when we read this attribute value.

The situation is not as smooth if we are using Active Directory, however. Our suggestion is to rely upon Windows native methods for converting SIDs to account names. We can use the `SecurityIdentifier` class and its `Translate` method to convert it into an `NTAccount` object. Simply return the `objectSid` attribute from the relevant FPS object and use one of the `SecurityIdentifier` constructors to build an `IdentityReference` object that can be used to translate between the formats. We demonstrated code like this in Chapter 10 when we were working with group membership for users.

SUMMARY

In this chapter, we focused on the specific issues of managing group objects in Active Directory and ADAM. We started by demonstrating how to apply our basic object creation knowledge to creating new group objects, including a discussion on group types.

We then discussed the various ways to manipulate group membership. There are several possible approaches, including direct modifications to the `member` attribute and invocation of the ADSI group manipulation methods.

Next, we focused on techniques for enumerating group memberships. Groups may contain many members, so we must often use special techniques to retrieve all of them. We demonstrated how to accomplish this in both .NET 2.0 and .NET 1.x.

We then discussed the other type of group membership in Active Directory: primary group membership. Primary groups work completely differently than normal groups and require a different set of techniques as a result.

We concluded with a discussion of foreign security principals, and how they relate to group membership, including a sample of how to create and read them.

∎12∎
Authentication

AUTHENTICATION IS THE PROCESS by which we validate a user's credentials in an attempt to verify who the user purports to be. That is, we are securely identifying our users using some sort of shared secret. For the scenarios we cover in this chapter, this shared secret is the user's password, although it really could be a number of things (once again, see *The .NET Developer's Guide to Windows Security*, referenced in Chapter 8, for a thorough discussion of authentication in general). As such, authentication really does not tell us much, other than "who" the user is choosing to represent.

In Chapters 3 and 8, we set the groundwork for connecting to the directory and understanding the binding process in detail. In this chapter, we take what we have already learned and apply it to the task of programmatic authentication.

When the user is a Windows or ADAM security principal, we have a number of options available to us for authentication. Since we will specifically be dealing with validating username/password combinations in this chapter, we will discuss the four primary means of password authentication we have available for us to use.

In each scenario, we will take input from the user in the form of a username, a password, and possibly, a domain name. A word of warning: The username can come to us in a few valid formats, so we should always be ready to contend with each one. Typically, we would filter the input or derive our own username format based on the input given to us by the client. For instance, the client might use any of the following formats for their username with Active Directory, as we discussed in Chapter 3:

- NT Login (`DOMAIN\Username`)
- NT Username (`Username`)
- UPN (`user@domain.com`)
- DN (`CN=User,DC=domain,DC=com`)

When using ADAM security principals (as opposed to using pass-through authentication with ADAM), we will typically see the username in only one of two formats[1]:

- DN (`CN=ADAM User,OU=Foo,O=Domain,C=US`)
- UPN (format varies)

It is our job as developers to anticipate that our clients will use any or all of the formats, and we need to be ready to either filter the format to our liking at input time, or deal with the format on the back end. Building the filtering through the UI is a good idea, but we should also be prepared to accept the different username formats on the back end.

Authentication Using SDS

One of the easiest methods available to us is to simply create a `Directory-Entry` object using our client's credentials and take some action that will cause a bind. If no error occurs, we have successfully bound to the directory and we can infer that the client's credentials are valid. However, the opposite is not quite true. That is, if an error occurs, we cannot automatically assume that the client's credentials were invalid. An error could occur because of other things, such as account lockout, being disabled, or log-on hours such that the client might not be able to authenticate successfully.

Before we get too deep into this discussion, we would really like to point out that using the `DirectoryEntry` object strictly for authentication is actually a nonoptimal solution. It is definitely easy, but there are a number of

---

1. In actuality, if we do not bind using the DN, ADAM will attempt to resolve the account using `DsCrackNames` (of which UPN is one format). This means it can accept any format supported by this API (and there are eight), but collisions are possible that prevent UPN from being used effectively. Only the DN format is guaranteed to get what we want.

LDAP Binding as Authentication

Is an LDAP bind appropriate to use for authentication? This seemingly simple question provokes no end of controversy in the community, with different camps falling heavily on one side or the other. Microsoft itself seems a bit divided on this point, with some documentation suggesting that it is not appropriate and other documentation showing you how to do it!

From a practical perspective, an LDAP bind is one of the easiest mechanisms to use to authenticate a client on Windows, especially for many higher-level languages such as VBScript. Microsoft's other APIs, such as Security Support Provider Interface (SSPI) and Kerberos, are quite a bit more difficult to program and are essentially inaccessible to some of these higher-level languages. Additionally, ADSI makes it very easy to use Simple Authentication and Security Layer (SASL) or "secure" authentication with LDAP binds, so it is not necessarily dangerous to use either.

If we always take care to secure the credentials (using SSL, SASL, etc.), there is nothing wrong, per se, with using this as an authentication mechanism. In fact, from the perspective of ADAM, an LDAP bind is the only way available to authenticate an ADAM security principal, so another method of authentication is not relevant.

The real debate surrounds whether using any given LDAP binding mechanism is appropriate for a given application architecture. We will attempt to address this issue a bit more in this chapter.

problems with using it. First, the `DirectoryEntry` object was not conceived for authentication use. In high-volume applications, we will find that using `DirectoryEntry` is impractical, as it cannot scale. In Chapter 3, we discussed how ADSI uses connection caching to reuse existing LDAP connections. Creating many ADSI objects with different sets of credentials works directly against ADSI's caching strategy and will cause us to run out of TCP/IP wildcard ports, resulting in seemingly random errors when trying to connect to the directory. This problem is especially insidious, as we often get great results during development, but things fall apart when we deploy to our production environment. Do not even consider using ADSI for authentication if the application requires high scalability with many concurrent users. It will not work.

It is also not the best-performing method, as there is a cost to building the schema for an object that will only be thrown away. For small or single-user implementations, the cost is probably tolerable, but using this technique, for instance, for larger ASP.NET web sites is probably a nonstarter.

Keeping in mind that the username can come in different formats, we should make sure that we have accounted for these. For a non-SSL Active Directory installation, the credentials can be passed securely using `AuthenticationTypes.Secure`. However, we are restricted to using the UPN format, or NT Login format, as the username. For ADAM, we can use `AuthenticationTypes.None` or `SecureSocketsLayer` (if SSL is configured). The username should be in DN format or UPN format for ADAM security principals. The UPN format for ADAM actually can vary widely, from the more common email format (`user1@adaminstance.com`) to simply a username or UID format (`user1`).

WARNING   Always Add Additional Security to Simple Binds

The username and password will be sent on the network unencrypted and vulnerable when using `AuthenticationTypes.None`. Always protect the credentials using `SecureSocketsLayer` in ADAM. If you have read this book cover to cover, you have probably already been warned about this a dozen times already. We apologize for beating you over the head, but simple binds are just not safe enough to let this go unmentioned.

Active Directory Authentication

Listing 12.1 demonstrates how we can use the `DirectoryEntry` object with Active Directory to authenticate credentials. The implementation shown is a fairly naïve implementation using `RootDSE`, but it is adequate for a variety of situations.

LISTING 12.1: A Naïve Active Directory Authentication Method

```
const int ERROR_LOGON_FAILURE = -2147023570;

private bool AuthenticateUser(
    string username,
    string password,
```

```
        string domain)
{
    //optionally add the domain
    string adsPath = String.Format(
        "LDAP://{0}rootDSE",
        (domain != null && domain.Length > 0) ? domain + "/" :
        String.Empty
        );

    DirectoryEntry root = new DirectoryEntry(
        adsPath,
        username,
        password,
        AuthenticationTypes.Secure
        | AuthenticationTypes.FastBind
        );

    using (root)
    {
        try
        {
            //force the bind
            object tmp = root.NativeObject;
            return true;
        }
        catch (System.Runtime.InteropServices.COMException ex)
        {
            //some other error happened, so rethrow it
            if (ex.ErrorCode != ERROR_LOGON_FAILURE)
                throw;

            return false;
        }
    }
}
```

We recommend RootDSE as the object to use in our ADsPath to test the bind. The reason for this is that the object is already known and is available anonymously, so no authorization demands are placed on reading it. We can be fairly certain that the underlying bind will simply test the user's credentials.

We mentioned earlier that using something like Listing 12.1 in a large ASP.NET site to authenticate credentials would probably not be a good idea. It is relatively slow for very high-volume applications and it tends to scale poorly. It is most appropriate for fat-client types of applications where we don't have to worry as much about other users or scaling requirements.

ADAM Authentication

We can just slightly modify our previous example in order to authenticate users in ADAM or bind proxies to Active Directory users using an LDAP simple bind. We will need to use the name of the server in conjunction with `RootDSE` in order to find our ADAM instance. Additionally, the domain parameter for our `AuthenticateUser` method does not make sense for ADAM. If we simply rename "domain" to "server" and fix up the references a bit, we are almost there. The last minor change will be to use `AuthenticationTypes.SecureSocketsLayer` in order to protect any credentials and to switch to a simple bind, as discussed in Chapter 8. With only a few minor changes, we have a working ADAM authentication mechanism using `System.DirectoryServices` (SDS), as Listing 12.2 demonstrates.

LISTING 12.2: **ADAM Authentication Using SDS**

```
const int ERROR_LOGON_FAILURE = -2147023570;

private bool AuthenticateUser(
    string username,
    string password,
    string server)
{
    //optionally add the domain
    string adsPath = String.Format(
        "LDAP://{0}/rootDSE",
        server
        );

    DirectoryEntry root = new DirectoryEntry(
        adsPath,
        username,
        password,
        AuthenticationTypes.SecureSocketsLayer
        | AuthenticationTypes.FastBind
        );

    using (root)
    {
        try
```

```
        {
            //force the bind
            object tmp = root.NativeObject;
            return true;
        }
        catch (System.Runtime.InteropServices.COMException ex)
        {
            //some other error happened, so rethrow it
            if (ex.ErrorCode != ERROR_LOGON_FAILURE)
                throw;

            return false;
        }
    }
}
```

The user's distinguished name (DN) is typically the name that we use with ADAM for authentication. However, our clients will most likely not remember or even know their DN. To cope with this, we can assign users a log-on name and store it in ADAM, using the `userPrincipalName` attribute. Once this attribute has been assigned, we can then use it as the username for our ADAM users. It can be passed instead of the DN for authentication in the `DirectoryEntry` object.

What if we want to use ADAM's pass-through authentication mechanism to authenticate Windows users? We discussed pass-through authentication in Chapter 8 and mentioned that to use it, we simply need to use a secure bind rather than a simple bind. As it turns out, Listing 12.1 will basically work for this if we specify the ADAM instance name correctly in our `ADsPath`, so we are already covered.

If we need to support both Windows and ADAM users, then we need to handle both secure and simple binds in our code. This can be tricky, as we essentially need a way to differentiate our users based on the username they supply so that we know which approach to take, or that we need to try both. Given that naming conventions will tend to vary from implementation to implementation, we do not have a specific sample to recommend beyond a combination of Listings 12.1 and 12.2. However, we do recommend choosing a naming convention for users in Active Directory and ADAM that makes this easy. A little planning will go a long way here.

Authentication Using SDS.P

Using the `System.DirectoryServices.Protocols` (SDS.P) namespace, we have access to a number of features that are not available using ADSI or SDS. We have much tighter control over the binding process and can more efficiently manage connections to the directory. This allows us to more easily scale where the previous SDS technique using `DirectoryEntry` would fall flat. If we recall from Chapter 3, `DirectoryEntry` will create a new connection to the directory for every permutation of credentials and `AuthenticationTypes`. Since we are specifically changing credentials for authentication, obviously this equates to creating a new connection for each unique authentication request.

SDS.P also gives us access to a feature called **fast concurrent binding**. Unlike a normal LDAP bind, this type of bind does not attempt to build a security token for the credentials. It simply validates the username and password. This allows the bind operation to complete in a fraction of the time a normal bind operation would require. This can yield important performance benefits, which may be especially important in server applications like ASP.NET.

Fast concurrent binding is available to us with Windows Server 2003 and ADAM when using a simple bind (`AuthType.Basic`). It cannot be combined with a secure bind. As such, we must take care, as usual, to encrypt the channel with SSL or another appropriate mechanism. Additionally, the client itself must be Windows Server 2003. While this sounds restrictive, in reality we typically would be using fast concurrent binding in server applications such as IIS, so deployment to Windows Server 2003 is reasonable. Developers will not be able to test this feature on Windows XP workstations, though.

Using the `LdapConnection` class, we will walk through a sample of how this can be done. Starting with Listing 12.3, we will bind to a server and start the process of determining what features we can use.

LISTING 12.3: Setting LdapConnection Options

```
class LdapAuth : IDisposable
{
    LdapConnection connect;
    bool fastBind;
```

```
bool useSSL;
bool isADAM;

public LdapAuth(string server, bool useSSL)
{
    this.useSSL = useSSL;
    this.fastBind = false;
    this.isADAM = false;

    this.connect = new LdapConnection(
        new LdapDirectoryIdentifier(server),
        null,
        AuthType.Basic
        );

    this.connect.Bind();

    this.connect.SessionOptions.ProtocolVersion = 3;
    this.connect.SessionOptions.SecureSocketLayer =
        this.useSSL;

    CheckCapabilities(this.connect);

    if (this.fastBind)
    {
        try
        {
            this.connect.SessionOptions.FastConcurrentBind();
        }
        catch (PlatformNotSupportedException)
        {
            //this will happen when clent is not W2K3
            this.fastBind = false;
        }
    }

    if (!this.fastBind && !this.useSSL && !this.isADAM)
    {
        //we did not get a fast bind or
        //SSL so we can try to at least
        //encrypt the credentials for Active Directory
        this.connect.AuthType = AuthType.Negotiate;

        this.connect.SessionOptions.Sealing = true;
        this.connect.SessionOptions.Signing = true;
    }

    if (this.isADAM && !this.useSSL)
    {
        //we are using ADAM with no SSL
```

```
            //try to use Digest to secure bind
            //Requires Win2k3 R2 ADAM
            this.connect.AuthType = AuthType.Digest;
        }
    }
```

Listing 12.3 is first binding to a server we provide, using a simple bind and SSL if it was specified. Ideally, we would want to use SSL here for both ADAM and Active Directory, as that in combination with a fast concurrent bind would provide the best performance while still protecting the credentials. If we are using Active Directory without SSL, then we would want to use `AuthType.Negotiate` (similar to `AuthenticationTypes.Secure` in SDS), along with `Signing` and `Sealing` options to protect the credentials. Lastly, if we were using ADAM without SSL, we would want to try to use Digest authentication. While SDS does not support Digest authentication with ADAM, it is supported with the lower-level control we have in SDS.P. The only caveat here is that it requires the Windows Server 2003 R2 release of ADAM as well as Windows 2003 SP1 clients and servers. We are intentionally not showing ADAM authentication without some sort of credentials protection (transport or otherwise), because it is just a bad idea and we would not want to see this in any type of production application.

To set all the connection options in Listing 12.3, we needed to know a bit more about the directory we were working with. Listing 12.4 contains our helper method used in our `LdapAuth` class. It demonstrates how we can read the `RootDSE` object using SDS.P to determine both the directory type and whether the server supports fast concurrent binding.

LISTING 12.4: Determining Server Capabilities

```
    private void CheckCapabilities(LdapConnection conn)
    {
        string ext = "supportedExtension";
        string cap = "supportedCapabilities";

        SearchRequest request = new SearchRequest(
            null, //read the rootDSE
            "(objectClass=*)",
            SearchScope.Base,
            new string[] { ext, cap }
            );

        //set 120 second timelimit
```

```
request.TimeLimit = TimeSpan.FromSeconds(120);

SearchResponse response =
    (SearchResponse)conn.SendRequest(request);

if (response.ResultCode != ResultCode.Success)
    throw new Exception(response.ErrorMessage);

SearchResultEntry entry = response.Entries[0];

object[] vals =
    entry.Attributes[ext].GetValues(typeof(string));

foreach (string s in vals)
{
    //OID for Fast Concurrent Bind support
    if (s == "1.2.840.113556.1.4.1781")
    {
        this.fastBind = true;
        break;
    }
}

vals = entry.Attributes[cap].GetValues(typeof(string));

foreach (string s in vals)
{
    //OID for ADAM
    if (s == "1.2.840.113556.1.4.1851")
    {
        this.isADAM = true;
        break;
    }
}
}
```

The first parameter to the `SearchRequest` object in Listing 12.4 specifies that we want to read the `RootDSE` object. We are checking two attributes, called `supportedExtension` and `supportedCapabilities`, to determine if fast concurrent binding is supported and if the directory we are using is ADAM, respectively.

Once we have determined what options are available to us and we have set our connection options, we can simply attempt a bind to the directory, as Listing 12.5 shows. We should also take care to clean up our `LdapConnection` instance at some point, although we probably want to keep it open for an extended period and reuse it repeatedly.

LISTING 12.5: LDAP Authentication

```
public bool Authenticate(NetworkCredential credentials)
{
    try
    {
        this.connect.Bind(credentials);
        return true;
    }
    catch (LdapException ex)
    {
        if (ex.ErrorCode != 49)
            throw;

        return false;
    }
}
```

`NetworkCredential` can be in any of the formats we covered previously in this chapter and in Chapter 3. We should also note that the `Ldap-Connection.Bind` method is thread safe, making it safe to use in multithreaded applications. We are omitting the final pieces to our `Ldap-Auth` class that implement the `IDisposable` pattern, but all of this code can be found on this book's web site.

For those who plan to use LDAP authentication in their application, we highly recommend an approach like this one that uses SDS.P. The ability to manage our LDAP network connections directly will allow our application to scale properly to many concurrent users, and the ability to use fast concurrent binding can give us an important performance boost.

Authentication Using SSPI

When authenticating against Active Directory, we can use a couple of techniques in order to validate a user's credentials using native Windows protocols rather than LDAP. One valid technique is to use the `LogonUser` API. This technique is fairly well understood, and resources like www.pinvoke.net have ready-made code snippets that demonstrate how to use the API successfully. We won't cover this technique, other than to say that for Windows 2000, this technique has some fairly significant limitations. This topic and more are covered in detail in *The .NET Developer's*

Guide to Windows Security. While these limitations have been removed with subsequent Windows releases, we feel that an easier technique is available that addresses all NT-based versions of Windows.

SSPI authentication has become much easier with .NET 2.0, and it is a handy way to sidestep any security issues that crop up with `LogonUser`. While this technique really is not LDAP or ADSI related in any sense, it is certainly useful enough to merit coverage. Essentially, we will use the new `NegotiateStream` class in .NET 2.0 to harness the Negotiate protocol directly. The trick here is to execute a trusted handshake, acting as both the client and the server. Listing 12.6 shows a sample of how this might work.

LISTING 12.6: Windows Authentication Using SSPI

```
using System;
using System.Net;
using System.Net.Security;
using System.Net.Sockets;
using System.Security.Principal;
using System.Threading;

class NTAuth
{
    TcpListener listener;
    int port;

    public NTAuth(int port)
    {
        this.port = port;
        this.listener = new TcpListener(
            IPAddress.Loopback, this.port);
        this.listener.Start();
    }

    private void CreateServer(object state)
    {
        try
        {
            NegotiateStream nsServer = new NegotiateStream(
                this.listener.AcceptTcpClient().GetStream()
                );

            nsServer.AuthenticateAsServer(
                CredentialCache.DefaultNetworkCredentials,
                ProtectionLevel.None,
```

```
                        TokenImpersonationLevel.Impersonation
                        );
        }
        catch (AuthenticationException) {}
    }

    public bool Authenticate(NetworkCredential creds)
    {
        TcpClient client = new TcpClient(
            "localhost",
            this.port
            );

        ThreadPool.QueueUserWorkItem(
            new WaitCallback(CreateServer)
            );

        NegotiateStream nsClient = new NegotiateStream(
            client.GetStream(),
            true
            );

        using (nsClient)
        {
            try
            {
                nsClient.AuthenticateAsClient(
                    creds,
                    creds.Domain + @"\" + creds.UserName,
                    ProtectionLevel.None,
                    TokenImpersonationLevel.Impersonation
                    );
                return nsClient.IsAuthenticated;
            }
            catch (AuthenticationException)
            {
                return false;
            }
        }
    }
}
```

The SSPI authentication technique will not work with ADAM security principals. As such, this technique applies only to Active Directory installations.

Discovering the Cause of Authentication Failures

It is a well-known fact that a user may fail authentication for reasons beyond incorrect credentials. In Windows and ADAM, a user's account may be temporarily locked out due to excessive log-on attempts with invalid credentials, or his password may have expired. There is a variety of additional failure modes as well. The issue for us as developers is that in some cases, we would like to be able to tell the user why the authentication failed instead of simply providing a yes or no response. The user may need to contact support in order to unlock his account or reset the password in order to begin accessing resources again, and this kind of feedback can make him more productive.

The downside for us is that none of the techniques we have detailed provides this information. LDAP, either through SDS or through SDS.P, simply throws an exception for any type of authentication failure, and Microsoft's `NegotiateStream` class seems to bury the underlying cause as well. Only the `LogonUser` approach (which we did not demonstrate with a code sample) can actually provide the details directly.

So, what are we to do? With LDAP-based approaches, one technique we might use would be to attempt to bind to the user's account in the directory with a service account (a trusted subsystem, as we discussed in Chapter 8) to read the account's properties, as we detailed in Chapter 10. From here, we can determine lockout status, password expiration, and other states that would prevent authentication. This approach is somewhat clunky, but in many cases, it is the best we can do.

With the SSPI-based approach, we seem to be out of luck, for now. Until the `NegotiateStream` class is reengineered to expose this information, we don't really have an option.

SUMMARY

We explored three different techniques to authenticate against Active Directory and ADAM. While we did not directly cover using the `LogonUser` API, that is also a valid option and it can be considered. Table 12.1 includes the four different choices, summarized by platform and version of .NET.

TABLE 12.1: Authentication Options Matrix

Operating System	.NET Version 2.0	.NET Version 1.1
Windows 2000	SSPI[a] SDS.P SDS	SDS
Windows 2003/XP ADAM	SDS.P SDS	SDS
Windows 2003	SSPI[a] SDS.P LogonUser[a] SDS	SDS LogonUser[a]

  a. Runs on client, not server.

We can make a couple of observations from this table. First, SDS.P is probably going to be our most compatible and perhaps best-performing choice across all platforms with version 2.0. However, the performance depends a bit on whether fast concurrent binding will be supported on our client and server. Regardless, it is a pretty good choice.

For version 1.1, we can see that only SDS is universal across all the platforms. The biggest problem, of course, is that this solution does not scale well. For small applications, SDS will be fine using version 1.1. Larger applications will need to consider writing a custom SSPI solution using managed C++ for Active Directory, or perhaps a native LDAP component for ADAM. Since these two options would be significantly more difficult, we do not show them as an option in Table 12.1.

While `LogonUser` can also be used on Windows 2000 clients against any version of Active Directory, we do not recommend using it unless it is called from Windows 2003 or XP clients, because essentially it must run as `SYSTEM` if we are to use it on this platform. Keeping in mind the limitations based on platform (e.g., `LogonUser`) and version of framework (e.g., SDS.P), this chapter and Table 12.1 should give you some useful guidance on what authentication method is appropriate for your own application.

PART III
Appendixes

■ A ■
Three Approaches to COM Interop with ADSI

T HROUGHOUT THE BOOK, we have mentioned that it is useful and occasionally even necessary to do some kind of COM interop with ADSI
when using System.DirectoryServices (SDS). For example, it is useful
for harnessing the IADsNameTranslate interface and it is necessary for setting attributes with the LargeInteger syntax (2.5.5.16, see Chapter 6).

There are actually three different approaches we can use for COM interop:

- The "standard" method, where an interop assembly is generated
  with tlbimp.exe or by setting a COM reference to activeds.tlb in
  Visual Studio .NET
- The reflection method, where we use types in the System.Reflection
  namespace to discover and invoke ADSI COM interface methods
  dynamically at runtime
- The "roll your own" approach of writing our own .NET declaration
  for a COM type by hand

The Standard Method

There is not much more to say here. In this case, we just create a runtime-
callable wrapper (RCW) interop assembly for the entire activeds.tlb type

library using tlbimp.exe or Visual Studio .NET. For Visual Studio .NET, this is as simple as using Project > Add Reference and selecting actveds.tlb from the COM tab. If we are not using Visual Studio .NET, we need to use the command-line tool from the .NET SDK, called tlbimp.exe. Here is a sample command line for using this tool (watch for the wrap):

```
tlbimp.exe actveds.tlb /out:actvedsNET.dll
 /namespace:ActiveDS
```

This will create an RCW called actvedsNET.dll that we should deploy with our application. If necessary, we can also provide a strong name for the generated assembly so that we can call it from our own strong-named assemblies as well. The .NET runtime includes a security restriction that prevents strongly named assemblies from calling into assemblies that are not strongly named. For more information about code access security (CAS) policy as it relates to strong names, see Chapter 8.

Advantages

The advantages of this approach are that it is easy and the performance is good.

Disadvantages

The downsides of this approach are as follows.

- We have an extra assembly to deploy with our code all the time.
- We may not like the way the default conversion renders some of the ADSI types. For example, none of the enumerations that can be combined bitwise has the `FlagsAttribute` attribute applied to it, and the `IDirectorySearch` and `IDirectoryObject` interfaces are not really useful with the default conversion.

Because of the ease of use of this approach, we have tended to use it throughout the book, even though it might not be ideal for all situations.

Microsoft could actually improve on the second point by providing what is called a **Primary Interop Assembly** (PIA) for actveds.dll, similar to what it does with the Microsoft Office automation libraries, which is handcrafted to address these problems and includes a strong name. However, Microsoft has thus far not elected to do this for us.

The Reflection Method

Reflection is simply the process of discovering information about a type at runtime and using that information to access the type programmatically. For example, we can determine method and parameter information at runtime and dynamically invoke this functionality for any object or type. There is a performance penalty to using reflection, so we need to decide when it is appropriate by application. We can oftentimes cache the type information to help offset this performance penalty as well.

The `DirectoryEntry` class already provides some easy access to the reflection-based approach through the `Invoke`, `InvokeGet`, and `InvokeSet` methods. These methods in turn use .NET reflection under the hood to call ADSI interfaces dynamically. The `NativeObject` property provides us with a `System.Object` reference that we can use for reflection against the underlying ADSI `IADs` interface as well, but all of that functionality is essentially available via the helper methods.

The more useful place for reflection is with values that are returned from `PropertyValueCollection` that represent `IADsLargeInteger` and `IADsSecurityDescriptor` types (and `IADsDNWithBinary`, to a lesser extent). If we are confronted with the need to simply read or write an `IADsLargeInteger` type, it seems silly to drag the whole activeds.tlb interop assembly around with us.

For that, we can simply use reflection to read the `HighPart` and `LowPart` members of the interface to get at the data in which we are interested. Listing A.1 shows what a simple function for conversion from `IADsLargeInteger` to `Int64` might look like.

LISTING A.1: Using Reflection to Read IADsLargeInteger

```
using System.Reflection;

public static Int64 ConvertToInt64(object largeInteger)
{
    Int32 lowPart;
    Int32 highPart;
```

```
        Type largeIntType;

        largeIntType = largeInteger.GetType();

        try
        {
            highPart = (Int32) largeIntType.InvokeMember(
                "HighPart",
                BindingFlags.GetProperty | BindingFlags.Public,
                null,
                largeInteger,
                null
                );
            lowPart = (Int32) largeIntType.InvokeMember(
                "LowPart",
                BindingFlags.GetProperty | BindingFlags.Public,
                null,
                largeInteger,
                null
                );

            return (long)highPart << 32 | (uint)lowPart;;
        }
        catch (MissingMethodException ex)
        {
            throw new ArgumentException(
                "Argument must be IADsLargeInteger!",
                ex
                );
        }
    }
```

This approach is also possible in Visual Basic .NET, with some simple conversion. However, Visual Basic .NET and other .NET languages that allow late binding offer an even easier approach. By disabling `Option Strict` in Visual Basic .NET, we can simply invoke the `HighPart` and `LowPart` properties directly and let the Visual Basic runtime do the heavy lifting, as shown in Listing A.2.

LISTING A.2: Using Visual Basic.NET Late Binding to Access IADsLargeInteger

```
Option Strict Off

'given an object largeInt that contains an IADsLargeInteger...
Dim highPart As Integer
Dim lowPart as Integer

highPart = largeInt.HighPart
lowPart = largeInt.LowPart
```

From there, we just take the high and low parts and reassemble them, as we instructed in Chapter 6. Note that we are not huge fans of Visual Basic .NET's ability to disable `Option Strict`, as it throws out lots of useful checking by the compiler that makes our code more robust. However, it can be applied at the file level, so if used surgically, it can be effective without sacrificing too much.

Advantages

The advantage of this approach is that it is easier to deploy for small situations.

Disadvantages

The downsides of this approach are as follows.

- It is slower than an interop assembly or declaration.
- It is probably too much work if we are using many types or members.
- Reflection-based programming can be somewhat tedious and error prone.

Handcrafted COM Interop Declarations

This is probably the least known of the three approaches, but it deserves some discussion. It is actually possible to declare our own types in our .NET language of choice that will work with .NET COM interop directly. For example, we can declare the `IADsLargeInteger` interface in C#, as shown in Listing A.3.

LISTING A.3: Handwritten .NET Type Declaration for IADsLargeInteger

```
using System.Runtime.InteropServices;
using System.Runtime.CompilerServices;

[ComImport]
[TypeLibType(TypeLibTypeFlags.FDispatchable |
    TypeLibTypeFlags.FDual)]
[Guid("9068270B-0939-11D1-8BE1-00C04FD8D503")]
public interface IADsLargeInteger
{
    [DispId(2)]
    int HighPart
    {
        [MethodImpl(MethodImplOptions.InternalCall,
```

```
                    MethodCodeType=MethodCodeType.Runtime)]
        [DispId(2)]
        get;
        [param: In]
        [MethodImpl(MethodImplOptions.InternalCall,
            MethodCodeType=MethodCodeType.Runtime)]
        [DispId(2)]
        set;
    }
    [DispId(3)]
    int LowPart
    {
        [MethodImpl(MethodImplOptions.InternalCall,
            MethodCodeType=MethodCodeType.Runtime)]
        [DispId(3)]
        get;
        [param: In]
        [MethodImpl(MethodImplOptions.InternalCall,
            MethodCodeType=MethodCodeType.Runtime)]
        [DispId(3)]
        set;
    }
}
```

OK, sure, it is a bit intimidating with all of those crazy attributes, and Microsoft's reference materials do not provide a lot of examples of how to write this kind of code. Still, it is definitely possible to do this. Additionally, we can take an interop assembly generated by tlbimp.exe and use a tool such as Lutz Roeder's Reflector to "reverse engineer" this declaration, which is what we did here.

Advantages

This approach combines the performance advantages of the first approach with the lightweight qualities of the second approach. It is ideal for small numbers of types and member declarations.

Disadvantages

The downsides of this approach are as follows.

- It is difficult to write this code without a book on the subject, although tools can help with this.
- It is probably too much work if we are using many types or members.

SUMMARY

There is more than one viable approach to doing COM interop with ADSI. Each has its advantages and disadvantages. It is helpful to know our options so that we can choose the appropriate approach for the type of program we are deploying.

▗ B ▖
LDAP Tools for Programmers

P ROGRAMMERS THE WORLD OVER recognize that having good tools for specific tasks makes them more effective, and LDAP programming is no exception. As such, we have listed here our "ultimate tools list"[1] for LDAP programmers.

LDP

LDP, packaged as ldp.exe and also known as the Active Directory Browsing Utility, is a graphical tool from Microsoft for performing LDAP operations against any LDAP directory. This utility is bundled with the Windows Admin Pack that comes with each version of Windows, and is distributed with ADAM. Microsoft does not charge separately for this tool or place any special licensing requirements on it (to our knowledge), but it is not available as a separate download.

LDP is often overlooked by administrators because it lacks graphical flash and polish and it does not provide any task-oriented features, such as unlocking or disabling accounts, or resetting passwords. It instead provides a fairly raw interface that is only a few steps removed from actually

---

1. Scott Hanselman maintains an excellent "ultimate tools lists" for .NET developers at his web site, www.hanselman.com/blog/ScottHanselmans2005UltimateDeveloperAnd-PowerUsersToolList.aspx. We suggest .NET developers of all flavors check out his site. Our material here serves to supplement his somewhat startling lack of LDAP tools, which we do not understand how anyone can live without!

writing code, and it demands that its users have a reasonable knowledge of LDAP programming in order to use it.

While this low-level utility may not be appropriate for a certain class of administrators, it is nearly perfect for developers writing LDAP code. LDP strips away nearly all of the layers of indirection and lets us execute LDAP commands directly in the tool. This type of interaction translates neatly into .NET directory services code in `System.DirectoryServices` (SDS) and `System.DirectoryServices.Protocols` (SDS.P). LDP provides us with a great place to prototype search operations and filters and try out nearly every type of operation LDAP offers, including some that are not available via ADSI. In fact, LDP does not use ADSI at all, but uses the LDAP API directly. This allows us to bypass any issues we might be having with ADSI.

LDP has these additional benefits.

- It is a single executable requiring no COM registration or other installation steps, so we can copy it from machine to machine easily.

- It takes advantage of all of the built-in Windows security features, such as login with current credentials, but it also works well on machines that are not joined to a domain.

- It provides a powerful set of built-in semantic attribute mappings, including conversion of binary GUIDs and security identifiers (SIDs) into their standard Windows string representations, conversion of numeric values back into their Windows enumerated constant names, and conversion of `LargeInteger` values back into Windows date values. In newer versions, we can also request the raw string version of the data, which is useful for determining how to build appropriate query filters.

- Newer builds have a useful, low-level security descriptor editor.

- New versions have special, built-in character sequences for supplying values in binary, Unicode, GUID, or SID format, and having those values converted into the proper format automatically. Attribute data can also be uploaded from a file. These options simplify some otherwise difficult tasks that might require the user to write some code.

This description only scratches the surface of what LDP can do. Both Ryan and Joe practically live in this tool for serious directory programming work. We suggest you just go get it and start using it right away.

ADSI Edit

ADSI Edit is another tool from Microsoft that provides low-level access to the actual attribute data in directory objects. As its name implies, ADSI Edit uses the ADSI API for interacting with directory objects, instead of using the LDAP API directly. It is much more graphical a tool than LDP is, using standard Windows tree views and property pages rather than the more "text-based" LDP approach. It is packaged as an MMC snap-in.

ADSI Edit has a useful security descriptor editor that does not hide some of the advanced settings, as does the Active Directory Users and Computers MMC (see the next section).

The ADAM version of ADSI Edit includes support for setting and changing passwords of ADAM security principals, which is difficult to do without writing code (although it can be done in LDP with the correct syntax).

ADSI Edit is distributed in the same manner as LDP (Windows Admin Pack and ADAM distributions).

It is possible to use ADSI Edit from a nondomain joined machine, but it works best when using Windows security features for binding.

Active Directory Users and Computers

The Active Directory Users and Computers (ADUC) MMC is Microsoft's primary graphical administration tool for user, group, and computer objects in Active Directory. ADUC focuses on providing task-oriented property pages and menus for performing common administrative tasks, such as creating and deleting users and groups, managing passwords and other account features, and maintaining group memberships.

While for programming work, we prefer lower-level tools such as LDP, ADSI Edit, and ADFind (discussed shortly), there is a lot to be said for using ADUC to get common administrative tasks done. We also like using ADUC for reverse-engineering work. It is often helpful to check the state of an object with LDP, perform a common administrative task in ADUC, and then check the object again with LDP to see what data changed. This type of approach is even more successful when applied to security descriptor modification, as it is often difficult to figure out how to achieve specific security behaviors simply by studying the SDK reference. With ADUC, we can use the friendly graphical UI to get the behavior we want and then reverse engineer the resulting security descriptor data with a lower-level tool to learn how to accomplish the same thing in code.

The ADUC tree view metaphor tends to break down when dealing with containers that contain many objects, but this is a limitation of nearly all browsing utilities. When a large number of objects are involved, search becomes the only practical way to deal with them individually.

ADUC does not work well at all on machines that are not joined to the domain. If we are using nondomain machines, we suggest using one of the tools we mentioned previously, or BeaverTail or Softerra's LDAP Browser, which we will discuss shortly.

Microsoft Exchange Server provides tight integration with ADUC via the Exchange System Management tools. When installed, these tools provide additional functions and property pages for common Exchange management tasks, such as mail- and mailbox-enabling groups and users. It also includes an extensibility mechanism that allows developers to add their own property pages and such, but this currently requires programming in unmanaged C++.

Microsoft also ships a variety of other task-oriented MMC snap-ins for Active Directory management, including Sites and Services, Domains and Trusts, and Schema. Depending on the task at hand, these other tools may also be of use.

LDIFDE

LDIFDE is Microsoft's command-line implementation of a tool for doing import and export of LDAP data using the standard format known as Lightweight Data Interchange Format (LDIF). LDIF files are the de facto standard for providing schema extensions to Active Directory and ADAM, so this tool is important for schema management tasks. In Chapter 7, we recommended using LDIF files exclusively for schema extension tasks.

LDIFDE is a useful tool in its own right for general export and import of LDAP data.

LDIFDE is also packaged with the Windows Admin Pack and with distributions of ADAM.

ADFind/ADMod

For command-line junkies, it doesn't get any better than ADFind and ADMod for searching and modifying Active Directory and ADAM. ADFind and ADMod are two of the many useful freeware tools offered by Joe Richards via his web site, www.joeware.net.

ADFind includes a huge number of advanced LDAP search features that to our knowledge are available only in LDP. None of Microsoft's command-line LDAP tools, such as dsquery, offers as much power, so we recommend ADFind instead.

In the interests of full disclosure, we should mention that Joe Richards graciously agreed to review this book and contributed a great deal to improving its quality. However, he does not receive any compensation for this tool, so this shameless plug represents no conflict of interest.

BeaverTail LDAP Browser

BeaverTail is a graphical Active Directory browser tool written in C#. BeaverTail is written and maintained by Marc Scheuner, a fellow Microsoft MVP, so this represents yet another shameless plug. We mention Beaver-Tail not so much because it is better than the previously mentioned tools, but because it is written in C#, it is freeware, and the source code is freely available. Even though we would like to believe that we have covered every possible LDAP programming scenario in this book, it is still often helpful to see example code in the context of a full-blown application.

BeaverTail is available as a free download from http://adsi.mvps.org/adsi/CSharp/beavertail.html.

Softerra LDAP Browser

The last tool we will mention is a free LDAP browser available from Softerra at www.ldapbrowser.com. There are actually two versions: the free version (called LDAP Browser), which allows read-only access, and the commercial version (called LDAP Administrator), which allows full editing and some more advanced features.

The free version is a polished LDAP browser that is compatible with any LDAP directory. It supports some nice searching capabilities and the ability to export objects as LDIF files. While not as powerful as LDP, it is definitely a more approachable tool.

SUMMARY

Most developers have a number of "must-have" tools under their belt that help them troubleshoot, manage, or generally simplify their tasks. We have presented a few of the tools we use most often.

We are sure that we have probably failed to mention a number of tools, but we think that the tools on our list are probably the best bang for the buck (especially since all of them are free!).

C

Troubleshooting and Help

SOMETIMES WE BUY TECHNICAL BOOKS because we are having specific problems and cannot find good answers elsewhere. However, we often find the answers to our questions buried within the text in places where we might not have known to look, and only after hours of reading. In the interest of finding answers to specific problems more quickly, we have attempted to cross-reference some of the key troubleshooting material in this book by the various Windows error codes we encounter in our daily work. This list is by no means comprehensive and it does not replace the book's index, but it should help many readers get "unstuck" more quickly.

All of the errors introduced by an error code will come from `System.Runtime.InteropServices.COMException` in version 1.1 and `System.DirectoryServices.DirectoryServicesCOMException` in version 2.0, which are the two standard exception classes used in `System.DirectoryServices` (SDS) for relaying errors from the underlying ADSI interface. In some other cases, another .NET exception may be thrown, in which case we mention it directly.

Error 0x8007203A: "The server is not operational."

This error is quite common and may occur for a variety of different reasons. The most obvious cause is that the server you were trying to contact might actually be down, it may be blocked by a network firewall, or it might not exist at all. However, given that there is a variety of different ways to specify a server to use with ADSI, there are many other ways this error may be generated.

Chapter 3 is where you will find most of the information about binding to the directory. If you are not specifying a server name at all in your binding string, check out the section titled Serverless Binding to Active Directory. If you are specifying some other information about the server in the binding string, the material on server name syntaxes is the place to start.

If you are trying to bind to a server using secure sockets layer, there are some additional things to know. Refer to the sidebar titled Troubleshooting Binds with SecureSocketsLayer, in Chapter 3.

Error 0x8007052E: "Login Failure: unknown user name or bad password."

This error is very common when supplying specific credentials in an LDAP bind. In many cases, this error simply indicates that the credentials supplied were incorrect. However, there are some other, subtler reasons why this error often occurs.

- The username is specified in the wrong format. See Chapter 3 for valid username formats.
- The format used for the username is not compatible with the authentication flags being used. Chapter 3 covers authentication flags in detail.

Furthermore, Chapter 8 provides useful information on general security issues with binding to the directory, and Chapter 12 provides an entire section on scenarios for LDAP-based authentication.

Error 0x80072020: "An operations error occurred."

This error shows up in various places and depends greatly on what operation we were trying to perform. As such, specific recommendations are difficult.

Our general guidance here is to look at what you were doing when the error occurred and refer to the appropriate chapters. For example, if the error occurred during an initial bind operation, Chapter 3 would be the place to start. Chapter 8 is a good second place to look in case the binding error might be related to a security problem. The stack trace produced by .NET in COMException will show what SDS was doing when the failure occurred, so use that for context clues.

If you were searching the directory, Chapters 4 and 5 are the best place to start. If you were reading or writing LDAP data values, Chapter 6 is the place to go.

Error 0x80072030: "There is no such object on the server."

This one is generally straightforward. Either the object you specified actually does not exist or the current user's security context does not have rights to see it.

If it is the former, you might want to refer again to the sections in Chapter 3 about binding string syntaxes. It may also be appropriate to refer to Chapter 4 for information on searching the directory if we know some information about the object in question (such as its name) but do not know where it is located.

For security-related issues, the first section of Chapter 8 is essential for helping you understand LDAP security. In some cases, you may need a more privileged account to access the object in question, but in other cases, you may have simply established your security context incorrectly.

Error 0x8007202F: "A constraint violation occurred."

This happens when you are trying to create or modify an object in the directory and the server rejects some aspect of the modification. This error can occur for a variety of different reasons, as the directory provides multiple levels of validation on modification operations. For example, the directory enforces rules defined in the schema, rules for naming objects in the directory hierarchy, and rules for certain attributes in the directory that must be enforced in order for the server to function correctly, such as the contents of specific attributes.

If this error occurs during object creation, Chapter 3 is the place to start for information about object creation and mandatory attributes. If this error occurs while updating an object, Chapter 6 provides a wealth of information about the various attribute syntaxes and rules for updating them.

It may also be worth reviewing some of the special rules for creating and modifying user and group objects in Chapters 10 and 11, respectively.

Error 0x80072035: "The server is unwilling to process the request."

This error is very similar to the constraint violation error, but it typically happens for other reasons. Once again, a review of Chapters 6, 10, and 11 is a good idea, depending on exactly what operation was being performed.

Error 0x80070005: "General access denied error."

As the wording implies, this is always a security problem. In some cases, this error occurs because we really did try to perform an operation that we were not allowed to perform. However, this error often occurs because of a problem with the way we established our security context.

Chapter 8 contains a variety of information about establishing a security context with the directory and discovering security information dynamically at runtime. A technique we like to use is to try the equivalent operation in a different environment or with a completely different tool, such as LDP (see Appendix B). If we can make it work in once place but not in another, then the difference usually lies in how we established our security context.

InvalidOperationException from DirectorySearcher

In .NET 2.0, a variety of new search operations are included in the `Directory-Searcher` class. However, not all of these options work with every single version of ADSI on each Windows platform. For example, Windows

XP as of Service Pack 2, and all previous operating systems, does not support extended distinguished name (DN) searches (see Chapter 5).

Trying to use an unsupported search feature will result in this exception with the stack trace pointing to the `DoSearchPrefs` method. Unfortunately, the error message does not explain that the option was unsupported on our platform, so we are often left scratching our heads. Now we know!

A future version of the .NET Framework may provide a more informative error message here. Additionally, future versions of the ADSI that are included with Windows service packs may introduce these features to down-level clients.

Getting Help

No book or article will likely ever solve all of your programming problems. That is where online communities come into play. Instead of struggling with a particular problem for weeks all by yourself, why not ask for help in an online forum?

Both of us are quite active in the Microsoft LDAP programming community and enjoy helping others. We also enjoy the opportunity to learn about the interesting things you are trying to do and discussing scenarios and ideas that we had never considered. Both of us attribute the depth of our knowledge in this field to our participation in these forums. We could not have written this book without the experience gained from trying to answer so many of your questions!

Joe is usually found hanging on the Microsoft NNTP-based newsgroups, such as microsoft.public.adsi.general and microsoft.public.dotnet.framework.aspnet.security, to name a few. You can reach these newsgroups using an NNTP client such as Outlook Express, or via the web-based interface on MSDN (http://msdn.microsoft.com).

Ryan runs the show on the ASP.NET forums in the directory services area. These forums are available on the Web at www.asp.net.

If you prefer a mailing list, both Joe and Ryan participate on the ADSI and Directory Services Yahoo! mailing list, along with a variety of other talented people. This list also has a useful files area and a search interface. Find it at http://groups.yahoo.com/group/ADSIANDDirectoryServices.

Before you post, remember a few etiquette tips.

- Please do not contact us directly via email for troubleshooting questions. Although we love to hear from you, contacting us directly prevents the conversation from taking place in public and helping others in the future. Additionally, it deprives other experts of the chance to try to answer, and it may take you longer to get an answer if we are away.

- Please conduct research before you post. A simple search of the Web or newsgroups with Google or whatever search engine you prefer may reveal 30 previous answers to the same problem.

- Please be detailed in what you are trying to do and in what the environment is. Always provide a relevant code sample. Try to tailor it to the smallest possible amount of code that demonstrates the problem. Snippets cut and pasted from larger frameworks with random member variables scattered all over are difficult to interpret.

Also, do not forget about the book's web site. While we do not plan to host discussions on it, the site will contain the samples from the book in both C# and Visual Basic .NET and will eventually contain other articles as the platform continues to evolve.

SUMMARY

We hope our attempt to cross-reference common errors with the book's content will help some of you use this book more effectively to solve specific problems. We obviously won't solve every problem this way, but sometimes we can save valuable time by narrowing down our options.

If that doesn't work, now you know where to find us too. We look forward to meeting you online and hope we can solve your problems that way. Perhaps something we learn from you will make it into a second edition someday. Happy directory services programming!

Index

Symbols and Numbers

BOOKS ONLINE

ENABLED

THIS BOOK IS SAFARI ENABLED

INCLUDES FREE 45-DAY ACCESS TO THE ONLINE EDITION

The Safari® Enabled icon on the cover of your favorite technology book means the book is available through Safari Bookshelf. When you buy this book, you get free access to the online edition for 45 days.

Safari Bookshelf is an electronic reference library that lets you easily search thousands of technical books, find code samples, download chapters, and access technical information whenever and wherever you need it.

TO GAIN 45-DAY SAFARI ENABLED ACCESS TO THIS BOOK:

● Go to **http://www.awprofessional.com/safarienabled**

● Complete the brief registration form

● Enter the coupon code found in the front of this book on the "Copyright" page

Addison
Wesley

If you have difficulty registering on Safari Bookshelf or accessing the online edition, please e-mail customer-service@safaribooksonline.com.